MOUNTAIN BIKE
MAINTENANCE

A FIREFLY BOOK

Published by Firefly Books Ltd. 2004

First printing

Publisher Cataloging-in-Publication Data   (U.S.)

Allwood, Mel, 1970-
     Mountain bike maintenance : the illustrated manual / Mel Allwood. —1st ed.
[256] p. : col. ill., photos. ;   cm.
Includes index.
Summary: Step-by-step guide to maintaining and repairing all types of mountain bikes.
ISBN 1-55297-734-X (pbk.)
1. All terrain bicycles--Maintenance and repair--Handbooks, manuals, etc. I. Title.
629.28/772 21   TL430.A55   2004

National Library of Canada Cataloguing in Publication

Allwood, Melanie
     Mountain bike maintenance : the illustrated manual / Mel Allwood.
Inlcudes index.
ISBN 1-55297-734-X
     1. All terrain bicycles--Maintenance and repair. I. Title.
TL430.A44 2004   629.28'772   C2004-900994-X

Published in the United States in 2004 by
Firefly Books (U.S.) Inc.
P.O. Box 1338, Ellicott Station
Buffalo, New York 14205

Published in Canada in 2004 by
Firefly Books Ltd.
66 Leek Crescent
Richmond Hill, Ontario L4B 1H1

Project editor: Nigel Matheson
Design & project art direction: Darren Jordan
Production: Lisa French
Jacket & layout photography: Karl Adamson

Printed and bound in Dubai
All photographs in this book are © Carlton Books

MEL ALLWOOD

MOUNTAIN BIKE
MAINTENANCE

THE ILLUSTRATED MANUAL

FIREFLY BOOKS

Contents

Introduction
Mountain bikes
Why do I like mountain bikes?

I became a cyclist originally because I live in a big crowded city, and I'm an impatient traveler. Bikes are by far the quickest way to get around and enable me to travel under my own steam. I can't stand to be sitting in a tin box in traffic or waiting for another piece of imaginary public transport.

My first mountain bike was the key to discovering a whole new kind of cycling. Early adventures were mostly around the bridleways of the North Downs in the South of England, a short train ride away from home. Many mountain bikes — and great trips to lots of fantastic remote places — later, it's still one of my favorite spots to ride. It doesn't have awesome scenery like Scotland or classic epic loops like the Lake District, but it does have plenty of hidden trails, enough short sharp climbing to keep you fit, and lots of warm cozy pubs just when you need them. Everybody likes their own backyard best.

One of the attractions of mountain biking for me is that it's a great way of getting to remote places that isn't noisy or intrusive and that doesn't do any lasting damage to the environment. The peace comes at a price though — once you're off the beaten track, if anything goes wrong with your bike, you need to be able to rely on your own resources to fix it. So it pays to be familiar with your machine and to carry basic tools and spare parts with you.

Like most bike mechanics, most of what I've learned about how to make bikes feel nice and work well comes from just taking things apart and putting them back together. I like fixing bicycles — they evolve, change and improve constantly, so that even mechanics have to learn new tricks and techniques all the time.

Bikes are relatively simple and seldom need complex or expensive tools. They respond magically to a bit of tender loving care — a nurtured bicycle feels better than a neglected one that costs twice as much. I feel like I've always been very lucky to have a job that I really love — I've worked at Brixton Cycles Co-op in south London for half of my life now, which means I get to hang out in the bike shop all day. Sometimes I do worry that one day somebody is going to find out and make me go and get a proper job that's not as much fun and doesn't involve fixing mechanical parts with oily things. If that ever happens, a big chunk of what I've learned is in this book.

One of my favorite things about mountain bikes is that they have so few superfluous parts. Since you're the power source for this transport, you don't want to be carrying around anything you don't have to. This advantage is a huge disadvantage at the same time. Anything you break while on a ride is probably vital and will have to be repaired before you're able to continue.

Fixing your bike

There are two good reasons for fixing your own bike, and a third more tenuous one. The first reason — where most bicycle repair careers start — is to help you get home when something goes wrong. Even if this is as much as you ever intend to do with wrenches, it's worth getting right. The difference between a glamorous repair story in the pub and a long dispiriting walk home is seldom more than a few basic tools and a bit of familiarity with the way your machine is supposed to work.

The second good reason often happens next — fixing your bike helps you get out on your bike. Adjusting it so that it does exactly what you want it to makes you more likely to go out on a ride, if only to test what you've done. The third reason could be less praiseworthy. Carrying out your own bike maintenance does save you money on getting your bike fixed — although I cannot resist the excuse to go out and buy my bike a nice present with the money I've saved doing my own repairs.

The unspoken goal of bicycle care is never to have to fix a broken bike at all — you've left it too late by then. One of the lazy reasons for spending some time looking after your bicycle is that careful nurture means fewer trail breakdowns. Regular mild care and attention is much more effective, and cheaper, than occasional guilty servicing frenzies. As you get more familiar with the workings of your bicycle, you gradually pick up a key skill: realizing that something is not behaving as it should and identifying where the problem is. This is still mechanics even if you then decide to pay someone else to fix it for you! Riding around with worn or damaged components is the quickest way to wear or damage whatever the parts are connected to, increasing the cost of the inevitable eventual repair. Learning to spot problems early will save you money.

For any mechanical task you decide to tackle, arm yourself with the necessary tools and spare parts before you take anything apart — tools are listed in the "toolboxes" in each section. It helps to clean your bike first. This saves you getting covered in grease and dirt as you work and makes it a lot easier to see what's going on. It means your bike looks all clean when you've finished too, which is always encouraging.

Whenever you're fixing your bike at home, give yourself enough time to work slowly and calmly. Trying to fix or adjust your bike with your friends waiting at the trailhead for you or knowing you're setting off on a cycling holiday the next day is a recipe for disaster. If possible, fix your bike before the bike shop closes too — that way everything is far less stressful if you suddenly discover you need spare parts or tools halfway through.

One of my intentions in writing this book has been to explain how parts of your bicycle work. All instruction manuals take you through a series of steps that will cure a specific problem; after a while it's easy to believe that there is only one way of doing each job. This is a myth though — every repair is slightly different so it makes sense to try and understand how your bicycle works before you dive in with your wrenches. You will always get better results from your labors if you learn to think like a mechanic, looking carefully at components before you start work, trying to understand how they work, then adjusting them for optimum performance. When something does go unexpectedly wrong, try to work out why it happened, so that you can stop it happening again. Sometimes the cause is obvious — if you wrap lightweight parts of bicycles around trees at high speed, something's got to give. Other times, there seems to be no immediate cause. Look at the broken or worn parts and see if you can work out what went wrong. Was it adjusted correctly? Did it have enough lubrication? This is the key difference between mechanics and fitters, who simply follow instructions blindly.

It's a commonly held myth that some people have a special touch with mechanical things, a bit like having green thumbs. While some people are definitely more dextrous than others, the most important quality you need to fix bicycles is the ability to assess the problem calmly and work out a good solution. Anyone can learn how to do this — it's not magic. Professional mechanics have more experience with similar problems to help them make choices and are just much quicker at it. Getting parts adjusted perfectly takes a little time, but you will get quicker with practice and patience. Bicycles are good to work on because almost everything you need to get at is exposed and accessible — you don't have to crawl underneath anything or shine flashlights into oil-soaked crevices. Bikes are light enough so you can turn them over or around without any fuss — if this doesn't seem like a big deal, you've never tried to fix a washing machine.

Throughout the book, instructions like front, left right, top, etc., are given as if you are sitting on the bicycle the right way up.

Who are you?

This book is intended as an introduction to fixing bicycles, for those who like to ride their bikes but feel daunted when something goes wrong. The more mechanically experienced rider should also find some of the tips useful though — bicycle mechanics are wonderfully complex, and you never learn everything however long you are involved. Once you've come to grips with the basics explained in the following pages, there are two books aimed at the more advanced mechanic — *The Bicycle Wheel*, by Jobst Brandt, and *Barnett's Manual — Analysis and Procedures for Bicycle Maintenance*. This one is intended as your first step towards mechanical confidence.

Mel Allwood

Basic tools and equipment

This chapter is divided into three sections — tools and workshop equipment, rescue repairs on the trail, and routine checking and maintenance. All the repairs, adjustments and routines in this chapter can be carried out with the basic toolkit listed on pages 14–15 and should make you self-sufficient in most situations.

Tools and workshop equipment

This section lists a basic toolkit (pages 14–15), which you will need to carry out trailside repairs and minor adjustments. It also contains a more comprehensive toolkit (pages 17–23), listing the tools you need to carry out more involved repairs.

Rescue repairs on the trail

The ability to carry out basic routine maintenance makes you much more self-sufficient. Sometimes, a simple repair can make the difference between a great ride during which you had to stop and fix your bike, and a really tedious day when you had to walk home from the furthest point on the trail. Once you've learned how to fix your own bike, you'll be able to fix other bikes in the same way — and once your trail buddies realize you're handy with your toolkit, they'll think twice before leaving you behind on a ride.

Routine maintenance — twelve safety checks, three comfort zones, one cleaning routine

This section guides you through some basic routines that will make your bike safer, more comfortable, and longer lasting. Check your bike is ready for you every time you go out for a ride. A quick but thorough safety check can prevent accidents and help you to catch potential problems before you set out. Careful bike set-up will make your machine feel more comfortable and will also make you a more efficient cyclist by converting as much of your energy as possible into forward motion. Cheap, clean components last longer than neglected, expensive ones, so if you want to save money, spend a little time keeping your machine clean.

Multi-tools — compact and lightweight, with all the tools you'll need on the trail

The language of bicycle parts

People who talk about bikes can sometimes sound like they're speaking a foreign language all of their own. Some of the words they keep using are completely unfathomable and bizarre, and some sound familiar but often mean something completely different than expected. The language of bikes isn't just a way of keeping in the clique though — it's vital to be able to identify specific parts.

Disc brake calipers: (aka disc brake units) These are bolted to special disc mounts on your frame or fork. Operating the lever forces thin, hard pads onto your rotor, the metal disc attached to your hub. Powerful and lightweight, these can be daunting to service because they're new technology. However they respond well to treatment with a few basic tools. Mechanical versions use normal V-brake levers and cables; hydraulic disc brakes use an oil-filled hose to force brake pads onto the rotor.

Cables and hoses: Connecting brake levers to calipers or V-brake units, these need to be kept in good condition to transmit an accurate signal. Speed control, as well as raw braking power, is vital. Steel cables run through lengths of outer casing from brake levers to V-brakes. Hoses are the stiff plastic tubes that transfer hydraulic brake fluid from hydraulic brake levers to calipers.

Rear derailleur: This moves the chain step by step across the cassette sprockets. Different-sized sprockets give you different gear ratios, so that you can pedal at a constant rate over a range of different speeds. The movement of the rear derailleur is controlled by a cable on the shifter on the right-hand side of the handlebar. Correct adjustment gives you slick shifting and ensures maximum life for your chain, chainset and cassette.

Chainset: This consists of three chainrings bolted together. Like the cassette sprockets, choosing a different-sized chainring gives you a different gear ratio. Larger chainrings give you a higher gear which is harder to push but propels you further on each pedal stroke. Smaller chainrings give you a lower gear, allowing you to climb steep hills. Chainrings will wear out over time, the valleys between the teeth stretching until the chain slips under pressure.

Cassette and Freehub: Your cassette consists of a set of different-sized sprockets bolted together. Currently nine-speed cassettes are most common and combine with the three chainrings on your chainset to give you 27 gears. Smaller cassette sprockets give you a higher (harder) gear for maximum speed, and larger sprockets give you a lower (easier) gear for climbing hills. The cassette is fitted to a freehub on your rear wheel.

Chain: The chain connects your chainset to your cassette, so that when you pedal, the back wheel goes around. It needs to be strong so it doesn't snap when you stand on your pedals and stamp up a hill, but it must also be flexible so that it can shift from side to side across the cassette and chainset. Chain width needs to match your cassette: for example, nine-speed cassettes have narrower, more closely spaced sprockets than older eight-speeds so you need a narrower chain.

Headset: The main bearing at the front of your bike, the headset connects your forks to your frame. This part is often ignored because it's mostly hidden in the frame. This bearing must be adjusted so it turns smoothly without rattling — any play or binding will affect your bike's handling. There are two types of headset: the newer "Aheadset" type shown here has almost completely superseded the older threaded headset. Regular servicing keeps bearings running smoothly and helps your headset last longer.

Bottom bracket: Bottom brackets are another "out of sight, out of mind" component. The bottom bracket axle connects your two cranks together through the frame. If worn and loose, the bottom bracket can lead to front gear shifting problems and cause your chain to wear out. Worn bottom brackets can be spotted by checking for side to side play in your cranks. Usually supplied as a sealed unit, this part must be replaced when worn or stiff. This repair needs a couple of specific but inexpensive tools.

Wheels: Building wheels can seem daunting, but it is very satisfying to ride around on a pair you have built yourself. Building a wheel consists of two steps: weaving the spokes together to connect hub and rim, and tensioning each spoke so that the rim is flat and perfectly round. A wheel jig is essential for this task. It holds the wheel steady and has indicators that help you decide which spokes need to be adjusted and by how much.

Hubs: Well-adjusted hub bearings let wheels spin freely and save you energy. When properly adjusted, your bearings will be tight enough to prevent any side to side play without being so tight they slow you down. Occasional servicing to clean out any grit and dirt that has worked its way in will keep your wheels turning smoothly. Fresh, clean grease helps keep moisture out of your hubs. Jet-washing is tempting after a muddy ride, but will drive water in past your hub seals, flushing out the grease.

Suspension: Suspension makes your ride smoother. Almost all new mountain bikes come with front suspension forks, and full suspension bikes (with front suspension forks and a rear shock unit) get lighter and cheaper every year. Suspension bikes are better because they absorb trail shock and make you faster over uneven ground. The suspension keeps your center of gravity moving forward rather than up and down. Front forks and rear shocks need setting up for your weight and riding style.

Pedals: Introduced from road bikes, clipless pedals have replaced toe clips: a key-shaped cleat on the bottom of your shoe locks into a sprung mechanism on your pedals. The idea of clipless pedals is daunting for the first-timer, but you'll appreciate the extra power once you are used to them. Because your shoe is firmly attached, all your energy throughout the pedal stroke is used. Clean, oiled cleats will release your shoe instantly when you twist your foot. Many riders prefer flat pedals with studs.

Gear shifters

Seat post

Saddle

Rear derailleur hanger

Cassette

Disc brake caliper

Rotor

Valve

Tire

Rim

Stem

Stem top cap

Headset

Suspension forks

Front hubs

Quick release

Pedals/cleats

Chainset

Chain

Dropout

Rear derailleur

Spokes

Tools and workshop equipment

Of course, everyone starts off with very basic equipment. Then gradually, as you get more confident fixing your bike, you find you need various other pieces of gear. Your toolkit grows and grows, until it reaches the happy point where you can tackle complicated tasks without investing in any more tools.

The evolving toolkit

Some tools are universal, like screwdrivers. Others are highly specific and only do one task, or even just one task on one particular make and model of component. When I was 18, I bought a socket to change the oil on my VW Beetle car. I sold the car a couple of years later, but the socket hung out in my toolbox until I didn't notice it any more. One day I cleared out my toolbox and realized I hadn't used it in 15 years — now it makes a nice candlestick on my bathtub. You can always find a new task for old tools so hang on to them.

The tools on the first list are good for a start and should allow you to carry out all the simple repairs in Chapter Two. Tools for the specialist jobs, found in chapters Four to Nine, appear under the comprehensive toolkit, pages 17–23 — buy these as you tackle the job. Same goes for your stock of oils and cleaning fluids — start with the essential list, and add to it over time as you take on major repairs.

As your toolkit grows, a clear distinction will develop between your trail tools and your workshop tools. Trail tools need to be small and light and, preferably, foldable so they don't stab you from inside a pocket when you fall off your bike. With workshop tools, the bigger and chunkier the better, first for proper leverage, and second so they last longer without wearing out. Neat and lightweight gadget tools will wear quickly if they get used frequently in the workshop.

Manuals and instructions are tools too

All new bikes and parts come with manuals or instructions. For some reason, it's traditional to throw them away without reading them. I don't know why. Don't do it.

Keep all instructions and manuals together: they're part of your toolkit. It is particularly important to keep the original manual for suspension parts as fitting and setting-up instructions vary between make, model and years.

Once you find yourself using the manuals, feel free to scribble your own notes and diagrams on them as your knowledge grows.

The simple toolkit

When I started working on this section, I wrote and rewrote for the better part of a morning, adding and deleting items I believed were essential until, finally, I was happy with the result.

Then a friend came round, and together we calculated that the total cost of all the tools came out to more than her bike. I started again. The result is two lists: one of indispensable tools and a second for when you get more confident.

The second list is broken down to match chapters of the book, so you can buy items as you go along. Some tools are bike-specific. Some are obtainable from hardware or tool stores. Good tools last for years, and are an investment. Cheap tools let you down when you least need it and can damage the component you're trying to fix. A plastic toolbox costs very little, and both keeps tools together and protects them from damage.

Don't lend your tools to anyone. This sounds harsh, but if you like someone enough to lend them a wrench, fix their bike for them instead. If you don't like them enough to fix their bike, you don't trust them enough to lend them your wrench.

◀ **Bikes, components and even tools come with manuals. Keep them — they're a vital resource**

◆ **Allen keys**. The best starter packs are fold-up sets of metric wrenches (keys) that include 2, 2.5, 3, 4, 5 and 6mm sizes. You can use the body of the tool as a handle and bear down hard on it without bruising your hand. I'd rather choose a set with a wider range of keys than you get with screwdrivers, which are intended for trail use. Later, you will want separate Allen keys as they are actually easier to use. Those with a ball at one end allow you to get into awkward spaces.

◆ **A long-handled (about 200mm [8 inches]) 8mm Allen key** is essential for most current crank bolts, which attach the pedals to the bottom bracket in the body of the bike. Occasionally you'll need a 10mm Allen key; older crank bolts take a 14mm socket.

◆ **Screwdrivers**: you'll need one flathead and one No.2 Phillips.

◆ **Metric wrenches. The 8, 9, 10, 15 and 17mm sizes** are the most useful, but a metric wrench set that's got all the sizes from 8 to 17mm is ideal. The best are combination wrenches, with a ring at one end (to grip all around the nut) and an open end at the other (easier to get into awkward spaces).

◆ **A big adjustable wrench**, also called a crescent wrench, with a 200mm-long [8 inch] handle is a good size to start with. The jaws must open to at least 32mm (1¼ inches). Always tighten the jaws firmly onto the flats of the nut before applying pressure to the handle to avoid damaging the nut and the jaws.

◆ **Good quality, bike-specific wirecutters** — not just pliers — can be purchased from your local bike shop. This tool can seem expensive, but both inner cable and outer casing must be cut neatly and cleanly.

◆ **Chain tool**. Again, quality really makes the difference. It's easy to damage an expensive chain with a cheap chain tool.

◆ **Chain-wear measuring tool**. An essential, this tool shows when your chain has stretched enough to damage other parts of the drivetrain.

◆ **A sharp knife with a retractable blade,** so you don't cut yourself digging in your toolbox for a wrench, is useful for cutting open packaging, releasing zipties (cable or electrical ties), etc.

◆ **A pair of pliers**.

◆ **A rubber or plastic mallet.** You can get these from hardware stores. A metal hammer is not a suitable alternative!

◆ **Puncture kit**, for standard and/or UST tubeless tires.

◆ **Track pump**. Frame-clipping pumps are intended for the trail, while a track pump gets plenty of air into the tires without you busting a gut. They're virtually essential for UST tubeless tires. Get one with its own pressure gauge, or buy a separate pressure gauge.

Sling a pen and notebook into your toolbox for making notes and drawing pictures as you take things apart. It will help you reassemble them later. It's also useful for noting tire pressures and suspension settings. (See page 25 for illustration.)

Adjustable wrenches · Repair kit, UST · Rubber mallet · 8mm Allen key · Tire-levers · Allen keys · Metric wrenches · Sharp knife · Chain tool · Wire cutters · Repair kit · Screwdrivers

Spare parts box

You need a box of spare parts as well. It's worth keeping bits and pieces in your house so you don't have to rush off in the middle of a job to pick them up.

◆ **Two tubes**: the right size, with the correct valve for your wheels.
◆ **Brake blocks or pads**.

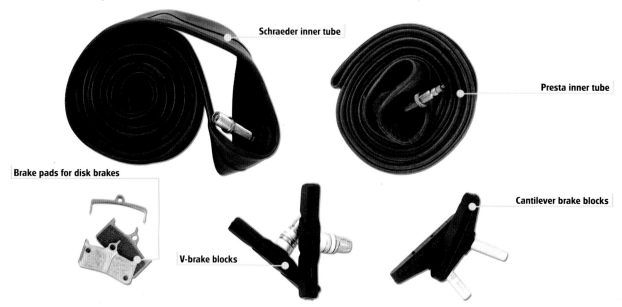

Schraeder inner tube

Presta inner tube

Brake pads for disk brakes

Cantilever brake blocks

V-brake blocks

◆ **Two brake cables** and a length of brake outer casing.
◆ **Two gear cables** and a length of gear outer casing.
◆ **Ferrules** (the end caps on casing) and end caps (the end caps on cables).
◆ **For Shimano chains**: chain-joining pins.
◆ **Zipties** (aka cable or electrical ties). These hold the fabric of the universe together. Before them we had string. Mountain biking couldn't exist until the ziptie was invented. Whoever invented it deserves a major international prize. No toolbox should be without a few of them.
◆ **Electrical tape**.

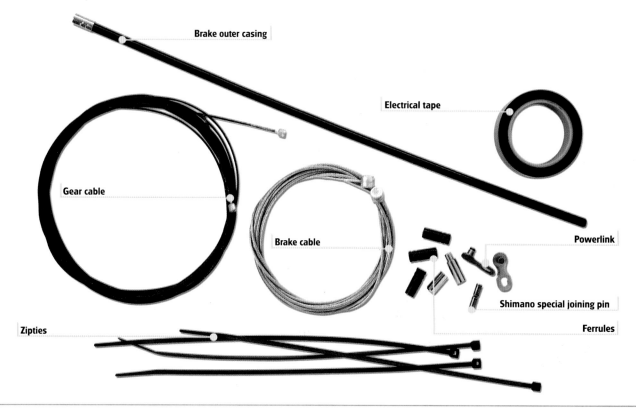

Brake outer casing

Electrical tape

Gear cable

Brake cable

Powerlink

Shimano special joining pin

Zipties

Ferrules

The comprehensive toolkit

As you start to tackle the major jobs, you have to add to your basic toolkit. (These items are broken down to match the chapters.)

Brakes

If you run disc brakes, you need a bleed kit. You can either improvise one from tubes and bottles, or buy a specific one for your brakes. If you haven't bled brakes before, a kit makes it a lot easier. You should be able to tackle everything else with the basic toolkit.

◆ **Good-quality wirecutters**

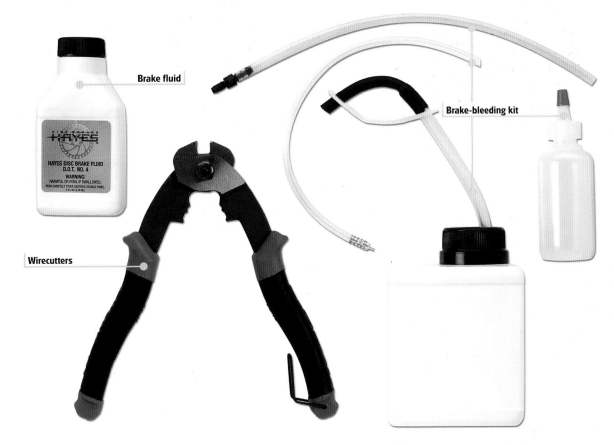

Brake fluid

Brake-bleeding kit

Wirecutters

Bottom bracket and headset
Headset wrenches

You only need these for older, threaded headsets, which come in three sizes: 32mm (formerly standard), 36mm (called "oversize" but actually standard now) and 40mm (Evolution size). Aheadsets are adjusted with Allen keys and don't need a wrench.

Bottom bracket tools

The most common style is the Shimano splined remover. This takes either a large adjustable wrench or a 32mm headset wrench. Remember, the right-hand side of the frame has a reverse thread. Facing the right-hand side of the bike, the righthand cup is removed clockwise. Facing the left-hand side, the left-hand cup is removed counterclockwise. Splined designs are wider than the older square taper ones; if you have an older version of the tool, the hole in the middle may not be big enough to fit over the splined axle. Sorry, you will just have to buy a new tool.

Headset wrenches

Shimano splined remover

ISIS splined remover

Transmission

◆ **Chain-cleaning box**.

◆ **Brush for chain cleaning**.

◆ **Crank extractor(s)**. Essential for removing cranks and accessing the bottom bracket. You will need a wrench to drive the inner part of the extractor once the body is firmly screwed into the crank. The cranks are refitted using just the crank bolts — you don't need the extractor for this. There are two types of extractor: one for the newer splined axles, the other for the older square taper axles. An adapter allows you to use a square-type tool with splined axles, but splined tools will not fit square taper axles.

◆ **Cassette-remover and chain whip**. The cassette-remover fits into the splines at the center of the cassette. You then need a big adjustable wrench to turn the tool. The chain whip fits around a sprocket and prevents the cassette turning as you undo its lockring. You don't need the chain whip for refitting the lockring; the ratchet in the middle of the cassette stops the cassette turning.

◆ **For freewheels** (how rear cogs were fitted on your wheel before cassettes were invented), you need the appropriate freewheel tool.

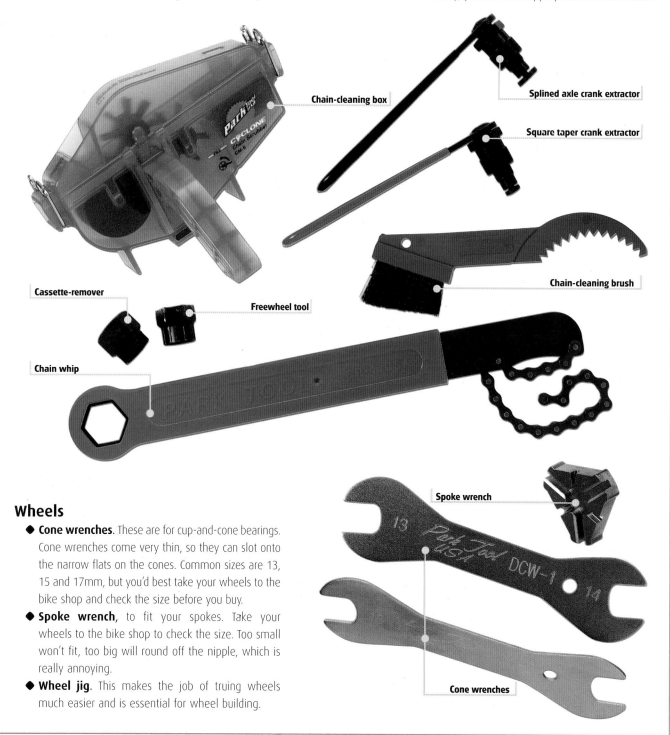

Chain-cleaning box

Splined axle crank extractor

Square taper crank extractor

Chain-cleaning brush

Cassette-remover

Freewheel tool

Chain whip

Spoke wrench

Wheels

◆ **Cone wrenches**. These are for cup-and-cone bearings. Cone wrenches come very thin, so they can slot onto the narrow flats on the cones. Common sizes are 13, 15 and 17mm, but you'd best take your wheels to the bike shop and check the size before you buy.

◆ **Spoke wrench**, to fit your spokes. Take your wheels to the bike shop to check the size. Too small won't fit, too big will round off the nipple, which is really annoying.

◆ **Wheel jig**. This makes the job of truing wheels much easier and is essential for wheel building.

Cone wrenches

Suspension
Shock tools

◆ These depend on the make and model of the shock. Check the owner's manual (which you have neatly filed) for the tool list. If you have lost the manual, most are available on the net. Check the list of resources at the back of this book for common web sites.

◆ **Air-sprung forks need a shock pump**. These have narrow barrels and accurate gauges to allow a precise volume of air into your shocks. If you buy a new air fork, it may include a shock pump. You can also get tiny trail versions to fit in your pocket when you're out riding.

◆ **A small plastic measuring jug** for shock oil or a **plastic syringe**. They sell these in drug stores for measuring out baby medicine.

Shock pump

Plastic syringe

Suspension fluid

Components
Pedal wrenches

All makes of pedals except Time use a 15mm wrench. Pedal wrenches are narrower than normal wrenches, so they can slot in between the pedal and crank, and are longer for extra leverage. Pedals must be fitted snugly, or they work loose and rip out the crank threads. Time uses a 6mm Allen key, accessed from the back of the crank. For these, you need a good-quality extra-long (200mm, 8 inch) Allen key or an extender bar.

Pedal wrench

Potions and lotions

A supply of cleaning and lubricating products is essential for routine maintenance. Your bike shop will usually have a choice. Ask for their recommendations, since they'll know what works well for your local environment. As you tackle more advanced jobs, you'll need some more specialized items.

Cleaning products

Always start with the least aggressive cleaning products, then gradually intensify.

- **A cleaning fluid**, for example Pedro's Bio Degreaser or Finish Line Bike Wash, both available in the US, or Muc-Off make washing much quicker. Spray it on and leave it to soak in. In dry, dusty conditions you can wipe it off. Otherwise, rinse with clean water.
- **Degreaser**. This is great for cleaning up dirty drivetrains. Spray or paint it onto chain, front rings, and cassettes; leave it to soak in; brush it off. Don't spray degreaser directly into wheel bearings, bottom brackets or headsets. It eats grease wherever it finds it, so if it does seep into bearings, you must strip them out and regrease them — a boring task. Also keep degreaser clear of suspension seals. Use a chain-cleaning box to keep the fluid contained.
- **Hand cleaner**. Essential! Most jobs start with a dirty procedure (like taking off an old broken part) and end with a clean one (such as adjusting a newly fitted part). Trying to assemble parts with new grease and dirty hands is a waste of time, so you need to be able to wash your hands in the middle of a job as well as at the end. Most hardware and auto parts shops sell cleaner that's specially designed for oily hands.

You'll also need plenty of cotton rags. The best source of this is often charity shops. They usually have bags of T-shirts they can't sell as clothes, which make perfect rags.

A sponge is better for paintwork than a brush.

Degreaser

Muc-Off

Hand cleaner

Polish   Grease   Oil

Lubricant and grease

- **Chain lubricant**. This is an absolute essential. Everybody has a favorite type: with me it's Finish Line Cross-Country. Ask the mechanics in your local bike shop what they use. Different lubes work in different climates. If you ride in a very wet and muddy place, you'll need a different lube from someone that rides in hot, dry climates. A dry climate requires a dry lubricant, to keep the drivetrain running smoothly while attracting minimal muck. In muddy, wet conditions you need a wet lube. These are stickier so they stay on in extreme conditions, but attract more dirt so you must be conscientious in your cleaning routine.

The important thing about chain lubes is that they should be applied to clean chains. Putting oil on a dirty chain is the first step toward creating a sticky paste that eats expensive drivetrain components for breakfast. If you haven't got time to clean your chain first, you haven't got time to oil it. Whatever you use for oiling the chain will also do as a more general-purpose lubricant for cables, brake pivots, and derailleur pivots — anywhere two bits of metal need to move smoothly over each other.

I always use drip oil rather than spray oil. Spray is messy and wasteful, and it's too easy to get it on rims and disc rotors by mistake, which makes your brakes slippery rather than sticky.

◆ **Grease.** Confusion surrounds the difference between grease and oil. Essentially, they're both lubricants, but grease is solid and oil is liquid. Grease is stickier and can't be used on exposed parts of the bike; dirt sticks to the grease, forms a grinding paste and wears out the bike rather than making it run more smoothly. Grease is used inside sealed components, like hubs. You don't get in there often so the stuff is required to last longer and remain cleaner. In an emergency almost any grease will do, but as you don't need much, get the good stuff from your local bike shop.

As your confidence grows, invest in a grease gun. This will keep your hands and grease stock clean. For a clean and simple system, I like the ones that screw onto the top of a tube of grease. To get the last bit out, though, you usually abandon the gun and cut open the tube.

Specific lotions

As with your toolkit, start with a stock of essential items and build up as you tackle specialist jobs.

◆ **Disc brake fluid.** Use only the fluid specified for your brake system. DOT fluid, an autoparts trade standard, deteriorates once the bottle has been opened so buy in small amounts and open as you need it.

◆ **Suspension oil** is formulated to have damping properties. Its "weight" is critical and depends on the make and model of your fork or rear shock. Damping occurs by oil being forced through small holes. Lighter, thinner oil (e.g., 5wt) passes through more quickly. Heavier, thicker oil (e.g., 15wt) takes longer. Your fork or shock only works properly with the correct weight of oil: check the manual (which is, of course, neatly filed in your workshop). You may mix two weights of oil to make an intermediate weight, but don't mix brands. See the Suspension section for a full explanation.

◆ **Antiseize** (also called Ti-prep).This prevents reactive metals from sticking together and is especially important for titanium components, which react and seize whatever they touch. Avoid skin contact with antiseize; this stuff is not good for you.

◆ **Vaseline** is often the best substance for applying to seatposts in carbon frames. Check with the frame manufacturer's recommendations.

◆ **Plastic components.** These need their own lubricants. SRAM Twistshifter gear-changers and the Sachs equivalent, Twistgrips, have to be cleaned with a suitable degreaser (e.g., Finish Line Ecotech) or warm soapy water, and oiled with a special plastic lube (e.g., Jonnisnot).

◆ **Loctite glue.** The generic name is threadlock, although the Loctite brand is pretty good. Used where bolts cannot rattle loose and between parts that may corrode together if moisture gets in, like rear hubs. Different colors indicate different strengths. Threadlock "#222" is red and is usually applicable up to M6 (6mm diameter) threads. Threadlock "#242", the most common, is blue and used for bolts M6 and above. Threadlock "#290", for holding pivot bushes, is green.

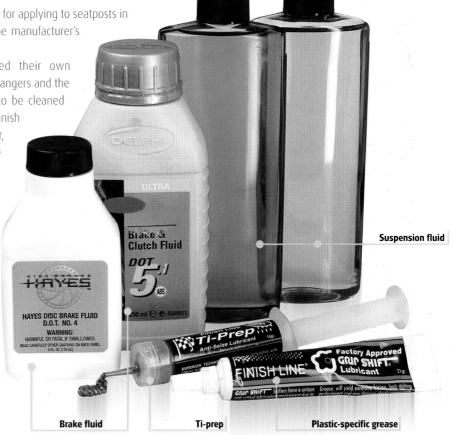

Suspension fluid

Brake fluid

Ti-prep

Plastic-specific grease

The tackle box

One of the most irritating parts of bike repair is being thwarted by a simple task because you're missing a simple but very specific part. Bike shop workshops always have racks of plastic drawers full of tiny little parts, many of which are essential for just one job. This is a luxury you're unlikely to have at home.

Your tackle box is essential but, like a good compost heap, it must grow over time and cannot be bought wholesale! Start one now. A tackle box is any container into which you drop odd nuts and bolts left over from other bike repairs. Then, when you shear off an essential bolt after the stores have closed, your box of bits can save your bacon.

The box should be bike-specific — surplus woodscrews and outdated distributor caps don't count. Useful things include M5 (5mm diameter) bolts in lengths from 10mm to 45mm, crank bolts, Aheadset caps with rude slogans on them, odd washers, valve caps, ball bearings and scraps of chain.

Your workshop

A proper workstand is probably your most expensive investment. Almost all the procedures listed in the main part of this book is easier if the bike is held steady with both wheels off the ground. Working standing up is easier than working crouched on the ground. A workstand also allows you to turn the pedals and wheels and observe everything working.

Take care where you clamp the bike into the stand. The best place is the seatpost. Try to avoid clamping onto the tubes — these are thin, and you can dent, or even bend, them too easily. Wipe the jaws of the stand before you clamp the bike into it, so you don't scuff the paintwork. If you're tight for storage space, look for a workstand that folds up when you're not using it.

The next level down from a full workstand is a propstand, which keeps the back wheel off the ground and holds the bike upright. These are relatively cheap compared to a workstand and a good compromise if you're not ready to commit to a workstand.

If you have nothing, then improvise. Avoid turning the bike upside down — bikes don't like it. Instead, find an obedient friend who will hold the bike upright and off the ground at appropriate moments.

You need enough light to see by, especially for close-up jobs such as truing wheels. Most repairs are messy too, so if you're working indoors, spread an old sheet on the floor before you start to catch things that drop and to protect the carpet.

Ventilation is important. Any time you use solvents or spray, you need enough air circulating to dilute chemical fumes to harmless levels. Anything powerful enough to sweeten your bike will probably damage your body.

The same goes for bodily contact with substances. Consider wearing mechanics rubber gloves. This saves loads of time cleaning your hands and reduces the quantity of chemicals absorbed through your skin. Lots of jobs involve removing something dirty, then either cleaning it or replacing it, and then fitting it. You must have clean hands for the last part of the job — there's no point fitting a clean component with dirty hands.

Torque

In order to measure how firmly we are tightening bolts, we use torque. There are two methods of doing this: the instinctive, common-sense version, and the scientific version. Both have their advantages. Traditionally, the manufacturer of a part indicated to the mechanic how firmly things should be tightened by fitting an appropriate bolt.

Delicate parts, which need just holding in place, come equipped with small bolts. The wrenches that fit these bolts are short so that you don't have enough leverage to overtighten the bolt. Parts that need to be clamped down firmly come with a big bolt that you can attach a nice hefty wrench to and lean on. This used to work well enough, but as riders we're demanding lighter equipment all the time, so manufacturers are designing components with less room for error. For example, replacing steel bolts with aluminum ones will save weight, but aluminum bolts are far less forgiving of overtightening: once stressed, they can snap without warning.

Overtightening bolts can also strip the thread that you're bolting into. This is a common problem with aluminum parts. For example, overtightening the bolts that hold the stem to the handlebars can damage the thread inside the stem, so that the bolt rotates uselessly rather than securing the bars.

The reverse problem, undertightening bolts, has a more obvious consequence: whatever you're trying to secure will rattle or work loose. Crank bolts often suffer from this — the left-hand one in particular needs to be tighter than people imagine. The first warning is usually a regular creaking noise as you pedal. If you ignore it, the crank bolt works loose, allowing the crank to shift about on the bottom bracket axle. This damages the mating surface between bottom bracket and crank so that even if you retighten the crank bolt, it works loose constantly.

As a consequence, it's becoming more vital to know exactly how much force you're putting on any specific bolt. This is especially true for suspension forks, where the bolts that hold the moving parts together are constantly being stressed by the cycling (moving up and down) of the fork. Most components now come with a tightening torque specified for every bolt.

Since torque specifications are a relatively recent obsession, most come quoted in Newton-meters (Nm). The Imperial equivalent unit is the inch-pound (in-lb). To convert inch-pounds to Newton-meters, multiply by 0.113.

However, it's one thing to find out how tight a bolt is supposed to be and quite another to be able to tighten it to exactly that amount. There is a workshop tool that allows you to do this — a torque wrench. It looks like a ratcheting socket handle and works in a similar way. Standard socket heads fit onto the wrench, which can then be set to the specified torque by turning a knob at the base of the handle. The wrench is then used to tighten the bolt as normal. When you reach the correct level, the handle of the bolt gives slightly, and you hear a distinct click, telling you to stop.

These tools are simple and reliable to use and are becoming more and more common in bicycle workshops. A well-equipped workshop will have two torque wrenches. A small one, with a range from about 4 to 20 Nm (35 to 177 inch-pounds), covers delicate applications such as cable clamps and rotor-fixing bolts. A larger one, with a range from 20 to 50 Nm (177 to 443 inch-pounds), covers those that need more force, like crank bolts. The two sizes are necessary because the tools always work best in the middle of their range. However, they are expensive to buy, relatively delicate and usually considered overkill for a home workshop.

Unless you're lucky enough to own a torque wrench of your own, if you ever get a chance to borrow one use it to tighten a selection of the bolts on your bike to the specified torque setting, to get a feel for how tight they should be. Many mechanics use torque wrenches to set bolts to the correct level regularly to remind themselves what the correct torque feels like.

When working by feel, be aware of the size of the bolts you're tightening and use this as an indication of the amount of force you should be using. Small bolts take small wrenches (or thin screwdrivers) and so should be tightened firmly but not excessively. If you're overenthusiastic with a delicate bolt, you'll strip the thread, snap the head off or round off the key faces. Large bolts or those that have to be tightened with chunky tools, like bottom bracket cups, should be wedged home with vigor.

The best place to find torque specifications are the instructions that came with the component, which will have the right torque for your specific make and model. New bikes come with a pack of booklets and leaflets, covering all the parts fitted to your bike. You may have to ask for it when you buy the bike. If you haven't got the instructions any more, use the Park Tools web site to reference general torque specifications. Park Tools' website is www.parktool.com, and the page address is www.parktool.com/repair_help/torque.shtml.

All specified torques assume that the bolt you are using has been greased so that it turns easily in the threads, and that both parts of the thread are clean and in good condition. A dirty, damaged bolt will be harder to tighten than a clean one and so will give a false torque reading.

Rescue repairs for the trail: how to be self-sufficient on a bike

This section deals with the repairs you may need to undertake while out riding — and for these you need a trail toolkit. Do carry your own, even if you ride with other people who are well-equipped. No one wants to be in a group standing around saying, "But I thought you'd have your pump." Also, ensure you can use everything in your toolkit, and immediately replace items that you run out of, like spare tubes.

If you've never tackled the following jobs before, practice the following in the comfort of your own home: (1) getting the wheels on and off your bike; (2) removing and refitting tires; and (3) splitting and rejoining chains. None of these repairs is difficult, but they're all much harder tackled the first time in the cold and wet.

Considering what we expect them to do, bicycles rarely go wrong. If you keep your bicycle well maintained, it will be unusual to face a trailside repair that is not on this list. However, you are occasionally faced with the unexpected. Once, miles from home with the night closing in, I had to make an emergency derailleur pivot. I succeeded using a spare pivot from the dismantled innards of an Allen key tool, held in place with a generous wad of electrical tape. The derailleur even changed gear quite effectively.

Keep your cool, be resourceful

Whenever you have to fix your bike by the side of the trail, think the task through carefully before you start.

If you're frustrated by a puncture or other repair, don't start fixing until you're less stressed. Do not, at any stage, throw your bicycle around, however petulant you feel. This improves nothing. You also look stupid.

Remember, everything you're carrying and wearing is a potential emergency spare part. Shoelaces, watchstraps, almost anything can be useful in ways you'd never think of until you really need them.

If you have to release your brakes to fix the bike, remember to refit them.

Spread a jacket out on the ground to catch pieces before you start work. Any part that falls off your bike or drops through cold, wet fingers can make a break for freedom, lying still and quiet in the grass until you've given up and gone away.

Your bicycle is on your side and really wants to get better, but it needs encouragement, not abuse. Swear if you have to, but don't kick it.

Repairing your bike after a crash

The first priority after you've crashed is to assess yourself as safe to ride once the bike is fixed. I'm lousy at this. I always stand up as soon as possible and say things like "I'm fine," even if I can't remember who I am.

Don't believe it when anyone else puts on the act either. You may be shaken even if you're not injured. Stop and recover before you get back on the bike. Once you've decided you are all right, check over the bike. Don't get sidetracked by obvious damage because there can often be more than one problem. Decide if you can safely repair the bike, or whether it will be quicker to walk out than struggle vainly for ages with the repair before limping home anyway.

Tools for the trail

Trail tools are things you carry around in the hope you never have to use them. When you ride with a group of people, it's worth being known as the person with a decent toolkit. Even on a bad day when you are really slow, you will never get left behind.

Keep your trail tools completely separate instead of raiding your toolbox for them so you know everything is there. Replace anything you run out of right away — there's nothing more irritating than realizing your spare tube has a hole in it that you've been meaning to fix. Portable tools often aren't ideal for the workshop. Small, light wrenches, for example, are great for the trail but are usually too flimsy for the workshop.

I use a seatpack. Lots of people carry their tools in a rucksack or bumbag, but they're heavy and painful to land on so I prefer to let the bike do the work. Seatpacks that clip on and off a clamp are best; it's annoying messing about with muddy Velcro straps on the trail. The following selection is a starting point rather than a definitive list. What you need still depends on your bike and riding environment.

For example, the bolts on most bikes are the Allen key type, but if yours has nuts, you need the corresponding wrenches. If you often get punctures — for example, because you ride thorny trails — carry extra tubes and patches. Carry a patch kit even if you have a spare tube; punctures can come in batches. For long rides in remote places, see the supplementary list. Ensure you know how to use what you're carrying! If you get desperate, you can stand by the side of the trail looking pathetic, hoping some kind soul who knows how to use your tools will ride past, but it's a risky strategy.

Trail tool pack

◆ **Spare tube,** with the correct valve (thin Presta or fat car-type Schraeder) for your pump.

◆ **Pump.** Make sure it fits your inner-tube valves. Double-action pumps put air in as you both pull and push, refilling the tire much more quickly. If you carry the pump on a bracket in your frame, use extra Velcro straps to ensure it doesn't rattle loose. After riding in muddy weather, clean the pump so the seals around the barrels stay airtight and won't leak. If you ride a lot in mud, carry the pump inside a backpack or bumbag to keep it clean. If the seals grit up and leak, the pump can't build up pressure.

◆ **Patch kit.** Once you've broken the seal on these, the glue dries out in about six months no matter how hard you screw on the lid, so make sure yours is fresh. UST tires require a special type of patch kit; make sure you have the right one.

◆ **Tire-levers.** If you're not confident about getting the tire off the rim with two levers, then carry three — they don't weigh much. Plastic levers are far better than metal ones, which damage the rims.

◆ **Allen key/screwdriver fold-up toolset.** I prefer the fold-up tools for trail use: they're easier to find if you drop them, and the body of the tool makes a comfortable handle for tightening and loosening bolts without hurting your hand. As a bare minimum, you need 4, 5 and 6mm Allen keys, a flathead screwdriver and a Phillips screwdriver.

◆ **Chain tool.** For Shimano chains you also need to carry appropriate spare rivets. You can also buy spare Powerlinks (see Split Links later in this chapter), which are a quick and easy way to split and rejoin chains, and weigh almost nothing.

◆ **A couple of zipties.** These are essential for emergencies and come out top in the weight-to-usefulness chart.

◆ **A strip of duct tape,** wrapped around the barrel of your pump. Like zipties, it weighs almost nothing and can come in very handy in an emergency.

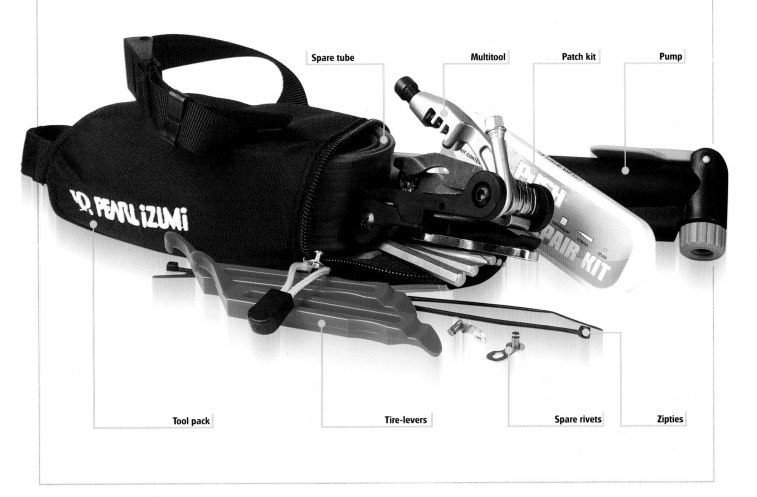

Spare tube   Multitool   Patch kit   Pump

Tool pack   Tire-levers   Spare rivets   Zipties

Punctures

Punctures are inevitable. The pressure inside the tire is higher than the pressure outside, and the world is full of sharp things. Don't worry if you've never fixed a flat before though; it's not as difficult as people make out. And, like learning to tie your shoelaces, it gets easier with practice.

There are ways to reduce the number of punctures you get. Occasionally you pick up a sharp object that cuts straight through tire and tube and causes a flat, but often objects take a while to work their way through the casing of the tire. Before you set out, check both tires: raise each wheel off the ground in turn, spin each slowly, and pick out foreign objects. Maximum and minimum pressures are printed or stamped on the tire sidewall. Make sure the tire is inflated to at least the minimum suggested pressure to reduce the chance of snakebite flats (caused when pressure from, say, a rock edge, squeezes two symmetrical holes in the tube against the sides of the rim). If you like running at very low pressure, choose a tire designed to take it. These tires have a thicker sidewall, which won't fold over itself and pinch the tube.

Problems with punctures at or around the valve can also be caused by low tire pressures. If there isn't enough air in the tire, it won't sit firmly against the inside of the rim. The tire will creep gradually around the rim, dragging the tube with it. The valve is held in place in the valve hole, so the tube around it becomes stretched and tears easily, ripping the valve out of the tube. Check your tires regularly for large cuts as well — under pressure, the tube will bulge out of these cuts and burst instantly.

Some people suffer from punctures more than others. If you feel unfairly cursed, consider investing in puncture-resistant tires. These have an extra layer of tough material incorporated into the carcass of the tire under the tread, which helps to stop sharp things working their way through. They do make the tire a little heavier, but it's worth it if you find punctures irritating. Also, think twice before buying tires that proudly proclaim their weight on the package — there will always be a compromise between weight and puncture-resistance.

Fixing a puncture by fitting a new tube in a standard tire

I always prefer to carry a spare tube as well as a puncture kit. It's much quicker than messing about waiting for the glue to dry or hoping that a glueless patch will hold. They don't weigh much or take up much room. Don't forget to check your tire carefully before you fit the new tube and to remove whatever caused the flat in the first place. Take the punctured tube home with you, repair the puncture in the comfort of your own home, and carry the tube around as your new spare. Once a tube has five or six patches, it's time to retire it.

If you're out on the trail, try to calculate how quickly your tire is going down. Maybe, if you're on your way home, you could pump it up and get there. Doesn't work that way very often, though! More likely, you're going to have to fix it.

REPLACING TUBES

Step 1: If you have rim brakes, you need to release them to get the tire out easily. For V-brakes, pull the black rubber boot off the end of the noodle, squeeze the brake units together, and pull the noodle out and then up to release it from its nest. For cantilever brakes, squeeze the brake units together, and push the cable nipple down and out of the slot in the unit.

Step 2: Turn the bicycle upside down. Undo quick-release skewer. Unless you have a fancy skewer set, do this by folding (not turning) the handle over the axle. If you're unsure how to use quick-releases safely, read the section on them before you go any further (page 69). For the front wheel, undo the nut on the opposite side of wheel several turns to get past the lawyer tabs (which stop the wheel falling out of the dropout slots if the skewer comes loose).

Step 3: The rear wheel is a little trickier to remove than the front. Stand behind the bike. With your left hand, pull the body of the derailleur backwards with your fingers, and push the cage forwards with your thumb, as shown. This creates a clear path, so that you can lift the rear wheel up and forward, without getting tangled up in the chain.

Step 4: Inspect the outside of the tire before you go any further to see if you can work out what caused the puncture. There may be nothing — you may have had a snakebite puncture, or the escaping air may have ejected whatever caused the puncture. If you find something sharp, pry it out. (Later you also need to examine the inside of the tire — see page 28.)

Step 5: If there's any air left in the tire, expel it. Remove the valve cap. For Presta valves (long and thin), undo the little thumb nut on top of the valve and press it down. For Schraeder valves (short, fat, car-tire type), use something sharp, like a key, to push down the pin in the middle of the valve. Stand the wheel upright on the ground, push down, and massage the tire. The more air you get out of the tube at this stage, the easier it is to get the tire off.

Step 6: Each side of the tire is held on by an internal wire, or Kevlar hoop, called the bead. This is smaller than the outside of the rim so the tire stays on when you pump it up. To remove the tire, lift enough of the bead over the sidewall of the rim. With care, this can be done by hand. Hold the wheel upright facing you. Work around the tire, pushing the side closest to you into the dip in the middle of the rim. This will give you enough slack to pull the bead off.

Step 7: With the wheel still upright and facing you, pinch a 10cm (4 inches) section of the side of the tire nearest you with both hands. Lift this section up and over the rim, towards you. Hold it in place with one hand, and work around the tire with the other gradually, easing the bead over the rim. Once you've got about a third of the tire off, the rest will come away easily.

Step 8: If you can't get the tire off by hand, you need to use tire-levers. Starting opposite the valve, tuck one tire-lever under the bead in line with the spokes. Fold it back and hook the tire-lever under the spoke to hold it in place. Move along two spokes and repeat with a second tire-lever, then repeat with a third tire-lever. Remove middle tire-lever, leapfrog one of the others and repeat, continuing until you can pull that side of the tire off with your hands.

Step 9: If the valve has a little nut screwing it to the rim, undo it. Reach inside the tire and pull out the tube. Leave the other side of the tire in place.

Toolbox

- **Spare tube** — check that the valve matches the tubes on your bike
- **Puncture kit** — backup in case you get more than one puncture
- **Pump** — make sure it works on your valve type. A pressure gauge is useful
- **Tire levers** — two is standard, take three if you're not confident
- **Wrenches** — any wrenches you need to remove your wheels
- **Tool pack** — carry these separately, so you can find them quickly
- **Warm clothes** — a hat to put on to keep you warm while you fix your bike — I get cold very quickly as soon as I stop riding

Refitting a new tube

It's vital to work out what caused the puncture before you fit a new tube. If the problem's still there when you fit a new tube, you'll puncture again right away — which is even more irritating if you haven't got a second spare tube.

Your first step is to inspect the tire carefully. Look around the outside for thorns, shards of glass or sharp stones. If you can't see anything from the outside, check the inside of the tire too. The easiest way to locate the culprit is to feel around inside the tire with your fingers, moving slowly and carefully to avoid cutting yourself. If you're still unsure what caused the flat, pump air into the tube and locate the hole. You may be able to hear it rushing out of a big hole. Smaller holes can be harder to find — pass the tube slowly through your hands so that you can feel the air on your skin. You can put the tube in a bowl of water and watch for bubbles, but I don't usually carry a bowl of water in my emergency toolkit. Sometimes you can use puddles as an alternative. Once you've found the hole in the tube, hold the tube up to the tire to locate the area of the tire where the puncture occurred, and inspect the tire again carefully.

Remove anything that you find. It's often best to push objects out of the tire from the inside, rather than forcing them through the tire from the outside and making the hole bigger. You won't necessarily find something in the tire because punctures happen in other ways too. Pinch punctures — also known as snakebite flats — happen when you don't have enough tire pressure. If you hit a rock hard, the tire squashes, trapping the tube between the rock and your rim. Pinch flats are usually easy to identify: you have two neat holes in your tire, a rim width apart. Check the tire sidewalls as well because a hole here will turn into a fresh puncture immediately. If you have rim brakes, the most likely cause of the puncture is the brake block sitting too high and rubbing on your rim. Either your brake block is set too high, or the wheel has been refitted crookedly in its dropouts so that it sits off to one side rather than neatly in the center of your frame.

"Booting" your tire

Big tears or gashes in the tire will need to be repaired before you fit a new tube; otherwise the new tube will bulge out of the split when you inflate it. The tube is much softer than the tire, so any bubbles will either scrape on the ground and tear or get pinched in the tire split as the wheel rotates. Both will cause another puncture immediately, which is irritating, especially if you don't have a second spare. Feel carefully around the inside of the tire. Any holes big enough to push the end of your finger into will cause a problem. You can buy tire boots — sticky-backed strips of plastic — but out on the trail, you'll have to improvise. The air pressure trying to force the tube out through the tire is high, so you'll need something fairly stiff. Ideally, choose something sticky so that it stays in place as you refit the tube. Duct tape is ideal for smaller holes; it's worth sticking a strip of it to the underside of your saddle for occasions like this. Ordinary tube patches will also help. For bigger holes, you'll need something stiffer to bridge the tear in the tire. This is a chance for you to use your imagination — try using food wrapping, cardboard, shoe insoles, whatever you have available.

FITTING THE NEW TUBE

Step 1: Now for the new tube. Remove the nut on the valve, if there is one. Pump a little air into the tube — just enough to give it shape. This will prevent the tube getting trapped under the bead as you refit the tire. Pull back the section of tire over the valve hole and pop the valve through the hole. Work around the tire, tucking the tube up inside it.

Step 2: Returning to the opposite side of the valve, gently fold the tire back over the rim. This gets tougher as you go. When there's just a short section left, you'll probably get stuck. Let a little air out of the tube again, and push the sections of tire you've already fitted away from the sidewall of the rim and into the dip in the middle, like you did to get it off. You should then be able to ease the last section on with your thumbs, a bit at a time.

Step 3: If you can't hand-fit the last section, use tire-levers. Work on short sections 5cm (2 inches) at a time, and take care not to trap the tube between the rim and the tire-lever as it's easy to pinch-puncture it. Once the tire is reseated, push the valve up into the rim so that it almost disappears (to make sure the area of tube near the valve is not caught under the tire bead).

Step 4: Pump up the tire. If you had a snakebite flat last time, put in a little more air. Once the tire is up, retighten the thumb nut on Presta valves, screw the stem nut back onto the valve stem, and refit the dustcap. Don't fit the valve stem nut until the tube is inflated, as you risk trapping a bulge of the tube under the tire bead.

Step 5: Refit the rear wheel. With the bike upside down, stand behind it and hold wheel in your right hand with sprockets on left-hand side. Put a left-hand finger in front of the guide jockey wheel (nearer the ground in this position), and your thumb behind the tension jockey wheel. Pull finger back and push thumb forward, then place wheel so sprockets are within the loop of the chain. Guide the axle into the dropouts, and secure by doing up the quick-release.

Step 6: Refit the front wheel. This is easier. Drop the wheel into the dropout slots; make sure there's an equal amount of space between the tire and the fork legs, and tighten the quick-release lever securely. Again, if you're not sure about your skewers, read the quick-release skewer section (page 69).

Step 7: If you have disc brakes, wiggle the rotor **(A)** into place between the brake pads before settling the wheel into the dropout slots. You need to check that the rotor is sitting centrally between the brake pads inside the caliper. If it's hard to see, hold something light-colored on the far side of the caliper as you look through. You may need to adjust the position of the wheel slightly so that the rotor is central.

Step 8: For rim brakes, don't forget to refit the brakes — it's easy to overlook this vital stage in the excitement of fixing your puncture. Pull the brake units together and refit the cable. If you have V-brakes, take care to seat the end of the noodle **(B)** securely in the key-shaped nest.

Step 9: Turn the bike back over and check that the brakes work properly: pull the front brake on and push the bike forward. The front wheel should lock, and the back one should lift off the ground. Pull the back brake on and push the bike forward. The back wheel should lock, sliding across the ground. Lift up the wheels and spin them. Check they spin freely, and that rim brakes don't rub on the tire.

Checklist: what caused the puncture?

Check for:
- Sharp things (thorns, glass, flint) cutting through the tire
- Cuts or gashes in the tire that allow the tube to bulge out — check both the sidewall and the tread
- Snakebite punctures — when the tire, without enough air, gets trapped between the rim and a rock
- Rim tape failure — when sharp spoke ends puncture the tube or when the tube gets trapped in rim holes
- Valve failure — when under-inflated tires shift around on the rim
- Overheating from rim brakes — although rare, this can happen on long mountain descents
- Worn tires — when tires get old, the bead can stretch, allowing the tire to creep out over the edge of the rim, where it will puncture
- Badly adjusted rim brakes — when blocks that are set too high rub on the tire rather than the rim, cutting through the sidewall of the tire in no time at all

Fixing a UST puncture by fitting a replacement tube

The simplest way of fixing a UST tubeless tire puncture on the trail is to use a new ordinary tube, which will fit fine (thus the mechanic's sarcastic name for the system: "Use Standard Tubes!"). You can fix the tire properly when you're home. See the Chapter 4 for instructions on how to do this.

◆ Remove the punctured wheel (see page 26). If you've only just had a puncture, the first thing to do is to locate the hole. If there aren't any obvious sharps or gashes, pass the tire in front of your face. You should hear the remaining air hissing out of the tire. You may also see bubbles if the ground is wet, or feel the cold air from inside the tube on your face. Once you've found the hole, mark it if you can, or note where it is in relation to any labels on the side of your tire.

◆ The UST design relies on the bead of the tire being airtight where it fits onto the sidewall of the rim. The tire and rim have matching profiles so that the join becomes more airtight as you put more pressure into it. This means that it can be tricky to break the seal. Try pushing the tire away from the sidewall with your hands. If you can't shift it, try laying the wheel on the ground and carefully stand on the sidewall of the tire where it joins the rim.

◆ Once you've released the seal, you should be able to pull one side of the tire away from the rim. Try not to break the seal on the other side so that you don't have to reseat it later. Unscrew the nut on the base of the valve stem, then pull the valve out from inside. Keep it somewhere safe — you'll need it again when you fix or replace the tire.

◆ Put a little bit of air in the tube, barely enough to hold its shape. Fit the valve into the valve hole and fit the valve cap to stop the valve disappearing inside the tire as you refit the tube. Tuck the tube into the tire all the way round.

◆ Start to fold the tire back onto the rim. An extra pair of hands can make the job easier at this point, particularly to hold down what you've fitted while you work on the next bit. Aim to finish at the valve stem. It's a lot easier if the opposite bead is still seated on the sidewall, so that there is space for the bead you're fitting in the well at the center of the rim.

◆ Don't use tire-levers on UST tires. The molding around the bead forms an airtight seal with the rim, which is damaged by levers so it leaks. Work a little at a time, lifting up a short section of tire sidewall with your thumbs, and pushing it up and over the rim. The last section is the most difficult; it may help to let some air out of the tube. To create enough slack in the bead, go back around and push the bead on the opposite side of the wheel into the well at the center of the rim.

◆ Once you've got the tire on, push the valve upwards into the rim, without losing it, to make sure that that area of tube is not trapped under the bead of the tire. Pull it back out and pump up as normal. If the valve has a nut or knurled ring that threads onto it, this should only be refitted once the tube is pumped up. Refit the wheel, as above.

The great grass myth

There's a long-standing story that if you puncture without a spare tube or patch kit, you can get home by stuffing the tire with grass. This sounds feasible in theory, but in practice it's either nonsense or requires a special kind of grass that I've yet to come across. I've tried it and just ended up spending an enormous amount of time harvesting grass by hand and trying to force it into the tire. This is trickier than you would imagine since the grass compacts as you pack it. Even if you can stuff enough in to give the tire some kind of shape, the tire rolls off the rim as soon as you cycle faster than walking pace anyway, shedding all your hard-won grass harvest instantly. If you try to cycle really slowly, the tire is so soft that it squishes all over the place, making your bike feel like you're riding through molasses. You might as well leave the grass growing happily where it is and start walking anyway.

Stiff links/split links

Often, the link you've just joined is stiff, although stiff links occur for other reasons: the chain may need lubricating, or you're riding in the wet. You feel a stiff link as you're riding — the pedals slip forward regularly, but at different places in the pedal revolution.

To find a stiff link, change into the smallest sprocket at the back and the largest chainring at the front. Lean the bike up against a wall, crouch beside it, and pedal backward slowly with your right hand. The chain heads backward from the top of the front chainring, around the smallest sprocket, then around the front of the guide jockey and the back of the tension jockey. Then, it heads to the front chainring again. The chain is straight as it travels across the top, then bends around the sprocket. The links should be flexible enough to straighten out as they emerge from the bottom of the sprocket, then bend the other way to pass round the guide jockey. But a stiff link won't straighten out as it drops off the bottom of the cassette and then passes clumsily around the derailleur. Once you've spotted the area of the chain that's causing problems, slow your pedaling right down and check each link as it comes off the tension jockey.

REPLACING STIFF LINKS

Step 1: Once you've identified the problem link, get your chain tool out. You need to use the set of supports nearest the handle — the spreading supports. Look carefully at the problem rivet to identify whether one side of the rivet sticks further out one side of the chain than the other. If it is uneven, start with the sticking-out side. If it looks even, start with either side.

Step 2: Lay the chain over the supports, and turn the handle clockwise until the pin of the chain tool almost touches the rivet on the chain. Wiggle the chain to precisely line up the pin with the rivet. Turn until you can feel the pin touching the rivet, then just a third of a turn more. Back off the tool and wiggle it to see if the link is still stiff. If it is not yet as flexible as those around it, repeat from the other side of the chain. The rivet needs to end up as even as possible.

Step 3: If you don't have the chain tool with you, hold the chain as shown and flex it firmly backwards and forwards between your hands. Stop and check frequently to see if you've removed the stiff link. The last thing you want is to go too far and twist the chain plates.

Split links

A split link, also called Powerlink, is a quick and easy way to split and rejoin chains. It is particularly useful if you like to remove your chain to clean it, since repeatedly removing and replacing the rivets in chains can cause weak spots. It's also a great emergency fix. You still need your chain tool for removing the remains of twisted or broken links, but the split link will not be stiff when you refit it and does not shorten the chain.

There are a couple of different types of split links; the best is the Powerlink, which comes free with SRAM chains. All split links work in similar ways. The link comes in identical halves, each half with one rivet and one key-shaped hole. To fit, you pass a rivet through each end of the chain, linking the ends together through the wide part of the hole. When you put pressure on the chain, it pulls apart slightly and locks into place. They never release accidentally.

To split the chain, locate the split link and push the adjacent links towards each other. The Powerlink halves are pushed together, lining up the heads of the rivets with the exit holes. You can then push the two halves across each other to release them.

Powerlink — the quick and easy way to split and rejoin chains ▶

Fixing a broken chain

After punctures, repairing a chain is the most common trailside task. Chains get damaged by rocks and pebbles flicking up and trapping between chain and sprocket (gear ring). A mistimed or clumsy shift of the gears can have the same effect, putting pressure on the chain when it's stretched. Old, worn, and neglected chains develop weak spots over time and are more likely to let you down under pressure.

Mostly, for any kind of chain problem, you'll need a chain tool. These are annoying to carry because they only do one job. But when you have a broken chain, nothing else will do — if you haven't got one, you're walking home. It can be shocking when a chain breaks — one moment you're stamping hard on the pedals, the next moment all resistance is gone, and you're left with spinning feet and no balance.

Your first step is to go back and retrieve the chain. They usually unroll in a straight line in the direction you were traveling, so if your chain is not immediately obvious, walk back parallel to the way you came and check your path. If you were moving fast, it may be some way back.

Checking a repaired chain

Once you've finished rejoining the broken parts, it's important to check that the repaired chain is still long enough to reach all the way around your drivetrain. It will be slightly shorter, since you will have removed damaged links. It is essential that there is still enough slack in the chain even in the largest sprocket, so that the derailleur is not strained or twisted. Otherwise, you risk tearing the derailleur off, damaging both the derailleur and the part of the frame to which it attaches.

Get someone to lift up the back of the bike for you, then change into the smallest sprocket at the back and the largest chainring at the front — pedal with your left hand and change gears with your right. Then change gears click by click toward the largest sprocket at the back, while watching the derailleur. As you move into larger sprockets, the derailleur will get stretched forward. Check the tension of the lower section of the chain, where it passes from the bottom of the chainring to the rear derailleur. If this section becomes tight, stop shifting. If you force the chain into a larger sprocket once the chain is tight, you'll damage the derailleur.

If the derailleur is struggling to reach the largest sprocket at the back, it's important not to change into this gear as you ride along. Try to remember not to use this gear. Personally, I prefer to readjust the end-stop screw on the rear derailleur so that I cannot accidentally change into the largest chainring, because it's all too easy to forget once you start riding. Shift click by click into larger gears until the chain becomes taut, then screw in the "low" end-stop screw until you can feel resistance — it will touch the tab inside the derailleur that limits further movement. Once you get home, replace the chain with a new, longer one (you'll almost certainly need a new cassette too) and readjust your end-stop screw so that the chain reaches the largest sprocket. For more about end-stop screws, see pages 109, 116.

MENDING A CHAIN

Wide segment

Narrow segment

One link

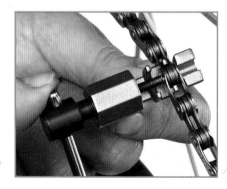

Step 1: Once you have the chain, look at both ends. One will be a narrow segment of chain, and the other a wide segment. A complete link consists of one wide and one narrow segment. You will usually find that the plates on the wide segment got twisted and damaged as the chain broke, so this complete link (the damaged wide one plus the narrow one adjacent to it) has to be removed.

Step 2: Look carefully at the chain to choose the right place to break it. When you come to rejoin it, you need to match up a narrow and a wide segment. Once you've selected the correct rivet, lay the chain over the chain tool as shown. Your chain tool probably has two sets of supports to lay chain over. Choose the set furthest from the handle of the tool.

Step 3: Turn the handle of the tool clockwise, so that the pin approaches the chain. When you get close, line up the pin very carefully with the center of the chain rivet. If the pin is not properly aligned with the rivet, you risk damaging the chain plates — creating a new weak spot on your chain— as you push the rivet out.

Step 4: As you continue to rotate the handle of the chain tool, it will start to push the rivet out of the chain. Be careful how far you push the rivet through. If the chain is a Shimano, and you have a replacement rivet, push the old rivet all the way out. However, with other makes of chain you reuse the original rivet and must make sure you don't push it out completely because they're awkward to replace.

Step 5: Ideally, you need to stop pushing the rivet when there's a little stub poking out just this side of the outer plate, well before it falls out. With a Park tool, wind the handle in until it won't go any further — this is exactly the right amount. You'll have to flex the chain slightly, as shown, to free the inner segment from the stub of rivet sticking out, then separate the chain.

Step 6: You'll have to take out a complete link — one wide section and one narrow section — so repeat the process, two rivets along, on the other side of your twisted link. You should now have a broken link and a slightly shortened chain; one end should end in a wide segment, the other in a narrow segment. Turn it so that the rivet at the wide end faces toward you.

One link

Step 7: Feed the end of the chain with the narrow segment between bottom tension jockey wheel and the tab at the bottom of the derailleur, then between the tab and the top guide jockey wheel. Don't go around the outside of the top tab; the shifting still works in a way, but things are noisy! If you have another bike, use it as a reference. Pass the chain around the front of the guide jockey, then over and back to the bottom of the cassette.

Step 8: Continue around behind the bottom of the cassette, up and forward over the top, and then forward toward the chainset. Pass the chain through the front derailleur. It will eventually have to sit on the chainrings but, for now, pass it around the front of the chainset, then drop it into the gap between the chainset and the frame to give yourself enough slack to rejoin the chain easily.

Step 9: If you're refitting a standard chain, ease the two ends together, flexing the chain so you can slide the inner segment of chain past the stub of rivet sticking through to the inside of the outer plates. Once you've got it, though, the stub will make it easy to locate the rivet in the hole in the inner plates, lining the two ends of chain up. For Shimano chains, see page 34.

Step 10: Lay the chain over the chain support furthest away from you. Turn the handle clockwise until the pin on the chain tool almost touches the rivet on the chain. Wiggle the chain to precisely line up the pin with the rivet.

Step 11: Keep turning the handle, while pushing the rivet into the chain, until there is an even amount of rivet showing on both sides of the chain. Remove the tool.

Step 12: Rejoining the chain usually squashes the plates together and makes the link stiff. See page 31 to free stiff links. Finally, reach around behind the chainset and lift the chain back onto a chainring. Stand up, lift the saddle up with your left hand, and push the pedal around with your right foot so that the chain can find a gear.

Shimano chains

Shimano chains need to be treated slightly different from standard chains. The rivets that join each link are very tightly fitted together, so it will usually damage the chain plates if you try to reuse an original one.

When splitting and rejoining a Shimano chain, the rivet must be pushed all the way out, then replaced with a special Shimano joining link. The rivets are different lengths to match the different chain widths used by eight- and nine-speed systems, so make sure to choose the correct replacement: the longer eight-speed rivets are grey, the shorter nine-speed version is silver.

The replacement rivet is twice as long as the original rivets and has a groove in the middle. The first section is a guide to locate the rivet correctly in the chain and must be broken off once the second part of the rivet has been driven home with the chain tool. This means you need pliers to snap the guide off, as well as a replacement rivet.

REFITTING A SHIMANO CHAIN

Step 1: Push the ends together until the holes line up, then push through the replacement rivet. The first half of the rivet goes through easily, holding things together while you use the chain tool. Lay the chain on the furthest supports of the chain tool, line up the chain tool pin with the rivet on the chain, and turn the handle of the tool clockwise. The groove in the center of the new rivet appears from the other side of the chain. Turn until the second half of the rivet emerges.

Step 2: Snap off the section of rivet sticking out, ideally with pliers. If you don't have any, trap the end of the rivet between two Allen keys on a multitool and twist.

Step 3: Wriggle the new link. Often it is stiff because the plates get stuck together. Lay the chain back over the chain tool, with the stiff rivet in the set of supports nearest the handle. Wind the handle in until the pin touches the rivet, then a further third of a turn to loosen link. Reach in behind chainset and lift chain back onto a chainring. Stand up, lift the saddle with your left hand, and push the pedal around with your right foot so that the chain can find its own gear.

Successful chain fixing — key points to remember

- Always use a good-quality chain tool. Cheap ones are fine for kids' bikes, but modern chains are manufactured so that the rivet is a very tight fit in the chain plate. This helps stop you from breaking them, but means that they will laugh at anything less than a proper chain tool.
- Big multitools sometimes include a chain tool. These are always better than nothing, but seldom as good as a proper separate one.
- Align the pin of the chain tool very carefully with the center of the rivet, otherwise you risk damaging the chain plates and mangling the link.
- Always check links that you've just joined. They'll often be stiff because the chain plates get squashed together as you push the rivet through them. Use your chain tool to spread the chain plates back out again, or the chain will slip over your sprockets as you pedal (see page 31).

Twisted links

Chain links usually get twisted when stones get kicked up by the tires, although if you're clumsy, you can also twist links with careless changes. You feel twisted links first — a regular, slight chain slip, but not always in the same place in your pedal stroke.

Twisted links

The gaps between the chain plates are only just big enough to fit a sprocket or chainring tooth into, so once a link is twisted it usually rides up over the tops of the teeth rather than dropping into the valley, causing your chain to slip under pressure. Alternatively, if the twisted link does mesh successfully onto a chainring tooth, it can get stuck and be sucked around the back of the chainring, getting jammed between the chainstay and the chainring. As well as being annoying, this damages the chainring and chainstay.

Even after you've worked out that you have a twisted link, it can be tricky to spot. The best place to see one from is behind the bike. Get someone else to hold the bike upright and pedal slowly backward. Get behind the bike and look along the chain from the same level as the cassette. You should see the chain stretching away from you, from the top of the cassette to the top of a chainring. The links should all be in the same line, with the two sides parallel. As your friend pedals, fresh chain is constantly fed up through the derailleur. Keep watching the top section of chain; the twisted link will make an obvious kink in the straight line of the chain.

You have two options for sorting out the twisted link. The easiest is to re-twist the link straight again. If it works, this solution is quick and simple, but leaves the repaired link weaker. You need an Allen key and a small screwdriver, or any other combination of two small pointy things. Insert one on either side of the twisted link and gently ease the chain back until it's straight. Try to straighten the link in one movement because working it backward and forward weakens the metal.

If you have a chain tool, a better option is to remove the twisted link for a permanent repair. This will shorten your chain, so check first that your chain will still be long enough to go around the big sprocket at the back and the big chainring at the front. If you shorten it too much and then shift into this gear, you risk damaging the rear derailleur and the part of the frame that it bolts onto.

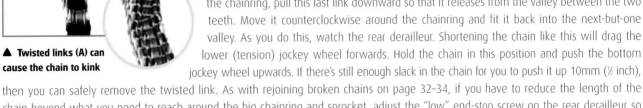

Check that you have sufficient length to remove a link by shifting into the largest sprocket and chainring. Looking at the bottom of your chainring, identify the last chain link that's meshed onto a chainring tooth. Holding the pedals still and making sure that the rest of the chain stays wrapped around the chainring, pull this last link downward so that it releases from the valley between the two teeth. Move it counterclockwise around the chainring and fit it back into the next-but-one valley. As you do this, watch the rear derailleur. Shortening the chain like this will drag the lower (tension) jockey wheel forwards. Hold the chain in this position and push the bottom jockey wheel upwards. If there's still enough slack in the chain for you to push it up 10mm (½ inch), then you can safely remove the twisted link. As with rejoining broken chains on page 32–34, if you have to reduce the length of the chain beyond what you need to reach around the big chainring and sprocket, adjust the "low" end-stop screw on the rear derailleur so that you cannot shift accidentally into this gear combination. Shift into the largest sprocket that the chain will comfortably reach, then screw the "L" end-stop screw in until you feel resistance. For more details on end-stop screws, see pages 109 and 116.

▲ **Twisted links (A) can cause the chain to kink**

Fitting chains

Find the twisted link, as above. You will need to remove a complete link — one wide section and one narrow section. Use the instructions on page 31 to split the chain twice, once on either side of the twist. The remaining ends of the chain should be different — one wide and one narrow end. For standard, non-Shimano chains, the wide section should still have the rivet sticking out of one side. Use this to rejoin the ends of the chain. For Shimano chains, use a special replacement rivet to rejoin the two ends of the chain. New chains are always supplied much longer than you will ever need them so that you can be sure to have enough. When fitting a new chain, I always like to make it long enough so that I can safely take a link out in an emergency.

Twisted link

Remove one complete link ▶

Shortening chain to singlespeed

If you destroy your rear derailleur in a crash, you are forced to run your chain on a single sprocket because you can no longer change gear. This repair tends to be more successful on hardtails (suspension forks only) than on full-suspension bikes, depending on how much of an effect the movement of the suspension has on the length of the chain. If you have to shorten the chain on a full-suspension bike, you have to measure the length of the chain that you need with the suspension at its full extension.

The first task is choosing a suitable gear. The one with the best chance of success is the middle chainring at the front and the smallest sprocket at the back. Choose a random place in the chain and use the chain tool to split the chain, as shown on page 31. Remember to leave a stub of rivet sticking out to locate the hole in the rejoined chain later. Separate the two ends.

Unthread the chain from the rear derailleur and reroute it to pass through the front derailleur, around the chainring of choice, back around a sprocket on the cassette while bypassing the rear derailleur altogether, and then forward to meet up with the other end of the chain. Match up the ends and choose where you're going to shorten the chain. Finding the perfect spot is sometimes tricky, but it's better to end up with a slightly slack chain than one that is too tight and binding. A binding chain will probably just break again.

Rejoin the chain, using the instructions on page 33. You have to ride carefully to keep the shortened chain in place without the tension from the rear derailleur, a component you don't notice until it's gone. Keep up an even pedaling pressure, and don't be tempted to stand up on the pedals because the extra jerkiness often throws the chain off.

Remember to save the section of chain you had to remove — you'll need to reuse it once you've repaired or replaced your derailleur. Chains and cassettes wear into each other, with the chain stretching at the same rate as the teeth wear, widening the valleys between teeth. You cannot just replace a chain, or a section of it, with a new chain, without replacing your cassette at the same time. Your new chain will just skip and slip on the old cassette.

◀ **Route the chain around the smallest sprocket, bypassing the rear derailleur**

Magic moment

I can't remember seeing many emergency bicycle repairs in movies, but I can recommend the ziptie repair from *Two Seconds*. The film is about a woman downhiller who quits racing. She packs her bike up and sets up to build a new life, but when she tries to put her bike back together, she finds she's lost the smallest sprocket from her cassette. I'm not sure why she had to take her cassette off the wheel to ship it, but after some pondering she replaces the missing sprocket with a ziptie. The ziptie neatly holds the other sprockets in place, allowing her to refit the lockring. In a short scene that must have been highly appreciated by a small section of the audience, she carefully readjusts the high end-stop screw to prevent the chain from shifting onto the missing sprocket. Top movie, and full marks for imaginative use of zipties.

Crank and pedal repairs

Every time you stand up on your pedals to haul yourself up the last steep bit of a hill, or you change into your biggest gear and sprint madly to beat your friends back to the car, you're relying on your cranks and pedals to stay firmly bolted onto your bike. Mostly they do the job, but sometimes they let you down.

The most common problem is crank bolts working loose and falling out, so that your crank drops off next time you lean on it. This is almost always a left-hand crank problem. These are both normal threads that tighten clockwise. As you pedal forward, the surface of each crank will rub on the underside of a loose crank bolt. This will tend to tighten a right-hand crank and loosen a left-hand crank. Once the left-hand side starts to work its way free, every pedal stroke will make it a little looser.

Of course, this won't happen if you tighten the crank bolt firmly when you fit it and check it regularly, but this kind of clever hindsight is a bit useless when your crank falls off in the middle of nowhere. It's also particularly unhelpful for anyone else at this point to ask you whether you'd checked the bolt regularly. Don't hit the speaker, though: smug people who ask questions like this when your bike breaks often carry useful tools — ones you might need to borrow.

Once your crank has fallen off or come loose, you have several options. If you still have the bolt, you're in business — retighten it firmly. Multi-tools often have the most common 8mm Allen key size but are far too short to apply enough pressure for a permanent repair. Wrap gloves or fabric of some kind around the tool, so that you can apply as much force as possible. Standing with one foot on the tool and the other on the pedal often works well, but you'll have to find something to lean the bike against while you do it. Most importantly, stop frequently to retighten the crank bolt, at least every twenty minutes.

If you can't find the bolt, your simplest choice is to remove the crank completely, balance your left foot on the side of the bottom bracket, and pedal with your right foot. This works better than you'd expect, but is surprisingly hard work going uphill when you'll be better off walking. This is least unpleasant if you have Shimano Pedaling Dynamics, or SPD pedals.

Securing your crank

If you have a way to go to get home, a little bit of time spent securing your crank will pay off. Even if you can't find the original bolt, you still have a spare — it's holding your other crank on. Remove the right-hand crank bolt and use this to tighten your left-hand cranks as firmly as possible onto the axle. Remove it again and refit it back onto the right-hand crank. Chainsets are more expensive than cranks and so are not worth sacrificing.

An emergency crank bolt will help keep the crank in place. If you can carve a short stub out of a handy-sized branch, then screw it into the end of the axle. Cut off any wood that protrudes out of the crank though — it will be in just the right position to take chunks out of your ankle. Pedal gingerly!

Damaged pedals

Pedals can also seize or break, usually in crashes. If the body of the pedal breaks off, leaving the axle still in the crank, just use the axle as a pedal. It's not very comfortable, but it will get you home.

Occasionally, the whole pedal tears out of the crank, usually a result of failing to tighten the pedal up firmly. This will strip the threads out of the crank — the permanent solution is going to involve buying a new crank. However, to get you home, call on your Boy Scout skills and carve a replacement pedal axle from a stick — see, you knew all those trees would come in handy some time. Don't go wild, this will only work with a very short pedal stub. Aim for something that you can get the ball of your foot onto. You won't be able to put much pressure on it, but it makes a bit of difference if you can use it to keep the crank turning through the dead spot when the other pedal is at the bottom of its stroke. Stay in a low gear and spin as much as possible.

Emergency wheel repairs

Wheels are excellent at resisting forces that are in line with them, like supporting your weight riding or jumping. However, they buckle easily under forces from the side, the kind of forces that are common when you crash. A common disaster is crashing and folding either wheel so badly it won't turn between the brake blocks. The temptation is to release the offending brake and carry on riding, but clearly this is a bad idea — you're careful for 10 minutes, then you forget you only have one brake and pick up speed. And suddenly you've crashed again.

Use these pages to straighten your wheel by adjusting the tension in your spokes.

Your rim is supported all the way around by the tension in your spokes. The tension in each spoke can be increased or reduced by tightening (counterclockwise) **(A)** or loosening (clockwise) **(C)** the spoke nipple, effecting the short section of the rim to which the spoke is attached. Alternate spokes are attached to opposite sides of the hub. Tightening a spoke that leads towards the right-hand side of the hub will move the rim toward the right **(B)**; loosening this spoke will allow the rim to move toward the left. Truing wheels is about adjusting the tension in each spoke, so that the rim runs straight with no side-to-side wobble. This process is not the magic art that it's often made out to be — as long as you're careful about three things:

1) Spend a little time choosing the right spokes to adjust. Spin the wheel and watch the rim. Identify the section of the rim that is most bent — you may be lucky and have one single bent zone that you can concentrate on, but if the wheel is really buckled, you'll have to estimate where the centerline should be.

2) Working out which direction to turn each spoke nipple is really tricky at first. Use the photo (left) as a guide. Watch the rim as you turn the nipple. If the bulge gets worse rather than better, you're turning the nipple the wrong way.

3) Adjust the tension in each spoke in tiny steps. It's much better to work a quarter of a turn of the nipple at a time. Cranking the spoke key around in whole turns is a recipe for disaster. Adjust a quarter-turn, check the effect that you've had on the rim, go back and repeat if necessary.

When to beat your wheel

There is an urban myth that you can straighten bent wheels by banging them on the ground, hard, at the point where they're bent. This myth is responsible for generations of gullible cyclists taking a slightly distorted wheel that could have been saved and beating it into a wreck.

The problem arises because there are, in fact, limited circumstances in which beating a wheel is worth a go. First, it must have a specific shape — it must look like a Pringle chip, with exactly four evenly-spaced bends, two in each direction. Second, the distortion must have been caused very recently. And third, the wheel must spring back into shape with exactly one firm tap. You will have a much higher chance of success (although, obviously, this takes all the fun out of it) laying the wheel flat on the ground and standing on the two high points. But don't try anything forceful at all. It usually doesn't work and is likely to make things worse — and more expensive to fix when you do get home.

Broken spokes

If you ride a wheel with a spoke missing and don't straighten it, you will bend the rim permanently. Yet, as only long-distance riders heading for the Himalayas ever seem to carry spare spokes, there's a limit to what you can do if one does break. Rear wheel spokes can't be replaced unless you have the tools to remove and refit the cassette, making an emergency fix unlikely. But you can adjust the surrounding spokes to make the wheel as straight as possible, getting your brakes to work better (if you have rim brakes), and making it more likely you will be able to fix the wheel properly later.

First, render the snapped spoke safe by preventing it from wrapping around anything else. If it's broken near the rim, wind it around an adjacent spoke to keep it from rattling around. If it's broken near the hub, bend it in the middle so that you can hold it still. Use a spoke key to unwind the nipple so that the spoke drops out of the end of the nipple. If it's broken in the middle, which is the least likely, do both.

Lift up the wheel and spin it gently to see how bent it is. There will usually be a single large bulge where the spoke is broken. Use a spoke key to loosen the spokes on either side of the missing one. It can be confusing working out which way to turn. Look at the spoke you want to turn and imagine you can see the top of the spoke nipple through the tire. To loosen a spoke, turn it so that the top of the spoke head turns counterclockwise.

With rim brakes, check the clearance between brake blocks and tire. You may find that the tire rubs on the brake block in the broken spoke zone. If this is the case, loosen the Allen key bolt that holds the brake block in place, and move the block down slightly so that it clears the tire.

Straightening a bent wheel

With a spoke key, you can sometimes get the wheel straight enough to ride safely. As a guideline, if the wheel has more than 2cm (1 inch) of sideways movement when you spin it, you are unlikely to be able to straighten it with a spoke key. One seldom appreciated advantage of disc brakes is that the brakes continue to work properly when the wheel is bent.

Turn the bike upside down. If it's the back wheel, get behind the bike; if it's the front, get in front so that you're in line with the wheel. Spin the wheel and look at the area where it passes between the brake blocks (or, if you have disc brakes, where brake blocks would be). If the wheel is too wobbly to pass between the brake blocks, release your brake units. If it's too wobbly to pass between the frame, pick your bike up and start walking home.

If you think you can straighten the wheel, spin it a couple more times and look at its shape. You need to identify the point where the wheel is most bent — the biggest bulge away from the center line. If you have V-brakes, use one of the brake blocks as a guide. Hold the brake unit still and spin the wheel, watching how the gap between the brake block and the rim changes. If the wheel is badly buckled, you're going to have to make a rough judgment about where the center of the wheel is, and work towards that. You won't get perfection in the field — just get it round enough to roll.

Adjustments of a quarter- or half-turn of the nipple are plenty. It's easy to start with a buckled but salvageable wheel and end up with a useless pretzel by going too fast. Much better to stick to small steps. Check the previous page if you're not sure which way to turn the nipple.

STRAIGHTENING A WHEEL

Step 1: If you don't have V-brakes, you will have to improvise a gauge to measure the wobble of the wheel against. Zipties are invaluable here — either ziptie a stick to the chainstay or fork so that it sits level with the rim, or zip a tie around the fork or stay, leaving a long tag hanging off. Use the tag as your gauge.

Step 2: Spin the wheel again and stop it when the middle of the biggest bulge is level with your gauge. Look at the spokes on the wheel. You'll see that alternate spokes lead to opposite sides of the wheel.

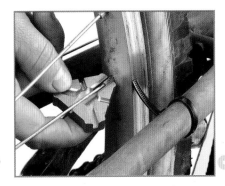

Step 3: Choose the spoke at the center of the bulge. If it leads to the same side of the wheel as the bulge, loosen this spoke and tighten the spokes on either side. A quarter- or half-turn should be enough. If the central spoke leads to the opposite side of the hub, tighten this spoke and loosen the spokes on either side by a quarter- or half-turn. Spin the wheel again, and pick out the biggest bulge.

Gear cable failure

Gear cables are specifically designed to pull against the resistance of a spring inside the derailleur. When the cable is released, the derailleur springs back to its default position, usually the smallest sprocket or chainring, although rapid-rise rear derailleurs default to the largest sprocket. If you do break a gear cable, one option is to allow the chain to default to the smallest sprocket and ride home in that gear, which still gives you flexibility because you can still use the other derailleur normally.

If the cable is broken and trailing wires, get rid of them so they don't catch anything. Either undo the pinchbolt that holds the cable on and remove it completely, or coil up the dangling wire and tape it to your frame. If you're removing the cable, coil it up and take it home — don't discard it on the trail.

Broken rear gear cables occur relatively frequently because the cable is long and passes through several angles, especially with dual suspension bikes. Occasionally the cable frays and breaks; more often the outer casing splits and gives way. Both breaks have the same effect: without the pull of the cable, the spring in the derailleur pulls standard derailleurs to the smallest sprocket, and rapid-rise ones to the largest. Broken front gear cables seem to happen less often, maybe because they don't work as hard as rear ones. The breakdown is still irritating because the spring in the derailleur will pull the chain to the smallest chainring, leaving your legs spinning furiously without making much progress.

Broken rear derailleur cable

Gear cables usually fray long before they break. It's worth getting into the habit of checking them whenever you clean your bike so that you can replace them at the first signs of wear and tear. But sometimes they catch you out and break unexpectedly. Without the balancing tension of the cable, the spring in your derailleur will pull the chain into its neutral position — the smallest sprocket (highest gear) for normal derailleurs, or the largest sprocket (lowest gear) for rapid-rise derailleurs. This may not be the most convenient gear for you to limp home in, so try these methods of temporarily locking your chain into a more useful sprocket.

If you'd like an easier gear than the smallest sprocket at the back, you can use the end-stop screws to reset the derailleur. Get someone to lift up the saddle to get the back wheel off the ground. Turn the pedals slowly with your right hand and use a Phillips screwdriver to screw in (clockwise) the high "H" end-stop screw. As you turn the end-stop screw, the chain will gradually change gear from the smallest

sprocket to the next one. It might even make it to the third sprocket. When the screw has gone in as far as possible, back it off (undo it, counterclockwise) so that the chain runs easily in the chosen gear, without clicking or trying to drop into another gear.

A spare scrap of cable can be used temporarily to set the chain to run in a lower gear. A spare brake cable will work if you have one; if not, remove the broken cable from the shifter and use the end with a nipple still attached. Feed the cable through the barrel-adjuster on the rear derailleur so the nipple sits in or over the barrel-adjuster. Next, push the rear derailleur across by hand so that it sits under a more convenient sprocket, and clamp the cable in the usual place under the pinch bolt. Use the barrel-adjuster to fine-tune the position of the derailleur so the chain sits directly under a sprocket without rattling. Coil up spare cable so it doesn't get caught in the chain or back wheel.

◀ **Using a scrap of cable to set the derailleur in a convenient sprocket**

Broken front derailleur cable

Your front derailleur cable pulls your front derailleur outward when you operate the shifter, shunting the chain from the smallest chainring to the middle and then largest chainrings. When you release the cable tension by clicking the triggershifters or rolling the twistshifters back, the spring in the front derailleur pulls the cage back, shunting the chain back into the middle and then smallest sprocket.

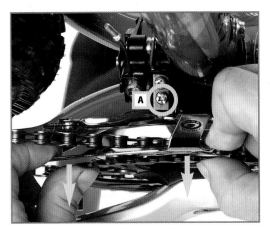

▲ **Pull the derailleur outward, over the middle chainring**

If your front derailleur cable breaks, the derailleur spring will simply pull the cage back over the smallest sprocket, leaving you with only your lowest range of gears. Cycling home in the smallest front sprocket is likely to be annoying. You will probably want to try to set the front derailleur so that it runs in the middle sprocket, rather than the small one, unless your whole route home is up a steep hill.

If the low "L" end-stop screw **(A)** will reach far enough, you can use it to set the derailleur position so that the chain runs in the middle ring. Reach in behind the chainset and lift the chain from the smallest chainring so that it sits on the middle chainring. Pull the front derailleur cage outward so that it is centered over the middle chainring. Holding it there, tighten the low "L" adjustment screw (turning it clockwise) as far as it will go. Release the derailleur cage with your right hand and assess where it sits.

The front derailleur is ideally positioned when there is a 1mm (⅟₁₆ inch) gap between the outer plate of the front derailleur cage and the chain, with the chain in the smallest sprocket at the back. If the cage is too far out, so that the gap is bigger than this, undo the "L" adjustment screw by turning it counterclockwise until the derailleur sits in the right place. You will now be able to use the rear gears normally.

You may find that even when it's screwed in as far as it will go, the "L" end-stop screw will not push the derailleur out far enough — not surprising, since this is not really what the end-stop screw was designed to do. If you can persuade it to sit mostly over the middle ring, you may still be able to use the larger rear sprockets normally. Avoid shifting into the smaller sprockets as this will cause the chain to rub on the derailleur, pushing it over so that you drop back annoyingly into the smallest chainring.

Alternatively, if you can't make any progress with the end-stop screw, you may be able to wedge something behind the front derailleur to hold it out from the frame. Nature is packed with suitable devices — sticks are perfect. Pull out the derailleur and tuck something in to hold it in place. This is one of those occasions when it's handy to have a sharp knife in your toolkit, so that you can shape the wedge. The spring in your front derailleur may be enough to hold your wedge in place, but zipties can help to stop it rattling free. You may even be able to set the derailleur so that your chain runs on the largest chainring. If you come to a hill, stop at the bottom and pull your wedge out, climb the hill in your small chainring, and refit the wedge at the top. Again, you should still be able to use your rear derailleur, but don't shift into gears that mean that the chain rubs on the derailleur cage — it will slow you down and wear out the cage.

Coil up the broken derailleur cable and secure it out of the way so that it doesn't get tangled up in your wheel, brakes or suspension. The frayed broken ends are surprisingly sharp. Make sure they don't stick out and stab your legs. Undo the cable clamp bolt and remove the stray piece of cable. Retighten the cable clamp bolt so that it doesn't rattle loose.

Derailleurs that have been badly bent in a crash may not respond to this treatment. If the cage is too twisted to allow the chain to pass through it, you will have to remove the derailleur completely. Undo the cable clamp bolt and coil the cable out of the way. Undo and remove the front derailleur fixing bolt. Your chain will still be trapped in the derailleur cage. Avoid splitting and rejoining the chain, which can be weakened. Instead, undo and remove the bolt at the back of the derailleur cage and slide the chain out from inside the cage. Sit the chain back onto one of the chainrings.

You would expect the chain to stay in whichever chainring you've chosen, but without the guidance of the front derailleur, it will usually jump off. Mostly, it will head for a smaller chainring. You can minimize unexpected changes by pedaling as smoothly as possible, and by staying in the larger sprockets at the back, which helps to keep the chain tension high.

Occasionally the bolt that holds the back of the derailleur cage together can rattle loose. This tends to make front shifting sluggish rather than hopeless, but you can secure the two halves together with a ziptie through the bolt hole to restore full function.

Twelve routine safety checks before you ride

Checking your bike every time you ride it can seem like a lot of effort, and also a little bit boring. It needn't take more than a few moments, however, and occasionally you'll appreciate the time it takes because you'll pick up a problem waiting to happen, which is far easier to fix before you set off. Looking carefully at your bike regularly also makes it easier to spot when something is wrong.

Specialized Enduro Expert

It's worth having a routine for checking your bike. Doing it in the same order every time means you're less likely to miss something. It's worth going through a mental checklist at the same time to ensure you have everything else you need for a ride. Your needs will depend how far you intend to leave civilization behind, but normal items include plenty of water, emergency food, appropriate clothing, sunblock, map, tools and pump, as well as checking that somebody knows where you're going and when you are expected back. If you can rely on coverage, a cell phone can be invaluable in an emergency. It's not a substitute for careful preparation though.

1) **Quick-release skewer:** Check both wheels are securely attached. Quick-release levers must be firmly folded to line up with the fork blade or rear stay; otherwise they can snag on things and open accidentally. Most levers have "open" and "closed" printed on opposite sides. Fold the lever so the 'closed' side is visible.

2) **Tires:** Check tires for bald patches, tears and sharp things. The glass and thorns, etc., which cause punctures often take time to work through the tire casing. Inspect your tires frequently and pick out foreign objects. It's tedious but quicker than fixing the punctures they cause!

3) **Spokes:** Check for broken spokes. Gently brush a hand over both sides of both wheels, with the ends of your fingers brushing the spokes. Even one broken spoke weakens a wheel considerably. A permanent repair is also much easier if the wheel hasn't been ridden on.

4) **Front wheel:** Lift front end of the bike off ground and spin the front wheel. Check it runs freely, and doesn't wobble between the forks.

5) **Rim brakes:** Check the brake blocks don't touch the tire or rim as the wheel turns. Rubbing blocks wear quickly and slow you down. Check position of the brake blocks. Each block should be parallel to the rim, low enough to avoid hitting the tire but not so low that any part of the brake block hangs below the rim. (N.B. Photo opposite is of a disc-brake bike.)

6) **Disc brake caliper:** Check disc pads. You should have at least 0.5mm ($\frac{1}{50}$ inch) of pad thickness on either side of both brakes.

7) **Brake levers:** Carry out a simple brake check every time you ride. Stand beside the bike, push it gently forward, then pull on the front brake. The front wheel should lock on and the back one lift off the ground. If not, don't ride!

8) **Brake levers:** Use a similar test for the back brake. Push the bike forward, then pull on the back brake. The back wheel should lock and slide along the ground. If not, do not ride.

9) **Chain:** Check the drivetrain. The chain should be clean and should run smoothly through the gears without falling off either side of the sprocket or the chainset. Turn pedals backward and watch the chain run through the derailleur. Stiff links flick the derailleur forward as they pass over the lower jockey wheel. It's worth sorting them out since they can cause your gears to slip under pressure.

10) **Cables and hoses:** Check all cables (brake and gear) for kinks in the outer casing or frays in the cable. Frayed cables should be replaced immediately. Clean and oil rusty or dirty cables. Check hydraulic hoses for links or leaks; inspect the joints between hose and caliper, and hose and brake lever.

11) **Stem:** Check that stem and bars are tight. Stand over the front wheel, gripping it between your knees. Try turning the bars. They shouldn't move independently. Try twisting the bars in the stem too. If you have bar ends, lean down on them. Tighten any loose steering components.

12) **Pedals:** Check the cleats in the pedals. Make sure you can clip into and out of both sides of both pedals easily.

Toolbox

Tools for three comfort zones (see page 44)
- 6mm Allen key to adjust saddle position
- 4 or 5mm Allen key to adjust saddle height
- 5 or 6mm Allen key to adjust bar and stem position
- 4mm Allen key to adjust cleat position

Tools for cleaning routine (see page 46)
- Muc-off or Finish Line bike wash
- Degreaser
- Stiff brush
- Sponge frame
- Chain oil to relubricate
- Plenty of warm water

Three comfort zones

You touch your bike in three places: at the handlebars with your hands, at the saddle with your butt, and at the pedals with your feet. If these points on the bike are in the right place, and of the right shape, you will be comfortable. If they're not, you won't.

Bike size

A bike that is the wrong size will always be uncomfortable. Always test-ride before buying a new bike and get the shop to help you choose. Different bike manufacturers measure frames in different ways so you can't assume that if one 18-inch bike fits you they all will. As a guide, stand over the bike with your feet flat on the floor. Lift up the seat and handlebars as far as you can. You should have 7–14cm (2¾-5½ inches) clearance between the tires and the ground. If you have to raise the seatpost above its safety mark to get enough leg extension, the frame is too small. When buying a new bike, don't just check for frame height. Try different models to find one that also feels a comfortable length, since this varies from bike to bike. You can make small changes to the reach by altering the saddle position and stem length, but it helps to start from a position close to the right one.

Specialized S-Works Epic

Saddle

Bars & stem

Pedals

The saddle

Get the height right first. Sit on your bike in the normal way with hands on the bars, leaning against a wall. Turn the pedals so the cranks are vertical, and put your heel on the lower pedal. Your knee should just lock straight in this position. Check the measurement with your other leg too; it's not unusual to have one leg shorter than the other. Set your seat height for the shorter leg. With this measurement, when you pedal normally — with the ball of your foot on the center of the pedal — your leg will be almost, but not quite, straight at the bottom of its stroke.

Next, set the saddle angle. For almost everybody, the most comfortable angle is with the top of the saddle exactly horizontal. If you find yourself tipping the nose of the saddle down more than a couple of degrees to be comfortable, think about swapping your saddle for a different one. Everybody has a different shape so you may have to try a selection of different models before finding the correct profile. See page 225 for help adjusting your saddle angle and position.

Finally, set the fore-and-aft position. Start with the saddle in the center of the rails. If you find yourself pushing over the back of the saddle when climbing, move the saddle backwards a little. Move the saddle forwards if you feel you need to be closer to the bars — this can be a good alternative to fitting a shorter stem if you feel too stretched out. A popular guideline is to sit on the saddle and use a plumbline to check that the front of your knee is directly over the center of the pedal. I prefer to sit slightly further forward than this, but it's a matter of personal taste.

Don't fool yourself into suffering an uncomfortable saddle. There are so many different kinds; at least one will fit you. Just as importantly, don't expect the saddle that comes on your new bike, or the first you try, to be perfect. If you have a saddle that suits you, transfer it to new bikes. Titanium rails are not only lighter but more flexible, giving a comfortable ride. Leather covers breathe better than plastic ones, which makes a big difference on hot days.

Women's saddles have become comfortable in the last five years; manufacturers have realized that not only do women buy bicycles, they also expect riding them to be a pleasant experience. Again, there are different types so try before you buy. Holes and slots cut in the center of saddles are good for relieving pressure but can be disconcertingly drafty on cold days.

Bars and stem

Reach (the distance between handlebars and saddle) and handlebar height affect how comfortable you are on the bike, as well as how effectively you can use your shoulder strength for control. Stem length and angle give a basic position for your bars. The ubiquitous Ahead stem doesn't have a lot of room for height adjustment but both height and length can be changed by changing your stem (see page 224). Shorter, higher stems are great for beginners. They encourage you to look where you're going, and the magic nature of bicycles means they usually go where you're looking (thus the common injunction, look at the path not the trees). Short stems are also favored for freeride and downhill bikes, where the extra control at high speed is a bonus. Flatter, longer stems help keep the front wheel on the ground while climbing and allow you to pull up on the bars while pushing down on the pedals. Such stems tend to be found on hardtail cross-country bikes, where they have the added advantage of transferring some of your body weight from the saddle to the bars. Unlike road biking, the aerodynamic advantage of tucking down low while mountain biking is rarely relevant.

Riser bars give an extra 3cm (1¼ inch) or so of height and can be rolled around to match the sweep of the bars to the angle of your wrists, which can make all the difference to sore shoulders. Handlebar material is also important for comfort. More costly bars are usually made of thinner tube, and so absorb the vibration that can leave you with tired wrists.

Bar ends give extra leverage when climbing and provide an alternative hand position so you can shift about on the bars to ease fatigue in your arms and shoulders. The easiest way to find the optimum angle for bar ends is to loosen them off so they rotate on the handlebars, sit on the bike, close your eyes, and grip them. Then tighten them securely in that position.

Take a bit of care when choosing grips. Your hand is going to spend a lot of time holding them. Match the grip diameter to your hand size. For hot weather, choose a pattern with ribs or grooves so they don't get too slippery when wet. If your hands get sore, choose a grip that supports the palm, to keep the blood flowing through your wrists.

Pedals

The third point of contact with the bike is through your feet, and, as with the other points of contact, a little care makes your machine more comfortable. Most SPD pedals are very small so they're light and don't snag on the ground. This can cause discomfort, with all the pedaling pressure concentrated on a small area of your foot. Use stiff-soled shoes so that the pressure is spread over the whole of the sole. Alternatively, consider using an SPD shoe with a cage, which can support your foot over a wider area.

Regular cleaning routine

Cleaning your bike is the best time to spot worn or broken parts that would otherwise fail and leave you stranded in the wilderness. Beware of jet washes though. Power hoses can leave your bike looking very shiny without much effort, but no matter how careful you are, they force water in through the bearing seals, flushing grease out. This shortens the lifespan of bottom brackets, headsets, and other components radically.

As a principle, start with the dirtiest bits and work up to the cleaner ones. That way, you minimize the amount of recleaning you may have to do.

If starting from scratch, here's a routine to transform your bike. Drop off the wheels and hang it up so you can reach everything.

MARIN Mount Vision

1) Start with the drivetrain: the chain, sprockets, chainset and derailleurs. If the chain isn't too dirty, clean it with a rag. See chain hygiene on page 95 for how to do this.

2) If your chain is too oily and dirty to respond to this treatment, give it a thorough clean. You can do a very respectable job without removing the chain from the bike, which is a lot of trouble and can weaken the link you remove. For the best results with the least fuss, tip a little degreaser into a small pot. Use a toothbrush or washing-up brush dipped in degreaser to scrub the chain clean. A chain-cleaning box (see page 18) is a good investment, making this job cleaner and quicker.

3) Sprockets and chainsets need regular cleaning too. They're close to the ground and exposed to whatever's going around. If they're oily and dirty, it's worth degreasing them. Oil is sticky and picks up dirt as you ride along, wearing out the drivetrain. As above, use a little degreaser and work it into the sprockets and chainset with a brush. It's very important to rinse things very carefully afterward to remove all traces of degreaser. Also, dry components carefully. Be careful not to get degreaser into bearings.

4) Once everything is clean and dry, relubricate the chain. I prefer drip oils to spray types because you can direct the oil more precisely, which ensures you can get it where it's needed without wastage. Drip a little onto the top links of the bottom stretch of chain all the way around. Don't use excessive amounts of oil. Leave the oil to soak in for five minutes, then carefully remove excess with a clean rag. Don't worry about relubing other drivetrain components as they need no more than is deposited by the chain onto the sprockets.

5) Next, clean the wheels. Muddy tires are best cleaned by riding your bike along a tarmac road (with your mouth shut) once the mud is dry. Use a sponge and a bucket of warm soapy water, hold the wheels upright to keep water out of the hubs, and sponge the hubs and spokes clean.

6) Rim brakes work much better on clean rims. They pick up dirt from the ground and from the brake blocks, which stops the blocks from gripping the rim effectively, causing both rims and blocks to wear out prematurely. Green nylon Brillo pads are ideal for this job. Wire wool is too harsh but nylon gets detritus off the rims without damaging the braking surface. While you're there, check for bulges or cracks in the braking surface. These indicate that the rim is worn out and needs replacing urgently. If your rim has rim-wear indicators, check them now too. (NB: Photo opposite is of a disc-brake bike.)

7) Disc rotors, the alternative braking surface, also work much better when clean. It's important not to contaminate them with oil. Use Finish Line for disc rotors. If they have become oily, clean the rotors with isopropyl alcohol (from a drug store), which doesn't leave a residue. Don't be tempted by car disc cleaner — this leaves a residue that cannot be scrubbed off by the brakes.

8) Brakes next. For rim brakes, release the V-brakes by pulling back the black rubber boot and pulling the curved metal noodle out of the hanger on the brake unit. Clean the block surfaces. Use a small screwdriver or knife (carefully) to pick out shards of metal. If the block surface has become shiny, use a strip of clean sandpaper to roughen it. When looking at the brake blocks, check they aren't excessively or unevenly worn. Most blocks have a wear-line embossed onto the rubber. If the blocks originally had slots, make sure the slots are still visible. Once they disappear, it's time for new brake blocks.

9) For disc brakes, wipe the caliper clean. Check hydraulic hoses for oil leaks. There should be no trace of oil at any of the connections. Also check for kinks in the hoses. Look into the rotor slot on the caliper, and check that the brake pad is at least 0.5mm ($\frac{1}{50}$ inch) thick.

10) Clean and oil the parts of your cables normally trapped inside casing.

11) For rear cable brakes, follow the black casing back from the brake lever to the frame. At the cable stop, pull the casing forward, to release it from the cable stop and wiggle the brake cable out of the slot. Use the same method to release the other sections of casing. Run a clean rag over the part that's normally covered by outer casing. Relubricate each section with a drop of oil. Refit the outer casing.

12) Repeat with the gear casing. You need to click your rear shifter as if changing into the highest gear, then push the derailleur away again (see page 109 if you are unsure how to do this). This creates enough slack in the cable to pull a section of casing out of its cable stop. Repeat with all the other sections of casing, cleaning and oiling — especially the last loop of rear derailleur cable. This loop is nearest to the ground and tends to collect dirt. Refit the outer casing.

13) Pull the front derailleur out over the largest chainring, click the shifter as if to change into the smallest sprocket, then release the casing in the same way. Clean, oil, and replace. A sticky gear cable causes sloppy shifting.

14) Pedals are often forgotten, even though they get more than their fair share of mud and abuse. Use a small screwdriver to clear all the mud from around the release mechanism. Make sure you do both sides of both pedals. Mud gets forced into the springs every time you clip in with your shoes, building up until you can no longer clip in and out properly. Lubricate the moving parts sparingly with a light oil, like GT85 or WD40.

Clean the frame and forks. You need a sponge and a bucket of warm water to rinse everything off afterward. All components work better and last longer if they're not covered in grime. Finally, a quick polish. Wax-based polish helps stop dirt sticking to the frame, keeping it cleaner for next time. Saddles also benefit from a polish — you might as well while you've got the polish out. Refit the wheels, reconnect the brakes. This is a good time to pump up the tires, just to finish the job off neatly.

Brakes

Brake blocks and pads are very small. Safe stopping depends on contact via a patch the size of a couple of thumbprints per wheel. It's vital that your brakes are adjusted to maximize this area — and that you can apply firm, controlled braking force.

The terms "brake pads" and "blocks" tend to be fairly interchangeable, but, generally, V-brakes and cantilevers use a thick chunk of soft rubber, called a brake block, and disc brakes use a much thinner, harder wafer known as a brake pad.

This chapter is divided into sections for each of the different types of brake. Cantilever brakes, where the brake cable splits into two parts just above the tire, were the original "mountain bike brake" and are still found on older mountain bikes, cyclo-cross bikes, and single-speed bikes. V-brakes have longer brake units, with the brake cable connecting the two units together across the top of the tire.

Both these types use the rim as a braking surface, which saves weight since the brake requires fewer parts. The design means you have to inspect the braking surface regularly to ensure the brake blocks have not worn through the rim. The air pressure inside the tire means that the rim will explode if it becomes too thin, which is dangerous and alarming to think about.

Disc brakes have become much more popular in the last couple of years. A small brake unit is attached to the frame or fork near the hub. Cables or hydraulic fluid force the brake pads onto the disc, a separate rotor attached to the hub. Consequently, hydraulically operated disc brakes are very powerful.

This chapter guides you through the basic procedures of braking systems: checking that your brakes work safely; adjusting them so that they don't slow you down when you're riding, yet stop you swiftly and with control when you need them to; fitting new ones; and servicing them to keep them working efficiently.

Disc brake rotors

Brakes: build your stopping power

Well-tuned brakes make you go faster. This might seem like a contradiction, but it's true. In order to be able to go fast, you need to be able to control your speed safely. Crisp, reliable brakes will make you feel more confident and get you out of trouble when you push things too far.

Brakes are very satisfying to work on. Their performance tends to deteriorate slowly, with pads and cables getting slightly more worn and dirty with each ride, but not usually so suddenly that you notice them getting worse. The good thing about this is that when you come to fit fresh parts, or clean and service units and cables, your brakes will feel significantly better — always very satisfying!

Brakes are obviously a mission-critical safety component. Always check them very carefully after you've done any work on them so that you can be sure you're safe to ride away. Make sure both brakes are working properly, then go back over all your nuts and bolts and check that you've tightened them all up. Anything that's left a little bit loose will rattle free as soon as you ride hard, likely leaving you in trouble.

V-brake and cantilever brake pads have universal fittings, but disc brake pads haven't settled down to a standard yet. Consequently, there are about thirty different patterns, with slightly different shapes, sizes and fittings. This is really annoying as the pads won't fit unless you get exactly the right kind. It's worth making sure you always have a spare set so that you don't get stuck.

Cable brakes are simpler to deal with than hydraulic ones, but the extra braking power you get from the hydraulics makes them well worth learning about. Dealing with brake fluid can seem a bit of a leap into the unknown, even if you feel very confident working with other parts of your bike. But it's not really significantly more complicated than other tasks, just a bit different. Treat brake fluid — whether it's DOT or mineral oil — with respect: it's not good for your skin. Both fluids will contaminate brake pads, causing them to have trouble gripping the rotors properly. DOT will also strip the paint off your frame if you spill it. Wear gloves, and work slowly and patiently.

V-brakes

Cable clamp bolt

Brake unit

Brake block adjusting unit

Brake block

Brake fixing bolt

Cantilever brakes

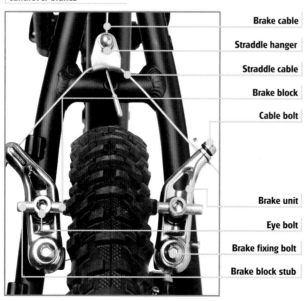

Brake cable

Straddle hanger

Straddle cable

Brake block

Cable bolt

Brake unit

Eye bolt

Brake fixing bolt

Brake block stub

Disc brakes

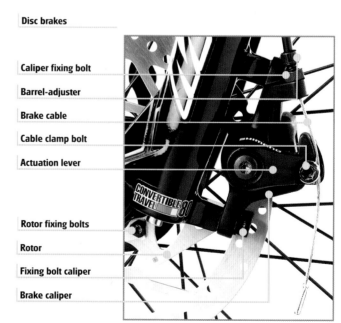

Caliper fixing bolt

Barrel-adjuster

Brake cable

Cable clamp bolt

Actuation lever

Rotor fixing bolts

Rotor

Fixing bolt caliper

Brake caliper

V-brakes: a general introduction and how to manage wear and tear

V-brakes have now become standard issue on mountain bikes. They have superseded cantilever brakes and will in turn be made obsolete by disc brakes. However, they are cheap and simple to maintain, so we will start with them. Here follows an outline of the advantages and disadvantages of this braking system.

V-brakes overtook cantilevers in popularity because they are more powerful. However, there has always been a trade-off in terms of pad wear — cantilever pads last much longer. V-brakes stop you faster because the way they are designed pushes them onto the rim harder than cantilevers, wearing out both the rim and brake blocks faster. So, enjoy the powerful braking but remember that as a direct consequence you are going to have to learn to inspect brake blocks frequently for wear and replace them. Depending on where and how you ride, you can wear out brake blocks at the rate of a set per day, and through a rim in a matter of months.

Regular maintenance

Keeping blocks and rims clean will make a huge difference to how long they both last. Dirty rims will wear out brake blocks, while flakes of grit and metal caught in your brake blocks will scour the rim surface. It's easy to forget that the rims are an integral part of the braking system. Unless they're clean and flat, the brake blocks will struggle to grip them and stop you in your tracks.

This section takes you through the processes of checking that your V-brakes are set up and working correctly, fitting new brake blocks, fitting a new cable, and servicing your brake units. Careful brake-block alignment and smooth cables will help you get the most power out of your brakes. You'll also get more feedback from them. Good set-up means that when your hands are on the brake levers, you will be able to feel what effect the brakes are having, increasing your control over the bike. Good brakes don't just lock the wheel up, they allow you to control your speed accurately.

One important thing to remember is that brake blocks and cables often need just cleaning rather than replacing. Cables can be cleaned rather than replaced as long as they're not frayed or kinked. Use the following procedure for replacing your cable. Keep to the instructions for removing the old cable, then clean it with a light oil like GT85. If necessary, soak congealed dirt off with degreaser. Cut the end of the cable off cleanly so that it can be neatly threaded through the outer casing. Clean the inside of the outer casing by squirting spray oil through it to flush out dirt. Replace any sections that are cracked, squashed or kinked. Replace bent ferrules. Then refit as a new cable.

Worn-out brake blocks

Brake blocks must be replaced if they're worn below the wear-indication lines stamped on the block. If there are no wear lines, replace the brake blocks when you've worn down to the base of any grooves molded into the block. They're also due for replacement if any of the metal over which the rubber block is molded is showing through. Otherwise, they can be cleaned and freshened up. Follow the instructions for removing the blocks. Use a sharp knife to cut off overhanging lips at the edge of the brake block, and use clean sandpaper to flatten the braking surface of the block. Pick out any flakes of metal or grit. Refit as new brake blocks.

V-brakes are bolted onto on your frame or forks by studs called brake pivots. Newer, disc-only frames and forks don't have these pivots, and so cannot be fitted with V-brakes. Currently many new bikes have both disc mounts and V-brake pivots, allowing you to upgrade from V-brakes to discs.

The brake units are designed to rotate around the pivots so the condition of the pivots is important. If the surface is rusty or corroded, your brakes won't pull smoothly onto the rim or spring back smartly. If your brakes are sluggish and fitting a fresh cable has no effect, see page 58 to service your brake units, and to clean and oil the pivots.

Crashing can also bend the brake pivots, preventing you from adjusting them properly. Look at the brakes from face on: the front brake from in front of the bike, the rear brake from behind it. You'll see the heads of the two brake-fixing units at the bottom of each unit. These should point straight out from the frame so that the bolts are parallel. Bent brake units don't just make it awkward to adjust the brake block position, they can also be a liability. Many fork pivots, and some frame pivots, can be replaced; check the manufacturer for spares. Although If you have disc mounts as well as V-brake pivots, this could be a good excuse for an upgrade.

V-brakes: a quick checkup to help ensure performance every ride

However casual you are about bike maintenance, you need to make sure that your brakes are working properly every time you set off on a ride. This doesn't need to be a lengthy procedure — just give your bike a careful visual check before you head off.

The steps below make up a quick and regular check to keep your brakes in good running order and they give you warning when it's time for a more serious overhaul.

Each of the steps below includes relevant page numbers, so that if any of the checks show a problem with your braking system, you can sort it out right away. Whatever you do, don't set off on a ride with brakes that don't work properly.

Lift each wheel and spin it, to check the brakes don't rub on the rims or the tire as the wheel turns. Look at the gap between the brake block and the rim on each side of each brake. See pages 53 and 55.

You'll need to disconnect the brake cable so that you can pull the brake blocks out from the rim. V-brakes are designed to make this easy. They also help when you want to remove and replace the wheels because you can get the tire out past the brake blocks without letting the air out.

The brake cable

The brake cable arrives at the brake unit via a short curved metal tube called a "noodle" or "lead pipe" (pronounced as in "leading in the right direction", not lead, the heavy metal). The end of the lead pipe has a pointed head with a raised collar. The brake cable passes through the noodle and then clamps onto one of the brake units. The other brake unit has a hinged hanger with a key-shaped hole for the noodle. The collar stops the noodle pulling through the hanger, so when you pull on the cable, the two brake units are drawn together, pulling the brake blocks onto the rim. The section of cable between the hanger and the cable clamp bolt is often concealed inside a black rubber boot that helps keep the cable clean.

To release the brake units, draw back the rubber boot to reveal the head of the noodle where it emerges from the hanger. Squeeze the two brake units together to create slack in the cable. Pull the noodle back and out of the key-shaped hole, then pull up to release the cable from the slot in the key-shaped hole. Let go of the brake units — they will spring right back from the rim.

To reconnect the brakes, squeeze the brake units firmly onto the rim. Pull back the rubber boot so that it's out of the way of the noodle, and guide the head of the noodle into the hole in the hanger. Make sure it's seated securely: the raised collar must be butted firmly up against the hanger. Refit the rubber boot back over the head of the noodle. Pull the brake lever to confirm that everything is seated correctly.

CHECKING V-BRAKES

Step 1: Inspect the condition of the pads. Release the brakes, pull each side away from the rim, and check that each braking surface is flat, has nothing stuck in it, and isn't worn through. Reconnect the brakes, checking that the brake noodle is firmly and securely located in its hanger. See pages 54–5 for brake block replacement instructions.

Step 2: Refit the brakes and check that each block hits the rim flat, square and level. Brake blocks that are too high will cut through the tire, causing explosive punctures. Blocks that are too low hang under the rim, wasting brake potential and creating a lip that eventually starts to snag on the rim. See page 53 for brake block adjustment.

Step 3: Run your hand along each cable, from lever to brake unit, checking for corrosion, kinks, fraying or damage to the casing. See pages 56-7 for tips on cable care. Pull the lever firmly towards the bars and check that each brake locks the wheel when the lever is halfway to the bars. See page 53.

Brake blocks: keeping your eyes open for regular wear and tear

Inspect your brake blocks frequently for wear, replacing them as they get thin and pick up grit and metal bits. Worn blocks make for a useless braking surface and eat expensive rims for breakfast. Ignore this important task and your rims will wear right through the rubber of the block to the metal innards of the molded pad. Brake blocks have a wear line indicating when they should be changed. If you can't see a wear line, change the pads when they've worn to the bottom of the grooves molded into the pad.

Even if you don't wear out blocks very quickly, you should still change them periodically as they harden with time and don't work as well. Every couple of years should do.

In between full changes, check on the condition of the pad and improve it. This is easiest to do with the wheels removed.

Release the brakes and remove the wheel. Look at the condition of the pad. It should be flat and even, without visible contamination. If you can see flecks of metal, use a sharp knife and carefully pick them out. If the pad had been sitting too low or at an angle, it will wear unevenly, leaving a lip that gets caught under the rim and prevents the brakes from letting go properly. This is a waste of brake block and braking potential. Carefully cut the offending lip off with a sharp knife, then follow the instructions to reposition your brake block so that it contacts the rim more evenly. If the brake block sits too high, it will wear through the tire — an expensive error.

Lightly sand the surface of the brake block with clean sandpaper. People often use a file for this, but shouldn't — it will hold metal flakes from whatever it was you last filed, and flakes that will embed themselves in the blocks. Clean your rims too. If they have sticky black streaks, use degreaser. Oil or tar on your rims will squeal alarmingly, allowing your wheels to slip through the blocks without slowing you down. A green nylon scouring pad works well for stubborn stains, and will scrub off contamination without damaging your rims.

Some brake blocks are designed with removable rubber blocks. The old, worn ones are removed by pulling out a retaining pin at the back of the metal cartridge and sliding the rubber part backwards. Replacement rubber blocks slide in in the same way and are held in place with the retaining pin. Always make sure the open end of the cartridge faces towards the back of the bike; otherwise heavy braking will rip the rubber out of the cartridge. The replacement blocks can be stiff to slide into the slots in the cartridge; it often helps to dip them in warm water.

ADJUSTING BRAKE BLOCKS

Step 1: Loosen the Allen key bolt at the end of each brake block. Keeping the Allen key there, use your other hand to maneuver the block to approach the rim at 90°, not overlapping the edge, top or bottom. The front of the block should be 1mm ($^1/_{16}$ inch) nearer than the back. Tighten the Allen key firmly and twist the block to check it is secure. Push the unit towards the rim so the block hits it, and check that you are satisfied with its position.

Step 2: Spin the wheel; if the brakes rub on the rim, the cable is too tight. Undo the lockring on the barrel-adjuster at the lever — two turns counterclockwise, looking from where cable enters lever. Loosen cable by turning adjuster clockwise. Turn twice, test again. When satisfied, retighten lockring. To loosen the cable further, return to brake unit, undo cable pinch bolt, and release 3-4mm ($^3/_{16}$ inch) of cable. Retighten bolt and fine-tune adjuster again.

Step 3: Pull lever firmly toward the handlebars. The brakes should lock when the lever is halfway there. If it travels too far, cable is loose. Leave enough space between lever and bar to hold the grips while braking. Undo lockring on lever barrel-adjuster, and roll adjuster outward. Test again and snug the lockring back to lever body. If you run out of barrel-adjuster, reset it: return to brake unit, undo pinch bolt, pull through 3-4mm ($^3/_{16}$ inch) cable, and retighten bolt.

Changing old brake blocks and adjusting their replacements

One of the points used to sell V-brakes originally was that changing the brake blocks would be easier than with cantilever brakes. This is slightly misleading — changing blocks is not difficult, but it can be tricky. I often find myself wishing I had smaller fingers — or more of them.

The key is to set up the brake units so that they're parallel and vertical before fitting the brake blocks into the units. Most new brake locks come with a new set of curved washers but occasionally you'll have to reuse the old ones. It's a good idea to clean your rims at the same time so that the new brake surfaces can get maximum grip.

CHANGING BRAKE BLOCKS

Step 1: Undo and remove Allen key nut on the end of the old brake block stud, then wriggle out the old block and its curved washers. The new brake block comes with fresh washers, but keep old ones as spares. Now look at the position of the brake units. They should be parallel and vertical **(A)**. Get the position of the units right before you fit new brake blocks. If they're not parallel, undo cable pinch bolt, and pull in or release cable. Retighten the pinch bolts.

Step 2: You may find the units are parallel but pointing off to one side. If so, use the balance screws at the bottom of each unit to even out the spring tension. This screw is normally a slot head but might be an Allen key. Choose the side that sits closer to the wheel and move screw half a turn clockwise. Pull and release the brake to settle the spring and repeat until brake arms are even. See page 59 for detailed explanation of the balance screw.

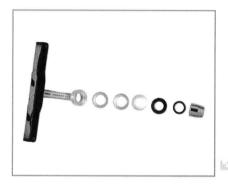

Step 3: Check whether the brake blocks are designed for fitting in a particular direction. Any arrows should point forward, and the shape of the block should follow the curve of the rim. Each block comes with a collection of curved washers to space and angle the block. Their order of use varies from bike to bike and depends on the distance between the brake unit and the rim.

Step 4: There should be a domed washer on the inside of the brake unit with the flat side facing the brake unit, and a cup washer between the dome and the brake block. Choose either the thick one or the thin one so that the block sits close to the rim, but not touching. A gap of about 2-3mm (around $\frac{1}{8}$ inch) is ideal.

Step 5: The adjustment does not need to be perfect at this stage, just approximate. With the stub of the brake block sticking out through the slot in the brake unit, fit the other domed washer, flat side against the brake unit. Then fit the remaining cup washer, followed by any flat washers. Finally, loosely fit the Allen key nut.

Step 6: You will find that with this arrangement you can alter the angle of the brake block, and also slide it up and down in the slot in the brake unit. Set the position of the brake block so that when you pull on the brakes, the block hits the rim with the fixing bolt at 90° to the surface of the rim. The block should be level, not higher at the front or back. None of the block should hang over the top or bottom of the rim.

Step 7: "Toeing-in": the front of the block **(B)** should be 1mm (¹⁄₁₆ inch) closer to the rim than the back, facing the same direction as the bike. Toeing-in helps stop your brakes squealing. Position the block and tighten the fixing bolt firmly. Check you cannot twist the block; the bolt must be firmly secured! Fit the other block the same way. The washer arrangement should be the same on either side, but may be different between front and back brakes.

Step 8: You will probably have to adjust the tension in the cable again to get the correct gap between brake blocks and the rim. For big changes, undo the cable pinch bolt again, pull though or let out cable, and tighten the pinch bolt. For a more subtle change, use the barrel-adjuster on the brake lever. Roll the lockring (if there is one) away from the brake lever. Now roll barrel-adjuster counterclockwise to bring the brake blocks closer to the rim.

Step 9: Roll barrel-adjuster clockwise to move brake blocks away from the rim **(C)**. Turn lockring so it wedges back up against the body of the brake lever. (Some barrel-adjusters don't have lockrings!) Pull the levers firmly to check the brake action. Brakes need to be fully locked when lever is halfway to the bar. If you run out of barrel adjustment, reset the barrel centrally, make a rough adjustment with the cable pinch bolt, and use the barrel-adjuster to fine-tune again.

Readjusting balance screws

Finally, you will probably need to readjust the balance screws. Turn the balance screw clockwise to pull that side brake block away from the rim, but remember that this also pulls in the opposing brake block towards the far side of the rim. Pull and release the brake levers frequently as you adjust the balance screw because they have to settle into place every time. For a more detailed explanation of how to adjust your balance screw, see page 59. Check every nut and bolt to make sure each one is tight. Pull on the brakes firmly, and check that the wheel locks up. Spin the wheel and watch the brake blocks — if the wheel isn't completely true, you might find that the tire rubs on the brake block as the wheel spins. Readjust the brake block position if necessary.

Choosing new brake blocks

This V-brake block set-up, using a threaded stud with curved washers, is used almost universally, making V-brake blocks completely interchangeable between makes and models. This might seem unremarkable, but the situation with disc brake pads is completely different. Every make and model requires a specific pad — and nothing else will do. The interchangeability of V-brake blocks has helped to keep the price down, since each manufacturer knows you can go elsewhere for replacements. Good makes include Aztec, Fibrax and Shimano. Longer or fatter brake blocks won't give you more braking power but are more durable. Slots cut in the surface of the block can help channel water away, but they can also collect grit if not cleaned regularly. Ceramic-coated rims need matching ceramic-specific brake blocks, which are harder than standard ones. Normal ones will wear away very quickly, as will ordinary rims if you use them with ceramic blocks.

Toolbar

Tools for changing or adjusting brake blocks
- Allen keys — almost always 5mm but occasionally 6mm
- New V-brake blocks

Tools for fitting new cable
- Allen key for cable clamp bolt — almost always 5mm but occasionally 10mm wrench
- New cable, casing, and ferrules
- Oil for lubricating cable — chain oil is fine
- Good wirecutters

Tools for adjusting balance screws
- Usually crosshead screwdriver, occasionally 2.5mm Allen key

Tools for fitting or servicing brake units
- 5mm Allen key for brake-fixing bolts
- Oil to lubricate pivots
- Wet-and-dry sandpaper to clean pivots

Maintaining your cables to help keep your brakes in good shape

You should check your cables regularly for corrosion, kinks and damage to the outer casing. Over time, dirt and water creep into the cables. It happens slowly so you hardly notice the brakes are getting harder to pull on and are not releasing properly. Fitting new cables is easy. You will feel the difference instantly.

Cables generally come in either standard or fancy versions. The luxury versions tend to be either lined or protected by a sheath that runs from shifter to brake. Luxury cables can make a significant difference if you ride in very muddy environments, as they stop grit from creeping into the gap between cable and outer casing. However, they are generally much more expensive. All cables come with comprehensive instructions though, so we'll stick to standard cables here. You can either buy brake-cable sets in a pack, with cable, outer casing and ferrules — Shimano make a good value pack — or you can buy the parts separately. Either way, you'll need a decent pair of cable-cutters to cut the casing to length; every bike has a different configuration of top tube lengths and cable-stop positions so the casing needs to be cut for each one. The key thing to remember when cutting casing is to make a square cut across the tube so that the end of the casing sits firmly inside the ferrule. Look into the end of the cut casing and make sure there isn't a stray spur of metal across the hole. This will catch on the cable every time you pull and release the brakes, making your brakes feel sluggish. Use the sharp point of a knife to open out the end of the white lining that runs through the casing as it gets squashed shut as you cut the casing.

Occasionally, you come across cheap, unlined casing. Don't fit this to your bike — it will feel terrible. It's fine for lawnmowers, but the extra money you spend on proper lined casing will make your brakes feel at least twice as good.

You'll notice throughout this text that I'm obsessed with ferrules. They cost almost nothing, protect the ends of your casing from splaying out, and make your brakes feel crisp. Yet they are often treated as an optional extravagance. The only place you won't usually need a ferrule is the end of the section of casing that fits into the V-brake noodle. The noodle has its own built-in ferrule.

Fitting new brake cable

Before you start taking things apart, have a good look at how the cable is currently set up because you need to recreate that later with the new cable. Snip the cable end off the old cable and undo the cable pinch bolt. Unthread the old cable from the brake noodle and outer casing, leaving the casing in place. When you get back to the lever, have a good look at how the cable fits into it. It helps to pull the lever back toward the bars, to look up at it from below.

FITTING BRAKE CABLE

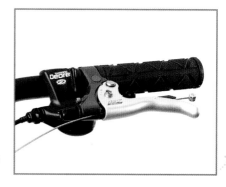

Step 1: Turn the lockring on the barrel-adjuster, and then the barrel-adjuster itself, so that the slots on both the barrel and the lockring line up with the slot on the body of the brake lever. Then pull the cable gently outward, or down, to release it.

Step 2: The nest, where the cable nipple sits, normally has a key-shaped hole so the nipple cannot pop out when you're braking. The most common fitting has a pivoted nest riveted to the lever blade, with a slot in either the front or the underside of the lever. Wiggle the cable so the nipple lines up with part of the hole that it can pass through, and pop it out. You may have to twist the cable so the end of the barrel lines up with the hole.

Step 3: Some Shimano levers use a variation where the nipple is trapped behind a lip halfway along the lever blade. Once again, line up the slots on the lockring and barrel-adjuster with the slot on the body of the cable. You will need to flick open the plastic cover on the back of the lever blade, then push the cable towards the outer end of the lever. Once there's a bit of slack, you should be able to wriggle the cable out from behind the lip.

Replacing outer casing

Clean out the brake lever; in particular, wipe dirt from the nipple nest. Remove each section of outer casing in turn. Measure and cut new sections to fit. Take care when cutting the sections of outer casing. It's important that the ends are cut square and that you don't leave a tang hanging across the opening. If the casing lining has been squashed where you cut it, use the point of a sharp knife to open it out again. Fit a ferrule on each end of each section, except the brake unit end of the final section because the noodle will usually have a built-in ferrule. Occasionally these are bigger than normal, so if the casing is floppy in the end of the noodle, try fitting a ferrule. If you can fit one in, you need one. The ferrules protect the end of the casing from splaying out and keep braking crisp. If there is no old casing to measure up against, you have to decide how long each section of casing should be. Ideally, sections should be as short as possible without binding.

Make sure the handlebars and suspension can go through their full range of movement without pulling on the cable. Sections of casing should approach cable stops so that they are already lined up with the cable stop. Sharp curves cause sluggish brake performance. Refit the nipple in the brake lever, using the reverse process you needed to get it out. Line up the barrel-adjuster slots and tuck the cable back into the barrel-adjuster, then give it a quarter-turn to trap the cable.

It's important not to let the new cable drag on the floor and pick up dirt as you fit it. Slide the cable through each section of outer casing in turn, with a drop of oil on portions of the cable that will end up inside casing.

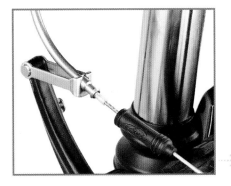  

Step 4: When you get to the final section, feel the cable through the casing, then through the noodle. Ensure the section of cable inside the noodle has a little drop of oil. Fit the noodle into the key-shaped hole in the brake unit. Make sure it's lodged securely, with the entire nose of the noodle sticking out of the hanger. Slide the black rubber boot over the cable and push it firmly onto the nose of the noodle. Pass the brake cable behind the pinch bolt.

Step 5: The cable normally clamps on above the bolt, but there will be a groove in the unit where you put the cable. Put it there. Pull cable through, so there is a gap of 2-3mm (around $1/8$ inch) between brake blocks and rim. Steadying the cable with one hand, tighten the clamp bolt with the other. Leave about 5cm (2 inches) of exposed cable, cut off the excess, and crimp on a cable end; i.e., "squash it with pliers." Tuck the loose end behind the brake unit.

Step 6: Test the brake; pull the lever hard twice. The cable might give slightly. Ideally, the brake should lock on when the lever is halfway to the handlebar. Use the barrel-adjuster to fine-tune; undo the lockring and turn it twice, away from the brake lever body. If the lever pulls too far, turn the top of the adjuster toward the handlebars. Do a couple of turns and retest. If the blocks rub on the rim, turn the top of the adjuster away from the handlebar.

Final adjustments

If you run out of adjustment on the barrel-adjuster (either it's adjusted so it jams on the brake lever body, or it's at risk of falling off), go back to the cable clamp bolt, undo it, pull through or release a bit of cable, and retighten. Then go back to the barrel-adjuster and make fine adjustments. Pull firmly on the brake lever again and check that it locks the wheel when it's halfway to the bar. Make sure that the brake blocks don't rub on the rims as the wheel turns. Check that every bolt is tight. You're done.

Barrel-adjusters

People are often confused by barrel-adjusters. They're a common feature of cable-operated brakes and are used to adjust the indexing on derailleurs as well so it's worth getting you head around how they work. The barrel-adjuster on your brake lever is easiest to deal with because you can see it all. The barrel-adjuster acts like a cable stop, holding the casing still, while allowing the cable to pass freely through a hole in the middle. Since the barrel-adjuster is threaded, whenever you turn it, it moves further in or out of the body of the brake lever. If you turn it so that it winds out of the brake lever, more of the barrel-adjuster thread is visible.

The cable inside has to travel this extra distance between the nipple, where it lodges in the lever, and the bolt that it's clamped to at the other end. This increases the tension in the cable, drawing the brake blocks closer to the rim. The lockring serves only to stop the barrel-adjuster rattling loose, so it is wound finger-tight against the body of the lever when you've finished adjusting.

Fitting new V-brake units

V-brake units get very tired if you use them hard. Every time you pull and release the brakes, the units rotate around the pivots, bending then releasing the spring. The pivots and springs won't last forever, particularly if you ride in muddy or dusty conditions. Simple, single-pivot types (like the Avid units in the pictures, or the Shimano Deore types) tend to last longer than those with a complex multi-pivot arrangement.

All V-brake units are made to fit the same size and shape of brake pivot, so you can swap between makes and models without running into compatibility problems. New brake units are supplied with a set of new brake blocks. Once you take the price of these into consideration, a new set of brake units is a good value upgrade.

FITTING NEW V-BRAKE UNITS

Step 1: Undo and remove the Allen key bolt that holds the units onto the brake pivots. It may be stiff to turn because Loctite is often used on these bolts to stop them from rattling free. The bolt heads can be quite shallow, so scrape them clean with a screwdriver before you try turning them with the Allen key—you risk rounding off the bolts.

Step 2: Pull the old units off the brake pivots. Clean the brake pivots carefully, removing all grease and dirt. If the surface is corroded, use wet-and-dry sandpaper to carefully smooth it. Put a drop of oil onto each brake pivot, and spread it over the surface. This helps the brakes return smoothly after you've squeezed them against the rim.

Step 3: Slide the new units onto the brake pivots. Line up the stub of spring on the back of each unit with the hole beside the brake pivot. You may have to undo the Allen key bolt on the back of the brake blocks, and twist the blocks out of the way to line up the spring properly. If you have three holes for the spring, use the middle one. Refit the brake fixing bolt, and tighten firmly.

Servicing V-brake units

Old brake units that are a bit tired can be revived with servicing. You'll need to release the brakes, then disconnect the cable clamp bolt. Undo and remove the fixing bolts at the bottom of each unit, then pull the brake units off the brake pivots. You may need to wiggle and pull at the same time, especially if the brake pivots have become corroded. Use a small brush (old toothbrushes are ideal) and degreaser to scrub all the dirt out from the gaps between the moving parts. Hold the unit still and wiggle the spring — if there's dirt in there, flush it out. You may find that you can pull the spring off the back of the unit. This makes it easier to clean behind, but remember to note the position and orientation of any washers or spacers.

It's best to work on one brake unit at a time; that way, you always have the other unit for reference if you get confused when reassembling the parts. Rinse the unit to get rid of residue from the degreaser, and oil the gaps between the moving parts. Move the spring against the unit to work the oil into the gaps, then wipe off the excess. Remove the cable clamp bolt and clean off any trapped dirt under the bolt head or the washer. Oil the threads of the cable clamp bolt and replace it. Clean the brake pivots carefully, removing any corrosion with wet-and-dry sandpaper. Oil the pivots, then refit the brake units as above.

The function of the balance screws

Each V-brake unit has a balance screw. You'll find it at the bottom of the unit, usually a crosshead bolt but occasionally a small Allen key. The end of each bolt rests on the end of the brake-return spring, so that the spring is forced against the bolt when you squeeze the brake unit towards the rim.

Turning the balance screw alters the preload on the spring, pushing its starting point further around the unit for a stronger spring action and releasing it for a weaker spring action. The confusing part is remembering which way to turn the screws for the effect you need.

▲ **Balance screws**

◆ Turning the balance screw clockwise **(A)** pushes it further into the unit, increasing the preload on the spring, making it springier and pulling the attached brake block away from the rim.

◆ Turning the balance screw counterclockwise **(B)** unscrews it from the unit, decreasing the preload, softening the spring and allowing the brake block to move nearer to the rim.

Since the two units are connected together by the cable across the top, adjusting one balance screw will affect both units: if one unit is pulled away from the rim, the other will be drawn towards it to compensate.

To adjust the balance screws, look first at each brake unit from face on — the front brake from directly in front of the bike, the rear brake from directly behind.

If the balance screws are badly adjusted, the units will point off to one side, rather than being parallel and vertical. There will be an uneven distance between brake blocks and rim, perhaps with one closer than the other, or even with one brake block dragging on the rim. To correct the problem, locate the balance screws. Start with the unit that's closer to the rim, and wind the balance screw in (clockwise) a couple of turns. You'll need to squeeze and release the brake lever every time you make a balance-screw adjustment to resettle the position of the spring. Look again at the angle of the two units. You should find that the adjustment has both pulled the closer brake block away from the rim and pulled the other block closer.

One confusing thing about the balance screws is that turning the screw has a different effect at different points — sometimes a couple of turns seems to make no difference at all, sometimes a quarter-turn makes a radical change. You'll have to experiment, adjusting the balance screws a quarter-turn at a time to find the central position.

Lever modulation

Modulation is just a fancy word for "how much the cable travels when you pull the lever." Adjusting the modulation means changing the distance between the point that the cable attaches to the lever blade and the pivot that the lever turns around. Increasing this distance means more power, but it also means more lever travel. Some levers have an adjustment for this, usually a thumb screw on the front of the lever. In the example (see picture at right), the red thumb nut situated on the front of the lever adjusts the position of the cable nest. Turning the thumbscrew clockwise moves the nest further away from the pivot of the brake lever, so that more cable is pulled through the lever when you move the lever blade. Turning the thumbscrew counterclockwise moves the nest nearer to the pivot of the brake lever, so that less cable is pulled through when you move the lever blade. Adjust the lever modulation so that it gives you a comfortable amount of lever swing. This will depend on the size of your hands.

The correct way to check rims for systematic wear and tear

It's easy to forget that the rims are just as much a part of the braking system as the brake blocks. Every time you brake, you're forcing your brake blocks against your rims. Powerful, controllable braking depends upon the condition of both blocks and rims. Whenever you brake, you wear both surfaces.

Rim design is subject to two competing demands. When you're trying to go faster, it helps to have rims that are as light as possible. Your wheels are spinning around as well as along, so saving weight on them makes the bike feel substantially faster than saving the same weight on a static part of your bike like the handlebars. Ideally, the rims should be as thin as possible so that they don't weigh much. Light wheels mean it's much easier to make your bike accelerate, as well as to make it change direction when you're moving fast.

If this doesn't make sense to you, take a wheel off your bike. Hold each end of the axle and move the whole wheel up and down. Then spin the wheel and do exactly the same thing again. Even though the weight of the wheel hasn't changed, you'll find it harder to move it where you want it to go when it's spinning.

But when you're trying to slow down, you need the rim material to be thick because the action of braking wears it out — and you don't want the brake blocks to wear through the rim. The deal is that rim manufacturers make their rims light so you buy them, but they expect you to keep them clean so they wear as slowly as possible, and to inspect them regularly so that you can replace worn rims before they blow on you.

Rim sidewalls

Rim sidewalls can be made to last longer without increasing their weight by covering the brake surface with a hard ceramic coating. This is expensive, but it radically reduces the speed at which the brake blocks can wear the sidewalls. Since the rim is much harder than normal, it's necessary to use harder brake blocks too.

Having a rim sidewall blow suddenly is very alarming. People can think they've been shot — there's a loud bang and suddenly they're lying on the ground, like in the movies. Because of the pressure inside the tire, the sidewalls don't give way gracefully. Over time, the sidewall gets thinner and thinner. One part of the sidewall gets too thin to hold in the tire. Then you brake suddenly — the moment of reckoning! Once one section of the rim starts to give way, it cannot support the next section, so within a fraction of a second most of your sidewall is ripped off. This punctures your tube, the resulting mess usually jams on your brake and you fall off the bike.

Rims also give way when you're pumping your tire up. The extra tire pressure on the inside of the rim sidewall is all it takes for the rim to finally give way. This is just as alarming and may also shower you with rim shrapnel.

Some newer rims come with indicator marks that show when the rim is worn out. The rim will have a small hole drilled from the inside, but not all the way through. The position of the hole is marked by a sticker on the rim with an arrow pointing to where the hole will appear. As you wear away the sidewall, the bottom of the hole appears from the outside; you can see your tire through it. Time to get a new rim! Another type of rim indicator consists of a groove milled all the way around the braking surface of the rim. When the rim is worn away to the base of the groove, it is worn out and should be replaced. To help you see it, the bottom of the groove will be a different color than the sidewall of the rim; for example, a silver rim will have a black groove in it, and a black rim will have a silver groove.

If you don't have a wear-indicator, check the condition of the sidewall by running your fingers over it. It should be flat and smooth, without deep scours and ridges. Check both sides because one sidewall may be far more worn than the other. Curvy, bulging or scarred rims are due for replacement. If they look suspect, ask your bike shop for an opinion (you know right away once you've seen enough of them). If you find any cracks in the sidewall when you inspect, stop riding immediately.

It's also worth checking the join where the two end of the rim meet. It's usually directly opposite the valve hole. Good-quality rims will have a milled sidewall. The wall is made slightly too thick and welded together in a loop. The surface is then ground off flat. Cheaper rims are simply pinned together, relying on the spoke tension in the built wheel to push the joined ends properly together.

Sometimes, the ends don't meet exactly, making a bump in the rim that knocks against the brake blocks. Small imperfections can be filed flat, but if the join protrudes by more than 0.5mm ($\frac{1}{50}$ inch), take the wheel back to your bike shop for inspection because overenthusiatic filing will just weaken the joint. Also check for cracks around the spoke holes and the valve hole. These are less dangerous but still mean the rim should be replaced.

Troubleshooting V- & cantilever brakes

Symptom	Cause	Solution	Page
Brakes squeak	Brake blocks set flat to the rim or with the back of the block touching first	"Toe-in" brakes so that the fronts of the brake blocks touch the rims first	55, 63
Brakes don't stop the bike or don't stop the bike quickly enough	Brake blocks are set too far from the rim	Set brake blocks closer	53
	Surfaces of brake blocks are contaminated or have picked up debris	Remove wheel, pick debris out of blocks with sharp knife, roughen surface with wet-and-dry sandpaper, replace wheel	53, 58
	Rims are contaminated or dirty	Clean rims with degreaser	46
	Brake blocks are worn out	Check wear on brake blocks — replace if necessary	51, 53-5, 63
	V-brakes — brake arms too close together, head of noodle jams on cable clamp when braking	Reset brake units to vertical, reorder brake block washers appropriately	58
	Cantilever brakes — link wires make unit angles too wide or too narrow	Reset straddle or link wire angle, readjust brakes appropriately	63, 66
Brakes pull on, but they don't spring back from the rim when you release the brake lever	Dirty or frayed brake cables, kinked brake outer casing	Clean and oil brake cable or replace it	51, 64-5
	Brake blocks are set too low and have worn so that a lip of brake block gets trapped under the rim.	Remove wheel, cut off offending lip with a sharp knife, replace wheel, reset brake block position	53, 55, 63
	V-brake noodle is squashed or full of grit	Flush out noodle with light spray of oil or replace	56
Brake blocks wear very quickly	Rim surface worn	Replace wheel or rim	60
Brake levers take excessive effort to pull, brakes don't release smoothly	Brake pivots worn, corroded or dirty	Remove brake units, clean and lubricate pivots	58, 67

Cantilever brakes

On new mountain bikes, cantilever brakes have been completely superseded by V-brakes. They are still standard on many cyclo-cross bikes (which are used for winter offroad racing). They are also popular with singlespeed riders who appreciate their simplicity and durability — and who often have an old serviceable pair lying around from five years ago when they had to convert to V-brakes. There are also a lot of "cantis" about on older mountain bikes, faithfully doing the simple job of slowing you down when you're going too fast.

Take care to use the correct brake levers for cantilever brakes because they are not compatible with V-brake levers. V-brake levers are designed with a greater distance between the lever pivot and the nest that the cable nipple sits in. This means that more cable is pulled through the lever with V-brakes than with a cantilever brake lever. You can see the difference if you compare a V-brake lever to a cantilever brake lever. For a cantilever brake to work properly, the distance between brake lever pivot and cable nest needs to be around 30mm (1¼ inches).

Cantilever brake blocks usually last much longer than V-brake blocks, but they will wear through eventually. Change them every couple of years whether they're worn down or not; the rubber hardens and ceases to work well after a while. This seems to be especially true if your bike lives outside or in outbuildings that get cold in the winter.

Check for wear by looking on top of the block for a wear-indication line. Usually stamped in black writing on the black surface of the block, they can be hard to spot, and you may be able to feel the line with a fingernail more easily that you can see it. There may not be an indication line; in this case, replace blocks before they've worn down to the base of the grooves molded into the blocks. Leave it too late and you risk wearing through to the metal bolt that the block is molded around. The bolt will scrape the surface off your rims.

The brake block is held in place by an eye bolt. The stub of the brake block passes through a hole in the eye bolt, which in turn passes through a curved washer then through a slot in the brake unit. On the other side of the brake unit is another curved washer, then a nut. When you tighten the nut, it pulls the eye bolt through the brake unit, squashing the stub of the brake block against the first curved washer, and holding it securely.

This design means that when you loosen the nut on the end of the eye bolt, you can move the position of the brake block in different and useful ways. You can move the eye bolt up and down in the slot on the brake unit so that the brake block hits the rim higher or lower. You can push the stub through the eye bolt, moving the brake block towards or away from the rim. You can roll the stub in the eye bolt so that the block approaches the rim at an angle. You can also twist the eye bolt on the curved washers so that the front or the back of the brake block touches the rim first. We use this flexibility to get the block precisely positioned.

The vital adjustment for cantilever brakes is setting the position where the main cable splits into two, just above the brake units. The split can be made with a straddle hanger bolted onto the cable, with a straddle wire that passes from one brake unit to the other via the straddle hanger, or with a separate link wire, through which the main cable passes, then clamps to the brake unit. Either way, it's important that the two sections of straddle cable, or the two arms of the link wire, are set at 90 degrees to each other. The best time to get this right is when fitting new brake blocks.

◀ **Four degrees of freedom**

Fitting and adjusting brake blocks

I find it easiest to work on one brake unit at a time, removing the old block then replacing it right away with the new one. This way, you will keep the washers and eye bolt in the correct order. If you take both units off at once, the washers and eyebolt have a tendency to drop off one unit when you're working on the other.

Hold the eye bolt still using a 5mm Allen key in the head of the eye bolt, and undo the nut at the back of the unit — usually with a 10mm wrench. You don't need to take the nut off, just loosen it enough to pull the old brake block out of the hole in the eye bolt. Feed the stub of the new brake block back through the hole in the eye bolt so that the brake block faces the rim. Most brake blocks will fit either way around, but if there are any arrows printed on the block, point these forward. The open end of the cartridge blocks faces backward. If one end of the brake block is shorter than the other, this goes at the front.

FITTING BRAKE BLOCKS

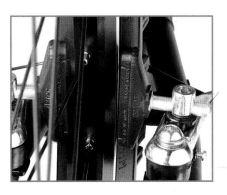

Step 1: Tighten the nut just enough so that the brake block doesn't fall out. Don't worry about adjustment at this stage, as long as the block is pointing vaguely towards the rim. Leave a generous gap between rim and brake block at this stage. Repeat with the other side. Now we're going to leave the brake blocks for a bit, and set the units up at the right angle.

Step 2: For straddle wire types, adjust the height of the straddle hanger and the length of the straddle wire, so that the two halves of the straddle wire are at 90° to each other. Link wires types are much simpler — undo the cable clamp bolt, pull in or let out until the two arms are at 90°, and reclamp. Most link wires are stamped or printed with a helpful guide line. See page 66 for more detail.

Step 3: Next, the balance screw. Cantilevers usually only have one. Pull brake lever and watch the units. If one sits closer to the rim, adjustment is needed. If the unit with balance screw is closer, turn screw clockwise to strengthen spring and move it out. If it is further away, turn balance screw counterclockwise. Start with half-turns, pulling the levers to ease things into place. At first there's no effect, then the spring gets sensitive to quarter-turns, so move slowly.

Step 4: Once everything else is set up, return to the brake blocks. Loosen the nut on the back of the unit so that you can manipulate the brake blocks. Push in each one until it's almost touching the rim. Each block should hit the rim at 90°, midway between the top and bottom of the rim.

Step 5: The front of the block should be about 1mm ($\frac{1}{16}$ inch) closer than the back. This is called "toeing in" and helps to prevent the brakes from squealing. People often mess about with bits of cardboard stuck behind the back of the brake block. This is just making work for yourself — look at the brake block and the rim, and set the angle of the brake block so that it's closer to the rim at the front than at the back.

Step 6: Hold the block in place with your hand and tighten the 10mm nut gently. Once it is fairly secure, hold the eye bolt still with a 5mm Allen key and tighten the 10mm nut firmly. Try to waggle the brake block — if it moves, it's not tight enough and probably needs a slight cable adjustment — see page 65.

Fitting a new brake cable

When you pull your brakes on, you can haul the brake cable through the casing with all the strength in your fingers. However, when you release the brake lever, you're relying on the strength of two small springs, one in each brake unit, to pull the units back out from the rim again. If your cables are gritty, rusty or kinked, they won't release freely, leaving you with sluggish, dragging brakes.

When cutting new lengths of outer casing, check that each section of is long enough; for example, the section that joins the handlebars to the frame should be long enough so that the bars can turn freely, without kinking the casing. The casing for the front brake should make a smooth, graceful curve. Cut new lengths, neatly and squarely with good, sharp cutters. Don't leave a ragged edge. If the lining gets squashed as you cut, pry it open with a sharp knife. Fit ferrules on each end of each section of casing.

LINK WIRES

STRADDLE HANGER

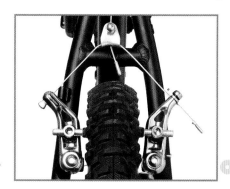

Step 1: Pull the quick-release nipple down and out of the slot on the brake unit. Cut off the cable end, and undo cable clamp bolt with a 5mm Allen key or a 10mm wrench. Pull cable out from under cable clamp bolt. Pull link wire gently. The V-shaped link wire should come away completely. Unless it is frayed or kinked, reuse it because they don't wear much. The section of outer casing may fall off. Don't worry, just reassemble it when you fit the new cable.

Step 1: One brake unit has a cable clamp bolt, the opposite unit has a slot for the straddle wire nipple. Hold this unit so the brake block is pushed against the rim, and pull nipple down and out to release it from the slot. Straddle wire and brake cable now hang loosely. Unhook straddle wire from straddle hanger, cut off cable end, undo clamp bolt, and pull the cable out. If it's frayed, replace it; cut off the cable end, undo the clamp bolt, and pull it out of the unit.

Step 2: Cut off the cable end on the old cable. Undo the cable pinch bolt that holds the straddle hanger onto the brake wire. You have to check what size tools you need, common sizes are 9mm and 10mm wrenches, and 5mm Allen keys. Irritatingly, they often use two 10mm wrenches— which is fine for workshops, which are usually filled with 10mm wrenches, but may ask too much of a home toolbox.

Replacing the brake cable

Pull the cable out of the outer casing a section at a time, leaving the casing in place for reference. Work out how the nipple on the end of the cable fits into the lever. As the nipple is attached to the lever blade, you usually need to pull the lever all the way in to see how it fits. Looking at the lever from below often helps. Undo the lockring on the brake lever barrel-adjuster until the slot on the adjuster lines up with the slot on the front of or underneath the lever body. Turn the adjuster to line up its slot.

Pull the old brake cable gently out of the slot, then pull the brake lever in toward the handlebar, and wiggle the nipple out of its nest. You may have to pull the cable forward to line it up with an escape slot for the nipple. Remove each section of outer casing. The front brake has just a single section, but the rear may be in a couple of parts that are separated by an exposed section of cable across the top tube. Refit the sections on the frame or cable hanger.

Take your new cable and sit the nipple back in the nest on the lever, then back through the slots in the lever. Feed the cable back through each section of casing in turn. Drip a drop of oil onto parts of the cable that end up inside the outer casing.

◀ **The brake cable pulls out through the slot in the lever**

Cantilever brakes: refitting the cable to the brake unit

Once you've got the cable attached to the brake lever, and threaded through the outer casing, you'll need to reconnect the cable to the brake unit. The procedure differs depending on whether you have link wire or a straddle cable. However, once you've connected the units, the procedure for adjusting the cable tension is the same.

Link wire

Look at the disc in the middle of the two arms of the link wire. Of the two different slots the cable could go into, one makes it easy to push the cable through by lining up precisely with the section of outer casing. Once you've fed the cable through the link wire, push it across to sit in the other slot on the link wire disc, and hang it at the right angle. Refit the nipple on the end of the link wire into the quick-release slot on the brake unit. Feed the brake cable under the cable clamp bolt, and pull through until the blocks sit close to the rim without touching. Tighten the cable clamp bolt firmly, cut off any excess, and fit a cable end. Pull the brakes firmly several times to settle things in place.

Straddle wire

Back at the brake, push the cable through the hole in the pinch bolt. With a standard hanger, the assembly order is straddle hanger, cable, washer, nut. The height of the straddle hanger is crucial to the effectiveness of the brake. Push up the brake units so the blocks touch the rim, and look carefully to estimate the correct hanger height. Clamp on the straddle hanger with the straddle wire arms at 90 degrees to each other. Firmly tighten the pinch bolt. This is critical, otherwise the straddle wire can slip down the brake cable and lock up the wheel.

Fit the straddle wire nipple into the slot on the brake unit, over the straddle hanger, and under the cable clamp bolt on the opposite side. Pull the straddle cable through so that the brakes are drawn in towards the rim. Ideally there should be about 2mm (⅛ inch) clearance on each side between the brake blocks and the rim. Hold the cable in place and tighten the cable clamp bolt firmly. Cut off any excess, leaving 5cm (2 inches) of spare cable, and then fit an end cap. Pull the brakes firmly several times to settle everything into place.

Adjusting the cable tension

Use the barrel-adjuster on the brake lever to fine-tune the adjustment. When you spin the wheel, it should spin freely without dragging, and it should lock when the brake lever is pulled halfway in toward the handlebars. If the blocks rub on the rim, you need to release tension in the cable. Roll the lockring away from the lever body and turn the barrel so it screws into the lever body **(A)** — clockwise,

looking from the direction that the cable enters the lever. Test, repeat if necessary, then roll the lockring to wedge it against the lever body.

If the lever moves more than halfway to the handlebars before the brakes lock the wheel, you will need to increase the tension in the cable. Undo the lockring a couple of turns, then roll the barrel-adjuster out of the lever body **(B)** — counterclockwise as you look from the direction that the cable enters the lever. Test by squeezing the brake lever again, repeat as necessary, then roll the lockring back so that it wedges against the lever body.

You may find that you run out of barrel-adjuster — either it's screwed completely into the body of the brake lever or it's screwed so far out that it threatens to fall off. Set the barrel-adjuster so that about half the thread shows. Make a crude adjustment by going back to the cable clamp bolt on the brake unit, pulling cable through or letting cable out. Then go back and repeat the fine adjustment with the barrel-adjuster.

◀ **Roll lockring away from lever before turning barrel-adjuster**

Cantilever brakes: adjusting straddle or link wire angle

The angle at which the cable connects the two brake units is critical since it determines how powerfully the brake blocks are forced onto the rim when the brake cable is pulled. Readjusting your cable angle will help you stop more quickly, but you may have to readjust your brake block positions. If you're fitting new cables and blocks, adjust the cable angle first, then fit the brake blocks to match.

The brake unit is attached to the frame by a single fixing bolt so that the brake unit can rotate around the bolt. The cable attachment points on the tops of the brake units move in a circle around the fixing bolts. This means the cable must be set up to pull the brake units around this circle — there's no point in pulling them in any other direction. This brake cable angle is best estimated by setting the sections of cable that connect the brake units so that they're at 90 degrees to each other — a right angle or square corner.

There are two different styles of cable fitting: link wire and straddle wire. Adjusting the cable angle is slightly different for each; adjusting brake blocks and cable tension is identical. To work out which you've got, check the last section of cable, where the single cable comes from the brake lever and splits into two cables, which each serve one brake unit. There are two styles of fitting. The older method was to bolt a straddle-hanger onto the cable, then run a short piece of separate cable from one side of the brake unit over the hanger, bolting it onto the other brake unit. The straddle-hanger is usually a metal triangle with a pinch bolt, but there was a fashion for purple anodizing and wacky shapes. Luckily, V-brakes put a stop to all that. I like this style because it is easy to adjust the height at which the cable splits in two. The downside is that if the brake cable breaks the spring in each unit pulls down the straddle wire onto your tire, where it can get trapped, lock your wheel, and throw you high over the bars. The link wire style was designed by Shimano to prevent this from happening. In this design, the straddle-hanger and straddle wire are replaced by a link wire. This is a V-shape set-up, with one arm of the "V" a short section of cable with a nipple at the end, and the other a short section of outer casing. The brake cable from the lever runs down to the link wire, through the section of outer casing, then bolting onto one brake unit. The other arm of the link wire hooks onto the other brake unit.

Both types of fitting tend to suffer from fraying just beside the cable clamp bolt. This part of the cable always gets squashed by the clamp bolt, and is then kinked and released every time you operate the brakes. Over time, the separate strands of the cable snap, reducing the number of strands carrying the load, therefore increasing the stress on each one. Replace cables as soon as they start to fray and inspect the clamped area regularly. Use these steps to set your straddle or link wire angle to 90 degrees, maximizing your mechanical advantage for powerful braking.

ADJUSTING STRADDLE OR LINK WIRE ANGLE

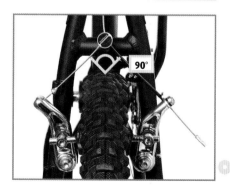

Step 1: Too low — with the link wire at this angle, your brakes feel spongy. Loosen the nut on the back of each brake unit and pull the brake blocks back from the rim. Undo the cable clamp bolt and pull through enough cable so that the link wires are at 90°. Retighten the cable clamp bolt and reset the brake blocks just clear of the rim.

Step 2: Too high — with the link wire at this angle, your brakes won't be particularly powerful. Undo the cable clamp bolt, release the cable until the angle between the link wires is 90°, retighten the cable clamp bolt, and readjust your brake blocks so that they sit closer to the rim.

Step 3: Just right! The pictures show a link wire type, but the principle is the same for straddle wire types. Play with the position of the straddle-hanger until the two sides are at 90°. Ideally, the brake block studs should be central on the eye bolt, with an equal amount showing on either side.

Fitting new brake units

Brake units usually last for years without complaint. Generally, the first thing to go will be the cover that protects and contains the spring. Spares for these are not generally available, but without the cover, the spring splays open under pressure rather than snapping the units briskly away from the rim. Replace units with broken spring covers; they cost barely more than a new set of brake blocks, which come supplied with the new units.

There is not as much choice available in cantilever brakes as there used to be once upon a time, although some very good-quality models are still made for cyclo-cross bikes; for example, Avid Shorties are light strong and powerful, though some people say they squeal too much.

FITTING NEW UNITS

Step 1: Pull the quick-release on your brake unit down and out to release it from the slot on the unit. If the slot in the brake unit has become squashed, use a thin screwdriver to carefully ease the slot apart so that the cable slides out without damage.

Step 2: Cut off the cable end, undo the cable clamp bolt, and release the cable from the units. Use this opportunity to check the condition of the cable, particularly where it gets clamped under the cable clamp bolt.

Step 3: Remove the bolts at the bottom of each unit and pull them off the frame. You may need to twist and pull at the same time; dirt that works its way into the gap between the brake and pivot can stick the two parts solidly together. For stubborn cases, try spraying a light oil into the gap, then work the brake back and forth.

Cleaning the pivots

Clean the pivots on the frame. If they're lumpy, uneven or gritted, use a scrap of wet-and-dry sandpaper. Oil the pivots and slide the new units on to them. Line up the spring that protrudes from the back of each with the middle of the three holes on the frame beside the pivot bolts. The new bolts may come with a stripe of Loctite glue, but if not, it's worth adding one since the last thing you need is your brakes rattling loose. A thin stripe will do, 2mm (⅛ inch) wide or so, for most of the length of the bolt.

Refit the cable, setting it up so that the two sections of link wire or straddle wire are at 90 degrees to each other. You may need to loosen the eye bolts that hold the brake block in place and push the brake blocks back away from the rim to give yourself enough space. Once you have set up the cable, follow the instructions for fitting new brake blocks on page 63.

Servicing units

If your brake pivots are dirty and corroded, your brakes will feel sluggish. Clean any oil pivots regularly for crisp braking.

Undo the quick-release and the cable clamp bolt, and pull the cable out completely. Undo the fixing bolts, and remove them completely. Pull the units off the frame and clean them. Use wet-and-dry sandpaper to clean the pivots. Undo one of the eye bolt nuts, remove the eye bolts, and clean all the curved washers. Put a drop of oil on each of the mating surfaces and reassemble. Just do one at a time so that you can refer to the others to put the unit back together in the right order. Oil the brake pivots, and slide the brake over the pivot, lining up the spring on the unit with the middle of the three holes beside the pivot on the frame. Refit the bolts that hold the units on, then follow the instructions for fitting new brake blocks.

Disc brakes: one day all bicycles will be fitted with these

Along with suspension forks, disc brakes have been the major source of innovation in bicycles over the last few years. Once the preserve of only the priciest and flashiest machines, they're now routinely specified on midrange bicycles.

There are two parts to a disc brake: the caliper, which bolts onto special mounts on your frame or fork, and the rotor (or disc), which bolts directly to your front or rear hub.

Disc brakes have two distinct advantages over rim brakes. First, they don't wear out your wheel by rubbing on the rim. Second, the hard surface of the disc rotor makes for powerful braking. Mechanical disc brakes are simpler to work on than hydraulic versions because they use standard brake levers and cables. Hydraulic disc brakes are more powerful but more expensive. Disc brakes of both types are getting lighter every year; new versions have barely any weight penalty over V-brakes. They still cost a fair chunk of extra money though.

Braking power

Braking power depends on rotor size. Large rotors, those with diameters of around 200mm (8 inches), are used for downhill racing, where high-speed control is paramount. Cross-country racing, where maximum speeds are lower but weight is at a premium, tends to favor smaller rotors of 150–180mm (6-7 inches) diameter. As well as being heavier, larger discs are more prone to bending, which causes them to drag in the caliper slot.

Disc brake calipers are relatively simple to mount, and need very little maintenance as long as they're kept clean. They're not in the direct firing line for anything that gets thrown up by your tires in the same way that rim brakes are, so they will work better for longer in most conditions. People sometimes find them intimidating because they're relatively new and don't look much like anything else, but they're no more difficult to adjust than V-brakes. Bleeding is tricky, but none of the procedures are difficult. Brake fluid has to be treated with care: it will strip off your paintwork if you spill it on your frame, and stop your brakes from working if you spill it on the rotor or brake pads.

Precise adjustment takes a little care. In order to work effectively, the caliper needs to be mounted so that there is a gap between the pads and the rotor on either side of the rotor. Since the rotor is bolted to the wheel, a location that cannot be changed, the gap is adjusted by moving the caliper so that it sits directly over the rotor.

Caliper adjustment

Caliper adjustment is the same whether the brake is mechanical or hydraulic. The caliper has to be bolted securely to the frame, with a gap between the rotor and the pads on either side. Most hydraulic brakes work by pushing both pads onto the rim at the same time. These work best if there is an equal gap between pad and rotor on either side. Most mechanical disc brakes, and some hydraulic ones, work by pushing the outer pad onto the rotor, which flexes and gets pushed in turn onto the other pad so the rotor ends up being trapped between two pads. The system is more effective than it sounds! It works best if the gap between the rotor and the stationary pad is as small as possible to reduce the amount of flex in the rotor to a minimum.

Emerging standards

The concept of standardized component manufacture was invented for gun-making by Guillaume Deschamps for the French army. It encouraged the interchangeability between individual parts rather than the making of each gun as an individual mechanism. However, artisan gun-makers were so resistant to a process that damaged their trade that they prevented the idea from realization for more than fifty years.

Bicycles are the same. Each manufacturer has its own way of doing things, and it takes a while for any one way to be universally accepted. A standard will emerge eventually, although it is not always the best of the options available. The two styles of caliper fitting are the Post Mount, where the bolts that secure the caliper point along the frame, and the International Standard mount, where the bolts point across the frame. Shimano took a few years to enter the disc brake market, waiting sensibly until everybody was sure it was a good idea. Their predominance in the market means that since they've chosen the International Standard, it has become the norm.

Disc brakes: the ins and outs of quick-release fittings

Disc brakes are more powerful than rim brakes (cantilever or V-brakes), slowing your wheel down rapidly. If your wheel isn't securely clamped into your frame, the braking force can be enough to tear the wheel out of the frame or fork. This is obviously to be avoided at all costs!

▲ **Hope mini disc brake**

The most secure wheel fitting is provided by slow-release designs, rather than the standard quick-release method. Many of these rely on a 20mm axle, which will only fit into a dedicated 20mm dropout, rather than the common 9mm (front) or 10mm (rear) sizes. Oversize axles are bolted onto the frame, usually with a couple of 4mm Allen keys on either side, although this varies between manufacturers. Standard wheels will not fit frames or forks designed for 20mm axles. Oversized axles are more difficult to get on and off the bike for fixing punctures and loading into cars, but the extra clamping security means that wheels cannot pop out under braking load. The wider diameter also makes the axle stiffer, which is especially useful for front wheels where it helps to brace the fork legs against twisting forces.

However, almost all bikes are currently being manufactured to use traditional quick-release skewers **(A)**. So follow these guidelines to minimise your chances of wheel pop-out.

Quick-release skewers

It's vital to ensure that your quick-release skewer is in good condition; the surfaces that lock onto the frame on each side should have crisp, sharp serrations that give a good bite on the frame. Your axle locknuts also need to be serrated so that they grip your frame or fork from the inside. The condition of the dropouts also matters. Torn, ragged dropout surfaces won't grip the axle or skewer properly.

When fitting your quick release skewers, the lever is secured by pushing it down over the center of the axle, not by twisting it around. The handle should close with a positive firm action, and should be tight enough so that closing it leaves a red mark on your palm. Once fitted, try pulling the lever open — it should resist flipping open. I prefer to use standard steel skewers in either black or silver on disc-brake bikes — this is not the place for pretty colors or fancy lightweight materials.

Skewers are designed to fit on the left hand side of the bike. Swapping them over to the right hand side stops the lever interfering with the rotor **(B)**, and also reduces the chance of burning yourself on the rotor if you remove the wheel during a ride as they get very hot. But if you have control knobs on the ends of suspension fork legs, you may find that the skewer won't fit properly on the right hand side. Avoid closing the skewer against rebound or compression adjusters.

The small volute springs on either side of the axle are there to help you line up the wheel in the dropouts when refitting it. They ensure that the skewer ends sit evenly out from the ends of the axle. If the springs get deformed, they'll get trapped between frame and fixing, reducing wheel security. Remove and discard damaged springs. If you're taking off one, remove both. They're only there for wheel fitting convenience and have no other function.

Check that your skewers are firmly tightened every ride. If you find your skewers come loose under heavy braking, immediately return to your bike shop and find out what's happening before you ride again.

Disc brakes: fitting International Standard calipers to your bike

With this fitting, the caliper is bolted onto the frame or fork from the side with bolts that pass through the mounts and then thread into the caliper. The sideways position is altered by inserting shims between the frame and the caliper. (I'm going to use "frame" through this explanation. If you're fitting a front brake, just substitute the word "fork" for "frame.")

"Shim" is a fancy word for an accurately sized washer. Shims have to be of precise thickness because the spacing between the caliper and the frame must be the same for each bolt. If the washer stacks are different thicknesses, the caliper sits crookedly over the rotor and drags as you ride. You'll need a selection of different washer thicknesses. Wider ones get the rotor passing through the caliper slot, while wafer thin ones fine-tune the position.

Front and rear calipers are fitted in the same way; the fronts just bolt to the fork rather than the frame. If you're reusing caliper-fixing bolts, put a narrow strip of Loctite glue on the threads. New bolts will have Loctite on already. Braking forces will twist and vibrate the bolts, so they need extra care to stop them rattling free.

To fit the caliper

With the rotor fitted securely to the wheel (see page 73 for how to do this if it's not already fitted) slide the slot in the caliper over the rotor, then line the holes in the caliper up with the holes in the frame. Fit a washer on each bolt, pass it through the holes in the frame, and thread the bolts onto the caliper. Watch the relative positions of the caliper and the rotor as you tighten the bolt. Look along the rotor, in through the slot in the caliper. It helps to hold up a piece of white card on the other side.

◀ **(A) Rear International Standard disc mounts**

INTERNATIONAL STANDARD CALIPER FITTING

Step 1: Tightening the bolts draws the caliper towards the frame. If the inside (nearest the wheel) pad starts to touch the rotor, you need to add shims. These come with a new brake or you can get some from your bike shop. Remove both bolts and add the same number of shims of the same thickness to sit between the caliper and the frame. Refit the bolts, tighten firmly, and repeat, watching the gap between the rotor and the pads again.

Step 2: Use thicker washers at first, then fine-tune with thinner ones. The gap between pad and rotor should be the same for models where both pistons are activated, and should be as close as possible to the stationary pad when one piston is activated. Looking through the gaps to estimate which side is bigger can be hard on your eyes. Hold a piece of white card on other side of the caliper and look though the gap at the card — it helps a little.

Step 3: Shimano calipers come with shims that represent a revolution in shim technology. (This might sound excessive praise, but if you're fitting several disc brakes, the time saving is huge.) The shims are shaped like tiny pitchforks, so you can fit them without taking off the entire bolt every time you change your mind about how many shims you need. The thinner shim has a notch so you can differentiate easily between the thickness.

Disc brakes: fitting Post Mount calipers to your bike

The Post Mount fitting system was developed by Hayes and is used on their brakes, Manitou forks, and some frames. It's not unusual to find bikes with a Post Mount fork and an IS (International Standard) mount frame, or the other way around. Adapters allow you to convert between types.

The caliper position is easier to adjust with the Post Mount, but it's important to ensure that the pads are parallel to the rotor before tightening the fixing bolts. It's possible to bolt the caliper on at an angle by mistake, so that one pad touches the rotor at the top and the other rubs at the bottom.

POST MOUNT CALIPERS

Step 1: These are even easier to fit! If you reuse bolts, put a drop of Loctite glue on the threads. New bolts come with Loctite pre-applied. Fit a washer to each bolt, then push the bolts through the holes in the caliper. Slide the slot in the caliper over the rotor, then line up the bolts carefully with the threaded holes.

Step 2: Screw in the bolts until they're almost tight; you should be able to wiggle the caliper from side to side, but you shouldn't be able to rock it backwards and forwards. Pull the brake lever and, while holding it, tighten the caliper-fixing bolts with the other hand. (A friend can be handy here, especially with the back brake). Release the brake lever and spin the wheel.

Step 3: You will usually find that this has spaced the caliper perfectly. Occasionally, it doesn't work, and the caliper rubs on one side or the other. If this happens, look along the rotor through the slot in the caliper to work out which side is rubbing. It helps to hold a piece of white card up on the other side of the caliper. Loosen off the fixing bolts a little bit, slide the caliper over, and retighten firmly. This is a little more tricky, but it's not difficult.

Sizing of disc brake mounts

The more common IS mounts are almost always 51mm (2 inches) apart. (An irritating exception, with 21.5mm (⁷⁄₁₀ inch) spacing, was used briefly.) The hole in the mount is not threaded — the fixing bolt goes through the mount, then threads into the caliper. Common brands of IS mount brakes are Hope and Shimano. The less common Post Mounts are a little more complicated and less standardized in spacing. They are found on Hayes brakes, Manitou forks and Trek frames, among others.

- ◆ Front Post Mounts — now 74mm (2⁹⁄₁₀ inches), has been 68.8mm (2⁷⁄₁₀ inches) or 70mm (2¾ inches)
- ◆ Chainstay mounts — 21.5mm (⁹⁄₁₀ inch)
- ◆ Seatstay mounts — 21.5 or 74mm

All fixing bolts, for both IS and Post Mount, are M6.

If you have Post Mount discs and IS mount frame or forks, or vice versa, you can buy adapters to convert from one type to the other. Your bike shop will be able to obtain the correct widget. The price seems alarming for a small and simple piece of aluminum, but you have to ignore that because without it your brakes simply won't work. Bolt the adapter firmly to the IS component, either the caliper or the frame/fork, then use the adjusting instructions for the Post Mount type. IS may be more common now, but Post Mount is easier to adjust!

At the beginning of the disc mount revolution, nobody was sure what the standard would be, so some manufacturers used non-standard mounts. If you have one of these, don't panic. Contact the frame manufacturer; you should be able to buy an adapter plate from them to convert your disc mount to something more standard.

In theory, it is possible to buy conversion kits to turn your non-disc frame into a disc-compatible frame. These are not often worth the trouble, and success depends on the precise size of your frame or fork. Go to your bike shop and get advice before pursuing this option.

Disc brakes: introduction to rotors, the heart of the system

The rotor is the proper name for the disc that gives the disc brake its essential *raison d'être*. As with caliper fittings, it has taken time for the manufacturers to adopt a universal fitting. They seem to be settling on the "International Standard" 6-bolt fitting with a distance of 44mm between opposite holes, as originally used by Hayes. The introduction of a single standard makes rotors interchangeable between hubs of different makes. Recent Shimano XTR brakes have gone off on a tangent and are fitted to a spline on the matching XTR hubs.

The rotor can get very hot, particularly on long downhills. Don't touch it until it's had a chance to cool down or you really will burn yourself. It's also easy to trap your fingers in a spinning rotor while fiddling about with the calipers. Simply don't go near the rotors when the wheel is turning. Blood will contaminate the rotor surface as will the oil from your fingers, so avoid touching the rotor surface when adjusting brakes.

Each caliper is designed to take a specific size of rotor — the diameter and thickness are crucial. A larger rotor will give you more braking power and leverage, a smaller one will be lighter. Generally, a diameter of around 160mm (6¼ inches) is good for cross country; downhill needs around 200mm (8 inches).

Thinner rotors are used for single-piston calipers, where a moving piston forces the rotor across onto a stationary pad. Thinner rotors are more flexible. They take less force to bend sideways and snap back into shape as soon as you release the brakes.

Rotors wear out eventually, although it takes a long time. Shimano say their rotors can be worn down to 0.5mm (¹⁄₅₀ inch) thickness, but I would change them before this. For efficient braking, the surface of the rotor must be smooth and shiny. Torn or rough surfaces mean inconsistent braking and fast pad wear. Rough surfaces are often caused by the rotor rubbing on the inside of the caliper slot, so check the alignment carefully if you have to replace a rough rotor to make sure the new one doesn't go the same way.

It's vital that the rotor bolts are fitted securely; otherwise they will rattle loose. For this reason, many manufacturers fit their rotors with Torx head bolts, which are a bit like Allen keys, but have star-shaped heads instead of hexagonal ones. The Torx type is no stronger than the standard type, but the unusual tool thwarts casual tinkerers. Newer multi-tools, like the Specialized EMT tool, come with a Torx key; otherwise they're available from car and hardware shops. Don't try to tighten the bolts with a screwdriver or Allen key, because you'll just damage the bolt head.

If you ride in muddy conditions, you may find that a wavy-edged rotor, like the Hope Mini, will stop the caliper from clogging. (Those people at Hope on the northern English moors have plenty of mud experience.) Having your name laser-cut in the rotor gives little mud-clearing advantage, but it does let you identify your wheels amid a pile of dismembered bike parts in the car park.

Braking efficiency

Your rotors are your braking surface — your braking efficiency will depend as much on the condition of the rotors as on the condition of your brake pads. Cleaning discs and replacing pads should be your first priority if you're not getting enough braking power. The majority of braking problems with discs are due to dirty or oily discs or contaminated pads, rather than more glamorous bleeding issues.

Cleaning rotors

Disc brake pads absorb grease or oil from any nearby source, with an immediate effect on braking power. Keep the rotor clean. It's best to avoid touching it with your fingers as they always leave greasy marks. Some people dab grease behind the brake pads to stop them vibrating and squealing. This is also a bad idea, since the grease will, without fail, work its way onto the surface of the pads. Clean the rotors with isopropyl alcohol, which doesn't leave a dirty residue. You can get it from drug stores. Car disc brake cleaning sprays are no good. Car disc brakes run much hotter, burning off the residue the sprays leave. Bicycle disc brakes don't get hot enough. Sometimes it can be worth cleaning new disc rotors straight out of the box to help reduce burn-in time. Bicycles that get a lot of city use need their rotors cleaned more frequently.

Bending back a deformed rotor

You can bend back slightly deformed rotors — up to 2 or 3mm (around ⅛ inch) of waviness can usually be pulled into shape. It's best to start by hand. Roll the wheel gently around, watching through the slot in the calipers to identify the biggest distortion. With a clean cloth over the rotor surface to protect both it and your thumbs, put both thumbs on the bulge and push it firmly back into shape. Thinner, lighter cross-country rotors respond well to this treatment. If you can't get enough force with your hands, you can ease the rotor very carefully back into shape with a crescent wrench. Protect the rotor from the jaws of the wrench with a cloth and proceed with extreme caution — it's very easy to make the distortion worse rather than better. Gauge the size of the wobble carefully before you start, then try to straighten the rotor in one movement. Bending the rotor back and forth will weaken it, which is dangerous. If you can't get it straight in one movement, it's too bent to straighten safely and must be replaced.

Replacing a rotor

Some rotors — for example, Shimano — have tightening plates under the bolts. These are small metal washers that you bend up and around the head of the rotor fixing bolts to prevent the bolts rattling loose. If you have these, before you start bend them flat with a small flat-bladed screwdriver so you can turn the bolts. Refit them under the bolt heads in adjacent pairs. Bend up the edges onto the flats of the bolt heads after you finish tightening the bolts.

Arm yourself with the correct size tool; for example, rotor bolts use Torx heads — never ever try to substitute the tool — if you haven't got the correct one, drop the job until you do. You can buy the right tool at hardware stores. If you round off the bolt head, it takes all sorts of messing about to recover. Undo each bolt a little bit, maybe a couple of turns. Once you can wiggle the disc on the hub go back around again and completely remove each bolt.

The new disc needs to be fitted facing in the right direction. Usefully, some have a rotation arrow printed on the outside. (You don't need to see which direction the arrow points — it is printed on the outside.) Otherwise, if the rotor has an offset arm, the arm at the top needs to point forwards.

If you reuse the old bolts, put a strip of Loctite glue on each one. New bolts come pre-glued. Fit each bolt loosely through the rotor then into the hub. Take up the slack in each bolt so the head of the bolt touches the rotor. Check the rotor fits snugly against the hub. The order in which you tighten the bolts is important. Don't simply go round in a circle, alternate across the hub as shown in the picture.

It is of utmost importance that these bolts are tight — loose ones will rattle out very quickly, which can be messy on the trail. Check they are still tight after your first ride, and then check again every 800 kilometers (500 miles).

▼ Tighten rotor bolts alternately across the center to hold tightening plates (A) in position

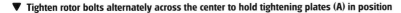

Mechanical disc brakes

These are often thought of as a halfway house between V-brakes and hydraulic discs. They're not as powerful as hydraulic discs, but they're much cheaper. If you are intimidated by maintaining hydraulics, the simplicity of cables is appealing. The advantages of not using the rim as the braking surface apply equally to mechanical and hydraulic disc brakes.

Mechanical disc units do tend to clog up quickly. Since they all work in slightly different ways, there isn't room here to show how to service all of them, but they're very satisfying to work on. Keep the instruction manual and get into the habit of stripping them down, cleaning them and reassembling them. You'll be able to feel the difference right away.

The most common design consists of one moving pad and one stationary pad. The moving pad pushes against the rotor when you apply the brakes, bending the rotor slightly so that it in turn is pushed against the stationary pad and trapped between the two. The moving pad is activated by pulling the brake cable. This pulls on the actuation lever on the brake unit, which twists the piston inside the unit. The piston is mounted on a shallow spiral, so that as it is turned, it moves towards the rotor. Since the pad is mounted on the end of the piston, it gets forced against the rotor. When you release the brake cable, a spring inside the unit pulls the piston back from the rotor, ready for next time.

Mud, dust, and salt can work through the seals, getting trapped inside the mechanism. This makes the piston action sluggish, so it's well worth taking the time to learn how to strip them down. Mechanical disc brakes respond well to being stripped, cleaned and reassembled.

Although all calipers work in slightly different ways, they're so similar that it's possible to generalize. Most brakes have a selection of small washers separating the internal components. It's vital that these all go back in the same order. By laying everything you remove out in a line, you can avoid the classic moment of discovering a stray washer after reassembling the caliper. For jobs like this, I like to set the parts out on a clean sheet of paper — you can draw diagrams on it as you go along to remind yourself which way round the parts went.

It's worth disconnecting the cable and removing the caliper completely from the bike, so that you can lay the brake on a flat surface and see properly what you're doing. If you can remove the pads by wiggling them out of the caliper slots, do so now. The stationary pad, the one nearest the wheel, may be held in place with a little steel washer. The teeth on the inside of the washer grip the post on the back of the pad. Use a small screwdriver to lever off the washer. Take care not to damage it.

Disassembly from here will vary, so make diagrams of what you're doing as you go along. Remember to make a note of which direction parts like seals face. Remove the actuation lever by undoing the bolt in its center. Take out any seals. Remove the innards of the brake carefully, there's a spring inside pulling the pad away from the rotor. You'll find a spiral groove inside the body of the caliper — this is

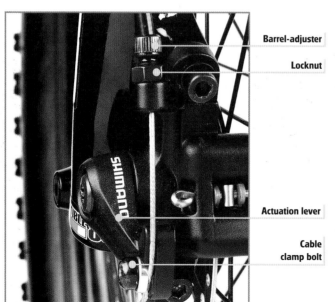

Barrel-adjuster

Locknut

Actuation lever

Cable clamp bolt

what pushes the piston against the rotor when you rotate the actuation lever and is normally the part that gets gummed up with mud. Clean the groove carefully. Cotton swabs are perfect. Wipe the inside of the caliper body and the other internal components clean, and reassemble according to your diagram. Don't regrease the piston head — the grease melts when the caliper body heats up, creeping onto the brake pads and contaminating them.

The actuation lever bolt needs a strip of Loctite to stop it from vibrating loose. Retighten firmly, then test the action of the brake. Squeeze the actuation lever, pinching the barrel-adjuster and cable clamp bolt together while looking into the caliper slot. The brake pad should move smoothly across the slot, springing immediately back when you release the actuation lever. If the actuation lever won't rotate easily, check that you've not left out a washer on reassembly. If the pad doesn't spring back smartly, your spring is misaligned, or there's still dirt in the spiral groove.

Shimano mechanical disc brake caliper

Changing and adjusting cables

Mechanical disc cables seem to drag in less dirt than V-brake cables. The latter are not in the direct firing line for debris thrown up from the tires in the same way — but corrosion and contamination in the cables still make your brakes feel sluggish.

Fraying or kinked cables also need replacement. Cut the cable end off the old cable. Undo the cable clamp bolt and free the end of the cable. Unthread the cable from inside the casing, leaving the casing in place. Keep any rubber boots. Once back at the lever, look to work out how the nipple is seated (it's usually in a pivoted nest attached to the lever blade). Pull in the lever and look at the exposed section from underneath. Most are variants on the type shown in the picture. Undo the lockring on the barrel-adjuster until its slot lines up with that on the front of the lever body, then undo the barrel to line up its slot too.

Pull the cable forward, so it slips out of the lined-up slots, then pull the lever towards the bars. The nest that the nipple sits in has a key-shaped hole so the cable cannot pull out under pressure. Wiggle the cable to line it up with the slot in the nest and pull it out gently. Remove each section of outer casing and cut a fresh piece to length. Cut the end of each section squarely, making sure you don't leave a ragged spur of metal across the hole. If the cable lining has got squashed where you cut it, use the point of a sharp knife to open it out. Each end of each section will need a ferrule. The cable stops on disc brake bikes are often larger than usual to accommodate hydraulic hoses. If you need to, reuse the ferrules from the old casing. The far end of the last section may not need a ferrule, but fit one if there is room.

Reverse the procedure you used for removing the old cable to fit the new cable back into the lever: line the nipple up with the key-shaped hole in the nest, wiggle it into place, line the slots on the barrel-adjuster and lockring up with the slots on the lever body, guide the cable into the lever body and barrel-adjuster through the slots, then turn the barrel-adjuster a quarter-turn to trap the cable in place.

Feed the cable through each section of outer casing in turn. If you're replacing the outer casing as well, cut each section carefully to length, making sure you don't leave a spur of metal across the hole at the end of the casing. Fit a ferrule on each end of each section. Make sure you don't allow the cable to drop onto the ground and pick up dirt. Drip a drop of oil onto any section of cable that will end up inside the outer casing. Feed the cable through the last section, then through the barrel-adjuster or cable stop on the disc brake. Lift the wheel and turn it. It should spin freely. A slight rub is fine, but the wheel shouldn't drag. The brakes should lock on when you pull the brake lever without the lever touching the handlebar. If either of these situations does happen, go to the adjustment section on page 78.

◀ **Line up slots in barrel-adjuster and lockring, then pull cable forwards**

CHANGING THE CABLE

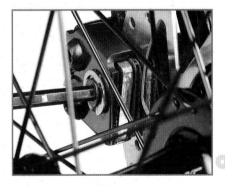

Step 1: Refit any rubber boots — give them a clean first if they're grubby — and slide the cable in under the cable clamp bolt. It is clear where it should fit — make sure it lies in the groove under the clamp bolt. Leave about 5cm (2 inches) of spare cable, cut the rest off and fit a cable end.

Step 2: Pull the cable through the clamp bolt to take up any slack, and hold it with one hand while you tighten the cable clamp bolt up with the other. Then pull the lever firmly several times to settle the casing and ferrules into place. You will probably find that the cable is so slack that you can pull the lever all the way to the bars without locking the wheel. If this is the case, undo the cable clamp bolt and pull more cable through. Retighten the cable clamp and retest.

Step 3: Usually, the stationary pad (on the inside, nearest the wheel) is adjustable. Most adjust by turning a 5mm Allen key on the back of the pad clockwise to move the pad closer, and counterclockwise to move it farther away. Get it as close as possible without touching the rotor.

Changing brake pads

Disc brake pads usually last much longer than V-brake pads. The material in the disc rotor is much harder than the material in the rim, allowing the disc brake pad to be much harder as well. Were you to use the material in the disc brake pad as a rim brake, the rim would wear away in next to no time. The harder material also means that the pad can touch the rotor as the wheel spins without slowing down significantly — so you don't have to worry about a slight rubbing noise when you spin a wheel with a disc brake.

Make sure you get the right pad for the brake; the fittings and shapes vary between makes, and between models from the same make. Take the old ones along to your bike shop for comparison if you're not sure. Even if you know the make, the shape will vary from model to model and from year to year. After fitting, new pads need to be burnt in — they don't work properly until you've braked a few times. Once you've got the new pads in, find somewhere you can ride the bike safely with limited braking power. Ride along slowly, haul on the brakes, and bring the bike to a halt. Repeat at increasing speeds, until you're satisfied. This may take 10 or 20 repetitions.

The pads on mechanical brakes sometimes wear unevenly. The most common design has the cable from the brake lever pull an actuation lever (mechanic's term for "lever that does something"), which pushes the outer brake pad onto the rotor. The rotor flexes under the pressure, gets pushed against the other disc pad, then ends up firmly trapped between two pads. This can cause uneven wear, but you must still change both pads at the same time even if one looks more worn than the other. They should be replaced when either of the pads has less than 0.5mm (1/50 inch) of thickness left from any direction. You may need to take them out to check how they're surviving. If in doubt, follow the procedure for removing them below, and refit them if they have life left. Clean your rotors whenever you fit new pads.

Changing brake pads

Drop the wheel out of the frame. Look at the brake caliper. You'll see that it has a slot into which the rotor fits. Most often, the pads will pull out in the same direction that you pulled the rotor out of the slot — towards the center of the wheel. Some will pull out of the top of the brake caliper, away from the center of the wheel. Have a good look at the caliper before you start and draw a picture if necessary to help you put everything back together. There will be a pad on each side of the rotor, and it will often have little ears or tabs to pull it out. Use these to manipulate the pads, rather than touching the pad surfaces.

CHANGING BRAKE PADS

Step 1: Often the pads will not pull straight out; they will have some kind of device that stops them from getting rattled out as you ride. This will normally be a pin that goes through the opposite side of the pad, so look on the other side of the caliper for a retaining pin or split pin.

Step 2: Pull out split pins, retaining pins or P-clips — keep them safe because you need to fit them back at the end. There may be one or two retaining pins. Split pins need to be bent gently straight with pliers before you can pull them out.

Step 3: Gently pull the pads out, either by grabbing the little ears that poke out of the slot, or by pulling on the corners of the pads. If you're not sure of the correct replacement pads, take the old ones to your bike shop to match them up.

Step 4: The pads may have a retaining spring; make a note of its position and orientation, and refit it with the new pads. Take care when fitting the new pads that the arms of the spring sit beside the pads, not over the braking surface. It's easiest to squash the spring between the pads, then fit both into the slot together, rather than trying to get the pads into the slot one at a time.

Step 5: Slide the new pads back into the caliper, pushing them in until the holes in the pad line up with the retaining pin holes in the caliper. Refit the retaining pin or pins, bending over their ends, so that they don't rattle out. Then pull the pads firmly to make sure they are held securely in place.

Step 6: Refit the wheel, wiggling the rotor back into the gap between pads. You may need to readjust the cable because new pads will be thicker than the old ones. Pick up the bike and spin the wheel. It should spin freely, without binding. However, it's fine if you can hear the pad rubbing slightly on the rim — this won't slow you down. If the rotor drags or the brake lever pulls back to the bar without braking, go to the adjustment section on page 78.

Brake-fitting tips

◆ Ensure you have the correct replacement pads, which vary between make, model and year of manufacture. Some packs come with a replacement pad spring, but, if not, you'll need to save the old one.

◆ Pads need replacing when they've worn down to 0.5mm thick.

◆ They will also need replacing if they've become contaminated with oil, which seeps into the brake pad material and prevents them from gripping your rotor.

◆ Some pad styles need a special metal spring that helps to force the pads apart when you release the brake lever. When fitting these, take care to ensure that the spring sits beside each pad, not trapped over the braking surface.

◆ Avoid touching the surfaces of the pads, they will pick up contamination from your fingers.

Magura single-piston brakes

Some mechanical disc brakes require you to extract the pads by completely removing the stationary piston and extracting the pads through the hole in the caliper body. The variation you're most likely to come across is Magura single-piston brakes.

To get the old pads out, remove the wheel and use a 5mm Allen key to undo the stationary pad-adjustment bolt. It's in the middle of the caliper body, facing the wheel. The pad cover comes off completely, revealing the back of the stationary pad. Use the little ears that protrude through the caliper slot to manipulate the pad through the back of the caliper body, twisting it slightly — there's only just enough room for it to come out. Now you can see the face of the other pad through the caliper body — get this out by the same route. It's magnetic, so it sticks slightly to the piston.

Clean inside the caliper body. Water is fine, and cotton buds are exactly the right shape and size for working out bits of grit. Then fit the new pads. The far one goes in first, facing towards you. Push the little ear in through the hole in the back of the caliper body, then use this to manipulate the pad into place — it will snap onto the magnetic face of the piston. Follow with the stationary pad, face to face with the one you've already fitted. Refit the stationary pad cover, then the wheel, then adjust so that the new pads don't rub on the rotor.

Mechanical disc brakes: adjusting brake pads for controlled stopping

The pad position will need adjusting after changing a brake cable, after fitting new pads, or as the pads become worn. Ideally, the pad position should be set so that you can lock up the wheel by pulling the brake lever halfway to the handle bar. This gives you enough lever movement for precise speed control, without the risk of trapping fingers between lever and bar during emergency stops.

Mechanical disc brakes can be tricky to adjust. The clearance between pads and rim must be small, without allowing the pads to rub on the rotor. A common source of confusion is that only the outer brake pad gets moved by the action of the cable, pushing the rotor against a stationary inner pad. This means that the two pads have to be adjusted in different ways.

You will really benefit from a workstand for this task. If that's not possible, get a friend to lift the wheel off the ground at opportune moments. Before you start adjusting, spin the wheel, look into the caliper slot, and check how much clearance there is between rotor and pads. If the brake binds as you ride, one or both pads are rubbing on the rotor and need to be moved away. If you're finding that you can pull the rotor all the way back before the wheel locks, one or both of the pads needs to be moved towards the rotor.

The caliper slot is quite narrow, and it can be tricky to see what's going on. Clean the caliper before you start trying to make adjustments. Then hold something white on the far side of the slot to make it easier to see the gap. Spin the wheel while watching the slot. Unless they're brand new, rotors will often have a slight wobble. Make sure you adjust for an estimated central position.

Adjusting pad position

Before you start adjusting the pad position, ensure that the rotors are not dragging on the side of the rotor slot — this will damage the rotors and slow you down. Adjust the caliper position (see the caliper fitting section, page 79), so that the rotor runs centrally before you adjust the pad position. Check that the wheel is properly and securely located in the dropout too — the rotor position will be affected if the wheel's not straight in the frame or forks.

It's worth keeping a spare set of brake pads. There is no standard size and shape (unlike V-brake blocks), so it can be tricky to find the right one. Spares are light and easy to carry for emergency replacement, but it's far easier to adjust pads at home than out in the open because the job involves too many small fiddly parts aching to start a life of freedom in the long grass beside your favorite trail.

Toolbar

Tools to fit new calipers
- Allen keys — 5mm or 6mm, to fit heads of fixing bolts
- For IS mount calipers — a selection of shims. Useful sizes are 1mm, 0.5mm and 0.25mm

Tools to change brake pads, and adjust pad position
- Depending on model, pliers to extract and refit split pins
- Fresh pads of correct make and model
- Allen keys for stationary pad adjustment bolt — usually 5mm
- Allen key for cable clamp adjustment — usually 5mm

Mechanical disc brakes: adjusting Shimano calipers

The most common arrangement is that used by the Shimano calipers in the pictures. The position of the outer pad, furthest from the wheel, is controlled by the cable.

Tightening the brake cable moves the pad towards the rotor; loosening it allows the piston spring to pull the pad away. The inner pad doesn't move when you operate the brakes, but its stationary position can be adjusted by turning an Allen key on the caliper.

Tightening the brake cable moves the pad towards the rotor, while loosening it allows the piston spring to pull the pad away. The inner pad doesn't move when you operate the brakes, but its stationary position can be adjusted by turning an Allen key back of the the caliper on the side nearest the wheel. The rotor may not be completely flat — spin the wheel between adjustments, so that you can account for any distortion.

FITTING SHIMANO PADS

  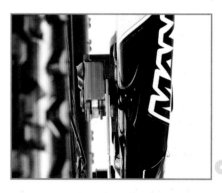

Step 1: The outer pad is controlled by the brake cable. If it rubs, release tension in cable so the pad sits further from the rotor. Use the barrel-adjuster at the brake lever. Roll lockring away from body of the brake lever and turn barrel to roll the barrel-adjuster into the brake lever, clockwise as you look from where brake cable enters brake lever. Repeat until the brake doesn't rub, and roll the lockring back so it wedges against the body of the brake lever.

Step 2: If you run out of adjustment at the barrel-adjuster, make a coarse adjustment by undoing the cable-clamp bolt, letting out a little bit of cable, then repeating the fine adjustment (Step 1) with the barrel-adjuster.

Step 3: If the inside pad is rubbing, you need to move the stationary pad away from the rotor. It usually requires a 5mm Allen key, which has to be threaded through the spokes of the wheel to get to the adjusting bolt. Normally, clockwise moves the pad closer, counterclockwise moves it away, but there are exceptions — watch the movement of the pad as you turn the adjuster. Quarter-turns are enough to make a difference to the clearance.

Alternative methods

Alternative arrangements for centering the pads over the caliper do exist, although the above method is now becoming standard since it's the easiest and most accurate way to set the clearance between pads and rotor.

Some older calipers have an integral adjuster, allowing you to wind the whole caliper sideways to adjust the gap between the pads. Turn the thumbscrew slowly. Once you get close, small adjustments make a big difference. Pull the brakes on hard between each adjustment to settle everything into place.

If the stationary pad is not adjustable, you will have to move the whole caliper sideways to set the gap between stationary pad and rotor. Then use the cable to adjust the clearance on the outside of the rotor. For Post Mount calipers, undo the two caliper mounting bolts just a little — just enough so you can move them. Ease the caliper sideways, checking the gap beside the inside of the rotor nearest the wheel. This needs to be approximately 1mm ($\frac{1}{16}$ inch). Hold a piece of white card on the far side of the caliper to make it easier to see the gap. Retighten the bolts firmly. You may need to readjust the outer-pad spacing after this.

International Standard (IS) mounts are trickier. Estimate how much more gap you need for the pad to clear the rotor. Undo the caliper fixing bolts and add an equal number of shims between each bolt and the caliper. With normal washer-shaped shims, you need to remove the bolts completely. Shimano pitchfork-shaped shims can be slipped between caliper and frame without removing the bolt.

Add shims until the inside pad clears the rotor, then retighten the caliper fixing bolts firmly. You may need to adjust the outer pad spacing after this.

Hydraulic disc brakes

Hydraulic brakes are much more powerful than cable-operated ones. The principle is simple: pulling the lever towards the bars pushes fluid down a narrow tube to the caliper, where the fluid pushes pistons outward. The fluid is incompressible; any movement of the lever is transferred directly to the pistons. The pistons have brake pads on their ends, which are forced against a rotor attached to your wheel, stopping your bike on a dime. The whole idea of dealing with hydraulic fluid can be daunting, but as long as you're careful and calm, it's not difficult.

There are a couple of different fluid types. You MUST use the correct type for your brake. Using the wrong fluid ruins the seals in the system, causing leaks. The two basic types are DOT car brake fluid and mineral oil. Mineral oil is easier to work with because it doesn't damage paintwork and is less environmentally unfriendly. DOT fluid has a higher boiling point and expands less at high temperatures. There isn't a significant performance difference between the two types, just don't mix them up. Both types of fluid will eventually absorb water from the air and become less effective, so buy small containers and keep them sealed. Don't use half-empty containers of old fluid that have been sitting around, even if the cap has been on. I wear rubber gloves to work with both types of fluid, as it is worth avoiding skin contact. Brake fluid is very corrosive and needs to be treated with respect.

Sometimes air gets trapped in the system: For example, if you cut a hose to shorten it or you crash and tear a hose out. If this happens, the brakes feel spongy. Air is far more compressible than brake fluid, so when you pull the brake lever, all bubbles have to be squashed before the force reaches the pistons and starts moving them. Luckily, air is lighter than brake fluid, so if you open the system at the top, the bubbles rise up and out. The process of opening the brake, letting air out, and replacing it with fluid is called bleeding. Bleeding is often treated as a complicated and mysterious process only to be carried out by druids. Actually, it's quite simple. Where people go wrong is treating bleeding as a universal cure for anything wrong with the brakes. It is only a useful method if you really do have air bubbles trapped in the system. It won't help, for example, if they have a leak somewhere or if dirt is hanging around your piston heads making them sticky. If bleeding your brakes make no difference, it's time to consider whether the problem lies elsewhere.

You must also take careful steps to not get brake fluid or mineral oil on either the disc rotor or the brake blocks. If you are bleeding or filling brakes, remove the wheel, and remove the pads from the caliper to keep them safely out of the way. Do not refit them until you've done whatever it is you need to do and the fluid is sealed back inside the system. If the system is open and the pads are nearby, you will undoubtedly contaminate them. If this happens, replace the pads, and clean the rotors with isopropyl alcohol. It may sound as if I'm trying to make you buy more pads by saying contaminated ones don't work well, but they don't.

Open and closed system brakes

A lot of fuss is made about the merits of open versus closed brake systems. I am inclined to believe that if you ride along worrying whether you have a diaphragm on your brakes or not, then you need get out more, specifically the sort of getting-out-more that you do without your bike. Both open and closed systems have a reservoir at the lever. Pulling your brake lever operates a piston inside the lever, forcing oil down the brake hose, and pushing the brake pistons inside the caliper towards your rotor. Under heavy braking, the fluid in the hose gets hot and expands, increasing the total volume of fluid in the system. Open and closed systems regulate this expansion in different ways to prevent the pads closing in on the rotor during long descents.

Open systems have a flexible rubber diaphragm inside the reservoir. As your brake fluid heats up and expands, the rubber diaphragm deforms to accommodate the extra volume. The piston inside the brake lever is designed so that as soon as it's operated, it blocks fluid flow from the brake hose to the reservoir. This is vital — brake fluid, like water, always takes the path of least resistance. If the fluid could flow back into the reservoir under pressure, it would simply crush the flexible diaphragm, rather than forcing your pistons onto your rotors. With an open system you cannot manually adjust the position of the pads.

Closed-system brakes have an adjusting knob on the reservoir. As you turn the knob, it changes the volume of oil that the reservoir can contain. Making the reservoir smaller forces fluid down the brake hose, pushing the pads towards the rotor. Making the reservoir bigger drags oil back up the hoses, allowing the pads to sit further from the rotor. This means that under heavy braking, like on a long downhill, you can back off the pads to completely eliminate drag on the rotor. However, the system won't automatically compensate for brake fluid expansion.

Adjusting hydraulic brakes

Every set of brakes works a little differently, making it impossible to give a comprehensive adjusting procedure without listing each individual type. Always keep the instruction book that came with your brakes and refer to it for detailed instructions for your particular brake. The basic principle is the same for all hydraulic brakes — the brake pads need to sit close to the rotors so that they bite firmly onto the rotor surface when you brake, but they need enough clearance so that the rotors can pass freely between the pads without slowing you down.

It is fine for disc rotors to rub a little on the pads. The disc pads are much harder than rim brake pads, so a little bit of contact will not slow you down. Don't become obsessed by a little susurration when you pick up the wheel and spin it — you won't be able to hear it above the ground noise out on the trail. But a badly bent rotor — one that rubs on both pads as the wheel rotates — makes the brakes really difficult to adjust the pad spacing satisfactorily. Slight bends can be straightened by hand, but warped rotors must be replaced. The most common set-up for hydraulic brakes features pistons which will both push a pad against the rotor from the pressure of the hydraulic fluid on either side of the rotor. The more powerful variation is to have a pair of pistons on each side of the rotor, four pistons in total. These are designed to fine-tune the action of the brake by making two of the four pistons slightly smaller. The smaller pistons will move first, followed by the larger ones. A single long brake pad fits over each pair of pistons. The extra length means more contact between pad and rotor, which also helps to keep everything cool. It also demands more precise caliper fitting because shorter pads are more forgiving of slight misalignments.

Adjusting pad clearance

Closed system brakes have a manual adjustment at the lever — usually a big knob that you can turn while riding along if necessary. For Hope closed brakes, it's the pretty silver wheel on top of the master cylinder. Magura brakes have an easy-to-find-and-use red knob on the front of the lever. For both of these, look into the gap between rotor and pad, and turn the knob to establish which direction moves the pads towards the rim and which moves them away. Squeeze and release the lever, then turn the adjusting knob so that the brake pads bite firmly onto the wheel when the lever is about halfway to the bars. This gives you enough lever travel for precise speed control, while ensuring that any fingers wrapped around your grips don't become trapped between lever and bar during emergency stops.

A few hydraulic brakes, for example Magura Louise, have a volume-adjusting knob on the caliper. Use a 5mm Allen key on the Allen bolt at the center of the outside face of the caliper. Magura Louise are single-piston brakes, where the hydraulic action pushes the outer pad against the rotor, forcing the rotor onto the stationary pad (nearest the wheel) and trapping it between the two pads. The stationary pad position needs to be adjusted separately, using the 5mm Allen bolt in the center of the inner face of the caliper body.

Open system brakes (which don't have an oil volume adjusting knob) often allow you to adjust lever travel instead. This is usually done with a small Allen key — a tiny 2mm or 2.5mm size — behind the lever blade. Again, adjust so that the brake bites when the lever is about halfway to the bars. If you've just bled your brakes or fitted new pads, you will often have to pump the lever a couple of times for the pistons to settle in place — do this before setting the lever position. If your lever is traveling all the way to the bars before the pads bite, you're short of oil volume, and may also have air trapped in your brake system. Follow the procedure for bleeding your brakes, remembering to use the correct type of oil for topping up the system. This will leave you with the right amount of oil and will eliminate any air bubbles. If your brake pads bind on your rotor, you may have a little too much oil in the system. With care, you can drain a little of the excess away. Remove the rubber cap on the brake bleed nipple, and fit a short section of rubber hose over it to prevent air being sucked back. Route the hose into a bottle or plastic bag. Open the bleed nipple, by turning it with a wrench a quarter-turn. Squeeze the brake lever gently so that 3–4mm ($\frac{3}{16}$ inch) of oil creeps up the hose — no more. Close the bleed nipple and carefully remove the hose. Test brake operation, then replace the bleed nipple cap.

◀ **Bleeding air bubbles from brake caliper**

Disc brakes: removing and changing brake pads

Brake pads must be changed if they're worn down to less than a third of their original thickness, so replace them if you only have 0.5–1mm ($\frac{1}{50}$ to $\frac{1}{16}$ inch) of pad left. You will also need to replace them if they've become contaminated with oil. This could be the result of spilling brake fluid on them or of careless chain lubrication for the rear brake.

Burning in newly fitted brake pads is vital. The surface of new brake pads does not stop the bike properly the first time you use them. For them to work safely, you need to get on the bike, ride along slowly, and pull on the brakes. First time, you'll be unimpressed. Repeat, gradually speeding up before you stop, until the brakes bite properly. This can take 10 or 20 tries. As you're doing this, be aware that the pads are going to improve suddenly. Once they're burnt in, barring contamination, the braking surface will stay good until the pads wear out. In fact, they often feel best just before they completely wear out, when the pad surface is very thin and gives a very positive feeling. This reminds me of the way favorite shoes get really comfortable just before they fall apart.

The way pads fit is similar enough with most models for it to be possible to give a general overview, but each model is also slightly different. It's worth having a good look at your caliper before you start taking out the old pads. If you haven't got a photographic memory, draw a sketch to remind yourself how to put it all back together again.

All pads for all makes and all models are different, which is very irritating. You have to get exactly the right kind, so keep a spare set in case you need them when the shop's closed or it has run out of your type. These general instructions cover most common models, the main exceptions being Magura Louise and Clara, where the pads do not come out through the rotor slot. See the box on page 83 for these.

Removing the old pads

As a general rule, the pads fit in position via the central slot in the caliper, either from the same direction as the rotor or from above the rotor. You have to remove the wheel to get at them. The pads sit on pistons, which are inside the caliper. The pistons are pushed out when the brakes are activated, forcing the pads against the rotor and slowing the bike.

Pads have a flat metal base with the braking surface stuck on top. The metal base has little ears sticking out. Always use these to manipulate the brake pads rather than touching the braking surface. Pads may be left- or right-specific — make a note of the orientation of the old ones as you extract them.

CHANGING BRAKE PADS

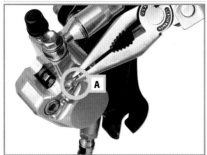

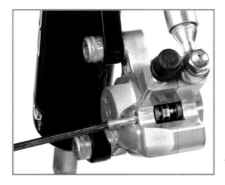

Step 1: The pads might be held in place by a magnet, a spring clip **(A)** on the back of the pads, or an exact fit in the slot. There is often some kind of secondary security device to stop pads rattling free. Look for some kind of screwed- or slotted-in retaining pin, which goes through the caliper and through holes in the far side of the brake block. The retaining pin may also be secured with a P-clip or spring. Start by removing any spring clips.

Step 2: Extract the retaining pin. In this case, the pin is held in place with a 2mm Allen key. Undo the Allen key to release it from its threads, then pull out gently.

Step 3: Pull the brake pads down out of the slots. Take care. Some have a spring that sits between the pads and holds them apart. Keep the spring as you need to reuse it; note its position. Have a good look at the pads as well — left and right may be different. Make a note so you can get the new ones back in the right way around. If old pads have any trace of life left, carefully wrap them up and store them for emergency use.

Adjusting calipers

The new pads will be thicker than the old ones, so you have to push the pistons back into the caliper. If you have an adjuster on the lever which controls the piston position (for example, Hope Closed types), wind it out until the heads of the pistons are flush with the caliper body. For types without an adjuster at the lever, you will have to manually press the pistons back into the caliper. It is important not to damage them. Hayes pistons have a central stud, around which the springs on the back of the pads clip. The stud will bend or snap if mistreated, so the ideal lever for these is a 10mm ring wrench. Sit the wrench so that the stud is in the middle of the ring and push back the piston firmly.

If the surface of the piston is flat, a plastic tire lever is ideal. Have a good look inside before you start though, and choose your implement carefully. Push back the piston firmly so that it sits evenly in the caliper with the surface of the piston flush with the caliper body.

FITTING NEW PADS

Step 1: Carefully clean inside the calipers. If dirt works its way in between the piston and caliper, the pistons will leak, allowing oil out and air in. The ideal implement for this task is a cotton swab (I wasn't brave enough to include this tool in the essential tools list). A twist of very clean rag also does the job. Don't use harsh solvents or brake fluid, which will destroy the delicate piston seals. Water is perfect. If you must, use some mild detergent.

Step 2: If there was a spring between the old pads, set it between the new ones, checking the orientation if left and right pads are different. Hold the pads and spring together, making sure the arms of the spring are beside, rather than on, the surface of the brake pad.

Step 3: Slip the pads into the slot in the caliper. Push them home until the holes in the brake pad line up with retaining pin holes, refit retaining pins, and refit the spring or P-clips. Tug the pads downward to check they are securely fitted. Refit the wheel. Check brakes. You may have to pump the lever a few times to settle it into place — don't worry if it pulls all the way back to the bars the first time. Your new pads now need burning in.

Magura Louise and Clara

The previous instructions cover most types of brake, but there are occasional variations in the pad-fitting procedure. The most common exceptions are the Magura Louise and Clara designs (named after the daughters of the guy who founded the company).

For these, remove the wheel, and then completely remove the adjusting plate on the inner side of the brake caliper nearest the wheel with a 5mm Allen key. Once it's out, you'll see the back of the inner brake pad. Use the pad ears that stick out of the caliper slot to wiggle the pad out of the hole where the plate was. This reveals the other pad, which wiggles out of the same hole.

The pads are magnetic, so use a magnet if you have one — it's tricky. Clean out the insides of the caliper with plain water. The magnet on the back of the adjusting plate usually does a good job of collecting shards of metal — clean these off.

To refit the new pads, use a 5mm Allen key to back off the volume-adjuster on the outer face of the caliper as far as it will go, then fit the first pad through the hole. Wiggle the pad so the ears poke out of the slot on the top of the caliper on the opposite side to where the rotor goes in.

The braking surface of the pad should face outward. Follow this with the second pad, with the ears in the same slot, and set the two braking surfaces facing each other. Refit the adjusting plate, screwing it in until the outer surface is flush with the caliper body. Refit the wheel and pump the brakes a few times to settle the pistons into place.

Hoses: shortening and clamping

When fitting new brakes, the hoses arrive in their box ready-bled. The folks at Hope, being hydraulic brake gurus, give good advice on this subject. They suggest you should fit them with the original-length hose, which will be too long, taped neatly to your bike. Once you've ridden and broken in the new brakes, you can cut down the hose. At least this way, you have ridden your bike and know how the brakes should feel and can ensure they feel the same after bleeding.

All brake hoses can be cut to length, apart from the first generation of Shimano-braided hoses, which have to be bought in the correct length. A little bit of graceful curve is fine, and you need to ensure hoses are long enough so that handlebars and suspension swingarms can move through their full travel without binding. However, hoses that get snagged as you ride need shortening. You might also need to disassemble your hoses to feed them through hose guides. If you're cutting the hose down, work out how much you need to remove before you dismantle anything and mark the length with tape. You don't want to be waving around open-ended hose trying to work out the right length.

The most common connection between lever and hose is a soft brass ring called an olive, which fits around the hose with a threaded shroud over the top. As you tighten the shroud into the brake lever, it squashes the olive onto the hose, making an airtight seal. The lever has a barbed fitting, which keeps the hole in the hose open. If you have this type, and a bit of patience, you can usually shorten or reroute the hose without losing any fluid or introducing air into the system. Other types, like Shimano cuttable hoses and Magura hoses, have a fitting in the end of the hose. These work well, but it's almost impossible to fit the fitting without losing fluid — and you always end up having to bleed the system. Better accept this at the beginning and drain some fluid from the system before you start to keep everything tidy. Follow the steps for shortening the hose, and don't forget to add the fitting before reconnecting everything.

If you're trying to reuse a barbed fitting from the remains of a shortened hose, hold the fitting carefully with pliers and slice away from you along the hose. Point the knife upwards, so it cuts through the hose without scoring the fitting. You can't simply pull the fitting out of the hose; the harder you pull, the tighter the hose clamps to the fitting.

You have to fit the new or recycled fitting back into the hose, which can be tricky because it is a necessarily tight fit. The correct method is to clamp the hose pointing upwards in a vice between two special guides, and to hammer the connector into the end. Chances are, you won't have a pair of these special guides. I don't either. To make a pair, drill a hole the same diameter as the hose all the way through a 2cm-deep (¾ inch) scrap of wood. Cut the wood in half down the center of the hole. You are left with two pieces of wood, each with a long semi-circular groove across it. Trap the hose between the pieces of wood, and clamp the wood in a vice or between the jaws of mole grips. Carefully tap in the connector.

Toolbar

Disc-brake tools: replacing brake pads
- Depending on pad securing system, pliers (for split pins) or 2 or 2.5mm Allen keys for threaded retaining pins
- For Hayes — 10mm ring wrench to push pistons back into caliper

Disc-brake tools: bleeding brakes
- Tool to remove reservoir cover — 2 or 2.5mm Allen key or Torx key
- Plastic hose to fit over bleed nipple — available in a manufacturer-specific bleed kit from your bike shop, or from hardware stores or auto parts shops — often in the brake and clutch bleeding section
- Bottle to route the hose into
- Plenty of duct or electrical tape to strap bottle and hose to your bike
- Wrench to turn bleed nipple — 7 or 8mm
- The correct brake fluid for your bike — DOT or mineral oil
- Cloth to mop up spills and to protect your paintwork
- Rubber gloves

Tools to shorten brake hoses
- Tools as above, in case you need to bleed the brakes afterward
- Sharp knife
- Replacement olives
- Small screwdriver
- Wrench to remove shroud — usually 8mm

Shortening Hope Minis

Shortening brake hoses involves dealing with brake fluid so wear gloves. They look stupid and feel funny but then again so do brake fluid burns.

The brakes hoses supplied with new brakes are always longer than you could possibly need so that you can cut them to length. It's best to be cautious when estimating the length — it's easier to do the job twice because you didn't cut enough off the first time than to have to start again with a new, longer brake hose. It's best to use new olives every time you refit the hose — the old ones often get deformed or split when you remove them. Buy new ones before you take the brake apart.

Ideally, when doing this job, you'll make a neat slice in the hose, then refit it without losing any fluid. Mark the place where you want to cut the hose before you start disconnecting the lever. If you have to mess about with connectors to refit the hose, tape the cut end to the bars, pointing straight upward. However careful you are, you'll often find once you've finished that you've accidentally introduced air into the system. Be prepared to have to bleed the brakes after shortening the hose.

REMOVING HOSE

Step 1: Undo the shroud, and push it along the brake hose, to reveal the brass olive. Slide the shroud along the hose, beyond the point you're going to cut it — that way you won't have to refit the shroud back onto the hose.

Step 2: The brass olive has a slot. Use a thin screwdriver to lever open the slot slightly and slide the olive along the hose away from the lever. This makes it easier to pull the hose off its barbed fitting on the lever. The chamfered end of the olive can get quite firmly wedged in the end of the lever.

Step 3: Use the thin screwdriver to gently lift the end of the hose off the lever. Don't simply pull the hose; it will tighten over the delicate barbed fitting that sticks out of the lever fitting and probably snap it. Don't wiggle the hose either. Normally the delicate fitting is protected by the shroud, but you have removed that. Cut the hose clean and square at your tape mark.

REFITTING HOSE

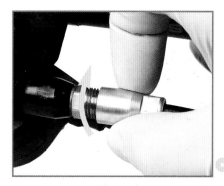

Step 1: Ideally, use a new brass olive. If you are reusing the old one, remove it carefully from the excess brake cable, holding the hose with pliers rather than your fingers to avoid stabbing yourself. The brass olive has a slot. Use a screwdriver to lever open the slot slightly, then slide the olive onto the shortened hose. Don't worry if the olive is a little loose; the shroud tightens over it, squashing it into shape.

Step 2: Carefully push the end of the hose fully over the barbed fitting, ensuring that the pointed end of the hose pushes into the middle of the tube. Again, don't be tempted to wiggle the hose at all as you fit it or the fitting will snap. Slide the shroud back up the hose to the lever.

Step 3: Wind the shroud onto the lever by hand, keeping it straight as you start it off. Tighten it snugly into the lever. Test the lever by pulling on it hard — it should come to a firm bite point and move no further. If it feels squishy, air has got in — head for the bleeding section.

Bleeding hydraulic brakes: an overview with examples

Bleeding isn't a regular task; as long as the system remains sealed, you can mostly ignore it. However, it does need to be done if there's been any break in the seal that might allow air in: for example, if you cut the hose to shorten it, or you crash and pull out a hose. If you use your bike hard — for repeated downhill racing or for long downhill rides with the brakes working hard — the fluid will eventually become worn out from heating up too many times.

The procedure is the same regardless of the fluid, although DOT lasts longer — a year if you work it hard, four years with normal use. Mineral oil doesn't last so long, but it discolors when worn out, making it obvious when a change is needed. Pop the lid off the reservoir every six months or so, look at the fluid, and change it when it is cloudy.

Don't be drawn into thinking that bleeding has to be done routinely — you won't get an improvement in performance by bleeding unless something is actually wrong. If you have to bleed your brakes frequently, there is something wrong. Look for leaks at all the joints, and inspect the hoses carefully. The smallest split in a hose will let out oil and suck in air, making the brakes feel spongy.

Regardless of the specifics, the point of bleeding is the same: you are opening the system to release air bubbles, replacing the air with oil, then sealing the system again without letting in air. Here are the general guidelines, followed by specific examples.

Arm yourself appropriately. Most importantly, you need at least one, sometimes two, short plastic hoses to pump oil into the system at one end, and to route surplus oil away from the bleed nipple at the other end. With open-topped reservoirs, the surplus will spill over, and you will need plenty of rags to mop up. Brake fluid is corrosive and will damage your paintwork if you let it spill onto frame or forks.

The easiest connectors come with Shimano and Hope types, which have a simple bleed nipple over which you can slip the end of the plastic tube. Other types of brake require a specific connector. You may have been supplied with the right connector when you bought the brakes or with the bike if the brakes were already fitted.

However, life sometimes isn't that simple, so prepare yourself for the bleeding operation by ordering the part from your bike shop. Plastic hose is easier to obtain because hardware stores stock it. Take the connection or your bike with you to ensure you get the right size. The larger common size of bleed nipple — like that found on the Hope brakes — is the same size as standard car brake bleeding nipples, so you will be able to use bleed hose from auto parts stores.

Plastic syringes are very useful for pumping oil into the system. You can improvise by taping the plastic tubes onto squashable plastic bottles, but it's easy to slip and introduce air into the system, causing the bleed operation to fail.

Once the syringe is filled with oil, hold it upright and tap the syringe to persuade air bubbles to drift upwards, just like in the movies. I often feel slightly foolish doing this, but it works. Once all the air has collected at the top of the syringe, squirt it out onto a clean rag so that the syringe contains only oil.

Surplus oil will be expelled from one of the tubes, so tape a bag or bottle to the end to catch it. Don't use thin plastic bags with DOT fluid — it's mildly alarming how quickly the brake fluid melts the bag. The tape is necessary to prevent it falling off as the weight of the oil increases, which can spread the stuff everywhere and spoil your bleed.

All systems have a port at the lever end and a port at the caliper end. Some systems, like Hayes, prefer to be filled through the caliper, with the surplus coming out at the lever end.

Others, like Hope and Shimano, work best filled at the lever end, with the surplus coming out through the bleed nipple at the caliper. Check your bike shop or your instruction book for the appropriate method for your particular brakes.

Trapped air bubbles make your brakes feel spongy ▶

Bleeding Hope Minis

The first time you bleed your brakes the job can feel tedious. But don't panic — it gets easier every time. You have to run around assembling equipment such as syringes and rubber tubing, but once you've worked it out, the items are there for next time.

Hope Minis are my favorite brakes, and are likely to be around a while. They work very well, weigh very little, look pretty and are made by the same nice people from the North of England who answer the phone in a reassuring Lancashire accent to respond to your technical questions with useful, friendly answers. I didn't need to do anything to mine for years after fitting them except change the pads.

The Hope Minis use DOT 5.1 fluid, which you can buy in small bottles from auto parts shops. Don't buy a large bottle because the fluid absorbs water and becomes ineffective once the seal has been broken.

BLEEDING HOPE MINIS

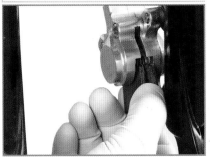

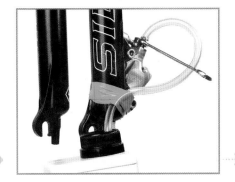

Step 1: Remove the wheel and the brake pads. The brake pads are secured with a retaining pin, which is itself secured with a spring clip. Pry off the spring clip, and undo and remove the retaining bolt with a 2mm Allen key. Pull the pads out of the rotor slot, and set them aside. This gets rotor and pads well out of the way in case of oil spillage.

Step 2: Remove plastic cover from the bleed nipple on the caliper. Put an 8mm ring wrench over the flats on the nipple, then push-fit a short length of plastic tube over nipple. Lubricate reluctant tubes with brake fluid. Tape the other end of the tube into a plastic bottle and secure to your frame or forks. Wrap a rag around lever to catch overspill, because brake fluid is corrosive. For rear brakes, take front wheel and pads off in case of an accident.

Step 3: Use a plastic tire lever to push the pistons gently back into the calipers until they are flush with the caliper body. You need to pack the gap between the pistons so they don't get squeezed back together as you bleed. A wedge of cardboard works fine. Check the pistons as you bleed to make sure they stay retracted into the caliper body, otherwise the pads will rub on the rotor when you reassemble.

Step 4: Set up the bike so that the top of the master cylinder on the lever is level and at the highest point in the system. Use a 2mm Allen key to remove the top cap on the lever and the rubber diaphragm. Set them aside where it's clean—you don't want them to pick up dirt. Start by tapping all the way along the brake hose to dislodge air bubbles. Air caught near the lever will bubble up through the open top of the master cylinder.

Step 5: Fill master cylinder almost to top with brake fluid. Open the bleed nipple a quarter-turn. Pull the brake lever gently towards you, forcing fluid through the system and out of the open-bleed nipple, taking the air bubbles in the caliper with it. With the brake lever held on, close the bleed nipple. Release brake lever gently, drawing fluid into the hose from the master cylinder. Top up master cylinder carefully, then repeat until there are no more air bubbles.

Step 6: Top up the master cylinder, open the bleed nipple, and carefully place rubber diaphragm on top. Press it into place, catching the overspill in a rag. Close the bleed nipple and replace the top cap on the master cylinder. Tighten the screws home; don't go mad, they only need to seal the diaphragm. Carefully remove the bleed tube and replace the bleed nipple cover. Refit wheel and brake pads, then pump lever several times to settle the pistons.

Disc brakes: bleeding Shimano Deore hydraulic brakes

The fluid used in Shimano hydraulic brakes is Shimano mineral oil. Don't use DOT brake fluid; it won't work and will eat the seals and leak. The oil comes in single-use packs, which contain enough fluid for one fill. Conveniently, this means that the container doesn't sit around absorbing water.

You'll be pouring fresh mineral oil into the reservoir, which can be messy. Wrap cloth or kitchen towel around the lever before you start, as a preemptive mopping exercise. The bleed nipple is narrower than the standard car size, so you'll need narrower plastic tube. You can find it in hardware stores, or buy a kit. Clear plastic is best — you can see the oil and air bubbles emerging from the bleed nipple.

BLEEDING SHIMANO DEORE BRAKES

Step 1: Start by removing the wheel and the pads of the brake you want to bleed to prevent them becoming contaminated by spillage. If you are bleeding the rear brake, remove the front wheel as well in case fluid spills out of the reservoir at the lever.

Step 2: Loosen the brake lever fixing bolts, and twist the lever, so that the top cover of the reservoir is level. Remove the top cover of the reservoir and the rubber diaphragm. Put these aside so that they stay clean.

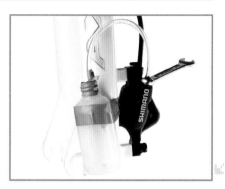

Step 3: Shimano recommends you remove the caliper from the bike and let it hang from the lever. However, bleeding seems to work well enough as long as you keep the bike propped up so that the lever is higher than the caliper. Fit an 8mm ring wrench around the bleed nipple, and then push a piece of plastic hose over the nipple. Tape the other end into the mouth of a bottle, and tape the bottle to your frame or fork.

Step 4: Push the pistons gently back into the calipers, ideally using a tire-lever. Wedge them in place with a block of clean cardboard. Open the bleed nipple a quarter-turn. Pump the brake lever gently, while keeping the reservoir topped up.

Step 5: Flick the hose to encourage air to bubble up and escape through the open top of the reservoir. Shaking it sometimes helps too. Close the bleed nipple and gently pump the lever to help the bubbles rise. Keep adding oil, and pump the lever gently until the lever goes stiff and only moves a quarter of its travel.

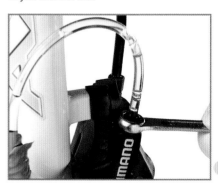

Step 6: Pull the lever back and close the bleed nipple. Fill the reservoir up to the top and replace the rubber diaphragm and the reservoir top. Fluid will overflow as you replace the cap, so be prepared to catch it. Gently tighten the reservoir-fixing screws. Remove the plastic tube from the bleed nipple and replace the cover. Remove the brake-spacing pad and refit the pads and the wheel. Pull and release the brake several times, then test brake operation.

Troubleshooting disc brakes

Symptom	Cause	Solution	Page
Brake pads don't pull back smoothly after braking	Brake cable gritty, corroded or frayed inside casing	Clean and lubricate brake cable or replace it	75
	Piston heads dirty	Remove pads and clean, or replace	75-7, 78, 82
	Dirt has worked its way into the caliper body, jamming the mechanism	Strip and clean caliper body	74
	Pads have become contaminated with oil	Replace pads	75-7, 78, 82
	Rotors have become contaminated	Clean rotors with degreaser, isopropyl alcohol or warm soapy water	72
	Pads are too far from rotors	Adjust pad position	78, 82
Brakes rub constantly on rotors	Rotor is warped	Bend back or replace rotor	73
	Caliper body is touching rotor	Adjust caliper body position	83
	Pads set too close to rotor	Adjust pad positions independently — outer pad using cable tension, inner pad using adjustment screw	78, 83
Brakes not very effective—cannot lock wheels by pulling lever	Pads have become contaminated with oil	Replace pads	75-7, 78, 82
	Rotors have become contaminated	Clean rotors with degreaser, isopropyl alcohol or warm soapy water	72
	Pads are worn out	Check pad thickness — replace if less than 0.5mm ($\frac{1}{50}$ inch)	75-7, 78, 82
Brake pads rub on rotor	Caliper misaligned	Refit caliper, with rotor central between pads	70, 71
	Rotor warped	Bend back or replace rotor	73
Brake levers feel spongy, brakes ineffective	Air in system	Bleed brakes	86-8
	Leaking hose	Inspect hose carefully, especially at joints, tighten leaking joints, bleed brakes	86-8
Brakes squeal	Contaminated brake pads or rotor	Clean rotor, replace pads	75-7, 78, 82
	Worn or roughened rotor surface	Replace rotor	73
	Loose fixing bolts causing vibrations	Check and tighten brake-fixing bolts and rotor-fixing bolts	73

Transmission

This chapter deals with the transmission — all the parts of your bike that transfer the pedaling power to your back wheel.

The parts that make up your transmission are relatively simple, but they are exposed to the elements all the time. They also have to be kept lubricated to work efficiently. If you don't clean your transmission regularly, oil and dirt will combine to form an abrasive grinding paste that quickly eats your transmission components. Since parts mesh with each other, they often have to be replaced together, so leaving your bike dirty can be a rather expensive habit.

In this section you'll learn how to adjust your gears so that they change slickly and quickly, how to check whether any of the components are worn, and how to replace or upgrade parts that are worn or crash-damaged.

Problems with your transmission can often take a little time to sort out, because some of the symptoms — like sluggish shifting, or gears that slip when you stamp hard on the pedals — can be the result of many different causes, or a combination of several of them. Since all the separate parts mesh with one another, ignoring small and irritating tics can lead to bigger problems. For example, a dirty rear gear cable will make your shifting annoyingly sluggish but it can also mean that your chain will not sit directly below the sprockets of the cassette. Consequently, in the longer term, both your cassette and your chain will wear out.

Fixing your gears is the area of mechanics where you will most appreciate a proper workstand. You have to be pedaling to change gear, so your back wheel will have to be held off the ground in order that you can turn the pedals to test the different mechanisms. You can improvise by persuading a friend to lift the back wheel off the ground at vital moments, but a workstand is easier.

It's best to start by learning how to adjust your gears so that they change crisply and transfer pedal power smoothly, then move on to learning how to replace parts. You will usually have to readjust your gears at the end of any fitting procedure.

SRAM cassette

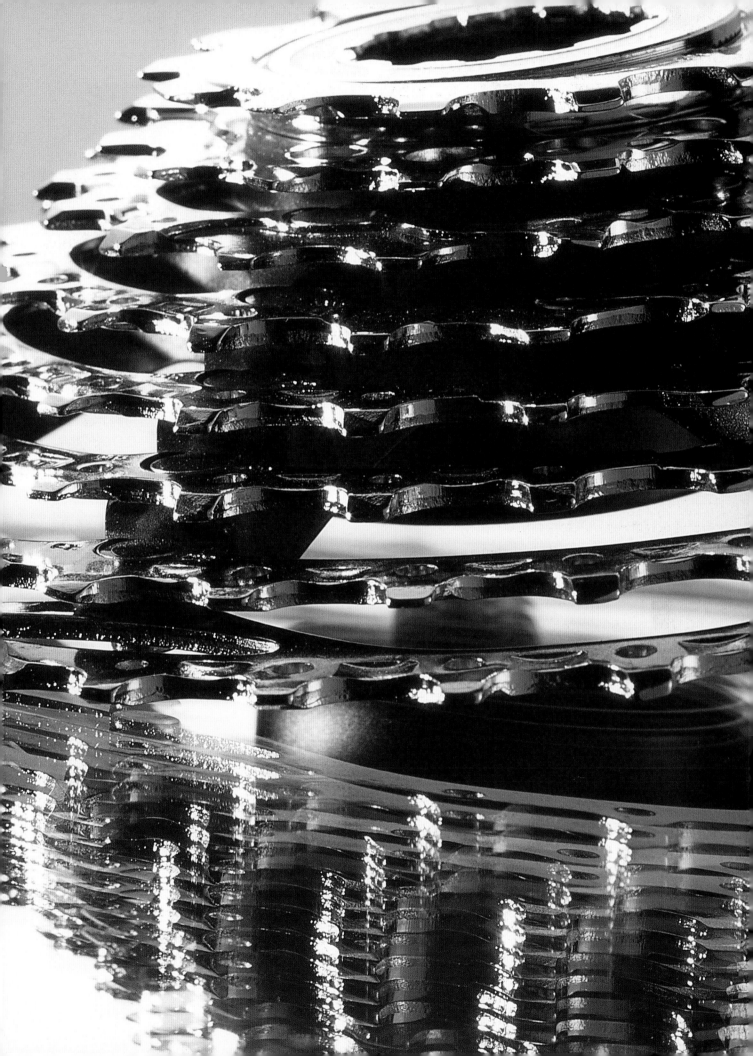

Gearing up — or down — for the smoothest possible ride

Bicycles have gears because people are lazy. To make the bicycle move, you have to push on the pedals. If you only had one gear, you could set the bicycle up so you had to push very hard, but each pedal stroke would make the bicycle go a long way. This is a called a high gear.

Alternatively, you could set it up so you didn't have to push the pedals hard, but one pedal stroke wouldn't take you far. You would have to do a lot of strokes to get anywhere. This is called a low gear.

Both extremes work in their own way, but your body is most efficient pedaling at a medium rate — pushing moderately hard and pedaling moderately fast — between 80 and 100 revolutions per minute. Gears were invented so that you can maintain a steady pedaling rate ("cadence" — roughly speaking, how fast your legs are going round) while the bicycle travels at different speeds.

Mountain bikes are designed to have a very wide range of gears so you can maintain an efficient cadence both when moving very slowly — for example, up a steep, rough hill at 2 mph — as well as when moving very fast — for example, plummeting downhill at 40 mph.

Small steps between the gears allow you to make subtle changes from one gear to the next, matching your pedaling speed precisely to the terrain you're cycling over. In recent years, manufacturers have steadily increased the number of gears on your cassette, giving you smaller, subtler gaps between gears, and making modern bikes more responsive than their old-fashioned counterparts.

Less haste, more speed

New cyclists — along with many who've been around long enough to know better — are seduced by the idea that in order to go faster, it's imperative to force the pedals around using as much strength as possible with every stroke. With experience, it becomes plain that this only gives an illusion of speed and, in fact, serves mainly to exhaust you in the short term and wear your knees out in the long term. Generally, you'll get where you want to go faster, feeling less exhausted, by using a lower gear: your legs spin around faster, but you don't have to press down so hard on each pedal stroke. It's worth watching the next person who overtakes you; chances are, their legs will be spinning faster than yours in a lower gear, and that's the main reason they're flying past you.

Turning on the power

There are some circumstances in which it makes sense to use a relatively high gear. For short bursts of speed, nothing beats standing up on the pedals in a high gear and hauling the bike forward. It means you can use your shoulder muscles, pulling up on the bars as well as stamping down on the pedals — perfect for keeping up momentum while you power up short inclines. Sometimes ground surfaces dictate gear choice as well. If you're approaching a sand trough or trying to cross a swath of deep, sticky mud, the best approach can often be to shift into a high gear, keeping your cadence low so that your tires have a chance to find the last scraps of traction without you getting bogged down.

By comparison, road-racing bikes have fewer gears, but they are very closely spaced. This reflects the fact that road-racing bikes are designed to be used at a much narrower range of speeds. Close ratios are vital to allow the rider to maintain a comfortable, efficient cadence while being able to ride at the speed of a tightly packed peloton (bunch of riders).

◀ **Shifting to a higher gear**

How gears work

What's great about modern gear design is that it allows you to keep pedaling at the same speed, regardless of terrain, by varying the amount of energy needed to turn the back wheel. Here, I'll explain it with math. Please ignore this page if it seems too technical — it makes no difference to how much you enjoy your cycling.

Imagine you no longer have a top-of-the-line, 27–speed bike. Instead, you have a model with only two chainrings at the front, which you turn by pedaling, and two sprockets on the back, which push the back wheel around when they are turned. This leaves you with a 10-tooth and 20-tooth sprocket at the back, and a 20-tooth and a 40-tooth sprocket at the front. These combinations aren't useful for cycling, but they make the math easier.

Start with your chain running between the 40 at the front and the 10 at the back. Begin with one pedal crank pointing upwards, in line with the seat-tube. Turn the cranks round exactly once. Each link of the chain gets picked up in the valley between two teeth. Since there are 40 teeth on the chainring, exactly 40 links of chain get pulled from the back of the bike to the front.

At the back of the bike, exactly the reverse happens. Since each link of the chain picks up one sprocket valley, pulling 40 chain links through will pull 40 sprocket valleys around. But the sprocket you're using has only 10 teeth, so it will get pulled round four times (4x10 = 40). The sprocket is connected directly to the wheel, so, in this instance, turning the chainring one turn means that the rear wheel will turn four complete turns. To measure how far this is, imagine cutting across an old tire to make a strip instead of a hoop, then laying it out along the ground. Measure the distance and that's how far the bike goes if you turn the wheel once. Turn the wheel four times, and the bike goes four times as far.

For comparison, leave the chain on the 40-tooth chainring, but move it to the 20-tooth sprocket at the back. Turn the cranks once and the chainring will still pull the 40 links around, but, at the back, pulling 40 links around a 20-tooth sprocket will only pull the wheel around twice (2x20 = 40), so the bike goes half as far as in the previous example.

Finally, leave the chain on the 20-tooth at the back, and pop it on the 20-tooth at the front. Now, turning the cranks around once only pulls 20 links of chain through, which in turn pulls the 20-tooth sprocket and the wheel around exactly once. Thus, turning the pedals around once moves the bike forward one tire length — a one-to-one ratio.

In the first example, the bike goes much further, but it is harder work to push the pedals around one turn. In the last example, it is very easy to push the pedals around, but you don't go far. Sometimes, you need to go as fast as possible, and you don't care how hard you work, so you use a combination of big chainring and small sprocket. You might be charging downhill, or trying to catch someone ahead of you, or sprinting for the sake of it.

Other times, like when you climb a steep hill or start off from rest, it takes all your energy simply to keep the wheels going round, so you need the easiest gear possible. Then you choose something like the last combination — small chainring and big sprocket.

Going back to the original bike, you have seven-, eight-, or nine-ring sprockets at the back, and three chainrings at the front. These allow subtle variations in how far the bike goes and how easy it is when you turn the cranks. The aim is to maintain a constant cadence, at a level that is most efficient for your body over varying terrain.

The two derailleurs (gear mechs — short for "mechanisms" — or changer arms) are controlled by separate shifters at the handlebars, the front by your left hand and the back by your right. These evolved by mechanical necessity but have proved very convenient.

On the back wheel you have a selection of sprockets on the cassette, as mentioned above, with small gaps between the sizes. Moving up or down from one sprocket to the next might make a gear 10 percent higher or lower, allowing very subtle changes in pedaling speed. You shift the sprockets (i.e., rear derailleur) most often, so it makes sense for the handlebar shifter to be on the right-hand side, since most people are right-handed.

Your left hand controls the front derailleur. You only have three chainrings on the front, but the differences between the number of teeth on the ring are far greater to allow a radical change to pedaling speed with a single shift. This is useful when the terrain changes unexpectedly — for example, if you turn a corner and the trail suddenly climbs. By moving the chain from the big to the little chainring, you can change into a much lower gear quickly enough to maintain momentum. Although it's possible to change into all the combinations of chainrings and sprockets, in practice, some should be avoided. Using the largest chainring and the largest sprocket means that the chain has to cut across from one to the other at a steep angle, which makes the chain wear faster and wastes pedaling energy. The same goes for the combination of the smallest sprocket and smallest chainring. Both these gears are duplicates — the same gear ratio can be found by switching into the middle chainring at the front and one of the middle sprockets at the back.

Chains: what are they made of?

Each chain is a string of simple components, joined in such a way that they don't pull apart even when you put all your strength into pulling around the back wheel. The design looks simple but is very cunning. A chain's enemy has always been wear, and early bicycle chains used to wear out very quickly. Every time a link of the chain dropped into the valley between two teeth, two metal surfaces rubbed on each other. Add pressure from the pedals along with dirt from the road, and you had the perfect recipe for chain damage.

The radical step forward came when the pin that joins each link was encased in a roller. You can see the rollers on the chain — they are the rings around each chain rivet. You should be able to push each of them around with your finger; they should move easily. This movement is important: every time a link of chain meshes with a sprocket or chainring, the rollers roll into position and prevent the two dirty metal surfaces rubbing and wearing. The inside surface of the roller rubs on the rivet, but this is protected from the worst of the dirt and stays lubricated longer than the outside surface.

There are three different components here: side plates, pin, roller. It is a remarkably clever but very simple design, and has to be exactly right. The cunning part is that, if everything is kept clean and well lubricated, there is no movement between the outside of the chain and the surface of the chainring/sprocket teeth. Movement means friction means wear, especially if the parts are exposed to dirt, as with the outside of the chain. The clever part is that friction occurs between the inside of the roller and the pin, which is far cleaner than the outside of the chain.

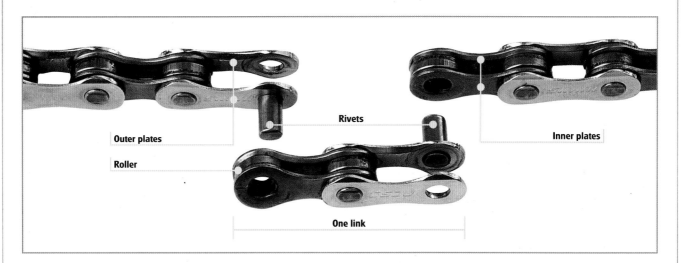

Outer plates

Roller

Rivets

Inner plates

One link

▲ **Outer and inner plates, roller, rivets and link**

Chains for mountain bikes all have the same pitch, namely ½ in. However, they have different widths, determined according to the number of sprockets on the cassette at the back. Sprockets on nine-speed cassettes are narrower (both the sprocket plate and the gap) than eight-speed cassettes so that the extra sprocket can be packed into the same space. The narrower chains are also more flexible, so they change more slickly. By the same token, they need to be kept clean and well-lubricated or they will wear more quickly. A chain that is too narrow for the block will stick, whereas a chain that is too wide won't shift properly. Both will wear down the sprockets very quickly.

Compatibility between parts is an important issue. You can be as careful as you like with adjustments for your front and rear gears, but if the components aren't compatible, the adjustment won't make any difference. Shimano is the undisputed giant in the transmission department; other manufacturers make their components compatible with Shimano parts. The most sensitive combinations are chain, shifters and cassettes. Nine-speed chains are considerably narrower than eight-speed ones, and have matching narrow sprockets, so there is no compatibility between the two systems.

Chain hygiene: regular chain wipe-down

A clean chain shifts neatly, whereas a dirty one shifts sluggishly and wears expensive chunks out of the drivetrain. To find out how clean your chain needs to be, try reading the words stamped on the side plates. If they are legible, the chain is clean enough. If you can't read them, the chain needs your attention.

Ideally, clean your chain little and often — catching it frequently enough to only need a wipedown. This is both the laziest and the best method — take advantage of this rare combination! Leave your chain dirty too long, and you need to look at the deep-clean section later in this chapter.

After a ride, lean your bike up against a wall and hold a clean, dry cloth or piece of kitchen towel around the bottom stretch of chain. Slowly pedal backward for 20 seconds, dragging the chain through the cloth. If it makes a big dirty streak, move to a clean bit of cloth and repeat. Job done. Simply do that every single time you ride and you maximize the chain's life without ever undertaking a boring major clean.

You need to lubricate the chain occasionally as well, but note that you can do as much damage by overlubricating as underlubricating. Chains need a little oil, but no more than dressing for a salad. If the chain is squeaky, you've left it too long, and the chain is gasping for lube. As a rough guide, oil the chain every 160km (100 miles). If the chain collects greasy, black gunk as you ride, you are over-oiling.

As above, wipe the chain with a clean cloth. Drip a drop of oil carefully onto each roller on the top surface of the bottom stretch of chain. (Drip oil is much better than spray. It goes where you want with little waste.) The important thing is to allow five minutes for the oil to soak in (have a cup of coffee), then wipe off any excess with a clean rag — drag the chain through it again. Oil is sticky. Leave it on the outside surface of the chain to pick up dirt, and it makes a super grinding paste.

Cleaning your chain little and often like this ensures that it never builds up a thick layer of dirt, which means that you don't have to use harsh solvents on it. This is well worthwhile — cleaning agents, degreasers and detergent will all soak into the internals of the chain, stripping out lubrication from the vital interface between the insides of the roller. Each roller needs to be able to rotate freely on its rivet so that the roller can mesh neatly with the valleys between the teeth of sprockets and chainrings as you apply pressure.

Wax lubricants are an alternative to conventional oils. Several manufacturers make versions that work in similar ways. The wax sticks to your chain, protecting it from the elements but providing a layer of lubrication. The wax is not as sticky as oil, so it's less likely that dirt will adhere. But if it does, the surface of the wax will flake off, taking the dirt with it. New layers of wax can be laid over the top since the surface should stay clean, saving you from having to clean the chain. This system means that your chain stays dry too, avoiding oily streaks on your clothes and in your home.

However, the system only really works if you start with a very clean chain — preferably a new one. A word of warning: never mix wax-based lubricants with normal ones — you end up with a sticky, slippery mess that adheres to everything except your chain.

◀ **Laziest and best: a regular wipedown**

Deepcleaning your chain

If your chain doesn't respond to the wipedown treatment, you must get serious. Dirty, oily chains need degreaser to clean them up. This is strong stuff, so take care not to let it seep into bearings, where it breaks down the grease that keeps things well-lubricated and running smoothly.

I prefer liquid degreaser, which you can apply with a brush, to the spray cans. Spray is more wasteful and harder to direct accurately. But whether you use spray or liquid, you need a brush. Dishwashing brushes work well; they're cheap, and you can buy them in regular shops such as Wal-Mart (don't wash up with them afterwards though!).

Bike shops sell special sets of brushes, but my favorites are paint brushes. I cut off the bristles about halfway down, so what remains is firm but flexible. Keep the brushes you use for your drivetrain separate from those for frames, rims and disc rotors. Use rubber gloves to protect your hands from the degreaser.

Take your bike outside, as this business always gets messy. Keep the bike upright, with the chain in the largest chainring at the front. Dip the brush into degreaser and work it into each link in the part of the chain that's wrapped around the front chainring. Do both sides, then turn the pedals around and work on the next section of chain. It takes a few minutes for the degreaser to work, so let it soak in, working around until you are back where you started.

Clean the chainrings next, front and back, picking out anything that's stuck between the chainrings or between the outer chainring and the crank arm. Clean up the derailleurs and the jockey wheels on the rear derailleur too, otherwise they dump dirt straight back onto the clean chain. Hold the back wheel upright and scrub the cassette clean. If there is compacted muck stuck between the sprockets, scrape it out with a stick or skewer. You can buy a special little brush if you want but remember: the world is full of sticks, which cost nothing. Be especially careful with the degreaser at this point: keep the wheel upright to prevent it from getting into the rear hub or into the freehub (the ratchet mechanism inside the cassette).

Using a clean brush, rinse off all the degreaser with warm water. Jet-washing may be tempting but don't — ever! The protective bearing seals cannot withstand jet-wash pressure, and the grease that makes bearings run smoothly is soon displaced by water. If your drivetrain is really dirty, you may now decide to repeat the job. Once everything is as clean as possible, dry the chain by running it through a clean rag and relubricate. Sprockets and chainrings don't need lubrication. Pop a drop of oil on the derailleur pivots, front and back, and wipe off the excess, otherwise, it just collects dirt.

Chain-cleaning box

A tidier option for regular cleaning is a chain-cleaning box. This is a case that fits over the chain, with little brushes inside that scrub the chain clean. Fill the reservoir with degreaser, then snap the box over the lower section of chain.

Pedal slowly backwards. Most boxes have a button that you press to release degreaser onto the chain. Don't pedal too quickly, or you'll splash degreaser out of the back of the box. Keep going slowly until you've used up all the degreaser. Unclip the box and take a five-minute break to give the degreaser time to break down the dirt.

Rinse off with clean, warm water. If your chain was extremely dirty, you might repeat the process. Dry your chain with a clean rag and relubricate. It's worth cleaning the chain box with a little fresh degreaser right away, so it is ready for next time.

A chain box helps keep you and your chain clean ▶

Measuring your chain for wear and tear

Your chain is under constant pressure as you pedal. A new chain arrives exactly the right size to mesh with the other components of your drivetrain.

Gradually, though, as time goes by and the miles rack up, the chain stretches. The gaps between each link grow, and the chain inevitably elongates. Eventually, if you keep riding, the chain starts skipping over them instead of meshing with the teeth on the sprocket.

That's when you find yourself pushing hard on the pedals, expecting resistance. Instead of gripping, the chain slips, and the pedal carrying all your weight gives way and spins like crazy, so you hurt yourself or even fall off. At this stage, your chain is already worn enough to damage other components.

Joining the chain gang

If you are disciplined about measuring your chain carefully and regularly with a chain-measuring device, you can replace just the chain before it has a chance to wear the other components of your drivetrain. This tool will tell you when you have reached this point. If you are attentive, you'll find it the cheapest option in the long term.

If you allow the chain to wear beyond this point, you will have to replace both the chain and the cassette at the same time. The old chain will have damaged the teeth on the cassette, so the new chain will be unable to mesh with it neatly. The consequence of changing the chain without changing the sprockets is that the new chain will slip over the old sprockets, and, even if you can make it catch, the old sprockets will wear the new chain into an old chain very quickly.

If you allow the chain to wear so that it starts to slip over the cassette as you pedal, you will definitely have to change the cassette and probably some or all of the chainrings as well. Look at the pictures on page 130 and compare them with your chainrings — if they are starting to look like the examples, change them at the same time as the chain.

Note that you cannot compensate for chain stretch by taking links out of the chain to make it shorter. The total length of the chain is not critical. It is the distance between each link that matters. If you take links out of a stretched chain, it is simply a shorter stretched chain.

MEASURING FOR WEAR

Step 1: A chain-measuring device is the quickest and easiest way of accurately measuring your chain. The best are from Park Tools and come complete with an easy-to-read dial. Buy one today — it saves you time and money.

Step 2: Alternatively, measure the length of 12 links. Twelve links of a new chain will measure exactly 12 inches (300mm). When it measures 12$\frac{1}{8}$ inch or less, you can change the chain without changing the cassette. More than that, and you have to change the cassette as well.

Step 3: You can get an idea of stretch without using a chain-measuring device. Put the chain on the biggest ring at the front and the smallest sprocket at the back, then lean the bike left-handed against a wall. Hold the chain at three o'clock and pull it outward. If the bottom jockey wheel of the rear derailleur moves, it's time for a new chain. If you can pull the chain off enough to see all or most of the tooth, you need a new cassette and probably new chainrings too.

Splitting and rejoining a chain

Every time you split and rejoin your chain, you risk making it weaker, so keep splitting to a minimum. For example, if you're fitting a new rear derailleur, undo the bolts that hold on the jockey wheels, thread the chain around the jockey wheels, and reassemble them with the chain inside the derailleur.

Make sure you tighten both jockey wheel bolts securely — the top one, particularly, is prone to rattling loose. For the front derailleur, remove the bolt at the back of the cage, slide the chain into the cage, and refit the bolt.

The chain tool is designed to support two adjacent chain plates while you push out the pin between them. It is important to do this carefully, as they may create a weak point and break later if you deform the chain plates. Shimano chains have to be treated differently from other chains — they need to be rejoined with a special rivet. See the separate section opposite.

SPLITTING A CHAIN

Step 1: Lay the chain onto the chain tool on the set of supports furthest away from the handle of the tool. Screw in the handle of the tool so that it approaches the chain. When it's close, line up the stud with the head of the chain pin. Screw in the handle to push the rivet.

Step 2: It's important not to push it all the way out, otherwise it's difficult to get back in again. With the Park tool, keep turning until the handle jams on the body of the tool. With other tools, keep testing to check you haven't gone too far.

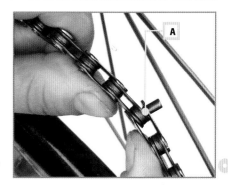

Step 3: Check you haven't gone too far by backing off the tool and trying to pull the chain apart. Ideally, you should have to flex it, as shown, to get the two halves of the chain apart. This is important because it means you have left a little stub of pin **(A)** inside the further chain plate, which you can then use to relocate the hole for the pin when you refit the chain.

REJOINING A CHAIN

Step 1: To rerivet, hold the chain as shown. Flex both parts away from the rivet and slide together. The little bit of rivet showing through the outer plate should snap into place, then hold the two parts together with the rivet aligned in the hole.

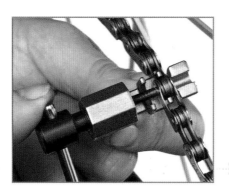

Step 2: Back the chain tool handle right off and place the chain back into the further supports.

Step 3: Turn the handle to push the rivet back through the chain so that an equal amount of rivet shows through each side. Here, you can see that one side of the rivet protrudes more that the other. Use the further chain supports to even up the amount that shows out of each side.

Shimano chains

These chains need to be treated differently to others because the rivets cannot be pushed out of the plates and reused. The original rivets that hold the links in place are made exactly the same size as the holes in the chain plates, which means that they have to be installed with enormous force and accuracy. Consequently they are very strong once in place.

However, if you try to reuse the rivets, you'll find that they won't press easily back through the chain plates — often, instead of reseating itself neatly in the hole, the rivet will tear open the chain plate hole, mangling the link beyond repair.

Shimano make a special replacement rivet that can be pressed back through the chain to rejoin it. Whenever you split the chain, the original rivet must be pushed out completely and discarded. This can be irritating, but the payoff is that Shimano chains are strong and change very slickly.

One of the rivets on your chain is the original joining link that was fitted when the chain was put together. You mustn't split the chain again at this link. You can identify it easily — most of the links have words printed around the rivet, saying "Shimano" and the code number of the chain. The original joining rivet has no words printed around it; avoid this one. Also avoid splitting the chain in the same place twice — any previously replaced rivets will have smoother heads. As long as you choose a different place every time, you can split and rejoin the chain as often as you need.

Shimano chains are not designed to be used with Powerlinks or other similar joining links, so if you have a Shimano chain, it's well worth making sure you always carry around a couple of replacement joining rivets. They weigh almost nothing, but if you need one, nothing else will do. Use duct tape to stick one under the bottom of your saddle so that it's always there in an emergency. Eight-speed and nine-speed chains are different widths, so they need different length replacement pins — they're not interchangeable.

New chains come with a spare replacement rivet in a little plastic bag (it's easy to lose this when you open the packet because it's very small) as well as a semi-assembled rivet attached to the chain for initial assembly. You can also pick up spares separately from your bike shop.

Inevitably, you may find yourself in a situation where you have to rejoin a Shimano chain without the proper replacement rivet. If you are forced to try rejoining a chain by reusing a link, take as much care as you can to when reinserting the rivet, so that it lines up with the hole in the chain plate. Be aware that the repaired link will be weaker, leaving the chain liable to break again. Therefore, you should always replace the repaired rivet or the entire chain as soon as possible.

SHIMANO CHAINS

Step 1: Line the chain up on the further set of supports. If you have a Shimano-specific chain tool, it may only have one set of supports. Push the rivet all the way out.

Step 2: To rejoin the chain, line up the holes in either end of the chain, and push the new replacement rivet through them. It will go most of the way through by hand. Use the chain tool to push it through until the first half comes all the way out of the far side of the chain. There's a groove between the two halves of the replacement rivet — keep pushing until you can see all of the groove and a trace of the second half of the rivet.

Step 3: Use a pair of pliers to snap off the exposed part of the replacement rivet. You may not have a pair of pliers with you out on the trail. If you have a fold-up multi-tool, you can improvise by trapping the protruding part of the rivet between two Allen keys, folding them down onto the body of the tool and twisting.

Stiff links

A newly-fixed link will often be stiff because the process of pushing through the rivet has jammed the chain plates together. You may also find that stiff links develop out on the trail. Heavy rain can do it, as can cycling through rivers. You can feel a stiff link when you pedal with moderate pressure — the chain regularly slips a little, enough to annoy you, but not always at the same point in the pedal stroke.

To locate the stiff link, lean your bike up against a wall with the chain in the big chainring at the front and the small sprocket at the back. Pedal slowly backward with your right hand and watch the chain as it feeds out of the bottom of the cassette, around the jockey wheels, and off the bottom of the bottom jockey. You see the bottom jockey wheel skip forward as the stiff link passes through the rear derailleur. Keep pedaling backward, and allow this section to pass through your fingers to pin down the stiff link.

LOOSENING STIFF LINKS

Step 1: Once you've found the stiff link, look at it carefully from above. You may find that one side of the rivet pokes out of the side of the chain more than the other. If this is the case, use the chain tool from the side that sticks out more to even it up.

Step 2: Lay the chain over the supports nearest the handle of the tool with the sticking-out end of the rivet nearest the handle. Wind in the handle until it lines up exactly with the center of the stiff rivet and touches it. Carefully wind in the handle another third of a turn. If the link is still stiff, repeat from the other side of the chain.

Step 3: If you don't have a chain tool, hold the chain in both hands, with the stiff link in the middle. Put both thumbs on the stiff link and flex the chain gently backward and forward. You should feel the stiff link gradually loosen off. Don't overdo it though — you don't want to end up twisting the chain.

Powerlinks

An easier way of joining chains is with a Powerlink. Both ends of the chain must be narrow segments, so remove any wide segments with a chain tool. Drop the chain off the chainring into the gap between the chainset and the frame for slack. Fit half of the joining link onto each end of the chain, one facing toward you and one facing away from you. Each part of the joining link has a key-shaped hole. Push one half into the other, then pull the two sections of chain apart to lock them into place. Replace the chain on the chainring. To remove the Powerlink, push the links on either side of the joining link toward each other. You may also need to squeeze the plates of the link together — one of those tricky moves that would be easier if you had three hands. The Powerlink rivets should pop back into the inner part of the key-shaped hole, allowing you to separate the chain by pushing half away from you and half toward you. Powerlinks are not designed to be used with Shimano chains.

Pull apart Powerlink to lock ▶

Correct chain length and routing

It's critical to get your chain length right. If the chain is too long, it flaps about and the derailleur folds up on itself when it's in the smallest sprocket at the back and the small chainring at the front. Too short, and the chain jams when you shift into the big/big combination. These are not recommended gears, but everybody shifts into them sometimes. The right length of chain gives you the smoothest shifting and means your chain will last longer too.

The correct length chain is just long enough to wrap around the biggest sprocket at the back and the biggest chainring at the front, plus one link (a complete link is one narrow section and one wide section).

Fitting a new chain

To fit a new chain, first route it. Shift the two derailleurs so the rear one is under the biggest sprocket, and the front one is over the biggest chainring. Start at the back at the lower jockey wheel and feed the end of the chain between the wheel and the lower tab. Next, feed the end between the top jockey wheel and the top tab. Route the chain around the front of the top jockey wheel, and then around the back of the cassette, forward to the chainset, through the front derailleur, around a chainring, and back to meet itself. Pull the chain as tight as it will go, as in the picture below — the rear derailleur will stretch forward to accommodate it. Add one link, and calculate how many links you need to remove.

If you're rejoining the chain with a split link such as a Powerlink, remember to take this into account — you only need to add an extra half-link, because the Powerlink is half a link. Including the extra link, this means that, if you have to shorten the chain to remove a twisted link, you are still left with a working chain that can reach all the gears. Join or rejoin the chain, and check through the gears. The chain should be long enough to reach around the big sprocket/big chainring combination with a little slack, but short enough so the rear derailleur doesn't fold up on itself in the small sprocket/small chainring combination.

Correct chain length

To check whether the chain you have is the right length, first make sure it's not too short. Step through the gears and check that the chain will stretch all the way around the big sprocket at the back and the big chainring at the front. It's fine for the cage of the derailleur to be stretched forward in this gear, but make sure the chain isn't too tight — there should be enough slack for you to lift the middle of the lower section of chain up at least 2cm (roughly ¾ inch). Then, check it's not too long. Change gear into the smallest sprocket at the back and the smallest chainring at the front. Look at the rear derailleur cage — the lower jockey wheel will be folded right back, taking up the maximum amount of slack. Make sure it's not folded so far back that any part of the chain touches any other part. The rear derailleur folds itself up in order to take up the extra slack created by shifting into the small sprockets and small chainring combination with the upper (guide) jockey wheel moving forward and the lower (tension) jockey wheel moving backward and up. If the chain is too long, the derailleur will fold itself up completely in the small/small combination. The lower section of chain can become entangled with the upper jockey wheel and the derailleur cage. As you pedal, putting pressure on the chain, the entangled chain will rip the rear derailleur off.

Similarly, if the chain is too short, shifting into the larger sprockets at the back while the chain is in the largest chainring will stretch the tension jockey wheel forward. If there's not enough slack, the tension in the chain can cause the back wheel to jam, kicking you off the bike, or it can twist or tear off the derailleur hanger, the part where the rear derailleur bolts onto the frame.

◀ **Measuring the correct chain length**

Why chains break and what to do about it when they do

Some people never break chains, while others seem to break them every time they ride. Chains break for different reasons, though, including bad luck, but sometimes it can be avoided. Sometimes small rocks or pebbles are kicked up by the tires where they get trapped between chain and cassette. As you put pedal, the chain breaks across the pebble. This is just bad luck and can happen to anyone.

Changing gears while stamping hard on the pedals puts a heavy strain on a few links. The links have to move sideways across your cassette to change gear, so they're at their most vulnerable because the pressure is applied at an angle. You do have to be turning the pedals to change gear, as this is what makes the chain derail, but your chain will shift across much quicker if you can slacken off the pressure as you change. Even when going uphill, try to anticipate gear changes so that you can build up enough momentum to lift off the pressure momentarily. A well-adjusted derailleur will change from one sprocket to the next in a quarter of a revolution of the pedals, as long as it's not under too much pressure.

Your chain will be even more likely to break if the extra pressure from shifting coincides with a weak spot. Weak spots include anywhere the chain is twisted and anywhere the chain has been split and rejoined, so split your chain as little as possible.

Treat your chain kindly

Regularly using a relatively high gear where you pedal slowly but with lots of force will wear and strain your chain (and your knees) much more than using a lower gear, where you spin the pedals around faster, but without stamping so hard on each pedal stroke.

A well-lubricated chain can cope with sudden loads better than a neglected one. Clean, oiled links will slide smoothly over one another, spreading peaks of force out over a number of links, so that none is taken beyond its breaking point. Excessive force will concentrate around stiff links. Over-oiling can be an enemy as well though — a sticky chain will pick up grit, wearing your chain faster and making it more likely to snap. Always clean excess oil off the outside of the chain once you've lubricated it. Only the thinnest layer of oil is necessary to stop the chain from rusting — all the friction that needs to be lubricated goes on inside the chain rollers.

As chains age, they collect more weak spots and become more likely to snap when you make sudden demands on them. Chains,

cassettes and chainrings all wear each other out as you ride. Rather than spreading the load over a number of chain links, worn chainrings and cassettes support only the first few links that they mesh with. This concentrates force over a few links, which may mean that the chain's maximum load is exceeded. The links may not look visibly damaged, but once this point is reached, wear will accelerate rapidly, with the stretched chain then wearing out the sprockets and chainrings in turn.

Finally, some people are simply stronger or heavier than others. If this is the case, ask your bike shop to recommend a tougher chain. These will always be more expensive than standard versions but need not be heavier — for example, the SRAM PC99 has hollow rivets to save weight and is much stronger than a standard chain. Under the same levels of abuse, it will stretch less, making your cassette last longer and less likely to snap under pressure.

◀ **New chains fit the chainring snugly over the chainring teeth**

Cassettes

Replace your chain every time you replace your cassette. Worn cassettes allow the chain to slip over the sprocket teeth, rather than to mesh securely into the valleys.

The standard fitting for attaching sprockets to the back wheel is the cassette. The cassette fits over the ratcheting mechanism, the freehub. This is bolted onto the hub, with the bearing at the outboard end. The freehub allows the wheel to go round on its own without pushing the pedals, that is to freewheel. The freehub makes a clicking noise when you freewheel. Cassettes and freehubs are made by different manufacturers, but all adhere to the standard Shimano-fitting pattern. The outer shell of the freehub is splined, a fancy way of saying it has grooves in it. The cassette has a matching set of grooves to slide over the freehub. Everything is kept in place with a lockring, that screws into the outer end of the freehub. The first common cassettes were seven-speed. When eight-speeds were introduced, they needed a longer eight-speed freehub, but seven-speed cassettes and freehubs are not compatible with eight-speed ones. However, a nine-speed packs more sprockets into the same space, so nine-speed and eight-speed cassettes both fit onto the same freehub. The lockring makes a horrible noise when it starts to loosen. Don't worry! The lockring has a serrated surface that locks onto the serrated face of the cassette. These crunch when separated.

REMOVING THE CASSETTE

Step 1: Remove the back wheel from the frame. Remove the quick-release skewer or nut, and fit the cassette-removing tool into the splines on the lockring. Make sure it fits snugly. Some tools have a hole through the middle so that you can refit the skewer or nut and hold everything in place, which is handy. Alternatively, for quick-release axles, use a tool with a central rod that slides into the axle and steadies the tool.

Step 2: Fit a chain whip around one of the sprockets on the cassette, in the direction seen in this picture. This will hold the cassette still while you undo the lockring. Fit a large adjustable wrench onto the tool — you need plenty of leverage so the handle will need to be about 30cm (12 in) long. Choose the angle so that it sticks out in the opposite direction to the chain whip.

Step 3: Place the wheel in front of you, with the cassette facing away. Hold the chain whip in your left hand, and the adjustable wrench in your right. Brace yourself and push down firmly on both at the same time. If you bolted the cassette lockring tool on, you need to loosen it once the tool starts to move, to make space into which the tool can undo. Remove the lockring, then slide the cassette off the freehub by pulling it straight out from the wheel.

Refitting the cassette

Wipe clean the splines of the freehub. (It is a mistake to use degreaser, as this drives grease from the axle bearings and freehub bearings.) Use the opportunity to check the wheel spokes, which are normally hidden behind the cassette — they get damaged if the chain comes off the biggest sprocket and catches behind the cassette, but you can't usually see the wear. If any are damaged, you have to deal with them — see page 156. Slide the new or cleaned cassette onto the freehub. One of the splines is fatter than the others and has to be lined up with the

corresponding spline on the cassette. Push the cassette all the way home. The outer rings are usually separate and must be correctly lined up. One of the separate rings may be narrower than the others and needs the supplied washer behind it. Grease the threads of the lockring, then screw it onto the center of the cassette. Refit the cassette-removing tool and the adjustable wrench, and tighten the lockring firmly. You do not need the chainwhip for this since the ratchet in the freehub stops the cassette rotating in this direction. When the lockring is almost tight, it makes an alarming crunching noise. This is normal! The inner surface of the lockring has friction ridges that lock onto the cassette to stop it working loose; they will click as you tighten it down.

◀ **Sprockets ahoy!**

Freewheels

For years, freewheels were the standard way of fitting sprockets to a back wheel, but they have now been superseded by the cassette design. You only come across a freewheel type on an older mountain bike or a on very basic new one. Axles on the freewheel type are more prone to bending and breaking, because the bearings that support the axle are much nearer to the center of the wheel.

Notches, splines and dogs

The most difficult thing here is choosing the correct tool. When freewheels were standard, there were a plethora of different designs, involving splines and dogs. Luckily, there are now fewer designs, and the only ones you're likely to come across commonly are the Shimano splined freewheel and the SunTour 4dog freewheel. (A splined tool has ridges that fit into matching ridges in the component running along the tool. A dogged tool has pegs, called "dogs," that fit into matching notches on the component.)

REMOVING FREEWHEELS

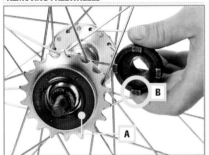

Step 1: To remove a freewheel, first choose the correct tool. If possible, take your wheel along to your local bike shop and ask them to help you identify the tool you need. Remove any nuts or the quick-release skewer, and locate the tool in the freewheel **(A)**. Splined tools hold themselves in place, but dogged tools need to be held in place with the nut or quick-release skewer. The tool in the picture is a 4dog freewheel remover **(B)**.

Step 2: Freewheels screw themselves into place as you cycle and are often very tight. You need a large adjustable wrench to turn the tool. Stand the wheel up, with the wrench horizontal in your right hand, hold the wheel steady and push down hard on the wrench. If you're using a dogged tool, you need to loosen the nut/quick-release a little when the freewheel starts to turn. Loosen the nut, unwind the freewheel a little, and repeat as necessary.

Step 3: Refitting is much easier! Grease the threads thoroughly, to make removal next time as easy as possible. Carefully line up the freewheel on the wheel — the threads are very fine, so it's easy to cross them accidentally (which means the freewheel starts to go on crooked and gets stuck). Screw on firmly by hand.

Additional advice on freewheels

Fit the wheel back on the bike and change into the lowest gear (largest back sprocket, smallest front chainring). It's important to make sure that the freewheel is firmly screwed on. With the bike on the ground, turn the pedals round so that the cranks are horizontal, then hold on the back brake and push down hard on the front pedal. You should feel the pedal move down a little, then stop when the freewheel is screwed fully home. Finally, check the gear adjustment and tune if necessary.

Freewheels contain a ratcheting device. It's this which allows that rear wheel to continue spinning after you stop pedaling, to "freewheel." Pawls inside the freewheel are sprung so that they are pushed constantly outward against a toothed ring. The pawls point away from the direction of the wheel rotation, so that as you pedal they catch on the toothed ring and force the wheel around. When you stop pedaling, the teeth on the spring push the pawls inward, so that they flap out of the way, springing back to be pushed out of the way again by the next tooth and creating a ticking noise as you pedal.

When the pawls become gummed up by mud or old oil, they fail to spring back and engage with the toothed wheel. If this happens when you pedal, the pawls won't catch, and your pedals will spin forwards uselessly. You can often revive freewheels without opening them up. Remove the freewheel from the bike and look at the back surface. The central part stays still while the outer part with the sprockets attached rotates. Hold the freewheel flat and squirt plenty of thin oil into the gap between the two parts — WD40 or similar. This will flush dirt out of the front of the freewheel. Relubricate with thicker oil — chain lubricant is exactly the right thickness. Hold the central part of the freewheel still and rotate the outer part to work the oil into the pawls. Replace the freewheel on the bike.

Derailleurs

Derailleurs are cunning bits of gear. The way they work is simple: they take advantage of your pedaling action to move the chain smoothly from one sprocket to another. The name comes from the French for "derail" (pronounced simply "de-railer" or "de-rail-yer"). It is known simply as an "S" in certain places.

The rear derailleur hangs underneath the cassette and feeds the loose chain that's returning from the chainset back onto the cassette. This is the part of the chain that isn't under pressure — it's the top part that's doing the work as you pedal. The important part for changing gear is the guide jockey wheel, the one that sits closest to the cassette. It's also called the top jockey, even when the bicycle is upside down. The derailleur works by using the cable to move the guide jockey across the cassette. Because this part of the chain is not under pressure, the chain will follow the guide jockey and move onto a different size sprocket as it is fed onto the cassette.

The chain needs to be moving to mesh with a new sprocket, which is why you have to be pedaling to change gear. If you pedal too hard, the chain will not be able to engage properly on the new sprocket, and will slip and crunch as you try to change gear.

The lower jockey wheel, also called the tension jockey, has a different function. It sits on the derailleur arm and is sprung so that it's always pushing backward. It is there because you need more chain to go around a combination of big chainring and big sprockets than for a combination of small chainring and small sprockets. The tension jockey is needed to take up the slack, otherwise the surplus chain would drag on the ground.

The next step is telling the derailleur what size sprocket you want to be in. In the pre-derailleur days of bicycle racing, road-racers had two different-sized sprockets, one on each side of the back wheel. When they came to a hill, they'd jump off their bikes, whip off the back wheel, turn it round in the frame, refit it with the larger-sized sprocket engaged, jump back on, and ride up the hill. At the top, they'd reverse the process. Derailleurs were invented because anyone who could avoid this nuisance saved enough time to win races.

In 1951, after experimenting with different styles, Tullio Campagnolo invented a derailleur called the Gran Sport, which looks pretty much like those we use now and works in a similar way. The derailleur is bolted on just below the rear axle. The top part stays still, but the knuckle, with the guide jockey attached, is hinged at an angle. This means that as the guide jockey moves across, it also moves down, tracking the shape of the cassette. There is a spring across the hinge, pulling the two halves of the derailleur together. Consequently, left to its own devices, the spring will pull the derailleur so that the guide jockey runs under the smallest sprocket.

Finally, here's where you tell the derailleur what you want. The shifter on the handlebars connects to a cable, which pulls the two parts of the derailleur apart. This moves the guide jockey across and down, and so pulls the chain onto a larger sprocket. Moving the shifter the other way releases cable, allowing the spring to pull the guide jockey and chain onto a smaller sprocket. This combination of cable and spring is common — V-brakes work the same way, with the cable pulling something into place and a spring returning it when the cable tension is released.

The two most important demands we place on our derailleurs are that they don't affect the transfer of power from the pedals to the back wheel, and that they shift the chain from one sprocket to the next as quickly as possible so that the change from one gear to the next happens without breaking the rhythm of the pedal stroke.

In order to be able to deliver these objectives, the movement of the derailleur as controlled by the shifter needs to be very precise. Derailleurs are right down near the ground, in a prime position for picking up all kinds of grit, dirt and mud. All that gunk will wear the pivots around which the movement of your derailleur hinges. It's not surprising that derailleurs, especially rear ones, have a relatively short life. Keeping them clean and well-lubricated helps, but if you ride hard, expect to replace them every year.

◀ **Slave to the rhythm: the derailleur**

Indexing: the delicate science of slipping from one gear to the next

In days gone by people used to be content just using the shifter to feel and listen for the right place under a particular sprocket when changing gear. Now indexed gears are universal. The shifter has notches instead of moving smoothly across its range and, if all the components are compatible and correctly adjusted, shifting one notch on the shifter pulls through enough cable to move the chain across exactly one sprocket on your cassette.

A few derailleurs are designed to work in reverse — the cable pulls the chain from the largest to the smallest sprockets and, when the cable tension is released, the spring in the rear derailleur can pull the cable back from the smallest to the largest sprocket. The Shimano Rapidrise (or Low Normal) derailleur is like this. Some people prefer it. I find it irritating. If you have a rapid-rise derailleur, see page 110.

The idea behind rapid-rise derailleurs is that the shift into a higher gear is controlled by cable action rather than spring action, so it's supposed to be better for split-second changes in races. If your transmission is working perfectly, there is a slight advantage — but this is offset by the design's inability to tolerate dirt or wear as well as the standard setup.

Adjusting your gears

Well-adjusted gears should be invisible — one click of the shifter and you should move into whatever gear you need without thinking about it. You need to lavish care on your gears to keep everything running smoothly, though. Indeed, after keeping your chain clean, the next most important thing is to keep your gears well-adjusted. They don't simply work better — your entire transmission lasts longer. Get used to adjusting your gears before you tackle any other gear work, as you have to make adjustments at the end of many procedures, especially fitting new cables or derailleurs. The rear indexing is the most important adjustment — proper tuning is not difficult, but practice makes perfect.

There are a couple of things to bear in mind as you learn to adjust your gears. The first is that your gear adjustment depends on transferring an accurate signal from your shifters to your derailleurs, so that when you take up or release a length of cable at the shifter, exactly the same amount of cable is pulled through at the derailleur. This will not happen if the cable is dirty or frayed or the casing is kinked. If you find that the adjusting instructions aren't working for you, check that cable and casing are in good condition.

All these adjustments require being able to turn the pedals to change gear, so you need to hold your bike up so that the back wheel is off the ground. Ideally, use a workstand. Otherwise bribe a friend to lift it up by the saddle at appropriate moments.

In the picture on the right, you can see the chain in the middle of a gear shift from a larger sprocket to a smaller one. The chain, dragged across to the right by the derailleur, has to climb up and over the teeth of the larger sprockets before dropping onto the next sprocket down. Careful design of both the sprocket profile and the chain links means that the chain will shift under pressure, transferring from one sprocket to the next without loss of power. Shimano chains have side links that bulge outward, allowing them to engage quickly with the sprocket teeth. Look carefully at the faces of the sprockets on your cassette, and you will see that these have also been cut away, making short ramps to help lift the chain up when shifting from smaller to larger sprockets. All these small design improvements, among others, help make your shifting instinctive and immediate.

Teeth that bite gently: shifting sprockets ▶

The best methods of adjusting the rear derailleur

Adjusting your rear derailleur can be tricky. The same problem could have one or more different — but similar — causes. Your derailleur is going to need adjusting if it's slow to shift up or down, if it changes gear all of its own accord when you're innocently cycling along, or if it rattles and clatters whenever you change gear. This is how you do it.

Adjusting your indexing: Derailleur types — standard and rapid-rise

Before you start adjusting, use the following method to check whether you have a standard derailleur or a rapid-rise derailleur. Change into one of the middle cassette sprockets. Take hold of any exposed part of the derailleur cable where it passes along the top-tube or down-tube of your bike, and pull the cable gently away from the frame. Watch the derailleur:

◆ If it moves towards a lower gear (larger sprocket), you have a standard derailleur — follow the instructions below.
◆ If the derailleur moves towards a higher gear (smaller sprocket) when you pull the cable, you have a rapid-rise derailleur — follow the instructions in the rapid-rise section on page 110.

Shifter types — twistshifters and triggershifters

When you adjust gears, you shift repeatedly through them to test what happens. Although there are different makes and models of shifter, they all work in the same way — adjusting your indexing will be the same process whether your handlebar gear levers are twistshifters or triggershifters. Start by experimenting to see what happens to the cable when you shift. Find an exposed part of the cable, like you did for checking whether you had a standard or rapid-rise shifter, and pull the cable gently away from the frame with your left hand. Holding it away, use your right hand to change gear. You won't need to pedal at the same time, just operate the shifter. One movement makes the cable slacker, the other makes it tighter. Change up and down a few times so that you begin to remember which does what. For standard derailleurs, shifting so that the cable is tighter pulls the derailleur towards the wheel and onto a larger sprocket. Shifting to release the cable allows the derailleur spring to pull the derailleur away from the wheel, toward a smaller sprocket. Once you are familiar with the action of your shifters, you can start indexing your gears.

People often get confused with gear indexing, mixing it up with adjusting the end-stop screw. This is also important, but it's different. The end-stop screws set the limit of the range of movement of the derailleur, stopping it from falling off either end of the sprocket. Sometimes they are set wrong and accidentally stop the chain from moving onto the sprockets at either end of the cassette.

If this is the case, you cannot adjust your indexing properly — go to the section on end-stop screws on page 109, adjust them, and then return here. Always check before you start adjusting the indexing that the chain reaches the smallest and largest sprockets, without dropping over the edge of either.

To tune the indexing, you have to adjust the tension in the cable so that one click of the shifter changes the cable tension precisely enough to move the chain across exactly one sprocket. Pulling the cable moves the chain toward lower gears, the larger sprockets near the wheel. Releasing tension in the cable allows the derailleur spring to pull the chain outward, toward the small sprockets.

Key points to check if you have trouble adjusting your cable tension

◆ Compatability — have you got the same number of clicks in your shifter as sprockets on your cassette? This is a surprisingly common cause of intractable adjustment problems.
◆ Derailleur hanger angle — the derailleur will only follow the shape of the cassette if the jockey wheels hang vertically below the sprockets. Crashes often bend the derailleur or the derailleur hanger inward, so that the derailleur sits at an angle and will not respond to adjustment.
◆ Crusty cables — the cable must be in good condition so that the shifter can pull through precise amounts of cable. This makes the most difference when the shifter releases a length of cable. The spring in the derailleur will not be strong enough to pull through cable that's gummed up with mud or rust.

Adjusting the cable tension on standard rear derailleurs

This is possibly the single most important adjustment that you will learn to make on your bicycle, and it's not difficult. There are always clear signs when you need to adjust the tension of your rear derailleur cable. If the derailleur doesn't respond to your shifter, if it shifts more than one sprocket when you click the lever, or if the chain rattles and clatters as you shift, it's time to look at your cable tension.

The important thing to remember during this procedure is to always start in the same place, with the cable tension at its slackest and the chain in the smallest sprocket. Otherwise, it's easy to confuse yourself, matching up the third shifter click with the fourth sprocket, or whatever. You will either need a workstand, to keep the back wheel off the ground, or the assistance of a friend, to lift the bike up for you at the appropriate moment.

Before you begin changing the cable tension, familiarise yourself with the action of your shifter. Follow the casing that emerges from the right hand shifter to where it joins the top tube or down tube, emerging as bare cable. Hook your finger under the middle of this section of bare cable, and operate your shifter — for trigger shifters, push and release one then the other. For twist shifters, rotate the shifter forwards then back. You'll feel the cable tension pull through, then release.

When the cable tension is exactly right, the chain sits exactly below each sprocket as you change gear. This maximises chain life, and stops the chain from clattering on the sprockets as you ride. Since the sprockets and shifter clicks are evenly spaced, once you have the adjustments for the two smallest sprockets, the others should work automatically.

Once you've worked out which action makes the cable tighter, and which makes it looser, shift so that the cable is as loose as possible.

Start by checking that the shifter is in the high gear position — turn the pedals, and click the shifter so that the chain moves all the way into the smallest sprocket. Keep clicking, in case there's slack in the system, until you run out of gears. Keep turning the pedals, and click the shifter exactly one click in the down direction, so that the derailleur moves towards the larger sprockets.

TAILORING THE TENSION

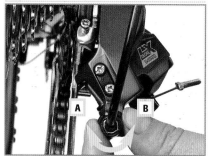

Step 1: The chain should move across to the next largest sprocket, and sit directly underneath it. Use the barrel-adjuster to make fine adjustments. To get the barrel to move, hold it as shown with your thumb on the top of the barrel. Turning it one way tightens the cable and moves the chain away **(A)** from you, onto larger sprockets. Turning the other way slackens the cable and allows the spring to pull the chain toward you **(B)**, onto smaller sprockets.

Step 2: If the derailleur doesn't move when you click the shifter, the cable is far too slack as often happens when you fit a new cable. Undo the pinch bolt, pull through a little more cable by hand, tighten the pinch bolt. Start again in the smallest sprocket, clicking the shifter several times to make sure it is at the slackest position. Now increase the tension by half a turn (turning away) and repeat until the chain lifts onto the second sprocket.

Step 3: Once you can move the chain from the smallest to the second sprocket, try shifting back from the second to the smallest. You may find you have to tune the position further — try a quarter-turn at a time. Once you've got the right tension, shift into the second-smallest gear and look at the chain from behind. The top jockey wheel, the one with the chain around it, should sit vertically below the second sprocket. Use the barrel-adjuster to finish off the tuning.

Adjusting the end-stop screw on your rear derailleur

The end-stop screws on your derailleur — also known as limit screws — prevent the derailleur from throwing the chain off either end of the cassette. This is a vital task: the end-stop prevents the chain from falling off both the largest sprocket into the gap between the cassette and the wheel, or the smallest sprocket so that it gets stuck between the cassette and the frame.

Either of these contingencies will damage your bike, cutting through the spokes where they join your rear hub or taking chunks out of your frame beside the cassette. The chain will get firmly wedged too, so the chances of you falling off and hurting yourself are quite high.

Only the heads of the end-stops screws are visible, the shafts of the screws are hidden inside the body of the derailleur. The derailleur is designed so that at either end of it, the tips of the end-stop screws come into contact with tabs molded into the pivoting part of the derailleur. Screwing the end-stop screws further into the body of the derailleur means that the ends of the screws hit the tabs sooner, limiting the movement of the derailleur and preventing the derailleur from pushing the chain off either end of the cassette. If you set the end-stop screws too far in, the derailleur won't be able to push the chain onto the largest or smallest sprockets.

It's easy to get confused when adjusting your rear derailleur because sometimes the same symptom can have more than one cause. For example, if you are having difficulty shifting onto the smallest sprocket, the cause could be that the "high" end-stop screw, which controls how far out the derailleur can move, is screwed too far into the derailleur. However, too much tension in the rear derailleur cable can provoke the same response. For this reason, I find it easiest to adjust the end-stop screw when there is no tension in the rear derailleur cable. If you're fitting a new cable, use these instructions to adjust the end-stop screws before you fit the new cable.

In cases where the cable is already fitted, release it from the cable stops on the frame so that it hangs loosely. To do this, first turn the pedals and change into the largest sprocket on your cassette. Stop pedaling, and shift as if changing into the smallest sprocket. The chain won't be able to derail because you're not pedaling, but the derailleur cable will become slack. Follow the outer casing back from the shifter, to where the outer casing joins the frame at the first cable stop, and pull the casing forward toward the front of the bike. Wiggle the cable out of the slot in the cable guide. This will give you enough cable slack to adjust the end-stop screws without getting confused by cable tension issues.

Once you've finished adjusting the end-stop screws, replace the cable. To create enough slack in the cable, you'll need to push the rear derailleur toward the wheel so that it sits under the largest sprocket.

SETTING THE END-STOP SCREWS

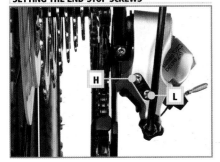

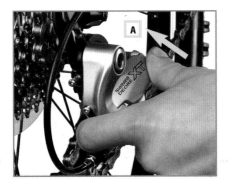

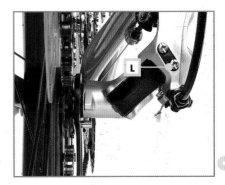

Step 1: Setting the high gear is easier, so we'll start there. Looking at the derailleur from behind, you see the two end-stop screws, marked "H" and "L," one above the other. Normally, the higher screw adjusts the high gear, and the lower screw the low gear. But, annoyingly, some SRAM screws work the opposite way around. The writing is often small and difficult to make out. Turn the lower screw so that the chain hangs exactly under the smallest sprocket.

Step 2: The low end-stop screw is trickier. With the back wheel off the ground, turn the pedals with your right hand. Position your left hand with first finger hooked behind the cable entry tab at the back and thumb over the forward set of pivots. Push your thumb away from you **(A)** while turning the pedals. Push the derailleur across, so the chain runs to the largest sprocket but not so far that it falls into the gap between the largest sprocket and the spokes.

Step 3: If you can't move the derailleur across enough to shift easily into the largest sprocket, you need to unscrew (counterclockwise) the lower (L) of the two adjustment screws. Small adjustments make a big difference, so take it easy. If the chain threatens to fall too far, wind the upper screw clockwise. Once set, you should be able to push the derailleur far enough by turning the pedals to let the chain sit vertically under the large sprocket, and no further.

Rapid-rise derailleur

Some models of derailleur are designed to work backward. Normally, the spring is set up to pull the chain onto the smallest sprocket of the chainring. Cable tension is needed to pull the chain toward the bigger ones. Several manufacturers have experimented with reversing this arrangement, so the spring pulls the cable toward a larger sprocket or chainring.

Adjustment is the same in principle as for standard derailleurs, but because the spring is reversed, you have to start the adjustment from the other end. Shift into the largest ring, making sure that the shifter is at the end of its range — turn twistshifters all the way or press triggershifters a couple of extra times to make sure. The chain should now be in the largest sprocket. Turn the pedals and move the shifter one click. The chain should move into the next largest sprocket. Note that this rarely happens the first time!

If the chain doesn't move into the next largest sprocket, the cable is too slack. Click back to the slack position at the shifter and tighten the cable by turning the barrel-adjuster so that the top of the barrel moves toward the wheel. A half-turn at a time is a good place to start. Test again.

If the chain doesn't move at all, the cable is very slack; return to the largest sprocket, undo the cable pinch bolt, pull through some cable by hand, and tighten the pinch bolt.

If the cable moves too far, shifting onto the third sprocket when you click once, the cable is too tight. Slacken it by turning the barrel-adjuster so that the top of the barrel moves away from the wheel.

Once you've got the tension adjusted so that the chain shifts from the largest to the next sprocket, try shifting back to the largest. Again, this should happen neatly with one click, but it rarely works perfectly the first time. Now turn the barrel in quarter-turns. Turn the barrel so that the top moves toward the wheel. This tightens the cable and makes it easier for the chain to hop onto the second sprocket. Turning it so that the top of the barrel moves away from the wheel loosens the cable, making it easier for the chain to return to the largest sprocket.

Compatibility

Shimano have set the standards for compatibility — their derailleurs are fitted to the vast majority of mountain bikes, so almost all components are made to be compatible with the Shimano standard.

The only significant exception is the SRAM ESP range. This is designed with a 1:1 cable actuation ratio, a term more complicated sounding than it is. It means that pulling 1mm (1/16 inch) of cable moves the rear derailleur guide jockey, and so the chain, 1mm under the sprocket. All the Shimano-compatible derailleurs have a 1:2 actuation ratio: pulling 1mm of cable at the shifter moves the derailleur 2mm (1/8 inch). Lots of people prefer the ESP 1:1 setup because using more cable to send the same signal to the derailleur means it is less subject to mud, grime and poor adjustment.

ESP components are only compatible with other ESP components, and they are all referenced by a number, for example, 3.0 or 9.0. All other SRAM components are compatible with Shimano and have names rather than numbers, for example, Centera or Quarz.

Setting the derailleur angle with the B-screw

Check the angle at which the derailleur hangs. The guide jockey needs to sit close under the sprockets for slick changing but not so close that the top of the jockey rubs on the bottom of the sprockets.

There should be two clear links of chain between the bottom of the sprocket and the top of the jockey wheel. Turn the B-screw **(A)** to adjust the gap. Turning clockwise increases the gap, turning counterclockwise allows the guide jockey to move closer to the sprockets.

If the chain sits too close to the sprockets, it will clatter on the cassette teeth as you ride. Too great a distance between the guide jockey and the cassette will cause sluggish shifting because the chain flexes sideways when you try to change gear rather than meshing with the next sprocket.

Fitting a new rear derailleur

There are many reasons you might want or need to change your rear derailleur. First of all, it might have snapped in a crash. Alternatively, it might simply have worn out from hundreds of gear changes.

Derailleur pivots will wear over time, causing sluggish shifting as the guide jockey struggles to respond to changes in cable tension. Take hold of the bottom of the derailleur cage and rock it sideways, toward and away from the back wheel. A bit of flex is fine, but if you can feel the cage knocking, replace the derailleur.

This task is easiest when you have as much chain slack to play with as possible. That's why you should change into the smallest sprocket at the back, while at the same time dropping the chain off the smallest sprocket at the front and into the gap between the chainset and the frame. Clip the end-cap off the cable.

FITTING A REAR DERAILLEUR

Step 1: Undo the cable clamp bolt and unthread the cable from the barrel-adjuster. If you reuse the same cable, there is no need to unthread it further, although you may find that a new derailleur will have a different configuration and need a longer cable. It is best to split the derailleur to remove the chain from it, as splitting the chain takes longer and weakens the split link. First, undo the guide jockey bolt slightly.

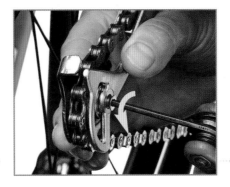

Step 2: Remove the tension jockey bolt, which is the one in the middle of the lower of the two jockey wheels.

Step 3: Slide the tension jockey wheel forward. It has a washer on each side. Don't lose these; they tend to drop out as you pull the jockey wheel out.

Step 4: Rotate the back of the cage slightly so that you can slide the chain out of the cage without splitting the chain. Undo the fixing bolt that attached the derailleur to the frame. Discard the old derailleur.

Step 5: Remove the tension jockey wheel on the new rear derailleur and loosen the guide jockey bolt. Hold the derailleur upside down, as in the picture. Fit the derailleur to the lower loop of chain, laying it over the guide jockey then trapping it in place with the tension jockey. Make sure it passes inside both tabs, so that the chain runs between the tab and the jockey wheel. Refit the tension jockey bolt. Tighten both jockey wheel bolts firmly.

Step 6: Turn the derailleur clockwise and pull it backward, so the fitting bolt is aligned with the frame-hanger. Bolt the derailleur to the frame, ensuring the bolt does not cross-thread. It's important that the small B-tab behind the derailleur sits behind the matching tab on the lower part of the frame-hanger, stopping the derailleur from swinging too far forward. Sometimes this is just a tab; sometimes the end-stop is the end of the B-screw **(A)**.

Servicing the rear derailleur

The rear derailleur does all the shifting work and dangles down close to the ground getting caught on twigs and picking up debris. It's also the part that your bike lands on first if you crash on your right-hand side or drop the bike. If you have time to think when you're crashing, drop the bike on the left — it's far cheaper!

If your shifting is still sluggish after you've adjusted the end-stop screws and the cable tension, then it's time to treat your rear derailleur to a little clean and relubrication. The separate sections of the derailleur need to be able to move freely, so that your shifting is crisp. The pivots that connect the parts work best if they're not jammed up with dirt and have a little oil to lubricate them.

The first step is to clean your rear derailleur. This is easiest with the back wheel removed, so you can get to everything. Wipe down the outside, then use a little brush to get mud and dirt out from inside the mechanism. You don't need to carry that muck around with you. You need to move the derailleur through its range to get inside it. With your left hand, hook a finger behind the back of the derailleur and push the front part of the derailleur body away from you.

Once you've got the dirt out from the inside, clean off the jockey wheels. They collect oil and mud and grind them together into an excellent chain-eating paste. Scrape this off with the end of a screwdriver. Next, check how worn the derailleur is. The teeth on the jockey wheels should have flat tops, not points. Take hold of the bottom of the derailleur and wiggle it towards you. It should flex rather than knock or flap about freely. When these things happen, it's time for a new derailleur.

Next, oil the pivot points. There are at least four on the derailleur body. Drop a bit of oil into the jockey wheel bearings, the knuckle where the derailleur rotates on the frame, and the point where the derailleur body meets the arm to which the jockey wheels are attached. Once you've oiled all these parts, move them to work the oil into the gaps. Push the derailleur away, as if it was changing gear, then allow it to spring back several times. Wipe off excess oil. Refit the back wheel.

If you feel like giving your bike a Christmas present, remove the rear derailleur (see page 111) and give it a thorough scrub. Undo the bolts that hold on the jockey wheels, remove them, and take the back of the cage off to clean properly between the cage and the jockey wheels. Push the bearings out of the middle of the jockey wheels, clean and oil them, then refit. Don't be tempted to swap the top and bottom jockey wheels — they're usually a different shape because they do a different job. The top guide jockey wheel pushes the chain sideways, from one sprocket to the next. The bottom tension jockey wheel pulls the chain backward, taking up slack. In addition, guide jockeys like the one in the picture, from a Shimano XT derailleur, have a rotation direction. Set this up so that pedaling forward makes the jockey wheel roll in the direction of the arrows. This can be achieved by bolting the jockey wheel into the derailleur so that the writing faces outward.

Use a small brush to scrub dirt from inside the body of the derailleur and oil the pivot points. Refit the derailleur, again using instructions for fitting a new derailleur.

Fixing bolt

Barrel-adjuster

Pivots x4

Cable clamp bolt

Spring

Cage

Jockey wheels

◀ **Shimano XT derailleur**

Rear hanger alignment

A lot is expected of your rear derailleur. You want it to be a precise, instant-shifting piece of gear even under pressure in a dirty environment. You need to be able to rely on it in all conditions and that's why it pays to nurture it.

One of the most common problems to be routinely ignored is the alignment of the rear derailleur hanger (the part on the frame that the derailleur bolts onto). The gears are designed to work when the two jockey wheels hang vertically underneath the sprockets. This vertical alignment is the first casualty of a crash, but it's often overlooked — you get up and brush yourself off, look at your bike and, if everything looks okay, you ride away. Bad things can happen next. If you've crashed and bent your derailleur inward, the gears may still work, but everything has shipped inboard a little.

Next time you stamp uphill in a low gear, you click the lever to find a bigger sprocket, but instead you dump the chain off the inside of the rear cassette, stuffing it into the back wheel just as you haul on the pedals. Likely results include falling off and hurting yourself — and expensive damage to your back wheel.

On a less drastic level, the shifting works best when the sprockets are aligned with the jockey wheels. The chain isn't being twisted as it runs off the sprocket; and the jockey wheels move in the direction they were designed to, rather than being forced up into the sprockets as they move across the cassette, which is what happens if the hanger is bent.

Look at the derailleur from behind. This way, you get the clearest view of whether or not the chain is running in one of the middle gears. The sprocket, chain and jockey wheel should make a vertical line. In the most common problem, the hanger is bent so that the bottom jockey wheel hangs nearer the wheel, as in the picture below.

It's not unusual for the hanger or the derailleur to be twisted rather than (or as well as!) bent, so that as you look straight at the sprocket, you can see the surface of the jockey wheels instead of just the edge. For precise shifting, the jockeys need to be flat and vertical to the sprockets. Because this is a common problem, all decent aluminum frames feature a replaceable hanger.

There are as many different types of hanger as there are makes of bike, and, even within a make and model, the hanger you need might depend on the year the bike was made. To make sure you get the right one, take the old one to your local bike shop for comparison. They are almost never interchangeable.

If you don't have a replaceable hanger, the frame will have to be bent back. You can do it yourself if you are careful, but if you are unsure, this is a job I recommend you take to your bike shop. You usually need to have snapped off a couple of hangers before you know how far you can go — an expensive experiment. If the bend is bad, it will be weaker after you have straightened it.

Leave the wheel in the dropout to support the frame. You have two options for bending back the hanger. The first is to clamp a large adjustable wrench onto the hanger — you need about 30cm (12 inches) of leverage to do the job — and to ease the hanger back into place. It is very important to bend in one movement — the last thing you want to do is work the hanger backward and forward to find the perfect place. It will snap off.

The other option, which is trickier but safer, is to screw a rear wheel axle into the thread on the hanger. They are the same size, an M10 thread. I've had a plenty of success bolting a whole wheel onto the thread, and using it for leverage. It's easy to see when you've got the angle right because the two wheels — your own, and the one bolted into the derailleur hanger — are parallel.

Some rear derailleurs come with a breakaway bolt. This means that the bolt that fixes the derailleur to the frame is designed to be slightly weaker than the hanger and the derailleur. In the event of a crash, instead of your hanger breaking or bending, your derailleur breaks off. Replacement bolts are still available, and are either push-fit or circlipped in, depending on the model.

◀ **Hangers need to be flat and vertical to sprockets**

Improving your shifting

It's often difficult to know where to start with gear adjustment. Sluggish shifting can result from a combination of factors, both constant and intermittent. The rear derailleur, in particular, relies on everything being set up perfectly so that all the components work together.

It's also tricky to adjust gears because they behave differently under pressure. Gears that feel perfect when you're trying them out in the garage can be disappointing when you try them out for real. Occasionally, the opposite situation occurs: you can't get the gears to shift properly at all in the shop, then you go for a ride anyway and unexpectedly they feel fine.

Adjust cable tension

If you're unhappy with the shifting, the most sensible place to start is with the cable tension adjustment. Click the shifters all the way into their neutral position (high gears for standard derailleurs, low for rapid-rise) and then shift over into the neighboring sprocket. If the chain doesn't sit vertically under the sprocket or doesn't shift crisply, you have an adjustment problem — see cable tension, page 108.

Check hanger alignment

Shift into the big sprocket and look at the chain from behind the bike. The chain should make a straight vertical line down the back of the sprocket and around the jockey wheels. If the jockey wheels are tucked in towards the back wheel, you have a hanger alignment problem — see page 113.

Replace or clean cables and casing

If your cable tension and alignment are correct, but your shifting is still sluggish, your gear cable may be dirty, kinked or corroded. In particular, check the section of outer casing that connects the rear derailleur to the frame as it is vulnerable to getting squashed or kinked.

Cables (the wires) are among the least expensive parts of the bike, so changing them doesn't break the bank. If you normally cycle in conditions where you need to clean your bike after a ride, think about changing cables at least four times a year. The rear derailleur cable is the bike part most susceptible to contamination because it transfers a very precise signal. Of all the repairs in this section, fitting and adjusting your rear derailleur cable is the best one to know. You can get all sorts of fancy cable sets that are designed to enclose the inner wire and keep it free from mud, but, in my experience, soil has an unrelenting urge to find its way into the piece of outer casing between my frame and derailleur where it lodges, specifically to make my gear changing feel terrible. Changing the cable is no complicated job, and the reward is instant: an improved bike and ride. The first part of the procedure depends on what kind of shifter you have, so we'll go through each of those in turn — see page 121. Once you have the cable installed in the shifter, the procedure for adjusting the derailleur is identical. Start with the shifter that's most similar to yours, then hop to the adjustment section on page 108.

Before you fit any new cable, you need to remove the old one. Cut off the cable end and undo the pinch bolt that clamps the cable onto the derailleur. Thread the cable back through each section of outer casing in turn, leaving the casing on the bike. Make a note of the cable route because the new one will have to go back the same way. If you replace the outer casing as well (which is not a bad idea — especially the last section that leads to the rear derailleur), then go to the section on outer casing on page 119. Cut the cable so that about 15cm (6 inches) is left poking out of the shifter, then follow the instructions for your shifter to get the old cable out and the new cable in.

Clean or replace your rear derailleur

Your derailleur will work much better if it's clean and oiled. See page 112 for servicing instructions. Give it a good scrub and oil it. Hold the bottom of the cage, near the bottom jockey wheel, and rock it gently toward and away from the wheel. Knocking, clicking or moving more than 4mm (around ⅛ inch) sideways indicates that the pivots in your derailleur are worn out — see page 111 to replace the derailleur.

Replace shifter

If none of these works, check that your shifter is sending crisp signals. Shift into a large sprocket, then click the shifter as if changing into a small sprocket, but without turning the pedals. This creates slack in the cable. Pull the section of casing that joins the bars to the frame forward and out of its cable stop. Slide the casing toward the back of the bike. This exposes the cable as it enters the shifter. Take hold of the cable and pull gently away from the shifter. Operate the shifter, checking that as you shift in either direction, the shifter pulls through little chunks of cable, and then releases them neatly, one at a time. If the shifter slips or misses clicks, service or replace it — see page 125.

Front derailleur

The front derailleur lies directly in the firing line of all the dirt and mud that get thrown up off your back wheel, so it occasionally deserves a bit of care and attention. Cheaper front derailleurs don't last that long. I find they are the components least resistant to winter, especially if you ride on salted roads.

They get covered in whatever the roads throw up, accumulating mud that is then forced into the shifting mechanism every time you change gear. Eventually, the spring that returns the chain to the smaller chainrings can no longer cope, and the derailleur stops returning when you release the cable.

◀ **Front derailleurs are less complex than rear derailleurs**

Front derailleur: adjusting the indexing

Like the rear derailleur, adjusting the indexing on the front derailleur is the same whatever type of handlebar shifter you have. Check what your particular shifter does by taking hold of an exposed section of cable to pulling it gently away from the frame. Change gears in both directions to familiarize yourself with the effect that the shifters have on the cable. One of the directions or levers will loosen the cable, the other will tighten it.

Lift the back wheel off the ground for this procedure. Turn the pedals and move the front shifter so that the cable is in its slackest position. As you turn the pedals, the chain should shift into the smallest chainring at the front. If it doesn't, the cable tension is too high. The barrel-adjuster for the front derailleur is up on the shifter. To loosen the cable, turn the barrel-adjuster so that the top of the barrel moves towards the front of the bike. Try a half-turn at a time to start with.

As with the rear derailleur, it is possible to get muddled between a problem with the cable tension or the end-stop screw adjustment. If you continue to adjust the cable tension, and the cable goes slack but the chain still doesn't drop into the smallest chainring when you change gear, you need to adjust the end-stop screws **(A)** — see page 116. Adjust the end-stops, then come back here.

Once you've got the chain into the smallest ring, keep pedaling and change gear at the shifter by one complete click. The chain should climb up into the middle ring. If it doesn't, or does so sluggishly, you need to increase the tension in the cable — turn the barrel-adjuster so that the top of the barrel moves towards the back of the bike. Once the chain moves onto the middle ring, adjust the barrel until there is 1mm (¹⁄₁₆ inch) of clearance between the outer plate of the derailleur cage and the chain, with the chain in the smallest sprocket at the back. The chain should now shift precisely between the three rings. If it won't reach the outer or inner ring easily, you have to adjust the limit screws. They are especially likely to need adjustment if you have changed the position of the derailleur on the frame.

You may run out of barrel-adjuster — you need to turn it further out, but, as you turn, it drops out of the shifter, or you need to move it further out, but it jams against the shifter. If so, you need to make a coarse adjustment with the pinch bolt, then restart the fine adjustment. Roll the barrel most of the way back in, then undo the pinch bolt on the derailleur and pull a little cable through — start with about 3mm (around ⅛ inch). Try the gears again.

Front derailleur adjustment is particularly sensitive to the position of the derailleur — if it's too high, too low or twisted, you won't be able to make it shift neatly by adjusting the cable tension. If you try the adjustment above and the derailleur still won't shift neatly, try adjusting the derailleur — follow the instructions for fitting a new one on page 117. Similarly, a bent derailleur will not shift neatly. Once you've bent one, it is hard to persuade it back into the right shape. You are usually better off replacing it than trying to reshape it. It does work occasionally, but not very often.

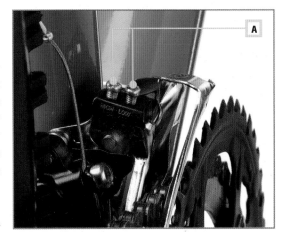

Derailleur position is vital for crisp shifting ▶

Setting the end-stop screws

End-stop screws limit the movement of the derailleur so it cannot drop the chain off the outside or the inside of the chainset. There are two separate screws. The "low" screw stops the derailleur swinging too far inward, dropping into the gap between the chainset and the frame. The "high" screw stops the derailleur swinging too far outward and falling off the outside of the chainset. If the chain won't travel far enough even with correctly adjusted tension, check your end-stop screws.

Each end-stop screw controls the limit of the derailleur movement in only one direction. Identify the correct screw first — the marks are often printed in black on a black background. Usually, the end-stop screw nearest the frame is used to prevent the chain from falling off the big chainring. The screw furthest from the frame stops the chain from falling off the smallest chainring.

SETTING END-STOP SCREWS

Step 1: Start with the chain in the middle ring. Check the shifter is in the middle of the three positions. Turn the pedals and shift into high gear. The chain should lift onto the big chainring as you turn the pedals. If it won't go, you need to unwind the "high" **(A)** end-stop screw (marked "H" on the derailleur, or with a wider line that is often hard to see since it's usually printed in little letters). Unscrew the "H" screw a couple of turns and retest.

Step 2: Once you've got the chain onto the big chainring, you need to make sure it won't go too far. With the chain still in the big chainring, gently roll in the "H" screw until you feel it touching the body of the derailleur — it will roll in fairly easily, then you will encounter resistance. At this point, back it off half a turn, and test again.

Step 3: Now try shifting into the smallest ring. Again, it should drop in first time. If not, you need to back off the low adjusting screw **(B)**. It will be marked with an "L" or with a narrower line. Test, adjust, then test again. Once the chain is in the small chainring, you need to set the "L" screw so it won't move too far. Wind it in, but watch the derailleur cage as you turn the screw, and stop as soon as you see that turning the screw is moving the cage. Test again.

Choosing the right type of derailleur

There are two basic types of derailleur: "conventional" and "top swing". The conventional type is the older design, where the clamp that attaches the front derailleur to the frame is higher than the derailleur cage. Top swing derailleurs have a cage that sits higher than the frame clamp. In most cases, the two are interchangeable, but some frame designs force you to use one or the other. This is especially true with full suspension frames, where the swingarm or pivots take up much of the available frame space in this area. If in doubt, replace your derailleur with the same type. Your frame will also dictate whether the front derailleur is "top pull" or "down pull." Down pull cables head down toward the bottom bracket, under the bottom bracket, and up the down tube. Top pull cables head straight upward, and along the top tube. As a small concession to simplification, some front derailleurs (for example, Shimano Deore) are made with a dual cable routing, so that they can be made to work with either down pull or top pull cables.

The third piece of information you need to know is your frame diameter. The three sizes are 28.6mm, 31.8mm and 34.9mm (1⅛ inch, 1¼ inch and 1⅜ inch respectively). Shimano Deore front derailleurs get points for simplicity since they come in one size (34.9) packaged with both the shims (spacers) needed to convert the derailleur to the smaller-frame sizes. An occasional variation are E-type derailleurs, which bolt onto the bottom bracket and are stabilized with either a clip around the seat tube or a bolt through a specific threaded hole on the frame. These types can be awkward: you cannot adjust the height of the derailleur since it is attached to the bottom bracket. Consequently they are only compatible with the chainring size for which they were designed. In summary, the three pieces of information you need to choose the correct bottom bracket are: 1) Conventional or top swing 2) Top pull or down pull 3) Clamp size (28.6, 31.8 or 34.9mm) or bottom bracket fitting type and chainring size.

FITTING A FRONT DERAILLEUR

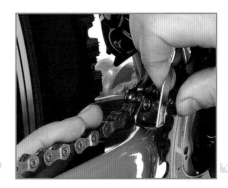

Step 1: Shift into the little chainring to release the tension on the gear cable. Undo the cable clamp bolt, and release the cable from the derailleur. Next, undo and remove the bolt that fixes the derailleur to the frame. Fold out the hinge that clamps around your frame and pull the derailleur away from the frame.

Step 2: The derailleur cage is still trapping the chain. Undo the small screw at the back of the derailleur cage. Ease the cage apart and slide the chain out. You will now be able to remove the old derailleur completely.

Step 3: Undo the bolt on the back of the new derailleur cage, then slide the chain into the cage, bending it as little as possible. Support the back of the cage on the chainstay, so it doesn't get bent as you refit the cage bolt firmly.

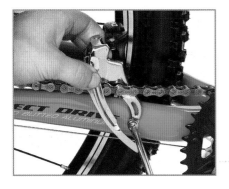

Step 4: Bolt the derailleur onto the frame. Start by positioning it at the same height as the old one. The correct height and angle have to be tested with the derailleur pulled out over the largest chainring.

Step 5: It's easiest if you test this by pulling it over by hand; things quickly get confusing if you connect the cable at this stage. If it won't pull over far enough, undo the outer end-stop screw (marked with a wider line or an "H"). Pull out so that the outer cage plate is directly above the outer chainring. The front part of the cage plate should be exactly parallel to the chainring. If it isn't, loosen the fixing bolt, swing the derailleur around, and check again.

Step 6: There should be a gap between the bottom of the outer derailleur plate and the top of the outer chainring of 1–3mm ($^1/_{16}$–$^1/_8$ inch). Test by pulling the derailleur out, then dropping it back and adjusting the height until it is right.

Adjusting a front derailleur

Turn the pedals and use the right-hand shifter to move the chain into the largest sprocket at the back. With the cable disconnected, the front derailleur should spring back toward the frame, pulling the chain onto the smallest chainring. If the chain doesn't drop onto the smallest chainring, you need to adjust the low limit screw (marked "L" on the derailleur). Undo the screw a turn, then turn the pedals again. Repeat until the chain drops into the smallest chainring. With the chain in the largest sprocket at the back and the smallest chainring at the front, adjust the "L" limit screw until there is 1–2mm ($^1/_{16}$–$^1/_8$ inch) clearance between the inside of the chain and the inner plate of the derailleur cage.

Pull the end of the still-disconnected gear cable gently and shift through the gears on the handlebars. You will feel the cable pull and release as you shift in either direction. Shift a few times to make sure the cable is in its most relaxed position. The chain should still be in the smallest chainring. Look carefully at the pinch bolt on the front derailleur, and check for the position of the groove under the cable clamp bolt. Lay the cable in place and pull gently with one hand, just enough to take up any slack in the cable. Tighten the clamp bolt.

Now use the instructions for fitting a new derailleur cable to adjust the cable tension (see page 115).

Servicing the front derailleur

Front derailleur cable tension pulls the cage outward, shifting your chain onto larger chainrings, but when you release the tension, the derailleur relies on a spring to pull the cage back toward the frame and to pull your chain onto smaller sprockets. If your pivots are dirty or worn, the spring won't be strong enough to pull back the change, and shifts into lower gears will be slow.

Front derailleur: clean and oil

If your front derailleur is on strike, your first remedy is a good clean with a long soak in light oil (WD40, GT85, Superlube). Periodically work the derailleur back and forth as far as you can — gradually increasing until you work across the full range of movements. This is easiest with the chainset removed. Dirt will probably ooze from the pivot points as you go. Wipe it off.

Oil all the pivot points carefully. Use the shifter to slacken off the cable; shift it into the smallest chainring position. Take hold of the derailleur cage, pull it out from the frame as far as it will go, and push it back. Repeat a couple of times to work the oil into the pivots. Once the cage is moving smoothly, wipe off all the excess oil — don't leave any oil on the surface of the derailleur: it's sticky and picks up more dirt. For extra points, clean the derailleur cable — see page 120.

Front derailleur: reshaping

The shape and condition of your front derailleur are crucial for reliable shifting. Old-fashioned front derailleurs consisted of two very simple flat plates, one on either side of the chain, which pushed the chain from side to side under the control of the front derailleur cable. Modern derailleurs are shaped to lift the chain quickly into place, allowing you to shift accurately under pressure. When new, they work faultlessly, but wear, crashes, and brutal gear changing will take their toll.

If you're having problems with your front shifting and adjusting the cable tension and end-stop doesn't cure it, it's worth inspecting the derailleur cage quite carefully. You can often identify the source of problems, and occasionally cure them, with some judicious bending. Check that the inside of the cage isn't worn out first though — the most usual problem area is the inside surface of the inner cage plate. This is the surface that pushes the chain from the middle chainring from the smallest one, and from middle to outer. It's tricky to get a good look, which is why wear in this area often goes unnoticed. Unless the derailleur is brand new, you'll see the marks where the chain has scraped across the cage. With time, these marks get deeper. If the marks are so deep that you can feel ridges with your fingers, the derailleur will need to be replaced — the chain will catch on these ridges as you change gear, twisting it rather than lifting it cleanly onto the next chainring. In extreme cases, the chain will wear all the way through the derailleur cage, and it will snap. Long before this, the clumsy changes will have worn and damaged your chain, so it makes good sense to replace worn derailleurs sooner rather than later.

If the derailleur isn't worn out, check the shape. The curve of the cage should match the shape of the chainring. The front section of the outer plate should be parallel to the chainring. The top section of the cage, which links the front plate to the back, should be flat and horizontal. Clumsy shifting bends the derailleur cage, preventing it from following the contour of the chainset.

Use pliers to bend the cage gently back into shape. Ideally, you need to reshape the derailleur with one movement — using the pliers to lever the cage backward and forwards will weaken the metal.

Check the condition of the derailleur pivots. Take hold of the back of the cage and wiggle it up and down. You will be able to feel the cage flex a little, but if you can rock it up and down, or you can feel it knocking, the pivots are worn out and the derailleur must be replaced.

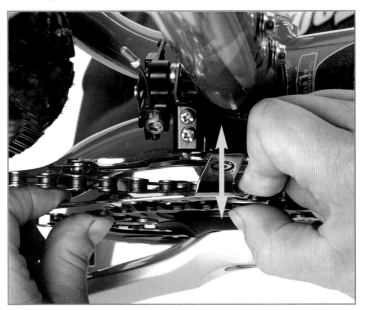

Work the derailleur back and forth ▶

Cable and outer casing

It's important to understand the differences between your gear and brake cables because they perform very different functions and require very different treatment. Here's the lowdown on these vital components.

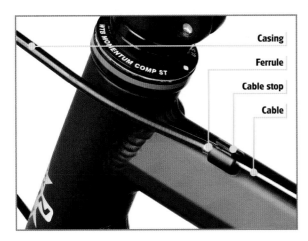

Casing

Ferrule

Cable stop

Cable

Cable: The wire that connects a shifter or lever to the component — it's usually silver

Casing: The cover that supports and guides the cable

Ferrule: A metal or plastic cap on the end of the casing that prevents the end of the casing from splaying out under pressure

Cable stop: The part of your frame that the outer casing slots into — a slot in the cable stop allows you to slide the cable out of the cable stop for cleaning

Cable end: A small metal cap that you squash over the end of the cable to prevent the cable fraying

Nipple: The blob on the end of the cable that fits into the lever or shifter, stopping the cable from pulling through

The outer casing used for gears is different to the casing used for brakes.

◆ Brake casing is made from tight spirals of square section wire.
◆ Gear casing is made from round section wire, formed into much longer spirals. It is covered in plastic (usually black), which protects the wire and keeps it in shape. It is lined with a Teflon tube (usually white) so that the inner cable moves smoothly inside.

The casings differ because they perform different functions. Brake casing must be very strong because it handles a lot of pressure. Gear casing must transmit a very accurate signal. When you shift from one gear to the next, you pull through mere millimeters of cable, so it is vital that the gear casing does not compress and influence the cable as you change gear or turn the handlebars. The long spirals prevent the gear casing from shortening under pressure, or as the sections of casing articulate with the bike.

The advantage of the tight spiral wind in brake casing is that while it is strong, when it fails, it does so gently. Gear casing cannot take so much pressure, but that's all right because gear levers are short, so you can't exert much pressure on them anyway. When the casing does fail, it tends to be catastrophic — the casing splits open and you get no shifting at all. Were this brake casing, this kind of failure would be bad news because the cable is likely to break under a strong braking force — that is, when you need it most.

Getting the cable and casing right is a cheap task that greatly improves your bike. It's worth changing the last section of outer casing (the piece that takes the cable into the rear derailleur) every time you change the inner cable, as it's nearest the ground. More expensive derailleurs have a boot (rubber gaiter) protecting the end of the cable and so they stay cleaner, but this piece of cable costs so little in relation to the importance of smooth changing that changing it is worthwhile.

The casing is really tough, so you need proper wirecutters to chop it to length — pliers won't do. It is important to cut the ends neatly and squarely — if you cut raggedly or at an angle the casing deforms as you change gear, making your shifting sloppy. Once you've cut the casing, check inside to ensure that the lining hasn't got squashed. If it has, open it out with the point of a sharp knife. Finish off the end of each length of casing with a ferrule. These protect the ends of the casing and stop them from splaying out.

Getting exactly the right length can be tricky. If the casing is too long, it adds friction to the cable, which again means sloppy shifting — the spring in the derailleur has to pull the slack that is created when you release cable at the shifter all the way back to the derailleur, so the less friction here the better. If the casing is too short, the inner cable will be constricted as it goes around tight bends. Care needs to be taken with sections of casing that join parts that move in tandem with each other; for example, the section of casing that joins the handlebars to the frame, or that join the frame to the derailleur. Dual suspension bikes need extra care with the sections that connect the main frame to the rear end. Make sure you have enough casing to allow suspension to move without stretching the casing. Ghost shifting is often caused by casing that is restricted or stretched. Replace these sections of casing every time you replace the inner cable. When the casing is the right length, it approaches the cable stops parallel to the frame and looks elegant. Check casing regularly for splits, cracks and kinks. Damaged casing should be replaced right away — it has a habit of being fine for a while, lulling you into a false sense of security, then it goes suddenly just when you're farthest from home, leaving you to limp back in the smallest sprocket or chainring.

The importance of cleaning cables and searching out hidden grime

The most common cause of sluggish shifting is the bits of the nice trail you rode down today that conceal themselves between cable and casing. Cleaning the bike can sometimes serve only to solidify the mud or dust so you have to be careful. Full suspension bikes suffer particularly badly — the loops of casing necessary to connect rear brake and gear cables across the central hinge are often a magnet for unwanted grit. Luckily, the cable stops on frames are slotted, allowing you to remove the casing and clean the sections of cable normally hidden within.

▲ **Pull casing forward and out of cable stop**

Inspect cable and casing before you start — if either are kinked, frayed or corroded, it's time to replace them.

For gear cables, lift your back wheel off the ground. Shift into the largest sprocket front and rear, then stop pedaling. Click your shifters as if changing into the smallest sprocket and smallest chainring.

For V-brake cables, squeeze the brake units together, slide back the rubber boot, and release the noodle from its hanger. For mechanical disc brakes, push the actuation lever upwards, as if applying the brake. This creates slack in the cable.

Follow the section of outer casing that emerges from the shifter or lever, to the cable stop on the frame. Pull the outer casing forward and wiggle the cable out of the slot in the cable slot. Repeat at all the other cable stops. Slide the sections of casing along the cable and clean all the concealed sections (a light oil such as GT85 or WD40 works well). Relubricate the cable with a heavier oil — whatever you use for your chain is perfect.

Slide the casings gently back into place, careful to avoid kinking the cable. Settle them back into the cable stops. For mechanical disc brakes, you need to pull the actuation lever up again to give yourself enough cable slack.

Reconnect the V-brake cable. For gear cables, lift up the back of the bike, and turn the pedals around to allow the chain to find a gear. You may need to operate the brake or gear levers several times to pull the outer casing firmly back into the cable stops.

Upgrade cable kits

The standard cable setup, with a steel cable running through a Teflon-lined casing, works well in most circumstances, as long as it's kept clean and lubricated. But a variety of upgrade cables are available that will last longer in messier environments. The simplest solution is to use a smooth inner wire that's been pre-coated with Teflon. These still need lubrication, but they will stay cleaner than standard cables and will reduce friction between cable and casing. They are slightly more expensive than standard cables but are no more difficult to fit.

Signed, sealed, delivered

A more extreme solution is to use a sealed cable kit — Gore-Tex cable kits are the most common example. These use a very smooth Gore-Tex coating (more commonly found as a waterproof, breathable jacket lining) on the cable. The kit comes with a plastic tube that protects the cable through its entire length. A rubber boot guards the end of the cable, stopping mud, grit or sand from creeping into the gap between cable and protective lining. The Gore-Tex coating has to be stripped off the end of the cable, so that it can be clamped securely. These sets are tricky to set up, so follow the instructions that come with the pack carefully. Once fitted, though, the cables and casings are good quality and last much longer than standard cables. They're worth the extra money and effort.

The advantages and disadvantages of different types of shifters

Shifters come in different types, but they all do the same job. When you move them one way, they pull precise amounts of gear cable to move your chain across your cassette. When you move them the other way, they release a precise amount of cable, allowing the spring in the derailleur to move the chain the opposite way across your cassette.

There are two main types: twistshifters rotate around the handlebars, while triggershifters have two separate levers, one to pull cable and one to release. Of the two big companies that make shifters, Shimano mainly make triggershifters, called Rapidfire, and SRAM make both.

Both types — twistshifters and triggershifters — have loyal fans because, in practice, they both work fine. In situations where your grip is likely to get very slippery, triggershifters have a slight advantage, but twistshifters are less vulnerable to damage in a crash because they don't have any protruding levers. Twistshifters also have fewer moving parts, so they are a little more reliable, and can be taken apart and serviced. The internals of triggershifters consist of lots of tiny parts, which were originally assembled by a huge triggershifter-making machine, and are too small to fit by hand.

Thumbshifters

Occasionally, you will still come across an old-style thumbshifter — a single lever that sits on top of the bars; you push it forward to draw cable through and pull back to release cable. Some of these, like old XTII seven-speed thumbshifters, have a capacity to generate misty-eyed moments of tender memory in old and cynical bike mechanics. They also work really well, performing a simple task in a simple way, without needing exotic materials or computer-aided design. The levers were big and chunky so they could be easily operated with frozen hands . . . so many advantages, they obviously had to go.

Combination units

Shifters are either separate from the brake lever or part of the same unit. They work the same whether or not they are connected. If you are fitting a combination unit, fit the shifter as if it was separate, then go to the brake chapter for the brake procedure.

Combination units are slightly lighter because brake and gear levers share a clamp, but the positions of the brake and gear levers obviously cannot be adjusted separately. Having combined brake and gear units also forces you to use the brake system specific to that manufacturer: for example, a Shimano XT combined brake and gear lever will be compatible only with Shimano hydraulic brakes.

Whichever type you have, remember that you are constantly working the shifter back and forth. The ratcheting mechanism inside, which holds the shifter in your chosen gear, will inevitably wear, so expect to have to replace your shifters every couple of years. The first signs are usually that your shifter fails to stay in your chosen gear, allowing the chain to slip back into the next smallest chainring or sprocket. You'll feel this start to happen first in the gears you use most often.

Whichever type of shifter you have, the derailleur adjustment works in the same way, so use this section to fit your cable or new shifter, clamp the new cable onto the relevant derailleur, then go to the derailleur adjustment section to tune your gears.

◀◀ **Triggershifters use two separate levers to change cable tension**

◀ **With twistshifters, rotating the grip changes the cable tension**

Fitting a new gear cable — triggershifters

Fitting a new gear cable is the easiest and cheapest way to upgrade your shifting. You'll need to arm yourself with a 5mm Allen key and a decent pair of cable cutters, as well as new cable, casing and ferrules for the ends of the sections of casing.

The procedure for changing cables is the same for front and rear shifters. Rear gear cables need changing more often because the section of cable near the back wheel gets filled with dust and mud easily, making your shifting sluggish. For either derailleur, cut off the cable end and undo the cable clamp bolt at the derailleur. Pull the cable gently out of each section of outer casing in turn. Work all the way to the shifter, so that you end up with bare cable hanging out of the end of the shifter.

Follow the three steps below to fit the new gear cable to the shifter, then route the new cable back through the outer casing to each derailleur. It's definitely worth changing the last section of outer casing on rear derailleurs every time, and on any other sections that are kinked, splayed or dirty inside. If in doubt, change it! Cut each new section to length, using the old sections as a guide. Cutting the casing often squashes the lining inside — use a sharp knife to reopen the end of the lining. Fit ferrules to either end of every section of casing.

As you feed the cable through the casing, check that it slides freely. If the inner cable doesn't run smoothly through the casing now, the gears won't work properly when you connect them. Replace any sections of casing that feel rough or sticky when you push cable through them. If you must use doughnuts (little protective rubber rings that stop the cable scratching the frame paint), use no more than two and make sure they're black. Feed the wire through the barrel-adjuster on the derailleur.

Check the action of the shifter by clicking through its range while pulling the cable gently away from the shifter — you should feel the shifter pulling cable through in steps. Release it in discrete jumps as you shift back. Replace any hatches that you removed from the shifter.

Now go to the sections on front and rear derailleurs on page 124.

'04 XTR

2004 XT and XTR shifters come as a combined unit with the downshift activated by the brake lever. The design is a cousin to the STI shifters that have become almost universal on road bikes. For cable fitting, follow the procedures for triggershifters, treating the brake lever as a gear shifter. To access the cable, remove the cover on these with a Phillips screwdriver.

FITTING A NEW GEAR CABLE

Step 1: The head of the cable may be hidden under a hatch on the back of the shifter, between and above the triggers. Use a Phillips screwdriver to undo the screw, and be ready to catch it as it falls out — it's quite short and will run away if you give it a chance. (Some Shimano pods — e.g. XT — have a hatch with two very small crosshead screws. These escape easily too.) Once you've removed the hatch, line up the slot on the barrel-adjuster with the slot on the shifter.

Step 2: Pull the old cable gently away from the shifter. Click the front trigger repeatedly. You'll feel the cable releasing a step at a time as you click. Repeat until you can't click any further — the cable will be in its slackest position. Push the loose end gently into the shifter. In this position, the head of the cable will emerge from the hatch. Pull it out. You may need to twist the cable slightly to free it. For shifters with a slotted barrel, pull the cable gently out of the slot.

Step 3: Without changing gear, look through the hatch from the end of the bar — you'll see the exit hole for the cable. Feed the cable through the shifter, pulling it firmly home so that the head of the cable sits snugly in its nest in the shifter. Next, feed the cable back through each section of outer casing in turn. Drip a drop of oil onto the cable as you feed it though each section, and push the ferrule at the end of each section firmly into its cable stop on the frame.

Fitting a new gear cable— twistshifters

SRAM GripShift cables have an undeserved reputation for being difficult to fit. The very first models were a bit of a three-dimensional jigsaw puzzle, but current designs are much easier. Check your old casing lengths as a guide to fitting new ones.

Remove old cable and casing, cutting off the old cable about 15cm (6 inches) before it enters the shifter. You'll need to shift into a particular gear to expose the head of the cable. When you look at your gear indicators, one may be a different color than the others, or one of the numbers may have a circle drawn around it. If all the numbers look the same, shift into the highest number on the right-hand shifter (8 or 9) and into 1 on the left-hand side.

FITTING TWISTSHIFTERS

Step 1: Pull gently on the cable as it enters the shifter through the barrel-adjuster, and shift into the correct gear. Remove the escape hatch or slide it to one side (sometimes this needs a little help from a screwdriver or pliers), and look into the shifter. You may see the head of the nipple, or the head of a 2.5mm Allen key grub screw, or a black plastic cover over half the nipple. If it's a grub screw, remove it completely. Careful not to lose the screw — they yearn for freedom.

Step 2: If it's a plastic cover, pry it gently back with a small screwdriver. Push the exposed cable into the shifter. The nipple will emerge through the hatch. Pull the cable out of the shifter.

Step 3: Without moving the shifter, slide the new inner cable in through the shifter. It will not feed in properly if the end of the cable is frayed, so cut off any untidiness. Pull it all the way through, make sure not to let the new cable dangle on the ground and pick up dirt. Replace the 2.5mm grub screw, if there was one, and tighten it firmly onto the nipple. Refit the escape hatch.

Other varieties of twistshifter

Some versions of twistshifters don't have a removable hatch — instead, the nipple is concealed under the edge of the rubber grip. Shift into the highest number on the right-hand shifter, or 1 on the left-hand shifter, and peel back the grip gently just below the row of numbers. You'll see the nipple — push the cable up through the barrel-adjuster, and the nipple will emerge from the shifter. Feed the new cable back through without changing gear.

The end of the cable needs to be in good condition to pass freely through the shifter. It's easiest with new cables, which usually have a small blob of solder at the ends to stop them unraveling. Otherwise, use a good pair of cable cutters to make a clean square end on the cable. It can also help to make a slight bend in the cable about 2cm (¾ inch) from the end. Then twist the cable slightly as you feed it through the shifter. As you pull the cable through the shifter, lubricate the last section, which ends up inside the shifter. Jonnisnot, or other similar plastic-specific grease, is ideal.

Fitting a new cable to the front and rear derailleurs

Fit the new cable into your shifters first, using the instructions on page 122, then follow these steps to connect the cable to your front or rear derailleur. You'll need to adjust the cable tension once you've fitted the cables; see page 108.

Rear derailleur

For the rear derailleur, push the cable through the barrel-adjuster on the back of the derailleur. Lift the back wheel off the ground and turn the pedals so that the chain returns to its neutral position — the smallest sprocket for most derailleurs, the largest for rapid-rise types. For rapid-rise, see below. Screw the barrel-adjuster all the way into the derailleur (turning it so the top of the barrel moves towards you), then back out a couple of complete turns. Look carefully at the cable-pinch bolt; there are often several possible ways to fit the cable under it, and only one of them makes your gears work properly. Look for a groove or a slot indicating the right place. The most common place is on the far side of the pinch bolt, pointing almost straight forward. Once you have the cable in the right place on the pinch bolt, pull it gently to the right, toward the front of the bike. Use the shifters to step all the way down and up through the gears. You should feel the cable pull your hand towards the derailleur as you shift down, then relax so your hand moves away as you shift up. Keeping a gentle pressure on the cable, change all the way up so that the cable is at its most relaxed and your hand is furthest from the derailleur. Guide the cable under the cable-clamp bolt, and tighten up with a 9mm wrench or 5mm Allen key. Turn the pedals and shift all the way across the gears and back again. This will shake out any slack, so undo the pinch bolt again, gently pull through any slack cable, and tighten the pinch bolt firmly. Cut off excess cable and fit a cable end. Now you have to adjust the indexing; see page 106.

Rapid-rise rear derailleurs

Push the cable through the barrel-adjuster on the back of the rear derailleur. Lift the back wheel off the ground and turn the pedals so that the chain returns to its neutral position — the largest sprocket. Screw the barrel-adjuster all the way into the derailleur (turning it so that the top of the barrel moves towards you), then back out a couple of complete turns. Pass the cable under the clamp bolt — a groove in the derailleur will indicate the correct place. Use the shifters to step all the way down and up through the gears. You should feel the cable pull your hand towards the derailleur as you shift up, then relax so your hand moves away as you shift down. Keeping a gentle pressure on the cable, change all the way down so that the cable is at its most relaxed and your hand is furthest from the derailleur. Guide the cable under the cable clamp bolt and tighten up with a 5mm Allen key. Turn the pedals and shift all the way across the gears and back again to the largest sprocket. This will shake out any slack in the cable, so undo the pinch bolt again, gently pull through any slack cable, and tighten the pinch bolt firmly. Cut off excess cable and fit a cable end.

Front derailleur

Pull gently on the cable and shift back and forth to get familiar with the effect the shifter has on the cable. You need to start with the cable in its slackest position, which will correspond to the chain being in the smallest chainring. Before you fit the cable, check the derailleur is properly fitted on the frame. The derailleur is harder to adjust if it's not fitted correctly. Take hold of the cage and pull it out from the frame so that the outer plate of the cage is level with the outer chainring. You may have to manually lift the chain onto the middle chainring.

The front section of the outer plate of the derailleur cage should be exactly parallel with the chainring. There should be a gap between the top of the chainring teeth and the bottom of the derailleur cage of 1mm–3mm (1/16–1/8 inch). If either of these needs adjusting, let the cage spring back towards the frame. Loosen off the derailleur fixing bolt (usually with a 5mm Allen key), move the derailleur, retighten the fixing bolt, and check again. You may need to repeat this several times. Feed the cable under the cable clamp bolt. A very common error is to fit the cable the wrong way around the bolt. Check the derailleur carefully — it has a distinct slot or groove where you are supposed to put the cable. Generally, if the cable comes up from below, it sits behind the clamp bolt. If it comes down from above, it sits in front of the clamp bolt. Keep a gentle pressure on the cable and tighten the clamp bolt firmly, making sure that the entire diameter of the cable is trapped between the clap bolt and the derailleur. Turn the pedals and shift through the gears several times. Don't worry if the chain won't reach the largest chainring at this stage. Shift back into the smallest chainring. Undo the cable clamp bolt, pull through any slack cable by hand, and retighten the cable clap bolt. Cut off any excess cable, bend it back so that it doesn't get caught in the chain, and squash on an end cap. Now you will have to adjust the indexing; see page 115.

Fitting triggershifters

Shifters will wear out over time. The levers can be vulnerable in crashes. Occasionally they have a tendency to get tangled up when you pack your bike into cars, snapping off when you pull them out. It's surprising how crisp new ones feel — you don't notice the old ones getting sloppy and sluggish until you replace them.

New shifters almost always come supplied with a new cable, already fitted, which saves you from having to load the cable into the shifter. It's worth taking a bit of care when fitting the new shifter though — avoid bending the cable where it emerges from the barrel-adjuster. Kinks in the cable will make it difficult to adjust your cable tension accurately. The boxes in which new shifters are packaged are carefully constructed to protect the cable; if you take the shifters out of the box to have a look at them, make sure you repack them carefully until you're ready to fit them to your bike. Don't allow the cable to drag on the ground, where it will pick up dirt. Keep it coiled up until you're ready to fit it into the shifter.

Since you're fitting a new shifter with a new cable, it's worth replacing the outer casing at the same time. The old casing will have picked up dirt, which will quickly transfer itself to the new cable, making it sluggish. Make sure to fit ferrules on either end of each section of outer casing. Some shifters come supplied with outer casing — you'll need good-quality cutters to shorten these to the correct length. Use your old casing as a guide when you cut the new lengths.

Once you've fitted the new shifter, use the instructions on page 124 to attach the cables to your front or rear derailleurs. Left-hand shifters operate front derailleurs, right-hand shifters operate rear derailleurs.

Fitting triggershifters

Remove bar ends and grips. Even if you're replacing the grips at the same time, don't cut them off, because you risk scratching the surface of the handlebar, which can weaken it. The ideal tool is a chopstick — slide this between the grip and the bar, spray light lube under the grip, twist the grip and pull it off the handlebar. (Chopsticks are very useful. Keep any you get with takeout noodles in your toolbox. If

you don't ever get takeout noodles, live a little more.) Slide the grip off the end of the handlebars. Undo the Allen key that fixes the brake lever on, then undo the fixing bolt for your old shifters. Slide both off the ends of the bars. If they won't slide off easily, use a screwdriver to lever the fixing clamps a open a little bit — just enough to get the levers and pods off without scratching the bars.

Slide the new shifters on, then slide on the brake levers, easing the clamps open in the same way if neccesary. Leave both fixing bolts loose, then refit grips and bar ends. Everyone swears by different stuff for this — spray lube, degreaser, hairspray (my favorite), Photomount, Renthal Grip Glue from motorcycle shops and more. If you don't have any such gear, pop the grips in a bowl of hot water for a few minutes, then slide them on, taking care not to burn yourself. Sit on your bike in your normal riding position, and roll brake and gear levers around to a comfortable position. If you're not sure, start with the brake levers at about 45 degrees to the ground, with the gear shifters tucked up close underneath them. If you have big hands, you might want to leave a gap between the ends of the grips and the brake levers. Once you've got the position right, tighten both brake levers and gear shifters firmly. Thread the cables through the outer casing, lubricating sections of cable that will end up inside casing with chain oil. Follow the instructions on pages 124 and 108 to attach cables to front and rear derailleurs and to adjust the cable tension.

Check that the grips have stuck firmly — don't ride away until you know they have!

▲ **Ease the shifter clamp open to avoid scratching the bars**

◀ **Experiment with a comfortable angle for the shifters, then tighten the fixing bolt firmly**

Fitting twistshifters

SRAM make two different types of shifter. Those with names, like "Rocket", are designed for a 1:2 actuation ratio and so are compatible with all Shimano rear derailleurs, as well as SRAM rear derailleurs with names. Shifters that are called by numbers, like "7.0" or "9.0," have a 1:1 actuation ratio, and are only compatible with SRAM numbered rear derailleurs. All front derailleurs work fine with either type of shifter.

Fresh twistshifters aren't difficult to fit, especially as new ones come complete with a cable already installed. Keep this coiled up until you've installed the shifter on the handlebar and are ready to slide the cable into its outer casing. This stops it from dragging on the ground, picking up dirt. ·

As you're installing the shifters, avoid kinking the cable as it enters the barrel-adjuster. It's a vulnerable point until you've supported the cable by sliding it through the outer casing.

Remove any bar ends and plugs. Then remove the short section of static grip — the section that stays still when you change gear. If you are replacing it, simply cut it off. Slide in a chopstick or similar instrument gently between the grip and the bar, without scratching the bar. Spray light lube under the grip and slide it off.

Find the clamp bolt for the twistshifters. These have come in a couple of different sizes over the years — usually small! Undo it enough to loosen the shifter — you don't need to remove the bolt completely. Then gently slide the shifter off. Slide the new shifter onto the bar and set its position so that the barrel-adjuster and gear cable run under the brake lever. I like to set the position so that the barrel-adjuster is as close as possible to the brake lever, but you have to leave enough room to turn the barrel-adjuster. Tighten the shifter clamp bolt.

Slide the plastic washer onto the bars so that it sits against the end of the shifter. Next, fit the static grip back on. These are shorter than standard grips, so you need to take extra care that they are firmly stuck. For extra grip, tighten a ziptie around the outboard end of the grip. If this doesn't do the job, your grips are worn out and should be replaced with new, tighter ones. Special short twistshift-compatible versions are available, but they're no cheaper than cutting a standard pair to length with a sharp knife or a pair of scissors.

Refit any bar ends and bar-end plugs

Next, the cable must be threaded through the outer casing. It's worth replacing this when you've got this far. It's only a little extra effort, and saves you transferring old dirt onto fresh cable. New shifters usually, although not always, come supplied with lengths of fresh outer casing. If they don't, pick some up from your bike shop, along with enough ferrules to fit on each end of each section of casing. Cut the new sections of casing to length by comparing them with the old sections, fit the ferrules, and slot the casing into the cable stops on

Barrel-adjuster

your bike. Check the length of each section of casing — they should make graceful but not excessive curves. Extra length just adds friction, but if the sections of casing are too short, the casings will kink, squashing the cable inside. Check particularly sections between handlebars and frame, and sections where the casing runs from the main frame of the bicycle to rear suspension section — the cable should be long enough to allow these parts to move freely. Slide the cable carefully through each section, with a little oil on parts that will end up inside casing. Exposed parts of the cable don't need lubrication, excess oil will only serve to pick up dirt. Once you've routed the cable back to the derailleur, use the instructions on pages 124 and 108 to fit the cable to the derailleur and adjust the tension.

◀ **Set the position of the shifter, so that you can still turn the barrel-adjuster**

Servicing triggershifters and twistshifters

Crisp gear changes rely on your shifter pulling through and releasing precise lengths of cable every time you change gear. Over time, the teeth that hold the shifter in each individual gear position become worn, so that your shifting becames vague. This is annoying, but it will also accelerate your chain wear whenever the chain runs at an angle off the sprockets rather than approaching the rear derailleur vertically.

Servicing triggershifters

There's little you can do with triggershifter pods once they are worn out; you can't get parts for them, and even if you could, your fingers need to be about half size if they are to have any hope of fitting them. This is particularly irritating if your shifter and brake lever are integral, as you will need to replace both levers and shifters. I prefer to fit separate brake levers and shifters — combined units are slightly lighter, but it's nice to be able to adjust the positioning of each independently and to replace them separately.

Servicing twistshifters

Only lubricate the shifters with plastic-specific grease, for example, Finish Line GripShift grease. Other lubricants may contain petrochemical traces, which affect the plastic in the componentry. It's easiest to do this job after taking out the old cable and before fitting the new cable.

Remove the shifters from the handlebars as described above. Different ones split apart in different ways. Commonly, there's a Phillips head bolt on the part of the shifter that curves down and has the cable coming out of it, which you remove along with the plastic cover through which it bolts. This releases the two halves. Gently pull them apart — you must see how the parts inside are assembled, especially the spring, which is a curved metal strip. This spring must go back in the same place, the same way round — draw a picture if you're not sure. Rocket shifters pull apart by squeezing the tabs at the outer end of the shifter — when fitted to your bike, the bars fit through the middle of the shifter and prevent the shifter from disassembling itself.

Clean the separated parts with soapy water, dry, and lubricate with a little plastic grease (see above). Reassemble the parts, according to your drawing (if you have made one). Gently wiggle the two halves back together. This is usually easiest with the shifter set to the lowest position. Refit the plastic cover and bolt, and refit the shifter onto the bar. Fit the cable and proceed as on page 124.

Toolbox

Tools for adjusting your cable tension
- 5mm allen key

Tools for fitting new cables
- 5mm Allen key, or 9mm wrench
- Good wirecutters

Tools to fit new rear derailleur
- 5 or 6mm Allen key for fixing bolt and cable clamp bolt
- Tools for fitting cables, as above

Tools to fit new front derailleur
- 5 or 6mm Allen key (see above)
- Tools for fitting cables, as above

Tools for fitting or repairing chains
- Good chain tool, e.g. Park or Shimano
- For Shimano—correct (eight- or nine-speed) special replacement rivet
- For SRAM chains – Powerlink

Tools for cassettes
- Chain whip
- Cassette tool
- Large adjustable wrench, to drive cassette tool

Tools for freewheels
- Correct freewheel tool—usually Shimano splined freewheel tool

- Large adjustable wrench, to drive freewheel tool

Tools to fit triggershifters
- 5mm Allen key
- Good wirecutters

Tools for chainsets and chainrings
- Crank-extractor, narrow version for square taper cranks, wide version for others
- Convertion plug for splined cranks
- Wrench or adjustable to drive crank extractor
- 5mm Allen key for chainring bolts
- Shimano chainring bolt tool

Removing and refitting chainsets for fun and profit

Why do you need to remove your chainset? There are several reasons. Either to fit a new one, to fit a new bottom bracket, to tighten your current bottom bracket in the frame, to fit new chainrings, or to clean properly behind the chainset. You might also need to access suspension bushings or bolts behind there.

Removing chainsets and cranks

◆ Remove both crank bolts. Most cranks are bolted on with an 8mm Allen key. Crank bolts must be snugly fitted, so you need a long Allen key for fitting and removal — use one that is at least 200mm (8 inches) long, otherwise you won't be able to free the bolt or refit it properly at the end. Both crank bolts have conventional threads that undo counterclockwise. Check inside the crank recess for any washers and remove them.

◆ Look into the hole that the bolt came out of. It is one of two types, an older square taper, or a newer splined taper, which will look like a notched circle. If you have an older crank extractor designed for square taper axles and a splined taper you need a special plug to pop into the end of the axle, so that the crank extractor doesn't simply disappear down inside the axle without pushing it out. If you need to get one, Shimano makes one: TLFC15.

◆ The crank extractor consists of two parts, one threaded inside the other. The outer part bolts onto the threads in the crank, the inner part then gets wound in, pushing the axle out of the crank. Before you fit the tool onto the crank, wind the inner part out so that it disappears inside the body of the tool. Hold the body of the tool steady with one wrench and wind the shaft counterclockwise.

◆ Clean the threads inside the crank and grease them. They are cut into the soft alloy of the crank and must be treated with respect. It's very easy to accidentally strip them with the harder threads of the crank extractor, an expensive mistake to remedy. Start the crank extractor in the crank threads by hand, then tighten home with a wrench. Don't go crazy.

◆ Wind in the extractor shaft using the correct size of wrench. It turns quite easily until the shaft touches the end of the axle, then gets harder as it starts to push the axle out of the chainset. Once it's moving through the crank, it should slide off easily. It helps to brace the crank against the wrench so they are as parallel as possible. Keep your arms straight and use your shoulder muscles to apply the force. On the chainring side, keep your knuckles well away from the chainrings — the wrench gives suddenly, and skinned knuckles are common.

◆ Once you've got the cranks off, look at them. Left-hand cranks are particularly prone to damage where they fit onto the bottom bracket axle. The thread is a normal right-hand thread, so if the crank gets a little loose, your pedaling action tends to loosen it further, until every pedal stroke deforms the mating surface between the crank and the bottom bracket axle. Square taper cranks are more prone to this than splined ones, but both need to be checked carefully. If the square taper or splines are damaged, the crank or chainset must be replaced — the taper splines will continue to work loose and will eventually damage the matching surface of your bottom bracket.

Refitting chainsets and cranks

Refitting is much easier than removing — the crank bolt acts as a refitting tool, so you won't need the crank extractor. Clean the ends of the axle and the hole in the crank or chainset. Some people like to grease the taper or splines, but I find this just makes the cranks creak as you pedal so I leave them dry. Titanium axles are the only exception to this — they need to be generously coated with Ti-prep.

Slide the chainset onto the axle. Grease the threads of the crank bolt, and grease under the head of the bolt. The crank bolts for splined bottom brackets use a fatter bolt with a separate washer, which needs a bit of grease on both sides. Older, 14mm wrench-type bolts have an integral washer. Fit the crank bolt and tighten firmly. You will not be able to get enough leverage with a standard length Allen key — use one with a handle that's at least 200mm (8 inches) long. Line the left-hand crank up so that it points in the opposite direction — this can be tricky with splined bottom brackets — and refit the crank bolt.

Retighten both cranks after your first ride.

If you have a torque wrench, this is one of the places where it's most useful — undertightened cranks will quickly work loose. Recommended torques for crank bolts are generally between 35–50Nm. See page 23 for more information on torque settings.

One-key release crank bolt

This part doubles as a crank extractor, so you can remove the cranks with just an 8mm Allen key. The crank cover is aluminum, rather than the standard plastic, and it is screwed into the cranks. The edge of the crank bolt head sits under the crank cover, so that as you undo the crank bolt it bears on the inside of the crank cover and pushes the axle off the crank.

With this, it's even more important to have a good long Allen key; you won't be able to undo the bolt with an ordinary-length key. Use the Allen key to undo the crank bolt. It will be stiff at first, then will turn quite easily for a short way, and will become stiff again as the crank bolt begins to force the crank off. Keep turning, and the crank will be pushed off the axle. You should take the one-key release gadget off periodically and grease the parts. These tools will only work if the threads are well-lubricated and the parts are clean. There are two small holes in the crank cover that you turn to remove the cover. You can buy a pin wrench to do this job, although a pair of needle-nose pliers also work fine. For fitting and removing details, see page 128.

Chainline

Your chain is at its most efficient when it's running in a straight line. Singlespeed bikes are always set up so that the chainring and chain are directly in line with each other to waste as little energy as possible.

For everyone else, in order for gears to work, the chain has to be able to move from side to side across the sprockets and across the chainrings. It will be running at an angle for most gear combinations. The most extreme combinations, in which the chain is on the big chainring and big sprocket, or on the small chainring and small sprocket, should be avoided, as chain, chainrings, and sprockets will wear quickly. Setting the position of the chainring so that the middle of the chainset lines up with the middle of the cassette will reduce the angle that the chain has to make to reach all the other positions to a minimum.

The chainset is bolted onto the bottom bracket axle, so changing the length of the bottom bracket will alter its position from side to side. A longer bottom bracket will move the chainset further out, so that it aligns with a smaller sprocket on the cassette, and vice versa. Bad chainline will cause unreliable shifting and accelerate chain wear.

To check your chainline, change gear so that you're in the middle chainring at the front and the middle sprocket at the back (or the fourth smallest for eight-speed sprockets). Look along the chain from behind the bike, so that you can see it pass over the cassette, forward and then over the chainring. The sprockets and chainrings should be in a straight line. A little bit of an angle is acceptable, but if the chain aligns better in the smallest or largest chainring, you will need to change the length of your bottom bracket to improve your chainline. Also look at the gap between your chainrings and your chainstay. There should be a clearance of at least 3mm ($^3/_{16}$ inch) **(A)** between the chainstay and any part of the chainring. The chainring will flex under pressure, and it will eat the chainstay if it's too close.

The position of the chainset on the bottom bracket will vary from model to model, so you may find that changing your chainset alters your chainline, sitting it farther from or nearer to the bike. When swapping chainsets, be aware that you may also need to swap your bottom bracket. To make things a little easier, all chainsets have a recommended bottom bracket length, which you will find printed in the chainset instructions.

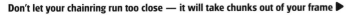

Don't let your chainring run too close — it will take chunks out of your frame ▶

Chainrings: removal, sizes, orientation, fitting and wear

All but the cheapest chainsets are made up of a spider and separate rings. The spider is the crank, with four or five arms onto which the chainrings bolt. There have been a number of different sizes and shapes of chainrings over the years, each with plausible reasons for existing, resulting in incompatibility between all the different versions. Whatever the science, it makes sense to take your bike or your old chainring to the shop when you buy a new one to make sure you get the right size.

Chainrings are machined to help the chain move across it when you change gear. The most difficult change for the chain to make is from the smallest to the middle ring, so good-quality middle chainrings are shaped to facilitate the change. They often have little ramps riveted onto the sides to lift the chain when it's halfway across. When the chain moves onto a bigger chainring, it has to lift itself up and over each tooth on the new chainring before it can settle in the valley between two teeth and do some work. Good chainrings are designed to make this shift as easy as possible.

Chainrings under pressure

The chain moves across the chainrings most easily when it's not under too much pressure, so chainrings are designed to encourage the chain to move across when the pedals are at the top or bottom of your pedal stroke, when you put least pressure on them. On many chainrings, these teeth are shorter than the ones on either side to make it easier for the chain to climb over them and drop into place.

It's all right for these teeth to be shorter. Because of their position on the chainring they don't get as much wear as those that are engaged when your pedals are level with the ground. It can be disconcerting though, to buy a new chainset and find that some teeth are shorter than you expect!

Chainsuck

Worn chainrings are a major source of chainsuck (for more on this, see page 132) — and a sign that you've been out riding having fun, so you're going to have to get used to replacing them. Worn chainrings also stretch your chain quickly, so changing them is a good investment.

You should be able to tell that your chainring is worn by looking at it and comparing it to these pictures. If you wait until a chainring is so badly worn that the chain slips across it, you're too late! You will usually find that one ring wears before the others, usually the one you use the most. It's fine to change rings one at a time, they don't have to be done all at once. When changing your cassette and chain, it's a good time to also change your most worn chainring.

Changing chainrings can be done with the chainset still on the bike, but the job is easiest if you remove it, saving yourself from bleeding knuckles too. Follow the instruction in the section on removing your chainset. The left-hand crank does not need to be removed.

Once you've removed the chainset, turn it over to see what type it is. The chainrings are either bolted to the crank arm using an Allen key, or are attached with a lockring and a retaining ring.

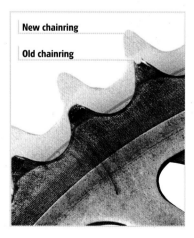

New chainring

Old chainring

Worn teeth mean the chain ▶ slips over the chainring

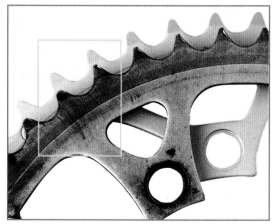

Replacing chainrings

Chainrings need to be replaced if they start to look like those on the previous page or if your chain skips across the teeth under pressure. The teeth that wear fastest are those under the most pressure — the ones at the top and bottom of the chainring when the cranks are horizontal. If your chainring teeth are worn sharp or the faces of the teeth are splayed outwards, replace the chainring.

Bent teeth will catch on your chain as you pedal, preventing the chain from dropping off the chainring at the bottom of each pedal stroke. This doesn't necessarily mean a new chainring though. Remove the chainring, as below, and clamp it flat in a vice. Support the chainring as near as possible to the bent tooth and ease it gently straight with pliers. Try to do this in one movement — sawing the bent tooth back and forward will weaken it.

REPLACING YOUR CHAINRING

Step 1: The smallest chainring must be removed first. Rest the chainset on a workbench or the floor, protecting the teeth of the largest sprocket with cardboard. Use an Allen key to undo all the bolts on the smallest chainring a half-turn, then go round removing them completely. Look at the orientation of the chainring. Note whether they face inward or outward. If any chainrings have spacing washers, note their location so you can refit them afterwards.

Step 2: Undo each of the Allen keys holding the middle and outer rings a half-turn each, and then go back around and remove them completely. Be careful undoing these bolts; they are hard to shift, then give suddenly, so mind your knuckles. Mostly, an Allen key does the job, but sometimes the nut on the back of the chainring moves around. A special tool, called a chainring bolt tool, is made for holding this and is available from your bike shop.

Step 3: As you remove the chainrings, note their orientation. There will often be a tab on the middle chainring and a peg on the outer chainring — both of these will have to line up with the crank when you refit the chainrings. Check which way the chainrings face — the middle chainring may have plates riveted to the inside face. Check also if there are any washers between the chainrings, as you will need to replace these correctly.

Step 4: Clean the chainrings and check them for wear. You put most force on your pedals when your cranks are horizontal, so the two areas of chainring at 90° to the crank will wear fastest. Hooked or pointed teeth, like the ones in this picture, will not mesh properly with your sprocket. This chainring will need replacing. Take worn chainrings with you when you go to buy new ones, so that you can match up the bolt pattern.

Step 5: Clean the crank, especially the arms that the chainrings bolt onto — clean out the bolt holes. Clean any of the old rings that you reuse. Check them carefully for bent teeth or teeth that have splayed under pressure. Bent teeth can be carefully bent back; the alignment is critical, so take your time about it. Splayed teeth are a sign that the ring needs to be replaced.

Step 6: Reassemble middle and outer chainrings. Be sure to get the orientation and position right — line up chainring tabs with your cranks. If your crank has a chainring bolt underneath it, orientate the chainring, so the tab is directly opposite the crank. Refit any washers. Grease the bolt threads, and refit them one at a time. Tighten each one firmly home, but don't go crazy — the bolts have a fine thread and snap if you overtighten. Refit the smallest chainring.

Chainsuck: causes and remedies

You don't realize how annoying chainsuck is until your bike is infected. Then you can't stop talking about it until it's cured — which can take patience as chainsuck has several different causes and is sometimes caused by a combination of factors.

What is chainsuck?

Normally as you pedal, you push down on the cranks, and the teeth on the chainrings mesh with the links on the chain, dragging it forward. The links on the chain also mesh with the teeth on the sprockets, dragging them around, which makes the wheel go around. As each section of chain is dragged around the chainring, it drops off the bottom and is pulled back around again.

Chainsuck happens when the chain fails to drop off the bottom of the chainset and, instead of heading backward toward the cassette, it stays stuck to the chainring, getting dragged up and around it as you pedal. It rapidly gets jammed in the gap between chainring and frame, the entire drivetrain locks, and you fall off your bike. To add insult to injury, the chain often takes chunks out of the chainstay.

The problem usually lies with the smallest chainring, but it can also happen in the middle chainring, and sometimes even in the big one.

Worn chain, chainring, or both

When both the chain and chainring are new, the distance between each link in the chain is the same as the distance between each tooth on the chainring. When you put pressure on the pedals, dragging the chain around the chainring, the pressure is taken up by only the top few teeth. The pressure gradually reduces in each link as the teeth progress round the chainring, until at the bottom of the ring the links are released entirely and drop off freely, as intended. The pressure from the pedals is spread over just those few teeth at the top of the chainring, reducing the amount each chainring wears.

Once either chainring or chain is worn, nothing works so well. A worn chain on a fresh chainring engages only a single tooth at the top of the chainring, accelerating chainring wear. The chain links at the bottom of the chain get caught too far back in the valley of the bottom chainring tooth and are dragged upward. As the chain wears and stretches, the distance between each link expands. As the chainring wears, the valleys between the teeth get wider and deeper, allowing the chain to slip back in each valley under pressure.

Chain and chainring damage

There is only enough room between the sprockets for a straight chain link. A twisted one always catches on the neighboring sprocket and causes the gears to slip or catch. A twisted link is also a weak point, so sort it out before it breaks and strands you in the middle of nowhere. With care, you can spot a twisted link by looking along the chain from behind while backpedaling gently. Check also for stiff links, which can easily cause your chain to slip under pressure, even when everything is adjusted correctly and none of the drivetrain is worn. To check for a stiff link in the chain, turn the pedals slowly backward, while looking at the chain. Squat beside the bike and hold the lower part of the chain between two fingers. Roll your hand so that one finger is slightly higher than the other. Pedal backward, so that the chain is dragged between your fingers. You feel stiff links as they pass between your fingertips. Use a good quality chain tool to spread the outer plates that restrict movement and cause stiff links; see page 100.

To get a good look, remove the chainset from the bike and the rings from the chainset. Check particularly for bent or damaged teeth. You can pick out the areas on each ring where the chain is having problems, as the adjacent chainring will be scarred. Twisted teeth are irritating — they can be tricky to spot, but will hook onto the chain and lift it up and around, rather than releasing it as they should. Bent teeth can be eased back straight with care. File off any tooth or part of tooth that protrudes sideways. Each tooth has a pulling surface, at the front of the tooth at the top of the chainring. When the chain is under pressure, this area of tooth can get splayed so a lip forms on one or both sides. As a temporary fix, these can be filed off, but it's usually a sign that the chainring is worn and needs replacing.

Lubrication and cleaning

First, try cleaning everything — the cheapest option, but one that may make things worse if it proves you have at least one seriously worn component, held together only by its own dirt. Or try an anti-chainsuck plate. This is an ugly aluminum plate that bolts to the bottom of the chainstay tube behind the chainset. Steps on it are shaped to fit the steps around the three chainrings, but without quite touching. The chain gets sucked up behind the chainring and hits a step on the plates instead of carving chunks out of your chainstay. Anti-chainsuck plates are a mixed blessing. Sometimes they help, sometimes the chain even jams in them too, and makes everything worse. I recommend finding the source of the chainsuck and sorting it out, rather than hoping the plates will bail you out. The only exception is with carbon frames, which should be permanently fitted with protection under the chainstay; chains make grated cheese from expensive carbon chainstays in seconds.

Singlespeed: hubs, chainline, appropriate gears and wear

Like vegetables, gears are a good thing but sometimes I just want to throw my gears away and eat chocolate instead. And just as it is difficult to explain to someone who has never eaten chocolate what an excellent idea it is, so it is hard to make a convincing case for riding singlespeed (one sprocket, one chainring, no shifters, equals one gear and therefore just one speed). You have to take my word for it — or, better still, try it yourself.

The first amusing thing about riding singlespeed is you instantly lighten your bike without spending a fortune on Space Age materials handcarved by astronomically expensive robots. The second thing is you realize how much ride time you spend futzing around changing gear. Having no distracting gears, you just ride along. Sometimes you cannot speed up because you don't have a high enough gear, and sometimes you have to get off and push because you don't have a low enough gear. These things happen to me on my geared bike as well. The final thing you notice is that riding is much quieter than normal. Still not convinced? That's fine — someone has to read the "adjusting gears" page to make writing it worthwhile.

There are two big issues. First, what gear to choose. In the end, your personal preference wins, but as a guideline, choose something around 65 inches. Gear size is equal to chainring size over sprocket size multiplied by wheel size in inches — so a 42-tooth chainring with a 17-tooth sprocket on a 26 inch wheel gives you 42/17 x 26 = 64 inch gear — which is as good a place as any to start.

The second big issue is chain tension. The chain mustn't slap or slip, nor can it be so tight that the pedals don't turn freely. Normally, the tension jockey on the rear derailleur does this job. On a dedicated singlespeed bike, the dropouts (where the wheel bolts to the frame) are horizontal, so you can adjust the chain tension by moving the wheel back in the frame. Almost all geared mountain bikes have vertical dropouts, so that the wheel cannot slip forward in the frame even if it isn't done up correctly. If you are converting your existing bike, you probably have to find a way to tension the chain. For initial experimentation, use your old derailleur.

Fit the derailleur and run the chain through it as normal. If you can, wind in the high end-stop screw so that the top jockey wheel sits directly under the single sprocket.

Often the end-stop screw won't go in far enough because it's not designed for this kind of use. Employ a little cunning, and use a piece of cable to hold the derailleur in place. Take a short section of gear cable, still with the nipple attached (it doesn't have to be in particularly good condition, since it's not going to move). Set the barrel-adjuster on the derailleur at the halfway position. Thread the cable through the barrel-adjuster so that the nipple sits in the barrel. Push the derailleur across so that the upper jockey wheel sits just under the single sprocket. Clamp the cable in place under the pinch bolt. Use the barrel-adjuster to set the position of the jockey wheel directly under the sprocket.

Remove your chainset and take off the smallest and biggest rings. Refit the middle chainring and the chainset.

Refit the chain

If you have vertical dropouts and are reusing the old derailleur to tension the chain, set the chain length quite short, so that the jockey wheels are at 45 degrees to the ground. If you're using a singlespeed chain-tensioner, the instructions in the packet explain how short to make the chain.

If you have horizontal dropouts, shorten the chain to take up all the slack, then adjust the position of the back wheel for at least 10mm (⅜ inch) of vertical movement in the middle of the top stretch of chain. The chain tension will change as you turn the pedals, so find the tightest spot and measure from there.

◀ **Singlespeed — simple and silent**

Troubleshooting transmissions

Symptom	Cause	Solution	Page
Chain slips, giving way suddenly under pressure	Worn cassette and chain	Measure chain for wear, replace if necessary, replace cassette at the same time	97, 101, 103
	Worn chainrings	Replace chainrings	130–1
	Damaged teeth on chainring	Realign bent teeth back	N/A
	Worn or damaged freehub body	Replace freehub body	149
	Twisted chain links	Straighten or remove twisted link	36
	Dirty or dry chain	Clean and lubricate chain	95–6
	Badly adjusted rear indexing	Adjust cable tension	108
	Incompatible chain, cassette or chainrings	Ensure compatability, especially between chain and cassette — don't mix eight- and nine-speed components	94
Rear derailleur doesn't index correctly	Incorrect cable tension	Tighten lockring and adjust gears	108
	Dirty cable	Clean and relubricate cable/replace cable and casing	119, 120, 122, 124
	Split outer casing	Replace casing	119
	Bent derailleur	Replace derailleur	111
	Bent derailleur hanger	Replace or bend back hanger	113
	Shifter worn	Disconnect cable from derailleur and test operation of shifter while pulling on cable as it emerges from shifter — replace if necessary	108, 114, 126–6
	Casette lockring loose, so that sprockets can move around on freehub body	Adjust cable tension	108
Rear derailleur usually indexes correctly but suffers ghost shifts when being ridden	Casing too short from handlebars to frame, or between sections of full suspension frame, so that movement of bars or frame tenses cable	Replace sections of outer casing with longer ones — you may also need to replace cable — ensure that casing cannot snag on parts of the frame	114, 119, 122, 124
	Chain worn	Measure chain wear, replace chain and cassette if necessary	97, 103
Chain won't shift into smallest or largest sprocket	End-stop screws are too far in	Undo end-stop screws so that chain can shift into the extremes of the cassette	109
	Incorrect cable tension	Adjust cable tension	108
	Guide jockey wheel too far from sprockets	Adjust B-tension screw	110

Symptom	Cause	Solution	Page
Rear gears index properly on smaller sprockets, but not on larger ones	Derailleur hanger bent	Replace or bend back hanger	113
	Chainline incorrect	Chainset too far out — fit shorter bottom bracket	128
Front derailleur doesn't index correctly	Incorrect cable tension	Adjust cable tension	115
	Incorrect front derailleur position	Adjust front derailleur so that the outer plate is parallel to the chainring, with 2–3mm of clearance between chainring and derailleur	115, 117, 118
	Bent derailleur	Bend back or replace derailleur	117, 118
	Dirty or corroded cable	Clean or replace cable	120, 122, 124
	Frayed cable	Replace cable	122, 124
	Split or kinked outer casing	Replace outer casing and cable	119, 122, 124
	Worn or broken shifter	Disconnect shifter from derailleur, pull gently on cable as it emerges from shifter, operate shifter to check for three distinct positions — replace if necessary	125-6
Shifting sluggish	Worn chain	Replace chain and cassette	101, 103
	Worn derailleur pivots	Clean and lubricate derailleur, replace derailleur	117, 118
	Ferrules missing from ends of sections of casing	Ensure that there's a ferrule at each end of each section of casing to help prevent the casing from shifting in the cable stops	119
	Cable in wrong position under clamp bolt	Remove cable and inspect area under clamp bolt — the correct position for the cable will be indicated by a groove in the derailleur	124
	Brake casing used instead of gear casing	Always use correct gear casing — brake casing is stronger but will compress slightly under load, causing erratic shifting	119
Front derailleur won't shift into largest sprocket	"High" end-stop screw too far in	Undo "High" end-stop screw to allow chain to shift onto large chainring	116
	Chainset sits too far out from frame, so that derailleur cannot reach at full extension	Fit shorter bottom bracket or fit chainset that sits closer to frame	128
	Incorrect cable tension	Increase cable tension	115
Front derailleur won't shift into smallest sprocket	Incorrect cable tension	Reduce cable tension	115
	"Low" end-stop screw too far in	Undo "Low" end-stop screw to allow chain to drop into smallest sprocket	116
Chain drops into middle or smaller ring randomly	Worn shifter	Replace shifter	125-6

Wheels

The quality and condition of your wheels make more difference to your bike than any other single thing. After all, you only need your gears when you want to change how fast they spin, and you only need your brakes to stop, but your wheels are going around all the time you're going along. Treat them right, and they'll roll along without complaining. Neglect them, and they'll make every climb feel like a vertical wall and every corner feel like you're riding on jelly.

Considering how little they weigh, bicycle wheels are incredibly strong. They are built to resist three main forces. When you sit on the bike, the wheels have to support your weight — this is a vertical force. In the same direction, but much stronger, is the force you subject your wheels to when you jump and land or hit a rock.

Sideways forces occur if you're moving fast and decide to change direction. Your wheel has to be strong enough to persuade your bike to follow the front tire without folding up.

The third type of force is rotational — you turn your wheels to make your bike move when it's still, and you drag your brakes on rim or rotor to slow yourself down

All wheels used to be built up from separate elements, but recently manufacturers have started to offer wheel packages, where you buy a pair of complete wheels, rather than choosing separate parts and paying a wheel builder to build them for you. These often represent good value, but some types of wheels use their own specific spokes and rims — be aware these can be more tricky to get hold of than standard parts. There isn't enough room here to go into detail on the different packages, but the basic principles for them are the same as for standard wheel sets.

This chapter looks at the elements that make up your wheel — hub, spokes, rims and tires — and how to make sure they're all working together effectively. The last part takes you step by step through building your own wheels, a task that takes patience but is not as hard as some people believe.

Mavic Crossmax.

How to remove and refit wheels

Even if you do no maintenance on your wheels at all, it's important that you know how to take them off so that you can fix punctures. It's even more vital to be able to refit them securely — you really don't want to lose wheels as you ride along. If you're not confident, ask your bike shop or an experienced rider to go through the procedure with you. When buying new wheels, if you're not familiar with the fitting system, ask your shop to show you how to remove and refit them.

The standard quick-release lever was designed for road-racing bicycles. It's a great system, allowing you to lock your wheels in place without tools. But the original designers of the quick-release lever had no idea what we would be doing with bicycles now. Suspension for bicycles existed already, but was a feature of butchers' and mail carriers' bikes, and they seldom tended to use their machines for hurtling around off-road with six inches of suspension. The design has been modified along the way to make the fitting more secure — the "lawyer tabs" at the bottoms of your fork dropouts force you to undo your quick-release lever nut a few turns before you can release the wheel. This gives you a little more time to notice that something is wrong before your front wheel jumps out and plants you face first in the dirt. Similarly, the move from horizontal rear dropouts, which allow you to adjust the chain tension, was necessary to make wheels more secure. Once common on mountain bikes, these are now seen only on singlespeed-specific frames. The arrival of disc brakes has meant that hubs are subject to even stronger forces. Therefore, quick-release skewers need to be tightened securely and checked regularly. Forks for downhill and freeride often have chunkier release mechanisms, which aren't as instant, but are more resistant to accidental release. If you find that your skewers work loose during rides, take your bike to your shop for a second opinion.

There is some disagreement about the best position for the lever. Traditionally, quick-release skewers were oriented so that the lever was on the left-hand side of the bicycle, and lay along one of the stays to prevent it getting caught. This is another legacy of road racing — the levers were always placed on the same side to save vital seconds after crashes — your mechanic could leap out of the team car and run with your wheel, already knowing which side your lever was on to reduce delay. Nestling the levers against the chainstay reduced the chances of your lever becoming entangled with someone else's bike and accidentally releasing your wheel.

On mountain bikes, it's important that the levers don't point straight forward, because they could get caught on a branch as you ride past and flip open. I prefer to fit them on the opposite side to disc rotors, as this reduces the chances of getting burned when fixing punctures. But the shape of your forks will often dictate where the skewer can fit, especially if there are adjusting knobs or fitting bolts behind the dropout. The most important thing is to ensure that the levers are firmly fitted. A ziptie around the skewer as an extra line of defence does no harm — I especially like Shimano XT skewers for this, as they already have a handy hole in them that's the perfect size.

FITTING QUICK-RELEASE LEVERS SECURELY

Step 1: Your skewer and hub locknut should both have deep, sharp serrations for gripping the dropout. Always use good-quality steel skewers, which should make dents in the frame where they clamp the dropouts. There should be a small steel spring (called a volute spring, after the similarly shaped sea shells) on each side — both of these should point inward toward the hub.

Step 2: Feed the skewer through the hub and screw the nut onto the other side. Hold the lever so that it sticks out at 90° to the wheel and tighten the nut finger-tight. Try closing the lever by folding it upward, not by twisting it. You should feel resistance right away. The lever has to be loose enough to close by hand, but tight enough so it leaves an imprint on your palm when you close it.

Step 3: If it closes too easily, flip the lever open again, tighten the nut a quarter-turn, and repeat. If you can't close the lever, flip it open again, loosen the nut a quarter-turn, and repeat. If you haven't done this before, ask your bike shop to check that you have secured your wheels correctly before you ride your bike.

Hubs: bearings

Bearings have been around since Roman times and appear in working drawings by Leonardo Da Vinci. His design for an early tank featured a device for enabling the gun turret to turn in different directions. He rested the upper part of the structure on a circle of wooden balls that allowed it to turn freely and support the weight (wood isn't the best bearing material, but is still used in cycle track racing rims). The modern ball bearing pioneer was Sven Wingquist, a visionary Swedish inventor who founded the SKF bearing company in 1907. The company still produces quality stainless steel bearings.

There are bearings in the center of your wheels. They take different forms, ranging from handfuls of cheap steel balls to fancy sealed units, but they all do the same job — keep the wheel securely fixed onto your bike with no side-to-side movement, while allowing it to spin as freely as possible. Well-adjusted bearings run for years without complaint. Bearings that are too loose or too tight slow you down either way and wear out in no time, so it pays to check them regularly.

Hub
Locknut
Seal
Cone
Bearings
Axle
Cone
Locknut

▲ **Shimano deore rear hub**

Pick up each wheel and spin it gently. It should continue rolling a couple of times on its own, even after a really gentle spin. If it slows down quickly, first check that the brake blocks or pads are not rubbing on the rim or rotor, which can have the same effect as overtight bearings. If that's the problem, go to the brakes chapter and sort them out first, then come back to bearings. If the brakes aren't the problem, then your bearing is too tight and it's slowing you down. Put the wheel down again and crouch beside the bike. Hold the rim of the back wheel where it passes between the stays (seatstays or chainstays on a hardtail, otherwise whatever lies between the main frame and the back wheel). Just pinch the rim between your thumb and finger. Hold onto the nearest bit of frame with your other hand, and rock your hands toward and away from each other, pulling the rim toward the frame then pushing it away.

The rim may flex slightly, but that's not what you're looking for. You need to check if there's a knocking feeling, or even a clicking noise, as you pull the rim back and forth. This indicates movement between the bearings and the surfaces supporting them, and means the bearings need adjustment. Repeat with the front wheel, holding the rim where it passes through the fork and rocking gently across the bike. Again, the rim may flex slightly, but it shouldn't knock at all. The wheel should spin freely, gradually slowing down over a couple of revolutions.

Bicycle wheel bearings can be divided into two types:

◆ **Cup-and-cone:** Traditionally, bicycle bearings were of the cup-and-cone type — a cone-shaped nut on the axle traps a ring of bearings into a cup-shaped dip in the hub. The cone can be adjusted along the axle, making enough space for the bearings to spin but not enough for the wheel to move sideways. The cones are locked into place by wedging a locknut against each one, then tightening the cone against the locknut. The advantage here is that the parts can be serviced and adjusted with a minimum of tools.

◆ **Sealed bearing hub:** The modern type is called a sealed bearing hub, although the name is a bit misleading because the cup-and-cone type usually has seals too — anyway, you're liable to open up either kind and find your bearings in a mess. Instead of the cup shape, this type has a flat-bottomed round hole on each side of the hub. The bearings and the races they run on come as a unit, which is then pressed into the hole. They are trickier to fit because the bearings on each side of the wheel have to be prefectly parallel to run smoothly. The advantage here is that both the bearings and the bearing surface can be replaced when they wear. With the cup-and-cone type, the bearings and cones can be replaced, but the cup is integral to the hub, and cannot be replaced cheaply.

Fitting and spacing hubs and sorting out hub seals

Before you start playing with wrenches and ripping your hubs apart, check that they fit neatly into your frame — ill-fitting hubs won't clamp securely into your frame or forks, and will wear quickly.

Hub spacing and fitting

Almost all mountain bike hubs come with the same spacing: the distance between the inside of the dropouts (technically called the "over locknut dimension" — OLND). This is 100mm (4 inches) at the front and 135mm (5¼ inches) at the back. A "dropout" is the part of the frame or fork with a slot for your axle. On forks, there's a dropout at the end of each fork leg; on frames, the right-hand dropout also has a hanger onto which your rear derailleur bolts.

It's important that the hubs fit snugly into the space between the dropouts. If the hub is more than a couple of millimeters wider or narrower than the frame or fork, the dropouts clamp it at an angle, rather than straight on. This puts uneven pressure on the hub bearings, wearing them out more quickly and, in extreme cases, bending or snapping the axle or the dropouts.

Each face of the dropout needs to be in good condition, so that the axle and skewer can clamp securely onto the surfaces. The locknuts on the outer end of the axle and the inner clamping face of your skewer are both knurled (notched) to increase grip. If you've ridden the bike with loose wheels, these notches will tear up the dropout surface, leaving the wheels less secure, even if you later tighten them correctly.

Care needs to be taken with your dropouts when you transport your bike too. They're very strong when the wheel is clamped in place, but are vulnerable when the wheel is removed. If you remove the wheels to put the bike on a plane, fit an axle support between the dropouts. You can usually pick one up at your bike shop — new bikes come packaged with them to protect the forks in transit.

Removing the front wheel and clamping the dropouts to transport your bike on a car roof rack can damage your suspension forks. Any movement between forks and clamp will twist the dropout, weakening it. Some fork manufacturers refuse to warranty forks with cracked dropouts if they've been carried in this way.

Hub seals

For me, getting muddy is a defining feature of mountain biking. It might not happen every time we go out, but there's no point pretending (as, ahem, in the photos in this book do) that we always stay clean. Muddy tracks aren't what designers working on bearings in clean studios consider as "running conditions," so your bearings definitely work best if you can keep the outside world out of them. Ideally, you create a completely watertight seal between your bearings and the world. Unfortunately, one of the features of bearing componentry is that one part needs to move smoothly against another. This means that at some point there's going to be a gap between the part of the wheel you want to move — the hub, rim and spokes — and the part you want to stay still attached to the bike — the axle.

But since we ride in grubby places, we raise the issue of trying to stop debris entering the gap between the hub and axle. Anything you put in the gap has to be carefully chosen to keep out dirt (so it has to touch both moving and stationary parts), but it cannot rub at all (so it's best if it doesn't touch either part). This is contradictory but true — a great deal of physics has gone into the problem. The practical upshot is that dirt gets into your hubs, and occasionally you have to get it out.

Different kinds of hubs

One major difference between cheap and expensive hubs is how well they're sealed. More expensive design and manufacture mean that the gap between moving parts can be made as small as possible, without the parts rubbing. Stronger, stiffer hubs also seal better — cheaper versions will flex under pressure, creating gaps around the seals. However, anything that completely keeps out the dirt won't spin around, so no seal is perfect, however much you spend on your parts. When you service your hubs, check the condition of the seals as you go along. Tears and cuts in the seals will allow rain and dirt into your bearings.

Many hubs have a large external seal protecting the exposed portion of hub and axle. It is often in the shape of a black cone and is usually found on the left-hand side of the rear hub and on both sides of the front hub. These help a lot, but if they get dry they squeak as they turn. To cure this problem, peel back the edge of the seal, clean it if it is dirty, and drop a drip of oil onto the interface between seal and hub. As for the rest, learn how to strip and rebuild your hubs, so they turn round smoothly without ever letting in a mud-grinding paste.

Checking and adjusting cones

Wheel bearings last longest when they are properly adjusted. The purpose of your hub bearings is to allow your wheel to spin freely as you pedal, while preventing the wheel moving from side to side in the frame.

The first part is obvious — hubs that bind instead of spinning will obviously slow you down and sap your energy. But play in your bearings will slow you down as well — if your wheel can move from side to side in the frame, your braking surface (the brake rotor for disc brakes, or the rim for V-brakes) gets constantly dragged against the brake pads or blocks. Loose bearings will make themselves felt when you ride as well, with wheels rocking within the frame rather than tracking your movement neatly around tight twists and turns. Your bike will feel uncertain, with small unnerving pauses, before it follows your directions.

Checking for loose bearings is the same procedure for front and back wheels. Hold onto your rim, near where it passes between the forks or the frame. Pull the rim gently toward the frame. If the bearings are loose, the rim will rock toward you — you will feel, and maybe even hear, it shifting on its bearings. It's OK if the rim flexes a little, but it shouldn't knock at all. Loose bearings need to be adjusted right away — as well as affecting your ride, they will wear quickly. If the bearings are allowed to bang onto the bearing surface, instead of rolling smoothly across it, they will create pits there. Check for tight bearings at the same time. Pick up each wheel in turn and spin it. The wheel should continue to rotate freely with just the gentlest encouragement. If it slows down prematurely, check the brakes first. If the brakes aren't the problem, your bearings are too tight. Use the steps below to adjust them. Front-wheel bearings are easier to adjust than rear-wheel bearings because both sides are accessible. With rear wheels, the right-hand cone and locknut are buried under the cassette.

Adjusting your bearings

Remove the wheel from the frame and remove your skewer — it just gets in the way. Spin the end of the axle between your fingers, then rock it from side to side across the wheel. If you found your bearings were too tight when you checked the wheel in your frame, the axle will feel gritty now — it may not move at all. If it felt loose in the frame, you will feel a slight rocking as you move the axle from side to side across the wheel. Since the axle runs through the center of the wheel, you only need to work on one side of the axle to adjust both sides of the bearing. The right-hand cones on the rear wheel are concealed by the cassette, forcing you to adjust from the left side. The front can be adjusted from either side, so just follow the instructions for adjusting the back axle.

Check that the right-hand locknut is locked securely onto the axle before you start. If this side shifts about as you work on the other side, you'll not be able to set the critical distance between the two sides accurately. Hold the short stub of threaded axle that protrudes out from the middle of the locknut and try to turn the locknut. If it moves easily with your fingers, you really need to service rather than adjust the hub. Dirt and water will have been drawn into the hub as the loose cones shifted on the axle. The pictures below show the hub on its own, without spokes, so that you can see both sides at once.

ADJUSTING HUBS

Step 1: Turn the wheel so that the left-hand side of the hub faces you. Remove any black rubber seals, so that you can see the locknut nearest the end of the axle and the cone behind the locknut. There may be a washer, or washers, between the cone and locknut. Slide a thin cone wrench onto the cone and hold the cone still. Use a wrench to undo the locknut one turn counterclockwise.

Step 2: The locknut and cone on the right-hand side of the hub are locked together, clamped firmly onto the axle, so you can hold the axle still by transferring your locknut wrench onto the right locknut. Leave the cone wrench on the left hand cone, and turn to adjust the bearings — clockwise to tighten, counterclockwise to loosen.

Step 3: Holding the cone still, transfer the wrench back to the left-hand side of the hub and tighten firmly onto the cone in its new position. Check the bearing adjustment again — it can take several goes to get the cone position right. Refit seals, skewer and back wheel. Check the bearing adjustment once you've got the wheel back in the frame — it's annoying, but you can often feel only slightly loose bearings at this point.

Cup-and-cone hub service: front

The front hub service is a good place to start — it's less tricky than a rear service because you have no gear clutter on the hub. If you haven't serviced a hub before, start on the front for practice.

If you have disc brakes, take care not to get grease on the rotors during this procedure. I've seen people stick a plastic bag over the rotor, then cut a hole in the bag through which to work on the hub. However, this does seem excessive — simply keep sticky fingers and bearings off the rotor. You need to check what size wrenches you need to adjust the cones. The cone itself need a special flat cone wrench because its wrench flats are very narrow. The size you need is normally 13mm or 15mm. The locknut is usually turned with an ordinary wrench, often a 17mm, but sometimes you also need a cone wrench for that. Enough variations exist to merit taking your bike to the shop to buy the size you need. While you've got it there, ask them for the correct size ball bearings for your hub. They're nearly always 5mm.

FRONT HUB SERVICE

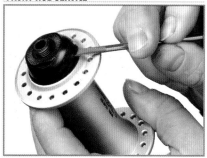

Step 1: Take the front wheel off and remove the skewer completely. Inspect each side of the hub. Seals may cover the cones, as in the picture. Peel them off by hand if you can to avoid damaging them, otherwise use a thin flat screwdriver to peel back the edges. In order, you can see the threaded end of the axle, the locknut with wrench flats, spacers, and the cone with wrench flats. Most of the cone is invisible, as it's inside the hub.

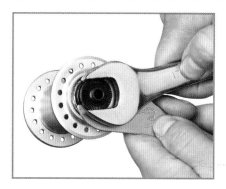

Step 2: Slide your narrow cone wrench onto the flats of one cone. Use the cone wrench to hold the axle still, then undo the locknut with the other wrench. Take it off completely. Remove any spacers. Lay them out in order on a clean rag so you can remember which order to put them back in. It's not difficult to work out the order for the front hub if they get jumbled, but it's good practice for when you come to the back one, which is harder.

Step 3: Switch the locknut wrench onto the other side of the wheel and use it to hold the locknut, and thus the axle, on that side still. Keeping your cone wrench on its original cone, undo that cone completely and take it off the axle. You should now be able to draw out the axle from inside the hub. Some bearings may drop out as you pull out the axle; be ready to catch them.

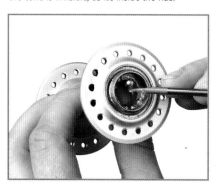

Step 4: Use a small flat-bladed screwdriver to extract all the bearings. Count them to be sure you replace the same number. Clean the axle and everything still attached to it. Wrap rag around the end of a screwdriver and use it to get grease off the bearing surface. For stubborn grime, you may need bikewash or degreaser. Rinse the bearing surface out and dry with a clean rag. Once all the old parts are clean, wash your hands to start fitting everything back.

Step 5: Inspect both the bearing surfaces on each side of the hub. A track will be worn in both cup and cone. Look for pits in the bearing surfaces. Any pitting prevents you adjusting the bearings nicely. Cones can sometimes be replaced individually, although you may have to buy a whole new axle. Pitted bearing surfaces in your hubs are more serious — you have to replace the hub, which means either buying a new wheel or rebuilding your rim around a new hub.

Step 6: Check the locknut is tightened against the cone. If the cone is pitted, note how much axle sticks out beyond the locknut, then hold the cone still with the cone wrench, and release the locknut. Wind all parts off axle. Fit the new cone, and replace any spacers and the locknut. Wind the locknut onto the axle so the same amount of axle thread pokes out the end, then wind the cone back up to the locknut. Hold the locknut steady and tighten the cone against it firmly.

Refitting the axle

It's always worth making sure the cones and bearing surfaces are really clean and dry before you refit the bearings. Any dirt left inside the hub will shorten the hub lifespan and make the cones more difficult to adjust. A light oil, like GT85 or WD40, will help to dissolve the old grease and dirt that becomes compacted onto the bearing surface — squirt a little into each end of the hub, then roll the wheel around so that the oil has a chance to soak into the whole bearing surface. A toothbrush is just the right size and shape to shift stubborn dirt stains. Clean the central part of the hub between the two bearing surfaces — it's easiest if you use a screwdriver to poke a thin strip of cloth right through the hub, then twist and pull to clean. Dry the bearing surfaces, so that the grease sticks to it properly.

Once everything is clean, check again for pits in all both bearing surfaces and both cones. Smooth worn tracks are fine — these just show where the bearings have been running. But any pitting at all — dents or rough patches on the bearing surface — means that the part must be replaced. Cones are slightly softer than the hub-bearing surface. This is so that they wear first, since they're easier and cheaper to replace. Take the old ones with you to the bike shop for replacement, since there are a number of variations in depth and diameter. Replace both cones at the same time — if one side is worn out, the other hasn't got much life left in it either. You may find that your hub cones are not available separately, so you may have to buy a whole new axle. If your hub surfaces are worn, you have no option but to replace the hub. If your rim is in good condition, you may wish to consider taking the wheel apart and rebuilding the rim onto a new hub.

 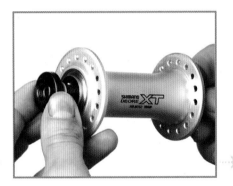 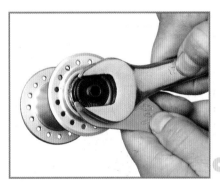

Step 7: Grease the cups on both sides of the hub. There should be enough grease for each bearing to sit in grease up to its middle. With clean hands, pop as many bearings back into each side as you took out. If you push a bearing into place and another pops out, that's one too many bearings. The grease should hold them in place.

Step 8: Slide the axle assembly back through the hub. If you have a rotor, slide through from the rotor side, otherwise it doesn't matter. Wind the new or cleaned loose cone back onto the axle all the way, so that it touches the bearings and traps everything into place. Now replace any spacers, and wind the locknut onto the axle so that it butts up against the spacer or cone.

Step 9: All the adjustment must be done from the side of the axle to which you refitted the cone; we'll call this the "adjustable" side. You tightened the locknut and cone onto the axle on the other side, the stationary side, before you refitted it, so you can use them to hold the axle still to adjust the cone on the other side. You don't adjust the cone on this side at all; it stays where it is.

Final adjustments

Now the tricky part. Adjust the space between cones and cups so the wheel can turn smoothly, but keep it tight enough to eliminate side-to-side play. Hold the cone still, and tighten the locknut against the cone so the cone can't rattle out of place. The problem is that tightening down the locknut usually shifts the adjustment. Test by rocking the axle across the hub, and then rotating. If it rocks from side to side, the cones are too loose. If it won't turn freely, the cones are too tight. Tighten up the adjusting cone gently against the bearings, so it can still turn freely, but without side-to-side wobble. Hold the axle by sliding your cone wrench onto the stationary cone and holding it still, then use your locknut wrench to wind the adjustable locknut gently up to the adjusting cone. When they touch, transfer the cone wrench from the stationary side of the hub to the adjusting side and wedge the adjustable locknut firmly against the adjustable cone. Test the bearing adjustment — twirl the axle between your fingers. It should turn smoothly with little resistance. Turn the wheel to face you and wiggle the axle from side to side — there should be no play. Occasionally you adjust it perfectly first time but this is rare — normally you have to go back and try again.

If the axle doesn't turn smoothly, move the adjustable cone out a little. Using your two wrenches, hold the adjustable cone still and undo the locknut one complete turn. Transfer the locknut over to the stationary side and use it on that locknut to hold the axle still. Undo the adjustable cone a little. Swap sides with both wrenches, hold the axle still with the cone wrench on the stationary cone, and tighten the adjustable locknut so it touches the adjustable cone. Swap both wrenches back onto the adjustable side, and tighten them against each other so they lock together. Test again, and repeat until satisfied. If there is play between the axle and hub, you need to undo the locknut; tighten the cone instead of loosening it, and lock the locknut back down onto the cone. Replace any seals you took off and refit the wheel.

Cup-and-cone hub service: rear

The rear hub adjusts the same way as the front one, but the job is complicated by the cassette that is attached to the back wheel.

You must remove the cassette to service the rear hub; see page 149. One complication is that the right-hand cone is recessed into the freehub body, forcing you to make adjustments from the left-hand side. The most common wrench sizes are a 15mm cone wrench and a 17mm ordinary wrench, and 18 6mm ball bearings. The rear hub needs servicing more often than the front: the rear wheel is forced around by the pedals, and it carries more of your weight, so works harder. It's also too close to the drivetrain for comfort, lying first in line for debris flying from your chain. The right-hand side can be messy. Service it frequently for best results and always replace bearings when you service a hub. If the cups in the hub are badly pitted, think about replacing your hub. It's often best to take the hub to your bike shop for an opinion. One option is to buy a new hub and spokes and rebuild your wheel around a new hub. See the wheel building section (pages 161–68) for instructions. Once you've removed and cleaned the dirty stuff, wash your hands so you can fit things back together without contaminating the bearing surface.

REAR HUB SERVICE

Step 1: Remove the wheel and the skewer. Peel off any external seals covering the cone flats. It's best if you can do this by hand — pinch the seal between two fingers to release it, then pull. Otherwise, slide a screwdriver under the edge of the seal and twist. Check the condition of the seal and replace if the edges are cut or torn.

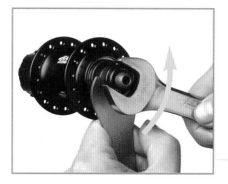

Step 2: Hold the left-hand cone still with your cone wrench, and loosen the left-hand locknut with your locknut wrench. Remove the locknut completely, then any spacers. Hold the wrenches so that your hands move apart as the locknut releases — it often gives suddenly and will trap your fingers painfully between the wrenches. Be careful.

Step 3: Swap the lockring wrench to the right-hand side of the wheel, and use it to hold the axle still while you wind off the left-hand cone completely. Line up the parts as you go, so you can replace them in the right order, the right way around. Draw the axle out from the right-hand side of the wheel, catching any bearings that come out too.

Step 4: Clean axle with the right-hand parts attached, along with the parts removed from the left-hand side, and the bearing surfaces inside hub. Wrap some rag round a screwdriver tip to get bearing surfaces clean. Use bike wash or degreaser for stubborn bits, but rinse and dry the hub afterward. Inspect the bearing surfaces. The bearings will have worn a track on both cups and cones, which is fine, but it should be smooth, with no pits. Replace pitted cones.

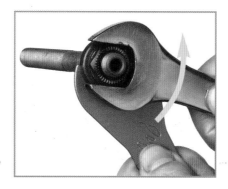

Step 5: If you're replacing a right-hand cone, note how much axle sticks out the end of the lump of cone, spacers and locknut. Hold cone steady on axle with cone wrench. Use the lockring wrench to remove the lockring. Wind old cone and any spacers off axle. Wipe axle clean and refit new cone. Refit spacers, then wind lockring onto axle to same position as before. Hold locknut still, and firmly tighten cone and lockring against each other.

Step 6: Put enough grease into the cups on each side of the hub so the bearings sit in grease up to their middles. Pop into each side as many bearings as came out. There will always be the same number in each side, and it's usually nine. If you push a bearing into the cup and another one pops out, you don't need another bearing.

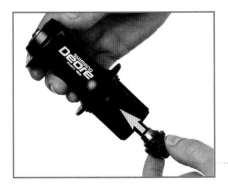

Step 7: Slide the axle, with the right-hand cone and lockring firmly tightened on to it, carefully into the hub from the right-hand side, making sure you don't dislodge any bearings. The cone will probably disappear completely into the hub.

Step 8: Thread the left-hand cone onto the end of the axle that's sticking out from the left-hand side, and tighten it down by hand so that it touches the bearings but can still spin freely.

Step 9: Refit spacers in order, followed by the locknut. Tighten the locknut down by hand so it wedges against the spacers, then use the two wrenches to tighten the cone and locknut together so that they wedge firmly onto each other. Test the adjustment — it is rarely right first time. The axle should spin freely with little resistance.

Step 10: Hold the wheel so that the end of the left-hand side of the axle faces toward you and rock the axle from side to side. There should be no play at all — you should not be able to feel the axle knocking from side to side. If the adjustment isn't correct, hold the left-hand cone still and undo the left-hand lockring a turn.

Step 11: Hold the axle still with a wrench on the right-hand lockring and adjust the left-hand cone — clockwise if there's knocking, to reduce the space between cups and cone, and counterclockwise if the axle is stiff to give the bearings space to spin freely.

Step 12: Holding the left-hand cone in its new adjustment, tighten the left-hand locknut against it. This often changes the adjustment, so play with the adjustment to compensate — a satisfactory adjustment often takes several goes, but it's just a case of trial and error. Once you're happy, replace any seals, and refit the cassette and skewer. Refit the wheel, tightening skewers firmly.

Toolbox

Tools for adjusting front cones
- Cone wrench — almost always 13mm

Tools for adjusting rear cones
- Cone wrench — almost always 15mm
- Locknut wrench — an ordinary 17mm wrench will work on most — however, those locknuts with two flats rather than six will need a 17mm cone wrench

Tools for servicing hubs
- Wrenches for hubs as above
- Good-quality bicycle grease, for example Finish Line or Phil Wood
- Degreaser and clean cloth to clean hub surfaces
- Replacement bearings — almost always ³⁄₁₆ inch (5mm) front and ¼ inch (7mm) rear — if in doubt take your old ones to the shop to size-up fresh ones

Sealed bearing hub service

Sealed bearing hubs use a pair of cartridge bearings pressed into the hub in place of the traditional cup-and-cone arrangement. The cartridges are more expensive than ordinary ball bearings, but the advantage of this setup is that the cartridge unit consists of both the bearing and the bearing surface — replacing the cartridge means that you've effectively got a new hub.

In some ways, servicing a sealed bearing hub is a lot easier than maintaining a cup-and-cone hub because there's no adjusting — you just pop out the old bearing, clean or replace it, and fit a new one.

Selecting the correct bearing size can be awkward because there are so many similar, but different, sizes. Bearings are identified by three measurements — the diameter across the outside of the cartridge, the diameter of the hole in the middle, and the thickness. The size is printed on the side of the bearing. When buying them from bike shops, ask them to reorder replacements from your hub manufacturer, which will guarantee that you get the correct replacement. Bearings are also available from specialist bearing and engineering shops, but it's well worth taking the old one along as an example.

We take a front hub; rear hubs work in the same way, apart from the fact that you have to remove the cassette to get at the axle properly. You may find that the axle covers have a small Allen key bolt that locks them onto the axle — undo the Allen key a couple of turns to release it from the axle, then treat as a push-fit axle cover. Once you've serviced the hubs, refit the axle covers as normal, then retighten the Allen key bolts gently — they won't need a huge amount of force to keep them in place.

The instructions specify a rubber mallet or a plastic hammer. If you don't have either of these, a block of wood works fine, but don't be tempted to use a metal hammer. It's not the same thing at all, and you will inevitably damage the ends of the axle.

You'll need to support the hub while you knock through the axle. My preferred tool for this job is a short piece of plastic plumbing waste pipe. The plastic is strong enough to support the hub but soft enough not to damage it, and it's just the right size for the hub to sit on, with a hole in the middle into which the axle can fall. Plumbing supplies stores usually have discarded scraps that they'll give you if you wander in and smile at them. Perfect.

When refitting the new bearing, take care to ensure that it fits flat into the hub so that an even gap shows all the way around the edge of the cartridge. The bearings will wear very quickly if fitted crookedly.

Check the condition of your axle at the same time. It will be specific to your hub, and a replacement for a damaged one will have to be ordered from the hub manufacturer by your bike shop. Cartridge-bearing axles seldom snap, since they are well supported by the cartridge, but the cartridge support shoulders and the axle ends can get worn. If the new bearings fit loosely onto the axle or can be wiggled about once you've seated them onto the axle, then the axle must be replaced.

SEALED BEARING HUB SERVICE

Step 1: Pull the axle covers off the axles. They will often come off by hand. If they're stiff, lever them off gently by sliding a small screwdriver underneath and easing them upward. The aluminum is soft, so work patiently to avoid damaging the cover.

Step 2: Stand the waste pipe on end, then balance the hub on top. Tap the top end of the axle through the hub. The axle has a raised section in the middle — the shoulder of this section rests against the inside of each bearing, so that as you tap the axle from one side, it pushes the bearing out from the other.

Step 3: The axle comes out with one bearing still attached. Place the axle in a vice, with the long end hanging through the jaws of the vice. Protect the jaws with wood or cardboard, then close the jaws so they almost clamp on the axle, but not quite. Tap the axle through the bearing to release it. Slide the axle back through the bearing that's still stuck inside the hub, and use the axle to tap out the bearing, supporting the hub again on your plastic tube.

Step 4: The axle will probably be stuck on that bearing now, so pop the axle back in the vice and tap it out again. You should now have two axle covers, an axle and two bearings. If you're replacing the bearings, take the old ones to your bike shop to get the right size replacements. If you're measuring them to order new ones, you will need to know the outside diameter, the inside diameter, and the thickness of the old bearing.

Step 5: Clean the inside of the hub thoroughly. Compare the depth of the bearing seat to the thickness of the bearing, so that you know how much of the bearing seat shows when the bearing is properly seated. Each bearing needs to sit flush with the bottom of the bearing seat. Dry the inside of the hub well. Spread a very thin layer of Loctite on the bearing seat; it helps to keep moisture out and holds the bearing in place without creaking.

Step 6: The new or regreased bearings now need to be tapped carefully into place, but it's important to support the bearings carefully as you do this to avoid damaging the bearing surfaces. You need to find a couple of bearing supports that sit on the outer ring of the bearing, with a hole in the middle wide enough for the axle to pass through. Sockets from a socket set are often perfect, as are bottom bracket fitting tools.

Step 7: Support the hub on your plastic pipe, then tap one of the bearings into place, using your bearing support to ensure that only the outer ring of the bearing is under load. Turn the hub over and rest the bearing on the bearing support. Tap the axle through the bearing you've fitted.

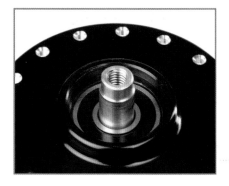

Step 8: Place the second bearing over the axle. Now comes the tricky bit: keeping both bearings lined up on their supports so that only the outer ring of each bearing is under load. Tap the second bearing into place, making sure both bearings are equally recessed into the hub, and that any gap at the top of the bearing is what you expected from your measurement of the bearing-seat depth.

Step 9: Refit the axle covers. If they were a press fit, simply slide them on by hand. They will get squeezed properly into place when you refit the wheel and tighten the skewers. If the axle covers have grub screws, fit them by hand, refit the wheel in the bike, tighten down the quick-release skewers, then tighten the grub screws.

Toolbox

Tools for sealed bearing hub service
- Allen keys for axle cover grub screws — most are press fit, though
- Rubber mallet, plastic hammer, or block of wood
- Replacement bearings
- Socket to support bearing — same size as outer diameter of bearing
- Loctite
- Hub support — plastic waste pipe or similar
- Vice with soft jaws, or improvised jaw protectors — scrap of cardboard or carpet

The importance of cleaning and regreasing sealed bearings

Worn cartridge bearings have to be replaced, but if they're just sticky and dirty, a quick service will keep your wheels running smoothly. Check whether they're worth servicing before you take the wheels apart — hold the wheel flat and rock the axle gently from side to side. If you can feel movement, or the axle knocks from side to side, the bearing is due for replacement. Otherwise, follow the steps for a clean and regrease.

The old grease inside sealed bearings can often be caked firmly onto the bearings and bearing surface; anything that finds its way in past the seal has no way out again, so it just becomes compacted onto the bearing surface. You will generally need to use degreaser to clean this stuff up.

Once the seals have been removed (so that the dirt has an exit route), soak the cartridge in degreaser. Ideally, pop cartridges in a small pot and cover them in degreaser, so that they're completely submerged. Leave for an hour, replace the degreaser, and soak for another hour, shaking occasionally. This should loosen all the old grease. Use a stiff brush to scrub the bearings clean. A toothbrush is perfect. Flush again with degreaser, repeat until the bearings come up shiny and you've got all the old grease out of the gaps between the ball bearings. Check your degreaser instructions — if it has to be flushed off with water, use plenty.

Drying the cartridge

Dry the cartridge. Properly, this should be done with compressed air, but nobody I know has a compressor at home. Fine substitutes are hot-air hand-dryers, and hairdryers. If the person you borrow the hairdryer from doesn't know what you're going to be doing with it, it's well worth cleaning greasy fingerprints off it very, very carefully before returning it.

Once dry, the bearings must be regreased immediately — the degreased surface is vulnerable to rusting because you've just stripped off its oily protective coating.

Good quality grease is well worth it — you don't get into the cartridge very often so it doesn't need much. Waterproof grease is best; I like the green Phil Wood stuff for this. The consistency is perfect. Pack the grease into the cartridge but don't overfill — you need to leave the bearings enough room to move.

CLEANING SEALED BEARINGS

Step 1: Place the cartridge flat on a clean surface. Hold it still with your finger, press hard, so it doesn't slip. Use a very slim blade to lift the edge of the seal, taking care not to bend it or cut the plastic. Make sure you direct the blade away from you — this sounds obvious, but I've carelessly and stupidly cut my fingers doing this too many times. Pull the seal off completely and repeat on the other side.

Step 2: Flush the bearings with degreaser. Use a small brush to get all the old grease out — an old toothbrush is ideal. Rinse the bearings to remove all the degreaser, and dry them. Repack the bearing with fresh grease. Don't overfill the bearing — there should be a little space for the balls to move in.

Step 3: Push the seals back over the bearing with your thumbs. The edges of the seals fit under the lip of the casing of the bearing. The fit is tight, so ease them carefully into place. When you've finished, there shouldn't be creases or folds in the edge of the seal. Wipe excess grease off the outside of the cartridge.

Removing and refitting cassettes for rear-hub services

Servicing rear hubs is trickier than servicing front hubs, since the right-hand side of the axle is concealed under the cassette. It is possible to service the hub without removing the cassette, but it's much more difficult — the bearing surface is behind the cassette, so it is tricky to clean properly. Use these steps to remove the cassette, then replace it after you've cleaned and regreased the hub.

Almost all cassettes use the same fitting method and the same tool, making cassettes easily interchangeable between hubs of different makes. The main body of the cassette slides over the freehub on "splines" — the freehub has long parallel grooves all the way around it, which fit into the identically shaped grooves on the inside of the cassette. When you pedal, forcing the chain around, the sprockets are supported all the way around by the leading edge of each spline. The cassette is held onto the hub with a lockring, that screws into the end of the freehub. Once this is removed, the cassette will slide easily off the freehub.

The standard fitting means that one tool will fit all lockrings. The tool also has a set of splines, which fit into matching slots in the lockring. The best type of tool for hollow, quick-release axles has an extra rod that extends out from the middle of the tool. This supports the tool under pressure, stopping it from slipping out when you turn it.

You'll also need a chain whip to hold the cassette still while you turn the lockring, and an adjustable wrench to turn the tool. You won't need the chain whip for refitting the cassette — the ratchet inside the freehub will stop it from turning. See the transmission chapter for more detail about cassettes.

◆ Remove the skewer completely. Fit the cassette tool over the end of the axle so it engages with the splined hole in the center of the cassette. Seat it firmly, so it doesn't slip off. If the tool has a rod poking out of its center, insert this into the hole in the end of the axle. If the tool has a hole in the middle, refit the skewer, and use it to clamp the tool onto the wheel. Otherwise just seat the tool firmly.

◆ Stand the wheel on the floor at your feet with the cassette facing away from you. Take the chain whip in your left hand. Wrap the loose end of chain around the cassette, so that it passes across the top of the cassette and back around the bottom, leaving the handle sticking out horizontally to your left.

◆ Fit a large adjustable wrench onto the cassette tool so that it sticks out horizontally to your right. Lean over the wheel and push down on both tools, steadying the bottom of the wheel between your feet. The chain whip will stop the cassette from rotating, so that the cassette tool can undo the cassette lockring. There will be a horrible crunching noise as it undoes. Don't panic, this is perfectly normal!

◆ Once the lockring is loose, undo it completely. Now you can slide the cassette gently off the freehub body — the sprockets simply pull straight out from the wheel. Some of the outer sprockets are separate; take them off carefully and keep them in order, together with any accompanying washers.

To refit the cassette after servicing the hub:

◆ Look at the freehub body, which the cassette slides onto, and the hole in the middle of the cassette. You see there are splines on the outside of the freehub body and matching ones on the cassette. One of the splines is slightly fatter than the others. Line up the fat spline on the freehub body with the fat slot on the cassette, and slide the big chunk of cassette onto the freehub body. Fit any loose sprockets with a washer if there was one originally.

◆ Refit the lockring, starting it off by hand. Once it's too stiff to turn, refit the cassette tool into the splines, and use a large adjustable wrench to turn it. It makes the crunchy noise as it tightens — again, this is fine. It still needs about a half-turn after the noise starts.

Removing and refitting Shimano freehubs

We will only deal with the Shimano freehub here. This is the single most common type and the most commonly available replacement part. You have to remove the rear axle for the job, so it's worth servicing the hub at the same time. A freehub doesn't last forever and can get clogged up with muck. It can also suffer badly if you catch it at the wrong angle with a jet hose.

The first sign of trouble is usually a regular slight slipping as you pedal. This feels very similar to a worn chain and cassette, so check those first, but if you measure your chain and it's in good condition, the freehub is the next suspect. Take your back wheel off the bike, and turn the cassette gently counterclockwise. You will hear the pawls of the ratchet click. Try to turn the cassette clockwise again — you should feel the pawls catch and stop you from turning the cassette. If the pawls catch, turn the cassette another click counterclockwise, and test again. You should be able to turn the cassette a complete turn counterclockwise, testing after every click, and the pawls should catch every time. If they slip, so that you can turn the cassette clockwise more than a tiny bit, you have sticky or broken pawls in your freehub body. Replace your freehub.

Follow the instructions for servicing a rear hub. Once you've removed everything — locknuts, cones, axle and bearings — follow these steps to replace the freehub. Then finish the hub servicing procedure.

Compatibility between freehub bodies

Back in the early days of mountain bikes, back wheels had old-fashioned freewheels with six sprockets. After a few years, this standard was replaced by a stronger design — a freehub with wider-spaced bearings and seven sprockets. Space was found within a couple of years for an extra sprocket by making the freehub body longer.

Seven-speed cassettes would not fit on the longer eight-speed freehub, nor would eight-speed cassettes fit on seven-speed freehub bodies. However, since the distance between each sprocket was the same, the two types could both work with the same width chain.

The next sprocket, increasing the cassette from eight to nine speeds, happened in a different way. Nine-speed sprockets are narrower, with less space between each one. So nine-speed and nine-speed cassettes will fit on the same freehub, but the nine-speed system uses a narrower chain that it fits into the reduced gap. Eight-speed chains won't work on nine-speed sprockets, nor will nine-speed chains work on eight-speed sprockets.

REMOVING FREEHUBS

Step 1: The freehub is bolted into the wheel with a 10mm Allen key bolt **(A)**. The bolt is recessed deep in the hub, so you'll have to wiggle the Allen key in there carefully from the right-hand side of the hub. Engage it securely.

Step 2: The freehub bolt should be done up very tightly, so you'll need to be firm with it to undo it. Stand with the wheel at your feet with the freehub facing away from you. Turn the wheel so the Allen key is horizontal, on your right-hand side. Hold the wheel with your left hand and push down hard on the Allen key with your right hand. You may find that you need more leverage. If you can find a tube that fits over the Allen key, use that for extra help.

Step 3: Once the freehub bolt **(B)** is loose, undo it completely and pull it out. Clean it; you can reuse it for the fresh freehub **(C)**. Clean the area exposed behind the freehub, line up the new one, and pop the bolt through. Tighten it really hard — as tightly as the one that came off. Use your "extension tube" again if you needed it to get the bolt off.

Tires: which type suit you?

Everybody makes tires. They all look different, and everybody claims theirs are the best. I don't know how they can all be the best, but many people are more loyal to their favorite brand of tire than to their favorite saddle manufacturer. Generally speaking, the tire pattern is determined by the terrain you ride and the type of riding you do.

If conditions are very muddy, broad tires — with widely spaced bars running across the rear tire — grip where nothing else can. For harder terrain, use something with closer lugs that has less rolling resistance. Heavier riders need a wider tire; lighter people can get away with something narrower.

Front tires perform a different job than rear ones, so their tread pattern is often different. Front tires are mainly concerned with steering, so the lugs on the tires are sometimes long bars pointing in the bike's direction of travel. This tread helps the front wheel grip as you turn corners, taking up the new direction and allowing the rest of the bike to follow.

Rear tires are mainly concerned with propulsion (although they obviously have a part to play in how your bike corners), and so they often have wide bars across the tire that grip the ground as you pedal. Different patterns work well in different terrains. Wide, deep paddles with big gaps are good for muddy conditions because they clear quickly. Closer, shorter lugs are better for harder terrain, rolling more smoothly so that you move faster.

However, your choice of tire matters far less than its condition. When tires are new, the lugs have sharp edges and grip the ground securely. Gradually the biting surface wears down, leaving the leading edge of each lug dull and chewed. Replace them and you ride more confidently right away. Whatever the debate over this tire pattern and that tire pattern, a fresh tire of any description always grips better than a worn tire.

Tire boots

Sometimes a tire gets so badly cut that the inner tube bulges out and punctures. In this case, you need to fit a tire 'boot' to stop the tube escaping. You can buy big dedicated strips of sticky-backed rubber for this, but more likely you will end up improvising. Anything flexible but strong will do: paper, cloth or cardboard, Folding money is great because the paper is very strong and fairly water-resistant. Plastic bags are useless — they are too flexible. A couple of layers of duct tape will work well.

I once surprised someone by successfully fixing their tire with a brown paper bag. I came across a cyclist with a huge gash in the side of his tire when I was in remotest Ireland. He'd fitted a spare tube, which had bulged out of the split and exploded right away. The paper bag (the wrapping from a candy bar) was in my jersey pocket. The paper was plenty strong enough for the task and helped keep the tube neatly in place. The stunned cyclist was suitably grateful, and had no idea that I was, if anything, more shocked than him that it worked.

Whatever you use, you need to put enough pressure in the tube before you fit it to hold the boot in the right place against the tire.

UST tubeless tires

The UST (Universal Standard for Tubeless) tubeless tire was developed to reduce weight at the wheel, and to stop the tube getting pinched between the rim and sharp rocks, by doing away with the tube altogether. The bead of the tire and the inside of the rim wall are designed so that when the tire is inflated, the two parts lock together, forming an airtight seal. Tire and rim manufacturers agreed on a common standard, called UST, to ensure that everyone's tires fit everyone else's rims.

The design is favored by people who race because the weight-saving makes most difference to them. The tires do lose air quicker than a standard tire 'n' tube, so there's a balance to be considered. (Personally, I'd rather live with the extra weight than mess about pumping up my tires daily, but I accepted long ago that there's no bike in the world light enough that someone as lazy as me is going to win a race on.) If every gram counts, or you like to run really low pressures for the extra grip, UST is worth it. If you like the convenience of jumping spontaneously on your bike without always pumping up the tires, stick to normal tube 'n' tire arrangements until they make USTs that don't leak.

Patching UST tubeless tires

Although flats are less likely with UST tires, they do happen. If you're out riding, often the easiest thing to do is to stick an ordinary tube into the tire and fix it when you get home. See emergency repairs on page 24 for tips. Once you get home, patch the tire. Tires are expensive, and patches work, so it's worth the effort.

Finding the hole can be the tricky part! Pump as much air as you can into the tire, and listen for hissing from the hole. Look carefully for a thorn or other spiky object sticking out of the carcass. Sometimes the hole is tiny and hard to locate, and you have to submerge the inflated wheel in water to look for the bubbles. This is much more awkward than doing the same process with a tube!

Once you've located the hole, mark it carefully or you will lose the place! I usually draw a circle in ballpoint around the hole, then draw an arrow pointing to it on the sidewall of the tire where it's easy to see. Undo the thumbnut on the valve and let all the air out of the tire.

It's important to do this next stage carefully. Both sides of the tire have an airtight seal against the rim. It's much, much easier to refit the tire if you only break one of the seals. If the hole is nearer one side of the tire, start with that side. Push the sidewall of the tire in and away from the rim. It will resist at first because the seal is tight, but once it's released the rest will pull off easily.

Sometimes the seal is very tight. If all else fails, lay the wheel on the ground and stand carefully on the sidewall of the tire, as close to the rim as you can get. Don't stand on the rim — you'll bend it. Pull off the released side of the tire all the way around and locate your hole from the inside. Pull out whatever it was that caused the puncture.

While you're in there, feel carefully around the inside of the tire for anything else sharp — there may be more than one intruder. Use clean sandpaper to roughen up the area of the tire around the hole. If you're used to patching tubes, don't underestimate this part — you need to make an area bigger than the patch much rougher than you would with a tube.

Spread the special UST glue around the hole. I start directly over the hole and work outward in a spiral, so that the patch ends up centered over the hole. Make the area of glue much bigger than the size of the patch. Then leave the glue to dry. Don't touch it or poke it, just leave it. It needs five to 10 minutes — if it's cold, give it the full 10 minutes.

The next stage

You'll find that your patch is now trapped between two layers of plastic, or a layer of plastic and a layer of foil. Peel off one layer, but don't touch the surface of the patch with your fingers at all or it won't stick. Use the other layer of packaging to hold it. Lay it carefully onto the glue. Don't move it about at all, just put it on. With the packaging still on there, press the patch firmly onto the tire. A tire lever is perfect for this, or the flat side of a wrench, or a spoon.

You can peel the backing off the patch now, but I usually leave it there — it doesn't weigh much, and you risk pulling off your carefully fitted patch if you try to remove it. Starting opposite the valve, refit the tire onto the rim. The tires are unwieldy, and it can feel like you need three hands, but once you've got most of the tire on, it stays in place.

This last part is harder. Don't be tempted to use tire-levers because if you do your tire will leak forever. Fold the tire onto the rim with your thumbs. Aim to finish at the valve. If it gets tough, return to the opposite side of the rim, and massage the bead of the tire into the well at the center of the rim to gain enough slack to pop it on at the top. Once it's in, ensure that the bead of the tire sits beside the valve, not on it, and pump it up. Be very vigorous at first to seal the tire and keep pumping until it pops into place.

Sometimes, if the tire is really tight, a bit of warm soapy water will help. Work in very small sections, lifting a 10–20mm ($^3/_8$–$^3/_4$ inch) length of tire at a time over the rim. The last bit will be a struggle and will pop into place just as you are about to give up.

Urban myths to ignore include pouring lighter fluid on the tire and applying a match. Don't do this. Tires are expensive, and this is not a time when setting something on fire helps.

Big workshop track pumps are better at getting the initial volume of air in fast enough; very small mini-pumps can make hard work of this. Air canisters can be hit-and-miss. If the tire seals right away, they're quick enough; if it doesn't, you waste the canister.

It definitely helps when reinflating tires if you can keep one side of the bead locked onto the rim. Fitting new tires is particularly frustrating; they're usually packed folded up and the kinks that result from their being folded usually make for air gaps. Take new tires out of the packet as soon as you buy them and store them unfolded until you come to fit them.

Even if you run very low pressures, it's worth pumping the tire up really hard to seal it properly — check on the sidewall to see how high it will go, then pump it up to that pressure before letting it down again to however low you want to run it.

Try to take a spare inner tube with you out on your bike

It's always worth carrying a spare tube when you go out for a ride, because it's much easier to pop a spare tube in than to fix a puncture by the side of the trail. But it's definitely worth backing the spare up with a patch kit. Punctures often come in batches and carrying more than one spare tube gets bulky. So, hold onto your punctured tube, and fix the puncture at your next opportunity. The repaired tube can become your new spare.

Fixing punctures

To repair a punctured tube, start by locating the hole. Pump up the tube to about twice the original diameter. You might be able to hear the air hissing out of the hole right away, and locate the puncture that way. If not, lick the palm of your hand and move it along the tube, about a centimeter away; you'll feel the cold air from the puncture on your hand. Roughen the area with the sandpaper from the patch kit; this helps the patch stick — and means you don't lose the hole. Let all the air out of the tube again. Spread glue in a spiral out from the center of the hole, making a glue patch that's generously bigger than the patch. This next step is the most important — let the glue dry completely. In average temperatures, this means five whole minutes. In the desert, you can wait two. If it's snowing, blow on the glue patch to keep it warm. Once the glue is dry, peel the foil off the back of the patch. Don't touch the rubber surface of the patch at all — use the clear plastic or paper to hold the patch. Drop it into place, then don't move it. Press it onto the tube with your hands. If it's very cold, clamp the patched part of the tube under your armpit to keep it warm enough for the glue to work, about another five minutes. You could peel the plastic or paper cover off next, but I normally leave it in place — it weighs nothing and saves you accidentally tearing off your neat patch. Refit the tube into the tire before putting pressure into it because the newly-stuck patch is vulnerable and won't stick properly until it's trapped between tube and tire under pressure. Puncture glue doesn't last long once the seal on the tube has been broken — it dries out in six months, however tightly you screw on the cap, so replace it regularly.

Schraeder inner tube/valve

Presta inner tube/valve

Valves

There are two types of bicycle valve: Presta and Schraeder. Presta is the thin one that road bikes always have. Schraeder is the fat car-type valve. Cheaper mountain bikes sometimes come fitted with car valves because they can be pumped up at gas stations. Presta valves are designed to work better at higher pressures and are more reliable — Schraeders leak if grit gets caught in them as you pump them up.

I always use Presta, but there is a bizarre law that says if you meet a stranger on the trail who's stuck because he can't fix his own puncture, he will always have Schraeder valves, so you can't help

him with your Presta pump. Luckily, most pumps now convert to fit either type of valve; with newer ones, you simply push any valve into the pump head and flick a switch. Many older ones require you to take the cover off the pump head, and remove a small rubber grommet and a small plastic thing. Turn both parts over and refit them into the pump in the same order they came out — plastic first, then rubber. Refit the cap, tighten it hand-tight, and you're ready.

Rims and rim tape

Punctures that happen because some sharp thing has worked its way through the outside of your tire and punctured your tube are annoying but fairly inevitable. On the other hand, those that happen because your tube has been punctured by your rim wall, or because your valve has shifted around in the rim and torn itself, are completely preventable.

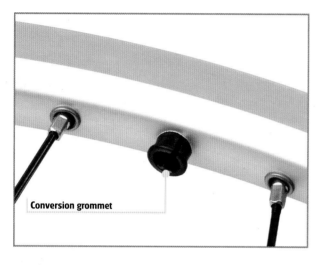

Conversion grommet

▲ **Schraeder to Presta rim-converting grommet**

Valve holes

Valves come in two sizes. The narrower Presta valve fits through a 6mm (¼ inch) hole in the rim, while the wider Schraeder valve fits through an 8.5mm (⅜ inch) hole. If you ride with low pressure in your tires (which slows you down but increases grip), you will find that the tube shifts about inside the tire. Since the valve is held in place by the valve hole, the area near the valve gets stretched and can tear. The retaining ring on the valve stem will help by reducing the amount of movement in the valve, but this is often not enough. A better solution is to buy one of the plastic or rubber rings that fit into Schraeder-size holes to reduce them to Presta size. This helps support the valve stem and stops water getting into the gap between valve and rim. They're properly called "Schraeder to Presta conversion grommets," but are more usually identified by a description of what they do: "those little black things you put in your valve holes if you run Presta tubes."

Some rims come with a narrowerd valve hole that is only big enough to take a Presta valve. You can drill these out if you want to run Schraeders — use an 8.5mm (⅜ inch) drill bit and drill through from outside. Cover the hub and cassette with a cloth so they don't get covered in metal bits. File off sharp edges around the valve hole or they will cut into the valve stem.

Rim tape

Rim tape sits around the inside of the rim to stop the heads of the spoke nipples cutting holes in the tubes. Make sure the tape sits evenly across the well of the rim, but that it doesn't run up the sidewall anywhere because this stops the tire seating properly. I like the thick plastic ones; they don't move around on the rim as you fit the tire and have to be stretched over the rim to fit.

Once it's fitted, check that the rim tape completely covers all the spoke holes — if there are any gaps at all, the tube will creep into them as you inflate it. The sharp edges of the spoke hole and rim tape will cut gradually through the tube, puncturing it. This may not happen right away — it's more likely that your tube will last until the furthest point of a long loop, just before it starts to snow.

When you've fitted rim tape, you will often find that the valve hole in the tape doesn't line up with the hole in the rim. Stick a screwdriver under the rim tape, lift it a little, and push it over to rest across both rim walls with the tape stretched over it. Roll the screwdriver around the rim until the holes line up, and remove the screwdriver.

Cloth tape is heavier than plastic tape, but it is a better solution for high pressures because it's less flexible. Thinner rim tapes will bulge into the nipple holes as you put pressure in your tires. If the rim tape has bubbles at every spoke hole, replace it with a thicker one. Don't double up the rim tapes, though — if you put one on top of the other, they fill up the rim well, making it tricky to remove and refit tires.

Wheel-truing: the science of keeping your wheels in balance

You get better at wheel-truing with practice. These instructions start you off, and they can rescue you if your wheel is too buckled to ride on. See page 38 for more detailed instructions in post-crash basics.

Rest the bicycle upside down, then remove the buckled wheel. Strip off the tire and tube. This makes it easier to see what you are doing, and also releases pressure on the rim, making it easier to true accurately. Replace the wheel in the frame. Spin the wheel and look carefully at the part of the rim that passes between the brake blocks. If the wheel is too badly buckled to pass between the brake blocks, slacken off the brakes as much as possible with the barrel-adjuster on the brake lever or unit. In extreme cases, remove one or both brake blocks.

Before getting out the spoke key, have a look at the rim to confirm what you're aiming to do. Look at the part of the rim nearest you, as well as the parts of the hub you can see behind it. You will also see spokes leaving the rim and heading for the hub. There are an equal number of these, connecting alternately to the left and right sides of the hub.

Tightening a spoke that connects to the right side of the hub pulls the small portion of rim that it's connected to across to the right. Tightening a spoke that attaches to the left side of the hub pulls that part of the rim to the left. The rim is held in tension between the right spokes pulling to the right and the left spokes pulling to the left.

Slackening a left spoke allows the right spokes to pull the rim over — just as with a tug-of-war team one team can move the central flag by pulling harder, but the same effect can result when the other team is tired and isn't pulling as hard. The aim of truing wheels is to balance the tension in all the spokes so that the lefts are pulling the same as the rights, holding the rim exactly central.

With this in mind, spin the wheel gently while watching the gap between the brake blocks and the rim. As the wheel spins, you will see that the rim moves from side to side. Imagine the centerline the rim ideally runs on, an equal distance between the brake blocks. Identify the area of the rim that has the biggest buckle.

Center of the buckle

Look closely at the buckled area and identify the spoke at the center of the buckle. You have to adjust the tension in this spoke to encourage the rim to sit more centrally. If the buckle pulls the rim to the right of the imaginary centerline, then spokes that go to the right-hand side of the hub must be loosened, and spokes that go to the left must be tightened.

Adjust the nipple at the center of the rim by a half-turn. The spokes are laced alternately to the left and right sides of the hub; if one spoke goes to the left, both its neighbors must go to the right. So, once you've adjusted the spoke at the center of the buckle by half a turn, adjust both its neighbors by a quarter-turn in the opposite direction. Spin the wheel again and look for the next biggest buckle. It may be in the same place or somewhere else. It's better to work slowly, adjusting three spokes then checking progress by spinning the wheel.

Working out which way the nipple turns to tighten or loosen the spoke confuses many people. If you get it wrong and turn the nipples the wrong way, you make each buckle worse rather than better. Eventually, if you persist, the wheel collapses. If you see things are getting worse and not better as you true, stop and think carefully about what you're doing.

Looser or tighter

When I was learning, I had to think about which way to go all the time. Eventually, I drew two circles on a piece of paper, one with a clockwise arrow that said "looser" in the middle and one with an counterclockwise arrow saying "tighter."

It lived in my toolkit for ages, and every time I had to true wheels, I put it on the ground underneath the wheel. I would spin the wheel to identify the buckle, then turn it so that the area I had to work on was at the bottom, over the paper. That way, I always knew which way to turn the nipples.

After a while, your hands remember, and you don't have to think about it any more. It's a good idea to get into the habit of using the spoke key in this position, since if a spoke breaks as you turn the nipple (which happens), it hits the ground harmlessly. Don't turn the wheel so you can see the head of the nipple you're turning, as this puts your eyes and face in the firing line.

It's possible you may not get the wheel completely straight. If the wheel stops improving, stop. As long as it passes through the brake blocks, you can ride the bike somewhere to get it dealt with properly.

Fitting a new spoke so that your wheels maintain their tension

Spokes usually break as the result of a crash, but they also break from being worn out. When you look at the wheel, it usually has one area with a big buckle. Run your fingers gently over the spokes and one may come away in your hand. It's important to fix it as soon as possible. Wheels rely on even spoke tension for strength. A broken spoke weakens the entire wheel structure, which then falls further out of true quickly.

Replacing broken spokes

If you have a broken spoke, remove the wheel, then the tire, tube, and rim tape. For rear wheels, remove the cassette (instructions on page 149). Locate the broken spoke and remove it. If it's broken near the head, pull the spoke out through the nipple hole, and push the head out through the flange of the hub. If it's broken at the nipple end, push the nipple out, and weave the spoke back so that you can pull it out of the hub. You may have to bend it to get it out.

Measure one of the other spokes to determine the length you need. Make sure you measure one from the same side of the same wheel as the broken one — lefts and rights can be different lengths. The spoke length is measured from inside the elbow where the head curves over to the very end, which will be inside the rim — look at adjacent spokes from the outside of the rim to estimate how far they protrude through the rim. The replacement spoke must be no more than 2mm (⅛ inch) longer or shorter than the others.

It's vital to weave your spokes back in in the right order. Look at your hub: you'll see that alternate spokes are "heads in" and "heads out." "Heads out" spokes on the flange nearest to you appear as circles because you can only see the heads (perhaps with the manufacturer's logo stamped on them), whereas "heads in" appear through the flange so that you can see the elbow of the spoke, which then points off toward the rim. Your new spoke must follow the pattern.

"Heads in" spokes are the easiest to fit. Start from the far side of the hub, post the spoke across the hub and through the hole. It will now dangle on the outside of the wheel, with the head between the flanges. Pull it gently all the way through so that the head of the spoke butts up the inside of the hub. Wiggle it around so that the spoke points toward the rim. It's important to ease the elbow of the spoke gently through the hole in the hub. The hole is only just big enough for the spoke, so that it can't shift about in use, which can make it awkward to get the elbow of the spoke seated in the hub hole without bending it.

The spoke pattern

The pattern repeats every four spokes, with all the "heads in" spokes on each side of the rim radiating out in the same direction. Pick out the next similar spoke and use it as a guide. Your new spoke crosses three others on its way to the rim. The first cross is over the adjacent spoke — the "heads in" one. These two spokes are very close so that the hub flange is between the two spokes. The new spoke passes over the next spoke it meets, but then has to be woven under the third. Try to curve it gently, rather than bending it, and avoid scratching the rim with the sharp end of the spoke. Line the spoke up with the empty hole in the rim, checking that the adjacent spokes in the rim head off to the opposite side of the hub.

"Heads out" is trickier — and more common! Post the new spoke a little way through the near side of the hub. Don't push it all the way through yet — it will end up stuck between the second and third spoke crossings on the opposite side of the wheel. Curve it gently outward from the hub and guide the end of the new spoke out of the far side of the hub, beyond the spoke crossings. It will need to be quite curved, and so will not slide easily through the hole in the hub. Push the head through with one hand, while maintaining the curve on the spoke with the other.

As with "heads in" spokes, the pattern repeats itself every four spokes. Count along three from your new spoke, in either direction, and use this one as a guide. Your new spoke crosses the adjacent spoke at the hub, passes under the next one it meets, and then has to be woven so that it passes outside the third. Line the spoke up with the empty hole in the rim, checking that the adjacent spokes in the rim head off to the opposite side of the hub.

For both types, put a drop of oil on the thread, post the nipple through from the outside of the rim, and thread the nipple onto the spoke. Take up the slack with a spoke nipple, and go to page 155 to true the wheel.

What makes spokes break?

Spokes usually break on the right-hand side of back wheels. The back wheel takes more of your weight than the front, since you sit almost on top of it. Derailleur gears mean the cassette sits on the right-hand side of the hub, so the spokes on the right approach the rim at a steeper angle. They have to be tighter to keep the rim central in the frame, so they are the most vulnerable to breakage.

They are also the most awkward to replace; the cassette has to be removed to fit a standard spoke into the holes in the flange. These spokes frequently get damaged by the chain.

A badly adjusted derailleur may allow the chain to slip into the gap between cassette and spokes. If you're pedaling hard at the time (which is quite likely, since you were already in a low gear), the chain acts like a saw on your spokes, cutting through them. If you have to take the cassette off to replace a spoke behind it, inspect the others at the same time for chain damage. Replace any that have been cut or torn. It's best to swap them one at a time, so that wheel tension and shape are retained. Tighten the nipple on each replaced spoke enough to support the rim before removing and replacing the next damaged spoke. The plastic spoke protectors that sit behind your cassette are ugly, but they do prevent the chain from dropping into the gap — always replace the spoke guard after fitting new spokes.

Rim damage

Rim damage is frustrating, and often happens as a result of punctures. If the tire deflates fast, there may not be enough time to stop before you're running on your rims. This is particularly damaging if the wheel is heavily loaded, or if you're bouncing down a rocky hill. The rim sidewalls can dent, ticking constantly on the brake blocks and making the bike difficult to control during braking. Sometimes the whole rim gets a flat spot so that, as the wheel turns, and the flat spot passes between the brake blocks, the blocks rub on the tire. Tire sidewalls are very soft, and the brake blocks soon wear through them and the tube, causing blowouts. One of the advantages of disc brakes is that your braking isn't affected by buckled wheels in the same way, but flat spots and bent rims will still weaken the rim.

Bent sidewalls can be bent back as an emergency measure, although they will be weakened and should then be replaced as soon as is practical. A small adjustable wrench is an ideal tool; clamp it tightly onto the bulge in the rim and ease it straight. If the bulge is big, do it in several stages, working inward toward the center from either side of the bulge.

If the rim has a flat spot, check that brakes are clear of the tire sidewalls. If not, adjust the blocks downward, so there is clearance even when the tire is at its lowest relative to the blocks. It's important to check with the tires pumped up because at higher pressures the sidewalls can bulge, throwing themselves into the path of the blocks. Once the wheel has a big flat spot, there's little you can do to correct it — if the rim bends inward more than a couple of millimeters (⅛ inch), you're looking at rebuilding the wheel with a new rim.

Toolbox

Tools for wheel repairs — post-crash wheel true:
- Spoke key — individual ones are better than those that come on multi-tools, which can be awkward to use

Tools for wheel repairs — tools for replacing spokes:
- Spoke key — as above
- Tire-levers — to remove and replace tire
- Pump — to reinflate tire
- Rear wheel — cassette tool plus chain whip to remove and replace cassette

Wheel words: learn the jargon

There is a proliferation of ready-built wheels on the market, but you still get the best value by attaching a hub to a hoop with a bunch of spokes yourself. If you do the weaving and tensioning yourself, you can spend the extra you save on a rim upgrade.

Your first attempt at building a wheel often takes some time, but it is a very satisfying experience. Once you've managed your first one, it gets easier every time. Don't be tempted to start with a second-hand rim and old spokes; it's much harder to true a second-hand rim, which will probably be dented and buckled, so will be frustrating since you find yourself doing the right thing without any effect.

Lacing, attaching the rim to the hub with all the spokes in the right place, comes first. This is easier than it looks. Next comes truing up the wheel so that it is round, flat and centered. This looks easier than it is and requires a fair bit of patience and care.

Front wheels are easier to start with than back ones. Back wheels have the cassette fixed on one side, which means the rim doesn't sit centrally to the hub. Therefore, the spokes on the cassette side have to be tighter than those on the other side. So begin your wheel building career with a front wheel if you can to ease yourself into it.

Disc brakes often come with recommended spoking patterns. This is because braking applies force to only one side of the wheel, so it's important that the spokes stressed by braking are those that best support the braking force. The lacing pattern given here works best for disc brake bikes and fine for the rest, so use it for everything.

Crossing patterns

Most wheels are built "three-cross" (3x). To see what this means, look at a wheel and follow a spoke from the hub to the rim. The spoke passes either under or over others on its way. If it crosses three other spokes, it's a standard three-cross wheel. The other common lacing pattern is "radial," where the spokes go directly from hub to rim without crossing any others. It is also known as a zero-cross (0x) pattern.

Radial spoking is used almost exclusively for front wheels. A crossed pattern is more suitable for the back wheel; you're using the pedals to force the rear hub to turn. The spokes transfer this rotation to the rim and tire. A crossed pattern means that the spokes leave the flange at an angle, which reduces the stress on both flange and spokes.

For both radial and crossed patterns, alternate spokes are connected to opposite flanges. This enables you to adjust the position of each section of the rim, moving it to the right by tightening spokes that connect to the right flange or loosening spokes that connect to the left flange, and moving it to the left by tightening left spokes or loosening right ones.

In crossed patterns, the spokes divide into pulling spokes and pushing spokes. The pulling spokes get tighter when you pedal and pull the hub around, dragging the rim behind them. The pushing spokes provide a counterbalancing force, thereby keeping the wheel in its strong, round shape.

When you're braking, the opposite happens — the pushing spokes suddenly have to do all the work, with the pulling spokes supporting them.

3 crosses

◀ **Three-cross is the standard pattern**

Spoke length

Whether you're building a new wheel or replacing a broken spoke, you need to choose the correct spoke. The length needs to be exactly right — a spoke that's more than 2mm (⅛ inch) too long or too short will not fit. Minor differences in flange size (the wider part on either side of the hub, with holes through which to thread the spokes) and rim profile will affect the spoke length.

When replacing a broken spoke, check the length by measuring another on the same side of the same wheel. Spokes are measured from the very end of the threaded end to the inside of the elbow of the head end. When measuring a spoke that's laced into a wheel, you have to take the rim tape off and look into the rim from outside to estimate how much of the spoke is inside the rim.

Spokes that are too long will protrude up inside the rim, where they can puncture the tube. You can file the ends off, so that they're flush with the top of the nipple, but that's still not good enough — only the end of the nipple is threaded, so if the spoke is too long, the nipple will have to cut its own thread on the unthreaded section of the spoke. This usually just damages the nipple thread, which then won't hold spoke tension securely.

Spokes must be long enough that they're threaded most of the way onto the nipple — if the nipple is only hanging onto the spoke by the last few threads, it will pull through as soon as the spoke is stressed.

When you build a new wheel, you start from scratch. You can work out the correct length using three-dimensional trigonometry, but it's hard math. It's easier to ask your bike shop to look it up for you — shops have tables of common hub and rim combinations, or computerized spoke-length calculating programs. Choose a quiet time, not a busy Saturday in July. The shops are most likely to help if you buy the spokes at the same time. In order to work out the correct length, the shop needs to know the hub model, rim model, number of spokes and crossing pattern, so either take along the components you're using, or buy them at the same time.

If you're building a wheel, buy a couple of extra spokes, so that you have spares later. Don't forget to pick up nipples at the same time — they don't automatically come with spokes.

Spokes come two types: "rustless" — meaning they are cheap — or "stainless." Always build with stainless. (The savings kept from using rustless will just be spent on more spokes sooner.) Good makes include DT and Sapim.

Spoke gauge

Spokes are usually either plain gauge (the same 2mm diameter all the way along) or double-butted (2mm at the ends where they normally break, and 1.8mm in the middle to save weight). Although spokes aren't a heavy component, saving weight here is particularly significant — wheels spin around their own axles, so weight saved here makes a big difference in how easily the bike accelerates. For heavier riders, plain-gauge spokes are less stretchy, so they help keep the wheel in shape when you bounce up and down on it.

The holes in the hub flanges are only just big enough for the spokes to fit through. If the fit is very tight, the spokes are more awkward to fit, but the wheel will stay true longer. Baggy hub holes allow the spokes to shift about, wearing the holes and releasing spoke tension. The width of the flange is also important. Once again, there's a compromise between ease of assembly and wheel longevity — if the hub flange is only slightly narrower than the elbow of the spoke, it will be tricky to ease the bend in the spoke through the hole. However the whole width of the spoke elbow will be supported by the inside of the hub hole, reducing the chance of spoke breakage. Some spokes are a smaller diameter at the threaded end. This does save a little weight, but means that you must use special 1.8mm nipples: while normal 2mm nipples will fit, they will work loose, usually over the first few miles that you use the nipples. Since a spoke gauge does vary from manufacturer to manufacturer, it makes sense to use the same make of nipple and spoke — even if they are supposed to be the same size, wheels built from mix-and–match components don't stay true as long.

Number of holes

Mountain bike wheels have mostly settled at 32 holes at the moment. The norm used to be 36, but as rims have become stronger, it's been possible to save weight by losing some spokes. Today, 28-spoke wheels are becoming more common, while 36 holes is still a good idea for heavier riders, or for those prone to trashing lots of wheels. The movement in expensive wheels is toward fewer spokes, but these are harder to build because, as you reduce the number of spokes, the tension in each becomes greater, and the precision balance between the tension in each spoke becomes critical. If you've not built one before, I recommend getting good at 32- and 36-hole wheels before moving onto the fancy stuff!

▲ **Rims with double eyelets stay true longer**

Eyelets

Rims are made of aluminum, which is light but relatively soft. Good-quality rims have an eyelet pressed into the rim at every spoke hole. These spread the pressure from the tension in the spoke over a wider area of the rim, and provide a smoother surface for the underside of the nipple to turn on. Single eyelets **(A)** sit on the inner surface of box-section rims. Double eyelets **(B)** are shaped to spread the pressure over both inner and outer surfaces, making the rim stronger but adding a bit of weight.

Lefts and rights

Once only rear wheels had awkward right and left sides, but the advent of disc wheels has sent fronts that way too. The lacing pattern is important because disc brakes are much more powerful than rim brakes. The spokes need to be arranged so that the strongest are lined up to resist the braking force. It's fine to build non-disc rims in the same way.

When you're building the wheels, there are lots of right and left directions. Discs are always attached on the left of the hub, cassettes on the right. Non-disc front hubs are the same both ways, but it's traditional to build them so that if you were sitting on the bike and looked down at the label on the hub, it would be the right way up. Rim labels are usually laced so that they can be read from the right-hand side. Again this doesn't really matter but it's a nice touch.

Off-center rims

There are several different makes of off-center rims, including Bontrager and Ritchey. Take care when building them — they are confusing. The spoke holes are not central but are set off to one side. Build front disc wheels so that the overhang is biggest on the left; for rear wheels the overhang should be on the right. The overhang compensates for the dish that the wheel is forced to take on because of the extra stuff on the hub — either the cassette or the disc mounting. Reducing this dish makes a stronger wheel. There will always be an arrow on the rim to help you get the right direction.

Deep-section rims

Deep-section rims are good for heavier riders because they keep their shape well, but they can be awkward to build. Good-quality rims are made of a shaped tube, bent around into a circle. With deep-section rims, it's easy to drop the nipple into the tube by mistake, instead of in one side and out the other. Once they're in there, you have to get them out, otherwise the nipple will roll around inside the rim, forever rattling. Sometimes the nipple will come out if you can shake it around until it's near the valve hole, otherwise you have to tease it out by poking it through of one of the holes with a spoke.

If the rim you're using is deep, screw the top of each nipple a couple of turns onto an extra spoke, and use that to insert the nipple through the rim hole. Unscrew the extra spoke, then screw the nipple onto the laced spoke. If you build lots of deep-section wheels, you can get a special little deep-section rim nipple screwdriver that grips the head of the nipple so you can pass it safely through the rim. (It's one of those special tools that seems extravagant to everybody except the person who has to use it . . .)

Nearing the end of the build, you have to bend spokes to maneuver them around those already fitted. This is fine, but ensure they don't get kinked. A gentle bend over most of the length of the spoke is far better than a sharp kink. You'll always need to bend the spokes slightly when lacing them onto the rim, but building with deep-section rims means fitting shorter spokes into a smaller space, so the bend must be tighter.

Disc wheels

Disc wheels are no more complex to build than non-disc wheels. The flanges are usually bigger, which makes it easier to lace them, but the front wheel must be slightly dished to allow space on the left-hand side for the rotor. The amount of dishing is minor, though, so the tension on each side of the wheel remains fairly even.

Building your own set of wheels is not as difficult as you might think

Wheel building is often treated as a mysterious art, unfathomable to mortals. It's actually not as difficult as it's made out to be. Producing a perfectly tensioned set of wheels that will run true for years in half an hour does take a lot of practice, but with a bit of patience, and a free afternoon, you should be able to make your own wheel out of a set of spokes, a rim and a hub.

Building your own wheels is a satisfying achievement, impressing other cyclists more than most other bicycle-fixing tasks. It breaks down to two parts: lacing and tensioning. Lacing — weaving all the spokes so that they join the hub to the rim — looks complicated, but is easy. Tensioning   tightening all the spokes so that they hold the rim round, true and centered — looks easy, but is complicated.

Follow the lacing steps carefully — they look confusing, but as long as you don't panic, you'll be fine. The key to lacing wheels successfully is remembering that there are four sets of spokes, each of which follows the same pattern. For each set, get the first spoke in the right place, then follow the pattern around the wheel until you come back to where you started. You really only have to think carefully about four spokes — not 32 or 36. On each side of the wheel, alternate spokes face in and out of the flange, and radiate clockwise or counterclockwise from the hub to the rim. At the rim, alternate spokes are connected to opposite sides of the hub.

Spoke key

Buy a nice spoke key with which to build wheels. The small ones on multi-tools are great for emergencies, but are awkward to use for more than a few rough nipple twists. Big dedicated spoke keys are more comfortable than little cheap ones that make the nipples hard to turn when putting the final bits of tension on, leaving you with sore fingers. There are two different common nipple sizes, refered to variously as "Japanese" and "American," "small" and "large," or "red" and "yellow," refers to the colors used to differentiate between the two sizes of the most popular spoke key, made by Buddy. These are great for wheelbuilding: they hold the nipple on all four sides, so that the flats don't get damaged. Check your nipples fit neatly into the spoke key before you buy it.

Wheel jig

Your most essential tool for learning to build good wheels is a wheel jig. A basic $80 model is fine for learning to build wheels on, although average workshop models cost $700. It is possible to build wheels without a wheel jig, using your bicycle frame as a guide, but it's a difficult way to learn. Splurge on a jig or borrow one if you can.

The wheel jig holds the wheel steady between two clamps. Different makes have slightly different features, but all work in the same way: an indicator arm comes out from the jig and sits beside the rim. The distance between the indicator and the rim can be adjusted, and is set so that the rim just touches the indicator. The roundness of the wheel is checked by spinning the wheel and watching how the gap between the rim and the indicator changes. The tension in the spokes is adjusted where the gap is smallest or greatest to reduce the total amount of wobble in the rim. The indicator is then moved closer, and the process is repeated until the rim is straight. Cheaper, more portable and storable models have an indicator on just one side of the rim, whereas more expensive types have an indicator on both sides.

Wheels are surprisingly heavy once they're spinning. If you can clamp or bolt the jig onto a workbench, it will help to stop it from wobbling around, making it easier to see the gap between your rim and the indicator gauge on the jig. Plenty of light also helps, as does a piece of white card or paper under the jig, so that you look through the gap onto the card.

These wheelbuilding guidelines take you through building a front and rear wheel in the most common three-cross style. If you want to know more about wheel building, get a copy of *The Bicycle Wheel* by Jobst Brandt. It's packed with technical information, explaining how spoked wheels actually work, how to build wheels in other patterns, and how to know when you should use other patterns.

The delicate art of lacing up the spokes for a new front wheel

We start with a front wheel, because they are much easier. The wheel is built up in four groups of spokes, one set radiating out in each direction from each side of the hub. Divide your spokes up into four equal batches before you start: four batches of eight for a 32-spoke wheel, four batches of nine for a 36-spoke wheel, and so on . . .

Assemble all components. If you're reusing a hub, clean it up, taking special care with the spoke holes. If they are dirty, the fresh spokes you push through them will get grit in the threads and become difficult to turn on their nipples. Oil each of the spoke holes in the hub and all of the holes in the rim, so the nipples can turn easily. Oil the spoke threads too. Hold the hub so that the right side of the hub is upward.

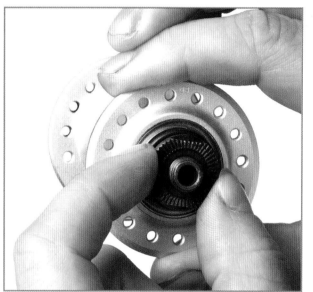

Servicing the hub

If you're rebuilding on an old hub, check that the axle spins freely, with no side-to-side movement. If the axle feels rough or knocks, service the hub before you start lacing the spokes onto it. It's easier to manipulate and clean the hub on its own, and this is a good time to check the condition of the hub.

It's better to discover that the hub is almost worn out before you start building than to realize that you've got a perfectly tensioned rim attached to a pepper grinder. Check the condition of the spoke holes in the flange too. They should be neat and round. Worn holes will have been pulled into a teardrop shape. Replace hubs once this happens — the spokes in your newly built wheel won't retain tension.

◀ **Check that the hub spins smoothly, with no side-to-side play**

LACING A FRONT WHEEL

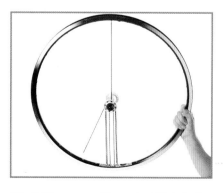

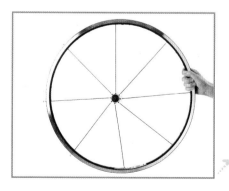

Step 1: Take the first group of eight spokes and drop them down through every other hole in the upper flange of the hub. The heads of the spokes go on the outside of the flange.

Step 2: Take any one of the spokes. This is the first spoke of the group, so you must get it in the right hole. Hold the hub vertically, with loose spokes hanging down. Hold the rim flat, label upside down. The correct hole is immediately to the left of the valve hole. Pop the spoke through the hole and trap it by screwing on a nipple a couple of turns.

Step 3: Take the next spoke counterclockwise around the hub. Moving counterclockwise around the rim, miss three holes, then pop the spoke in the next one. Trap it with another nipple. Take the next counterclockwise spoke, miss three holes, and take the next. Continue until you arrive back at the valve hole. Because each wheel consists of four sets of crossed spokes, the ritual of fitting the spoke into every fourth hole holds true regardless of the number of holes in the rim.

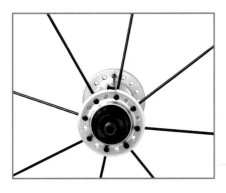

Step 4: Keep the rim facing toward you. See the far side of the hub has the same number of holes as the near side, but they are offset; each far-side hole falls between two near-side holes. Find your first spoke again, next to the valve hole — we'll call it spoke 1. Hold the wheel upright, with the valve hole at the top. The next spoke drops into the flange hole just left of spoke 1, and laces onto the rim on the next hole to the left of spoke 1.

Step 5: Drop a spoke through alternate holes on the further flange, and follow the pattern around the rim, fitting a spoke in every fourth hole. Now, starting with the valve hole and moving counterclockwise, you should have spokes in the next two holes, then two gaps, then two spokes, two gaps, all the way round. You should be able to see the heads of all the spokes. Hold the rim still, and twist the hub counterclockwise so it looks like this picture.

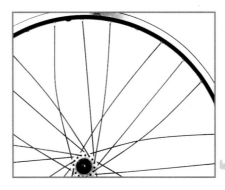

Step 6: Turn the wheel so the other side faces you. Shake the hub lightly to settle the nipples into the rim, but make sure you keep the twist in the hub. Drop a spoke through all the remaining holes on the flange nearest to you. Take one of these spokes. It will currently be hanging down between two of the pairs of spokes already laced, but you have to send it clockwise around the rim. Curving it gently, ease it between the spokes.

Step 7: It crosses three spokes on its way to the rim, passing under two and over the last one. The first one it crosses, near the flange, is its neighbor. It goes under the next one too. Weave it gently over the next spoke. Check where this crossing spoke meets the rim — your spoke fits in the hole that's two further around clockwise. Complete the pattern, fitting in each spoke four holes on. N.B. count all holes with or without a spoke, but never count the valve hole.

Step 8: Without turning the wheel over, drop a spoke through all the remaining holes on the far side of the hub. Lift up each one in turn. It passes over the first two spokes it meets, starting with its neighbor, and under the third. It should be obvious which hole it fits into, because there aren't many left. It's the one "two further on" from the last one it passed over.

Step 9: Complete the pattern, weaving each spoke at a time over two and under one. You're all laced now. Starting at the valve, tighten each spoke until the thread just disappears inside the nipple. A screwdriver or a spoke key speeds this up. Now you are ready to put tension into the spokes. Go to the truing and tension section on pages 166–68.

Toolbox

Tools for wheelbuilding
- Decent, well-fitting spoke key
- Wheel jig — basic models are fine
- Oil for spoke threads
- Threadlock to be applied to spokes after final tensioning (optional)
- Fresh rim tape if necessary

Lacing a back wheel

Now you're ready for the next step. If you can build a front wheel, you can build a back one, but there are complications because of the cassette.

The right-hand flange (the shoulder on the hub with holes for the spoke heads) has to be shoved over toward the center of the hub to accommodate the sprockets, so that the spokes on that side are doing a harder job. That's why when you break a spoke, it's usually on the drive side, where the cassette is attached. It makes sense, therefore, to start with shorter spokes on the drive side. The length difference is usually about 2mm (⅛ inch), which may not seem a lot, but it matters.

That there are two lengths of spoke makes things a little more complicated when lacing the wheel; you must be careful not to mix up the spokes. It helps to make up the four groups before you start lacing, two batches of shorter ones for the drive side, and two batches of longer ones for the non-drive side. Each group has a quarter of the total number of spokes, so if you're building a 32-hole wheel, each group has eight spokes; if you're building a 36-hole wheel, each group has nine spokes. The ritual of lacing is slightly different for a back wheel.

LACING A BACK WHEEL

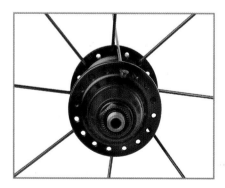

Step 1: With the drive side (the side on which the cassette fits) of the hub facing upward, drop the first batch (7, 8, or 9) of shorter, drive-side spokes into every other hole in the top flange.

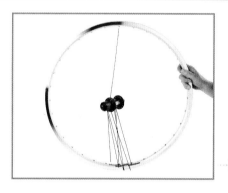

Step 2: Hold the rim upright. For extra points, make sure any labels are facing toward you. Take any one of the spokes and put it through the rim hole immediately to the left of the valve hole. Trap it with a nipple.

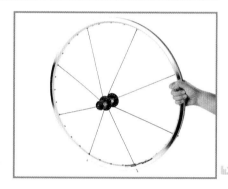

Step 3: Working round in an counterclockwise direction, fit each successive spoke into every fourth hole, i.e., miss three holes, fit a spoke, etc. Count all rim holes with or without a spoke, but never count the valve hole. Turn the wheel around so that the non-drive side of the hub faces you, keeping the valve hole at the top.

Step 4: Take a batch of the longer, non-drive side spokes. Look at the alignment of the holes in this side. You'll see that each hole on the far side falls between two holes on the near side. Choose a hole in the near flange, so that when you push a spoke through, it hangs to the right of the spoke already fitted next to the valve hole.

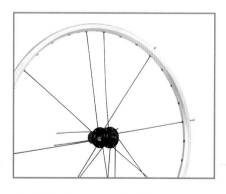

Step 5: Fit this spoke to the right of the spoke beside the valve hole. Secure it with a nipple. Drop longer spokes through every other hole around the hub.

Step 6: Follow the spoking pattern clockwise, missing three holes then fitting a spoke until you reach the valve hole again. Check the pattern — starting at the valve hole and working around clockwise, you should have two spokes, then two gaps, all the way back around to the valve hole.

Step 7: Without turning the wheel around, drop the next batch of shorter spokes through the remaining holes in the far flange so that the heads are between the flanges. Take the hub and twist it clockwise while holding the rim still.

Step 8: The spokes you've already fitted radiate out counterclockwise from the rim. The next spoke has to go the opposite way. The first spoke it crosses is its immediate neighbor — they cross with the flange between them. Keep outside the next spoke, then weave the spoke under the third. Check where this spoke meets the rim. The adjacent rim hole clockwise will already have a spoke in it — fit your spoke into the next hole clockwise.

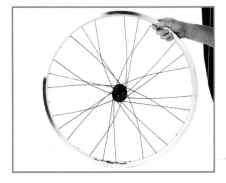

Step 9: Repeat with the rest of this group, fitting each successive spoke four rim holes on from the last, counting rim holes whether they have spokes in or not. Check your pattern again. Starting at the valve hole and working clockwise, you should have three spokes then a gap, all the way back around to the valve.

Step 10: Take the final set of longer non–drive-side spokes. Push them through the final set of holes from the drive side so that their heads are between the flanges. The hub area is quite crowded now, so ease the spokes through the flange holes as carefully as you can with a minimum of bending.

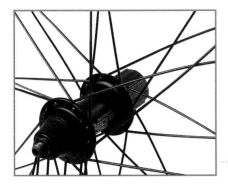

Step 11: Facing the non-drive side of the wheel, this spoke radiates out clockwise. The first spoke it crosses is its immediate neighbor, with the flange between the crossed spoke. This spoke passes over the next spoke it meets. Curve it gently to pass under the next one. Pop it into the next available hole and keep it in place with a nipple. Repeat with the other spokes in this group, fitting the spokes into the remaining holes.

Step 12: When you come to truing, the rear wheel takes a little longer than the front. Take it slowly, in very small steps. The drive side spokes end up a lot tighter than the non-drive side; typically, the non-drive side will have two-thirds the tension of the drive side. Dishing is also an issue; the wheel wants to start further to the left, and you have to pull it back.

Spoke-lacing — quick guide

Rear wheel:
- Drive side up, drop spokes through top flange
- Hold rim upright, valve hole at top
- Hold hub drive side toward you, lace any spoke in rim hole adjacent to and left of valve hole
- Continue pattern counterclockwise, lacing spokes into every fourth hole
- Turn wheel around so non-drive side faces you
- Feed spoke through nearest flange so that it passes immediately to the right of top spoke on far side of hub
- Fit this adjacent to and onto the right of the first spoke you fitted, on the far side from the valve hole
- Continue pattern clockwise
- Twist hub clockwise
- Keep wheel same way around, push spokes through remaining holes in further flange
- Turn wheel over, then take any spoke, cross it over its neighbor (with the flange between the two), over the next spoke, and under the third
- Count two from the last spoke you crossed and fit the spoke in the next hole
- Continue the pattern with the rest of this batch
- Push spokes through remaining holes in far side of flange
- Turn wheel over, then take any spoke, cross it over its neighbor (with the flange between the two), over the next spoke, and under the third
- Count two from the last spoke you crossed, and fit the spoke in the next hole
- Continue the pattern with the rest of this batch

Building your own wheel: tensioning and truing the spokes

This is the part that looks easier than it is. The spokes must all be tight, so that the wheel is strong and perfectly balanced and the rim runs true. The balancing comprises four separate operations: correcting the true, correcting the hop, correcting the dish, and correcting the tension. Part of the reason wheel building has always been considered difficult is that adjusting one of these factors affects all the others.

The four operations listed above break down as follows:

True

The spokes are laced alternately to the left and right sides of the hub. For example, a zone of the rim that is too far to the left can be corrected by tightening the spokes that go to the right. Since every other spoke is connected to opposite sides of the hub, this can be broken down into a series of very small steps, always truing just the part of the rim with the worst bulge.

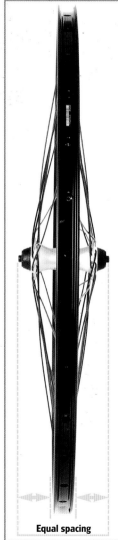

Equal spacing

Hop

The rim must be an equal distance from the center of the hub all the way around. If it isn't, the brake blocks will be hard to set up, and you will kangaroo down the road, your wheel falling apart in no time at all. If a section of the rim hops outward, i.e., is too far from the hub, it can be drawn inward by tightening two or four spokes centered around the peak of the hop. Tighten the same number of right-hand side spokes as left. Adjusting the hop always throws the wheel slightly out of true, but try to minimize the effect.

It's easier to correct an outward hop, where a section of the rim is too far from the hub, than it is a flat spot.

Dish

The rim must end up centered between the locknuts, so that when you put the wheel into the bicycle frame, the rim runs evenly between fork legs, between seat and chainstays, and between swingarms. Tightening all the spokes on the right-hand side will move the entire rim to the right; tightening all the spokes on the left will move the entire rim to the left. The rear wheel has a cassette bolted onto the right-hand side so that the heads of the spokes on that side are closer to the center of the hub. This means that the right-hand spokes have to be tighter than those on the left, in order to keep the rim central — that's why they're more likely to break than those on the left-hand side of the rear hub.

Front disc hubs also have to allow a little bit of extra space on the left-hand side, but the dishing required is minor.

◀ **Dish: these two distances must be the same in width**

Tension

Tension is tricky to get right. You can easily destroy a rim by overcranking the spoke tension until the rim collapses. For the home mechanic, the easiest way to ensure the tension is correct on the wheel you're building is by comparing with another set of wheels.

Take hold of a pair of almost parallel spokes on a completed, functioning wheel, and squeeze them. Then do the same with a pair of almost parallel spokes on a working set. Be sure to compare like with like; front-wheel spokes have lower tension than backs, and the right-hand side of back wheels has higher tension than the left when the dishing is correct.

Tightening the spokes

Once your wheel is laced, the next step is to tension it. It's important to take this in small steps, increasing the tension gradually and evenly, while constantly checking that the wheel remains round. The most common mistake is to crank up the tension too fast, without straightening the rim between each round of spoke tightening.

Follow steps 1–6 below for a wheel that is fairly round, true and dished. Then start again at the valve hole, and go methodically around the rim, tightening each spoke a quarter-turn. Repeat steps 3 to 6, truing the wheel more precisely. Go round again, tightening each spoke a further turn.

Refer to a set of working wheels, so that you can compare spoke tension. Keep tightening all spokes, then correcting true, dish and hop. Once you get close to the tension in the working wheels, stress-relieve the spokes; see page 168.

TIGHTENING THE SPOKES

Step 1: If you've just built your wheel, most spokes will be loose. Give all spokes an even amount of tension. Tighten each nipple until the spoke thread just disappears. Set wheel in the jig and spin. Pluck the spokes with a fingernail. To start the truing process, most need to be tight enough to get a note from. If most do, skip to next step. Otherwise, start at the valve hole and tighten each one a quarter-turn. Repeat until the wheel has some tension.

Step 2: Once you have a degree of tension in the wheel, you can start truing it. Spin the wheel again. It probably doesn't look round at all. Your jig has an adjustable indicator — set this so that when you spin the wheel, the indicator only touches the side of the rim in one place. This is the most out-of-true section.

Step 3: Find the center of this biggest bulge. Loosen the spoke at the outside of the bend a half-turn, and tighten the spokes on either side a quarter-turn. This won't make much difference, but that's okay. This step has potential for going horribly wrong, so we'll take it in very small stages to maximize our chances of success.

Step 4: Repeat the procedure. Spin the wheel, identify the worst bulge, loosen the spoke at the center, tighten those at both sides, until the wheel moves from side to side no more than 10mm ($^3/_8$ inch). This can mean working repeatedly on the same area; don't worry as long as you are always attacking the biggest bulge.

Step 5: Once you have the wheel vaguely true, spin it, and check for hops. Move hop indicator on your wheel jig as close as it will go; watch the gap vary as wheel turns. It's easier to draw rim nearer to the hub than force it away, so concentrate on areas where rim hops outward. As with truing the wheel, work on the largest hop. When you find it, tighten the two spokes at its center a half-turn. Repeat until the total hop in the rim is less than 3mm ($^3/_{16}$ inch).

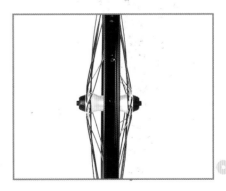

Step 6: Check the dish is correct; see page 166 for details if you're unsure how dish works. Turn the wheel over in the jig or in the bike without moving the indicators. If the wheel is perfectly dished, the rim sits in the same place again. If it's off to one side, it moves over in the jig. Correct by tightening all the spokes on the outer side one quarter-turn. If this is not enough, loosen all the opposite spokes a quarter-turn. Repeat until the wheel sits centrally.

Wheel building: how to make sure the tension in your spokes is right

When you put tension in the wheel and true it, the spokes can get twisted. Instead of the nipple turning on the spoke thread, it can twist the whole spoke. The tension may look correct, but the first time you cycle down a bumpy road on your new shiny wheel, the twisted spoke will unwind as the tensions in the spokes change, and the wheel will immediately drop out of true.

When your wheel is almost fully tensioned, it's a good idea to go around the wheel and relieve the stress in the spokes. Start at the valve hole, and choose a pair of nearly parallel spokes from the same side of the hub. Squeeze them firmly together. Work around the wheel, first from one side of the wheel, then the other.

You may hear the spokes creaking or pinging as you do this. Once you get back round to the valve hole, check the wheel again for side-to-side wobble. You may need to true and then stress-relieve several times. The wheel is ready when you can stress-relieve all the spokes without affecting the truth of the wheel and the tension is similar to that of a functioning wheel. Some people swear by standing on the rim at this point as a final stress-relief procedure. I say don't do this — it's excessive and unnecessary.

Freshly built wheels last longest if given two or three trues as they settle in; it's worth popping the wheel back into the jig after 160 kilometers (100 miles) to keep it exactly straight.

▲ **Squeeze hard to stress-relieve the spokes**

Spoke length L

Effective rim diameter . . . . .D
Flange hole circle diameter . . . . .d
Flange width . . . . .W
Flange hole diameter . . . . .S
Crossing pattern X
Number of spokes . . . . .N

Work out first:
$T = 360 \times X/(N/2)$
$A = (d/2) \times \sin(T)$
$B = D/2 - ([d/2] \times \cos[T])$
$C = W/2$

Spoke length:
$$L = \sqrt{(A^2 + B^2 + C^2)} - \frac{S}{2}$$
Alternatively, to save time, search the Net.

Spoke-length mathematics

◆ Effective rim diameter — This is the distance directly across the rim, measured from the underside of a nipple head to the underside of the opposite nipple head. This is tricky to measure directly, as the underside of the nipple head is inside the rim. I measure the length of a nipple, from under the head to the end; i.e., the total length minus the head. For DT nipples, this measurement is 10mm (⅜ inch). Then drop the nipple through the rim and measure the amount that's exposed. Take one from the other, which gives you the length of nipple inside the rim. Measure across the inside diameter of the rim, between opposite spoke holes, and add twice the concealed nipple length — once for each end. This gives you the effective rim diameter.

◆ If you look at the hub from one side, the hub holes make a circle. Measure across this circle for the flange hole circle diameter, from the middle of a hub hole to the middle of the opposite hub hole.

◆ The flange width is measured across the hub, from the center of one flange to the center of the other.

◆ The flange hole diameter is the size of the spoke holes in the hub — usually about 2mm (⅛ inch).

Troubleshooting wheels

Symptom	Cause	Solution	Page
Bike feels slow, you feel tired after short rides	Cones too tight on front or rear wheels, or both	Adjust cones so that wheels spin smoothly	141
Bike feels uncertain when cornering	Cones too loose — wheel will wobble from side to side on the frame	Adjust cone so that the wheel can't rock from side to side in the frame	141
	Wheel is buckled	True wheel so that rim runs true and doesn't wobble from side to side as the wheel spins	155
	Insufficient tire pressure	Inflate tire to minimum pressure marked on the sidewall of the tire	N/A
Rim brakes — rim rubs on V- or cantilever brake blocks	Wheel is buckled	True wheel, so that rim runs true and doesn't wobble from side to side as the wheel spins	155
Brake blocks wear quickly	Rims dirty	Clean rims with degreaser	46
	Rims worn	Check rims for scours, grooves or ridges — replace rims or wheels	138, 160–8
Spokes loosen repeatedly	Rim buckled	Uneven spoke tension in buckled wheels causes spokes to loosen — rebuild wheel with new rim	160–8
Frequent punctures	Tire still has sharp things stuck in it	Check tire carefully, feeling around the inside for protruding thorns or glass — fold the tire inside out, so that you can see more clearly	153
	Spokes poking through the rim	Run your fingers around the inside of the rim, checking for sharp spoke ends — file sharp ends off	N/A
	Rim tape shifting, exposing spoke holes	Replace rim tape with wider, tighter one	154
UST tires leak	Tires need pumping before every ride	This is normal! Fit tubes for normal riding, take them out again on race days — an unexpected training bonus!	151

Suspension

There isn't room to cover every procedure for every type of fork here — that would take a whole book on its own. This chapter gives you an overview of current technology, deciphering the jargon that makes suspension so tricky to talk about. The most important process for a pair of forks, or for a shock, is to set it up to suit your weight, your bike and your riding style. This is not as complicated as it sounds!

You'll need to use these instructions in conjunction with the owner's manual for your forks, so if you haven't got the original, you can check your bike shop for a spare, or download one from the Internet — web addresses for all the major manufacturers are in the contact list on page 240. This will help you identify the correct adjusting knobs, levers and dials, and give you starting points for the correct sag and damping settings. This chapter takes you through the process of adjusting your suspension so that you get the most out of it by testing and tuning the settings and carrying out basic maintenance.

Fork and shock manufacturers have become much more wary of encouraging you to go too deep into your own forks in recent years. The instruction manuals for some early forks suggested that you should completely strip and rebuild your own forks after every eight hours of riding time. Service intervals now are much longer, but in many cases stripping your own forks at home will void your warranty. In the case of rear shocks, you should never disassemble nitrogen-charged damping units yourself — the high pressures inside make this dangerous, and they have to be refilled with nitrogen once you're finished, a substance you won't find lying around in a normal home workshop.

Concentrate on the most basic aspects of setup, cleaning and inspection. I've included a fork service to give you an idea of what this involves, but always follow the manufacturer's recommendations about how far you should go. All the major manufacturers have authorized service centers, where you can send your shocks or forks for repairs that, if you did them yourself, would void your warranty.

Fox Float rear suspension unit

Suspension: why you need it and how it works

Suspension technology is moving very quickly. What is currently state of the art is actually more likely to be part of a great work in progress than the final form. One happy result of this is that good, reliable designs constantly get cheaper and better. It's easy to forget how much better suspension forks are now than, say, six or seven years ago, and to realize that for the same amount you paid for the fork back then, you can now get a whole bike with a better fork.

Many people originally resisted suspension forks — the extra weight was a high price to pay for the clunky suspension, which seemed to need an hour of servicing for every hour it was ridden. But even the early forks made bikes feel so much faster, and helped them stick to the ground much better.

Although we now see fewer completely weird designs, radically different approaches continue to evolve, and there is no sign of suspension shaking down into just one clear "best design." In fact, sometimes the easiest way to tell what the next favorite design will be is by checking which one is currently being slagged off as outdated.

You would have thought that once we'd decided to fit suspension to bicycles, we could borrow the technology from other disciplines. But it didn't seem to work out like that. Although many of the best designers working on the problems come from other areas, like John Whyte from Formula One racing cars and Keith Bontrager from motocross, the bicycle seems to need to be thought about in different ways.

One reason is that the power source — the rider — has a low output, and you can't just slap on a bigger engine. The other is that rider weight makes up a big proportion of the suspended weight, but that weight might vary considerably from one rider to another, even on the same sized bike.

Suspending disbelief

So, what does it all matter? You can hardly buy a decent mountain bike with rigid forks any more, and full suspension goes up in quality and down in price all the time. All those people who used to say, "It's all very well for the kids, but it's so heavy you can't climb at all on it," used to be right. Early suspension was heavy, and bounced so much when you climbed that you might as well be trying to hop up on a pogo stick. Some people are still saying this, but we can't hear them any more because we've left them behind at the bottom of the hill.

Full suspension is light enough to climb on now, and good design means that full suspension helps you climb by keeping the back wheel pressed down into the ground, finding whatever grip there is to help you up hills. Suspension isn't just for people who want to jump off roofs — it allows you to blast over rough ground without carefully picking a line as you would with a rigid bike.

Suspension does need more care and attention than other parts of your bike. The first surprising thing is that when it's new, it needs attention right away. When you buy a new fork, or a new bike with forks and a rear shock, you need to spend a little time adjusting it. The adjustments are very personal — nobody can set it up for you because adjustments must be done to your weight and reaction speed. It takes maybe upward of half an hour — and you need to take your bike somewhere you can play safely without traffic. Follow the instructions in the sections on setting up your forks (page 180) and setting up your shocks (pages 189–90).

Once your suspension is set up correctly, check and clean it regularly — shocks don't respond at all to neglect. A check and clean needs no special tools and is easy to do, but it should be done regularly. There's no harm in checking shocks after every ride, but they also need a thorough inspection once a month — see pages 182–6 for forks and pages 191–3 for rear shocks.

Doing a full service on suspension forks and shocks is more advanced and often requires special tools particular to the make and model of your bike. Previously, the instructions that came with forks were very comprehensive — manufacturers positively encouraged everybody to get in there and get dirty — but in the last few years there has been a clear move away from this. Indeed, most manufacturers now take the opposite stance, with clear injunctions for you to not go further than the basic maintenance and regular inspection set out in the owner's manual. However, your forks and shocks still have to be serviced frequently, so either go to your bike shop or send the fork or shock off to a shock specialist — see contact details in the back of the book. The strip-down of a fork on page 182 is to show you the kind of thing that happens when an authorized agent services them.

The same applies to rear shocks — you are expected to keep them clean and lubricated, but not to delve too deeply into their innards, as this will void your warranty.

Remember to increase the frequency of servicing if you ride in sandy, salty or muddy conditions, if you cover a lot of miles, or if you have a reputation for breaking parts of your bicycle.

Part of the mystery of suspension is that talking about it demands all kinds of jargon: terms for the parts, for the adjustments and for how the fork reacts to the terrain. Much confusion arises because most of the words have both a real-world meaning and a suspension-world meaning, which, while not altogether different, is a lot more precise.

Vital elements

Everybody claims their design is the best and most unique, but all suspension does the same job. A fork needs only two elements to work: a spring, which allows the wheel to move so you don't have to, and damping, which controls the speed at which the spring moves.

The spring can be a chamber of air, a coil spring, a rod of springy elastomers, or a combination of all three. The spring performs the visible function — shock absorption. When you hit something, the spring gets shorter, absorbing the pressure. The stiffness of the spring controls how far it moves when you hit something — a soft spring gives a lot; a stiff spring gives a little.

The more mysterious element is damping. Damping is vital because it controls the speed of the spring action. Pogo sticks are an example of springs with no damping — if you bounce on them, they keep bouncing. This is great fun on a pogo stick but terrible on a bike. Damping controls the speed of the spring movement. You may be able to control the speed of the damping with external knobs, or it may be factory-set. More expensive forks allow you to control the speed of the fork compression separately from the speed at which the fork rebounds.

Buttons, bells and whistles

More controls doesn't always mean better. One of the problems with buttons, bells and whistles is that there are as many wrong positions as right ones and, if you're not systematic, you can make things worse rather than better.

The least familiar function is lockout, which does exactly what it says on the packet. It locks out the suspension, so the bike doesn't bob around and is particularly useful for smooth climbs and road riding, where you don't need the suspension. Most useful for climbing are forks that lock out in the compressed position, which helps you to keep your weight over the front wheel on steep bits.

Learn the language: travel

Travel is one of those suspension jargon words that means exactly what it says: how far your fork travels from its most extended to its most compressed position.

Many early suspension forks were proud of traveling all of 63mm (2½ inches). Today, 100mm (4 inches) is a common fork travel, and travel of 150mm (6 inches) or so is not uncommon.

These longer travels come at a price though — they're always heavier because you've got more fork material, and they have also to be beefier, otherwise they flex too much. Flexible forks are no good because they don't corner confidently, and they waste your pedaling energy. The other advantage of shorter forks shows up when you climb: long forks lift the front of the bike up, making it difficult to keep the front wheel on the ground during steep ascents. Similar compromises exist for rear suspension: loads of travel is great for jumping off things, but it is not as handy for climbing up them.

Forks with 130mm (5 inches) or 150mm (6 inches) of travel are for freeride and downhill use, as the long springs will absorb big landing forces without too much stress.

Adjustable travel

This is an effort to reconcile the compromises between long travel, which is great for absorbing big bumps, and short travel, which is more efficient for climbing. Certain kinds of suspension forks and shocks are available that allow you to change your travel on the move without getting off the bike, although personally I prefer not to be fiddling around with travel-adjust knobs while whizzing along. Including adjustable travel in a fork adds cost, but it's worthwhile for versatility. Be aware that in some forks the adjustability in the travel is obtained by preloading the spring, leading to a higher spring rate for shorter travel settings. This should be an advantage — stiffening the spring in its short-travel, climbing mode — but some people don't like the way it changes the feel of the bike. Test-ride adjustable travel forks through their range before you commit yourself.

Learning the language of suspension: sag and preload

Your suspension is there to do a simple job — taking short, sharp shocks, and turning them into smoother, more controllable forces. This allows you to travel fast over uneven terrain, maintaining as level a path as possible, saving your energy. and allowing you to pick shorter, quicker lines on the trail.

Sag

Suspension moves up and down as you go over bumps and through potholes in the trail. Since the ideal is for your body to move in as straight a line as possible, ironing out the irregularities, it makes sense for the resting position of your suspension to be around the middle of its travel — so it can extend into dips as well as compressing over bumps. If the fork extends into dips so that you don't fall into them, you don't have to ride out of them, saving you some energy.

Sag is the distance that your fork or shock compresses when you sit still on your bike in your normal riding position. It's worked out by measuring the length of your fork or shock with and without you on the bike, then subtracting one number from the other. This tells you how much your weight has compressed the fork or shock.

The amount your forks compress when you sit on the bike depends partly on how much you weigh, and partly on the geometry of the bike, so it needs to be set up individually for each person on his own bike. For those who can't be bothered to measure and adjust, new forks and shocks are supplied preset with an average amount of sag, but your suspension will work much better when tailored to you and your bike.

Each suspension fork manufacturer recommends an ideal amount of sag for your particular fork. There's no hard-and-fast rule, and suggested starting points range from 10 to 40 per cent of your total travel.

You also need to take into account what kind of ride you want — if you race, you set your forks up with a little less sag to minimize the amount of energy lost bobbing up and down. If you ride all day, you set them up with slightly more sag so your bike is comfortable to ride, absorbing trail noise so you don't get as tired. Rougher trails need still more sag and, if you jump around, you set your forks soft to absorb the force of landing.

Preload

This is the adjustment you make to the spring to alter the amount of sag. Increasing preload by pumping air into an air spring or compressing a coil spring will make the spring stiffer, keeping you higher in the air — less sag. Reducing pressure in an air spring, or unwinding the preload on a coil spring, reduces the sag and sits you lower down.

Altering the preload is the single most important adjustment for you to make on your forks or suspension because it sets the fork or shock up to match your weight and bike geometry.

Coil springs will keep their adjustment once you've set it, but air spring forks tend to leak slowly, so they need to be checked every couple of months. You need a shock pump to measure and adjust the air pressure. Occasionally air forks come supplied with a pump, but it's more common for you to have to buy one separately. Shock pumps have narrow barrels and pressure gauges so that you can set the pressure accurately.

Topping out and bottoming out

Both these terms mean "hitting the end of your available travel." Bottoming out is when you hit something hard, and your forks or shock compress completely. Topping out is when your fork or shock extends and reaches the limit of its travel. First generation suspension forks used to let you know this in no uncertain terms — the end of the stanchion hit the inside of the fork with an alarming thwack. This was so unsettling that fork manufacturers soon designed a form of stop at each end of the travel, so that now you run into the buffers at the end of the track rather than crashing into the barrier. It's often considered a bad thing to top or bottom out — but don't be concerned. Ideally, your forks should be set up so you bottom out about once every ride — otherwise you're not using the full extent of your fork or shock travel. Put a ziptie loosely around the shaft of your shock or the stanchion of your fork, and push it down to the seal before you ride. The fork or shock will push it up again as it travels, and show you how far the shock is moving.

Learning the language of suspension: the spring thing

The spring in your fork is in many ways the simplest component — when you compress the fork, the spring resists the compressing, and it re-extends the fork as soon as you release the compressing force.

Air springs, coil springs, elastomers

It may be freely available, light, and highly adjustable, but air can be pesky because it doesn't like being trapped inside the fork. The fork manufacturer has to spend your money ensuring it doesn't leak. An air spring works by trapping air in a chamber at the top of the fork leg. As you compress the fork (by riding into an obstacle), you squash the air into an even smaller space, which it resists, responding by pushing out the fork again to make more space for itself and acting like a spring.

Coil springs are very simple, and neither leak nor get affected by temperature. But if you want to change their springiness much, you either have to buy a new one or exchange it. If you buy a bike or a fork with a coil spring, make sure it's the right stiffness when you buy it by checking that you can adjust the sag for your weight. You can tune in a small amount of stiffness by altering the preload, but you can't make major changes — the spring has to be the right stiffness from the beginning. Exchanging steel springs for titanium ones is expensive but saves a little weight.

Elastomers used to be the most common spring type, but they have been largely superseded by coil springs. Elastomers are made of rods of urethane, usually in differently colors to denote their stiffness. Elastomers are a cheap spring medium, but their spring rate is affected by temperature, so they become much stiffer when cold and much softer when warm. Fine-tuning tricks for the first generation of elastomer-sprung forks included drilling holes across the elastomers to make them softer.

Your forks may have springs in both legs, but it's also common to have springs in one leg and a damping mechanism in the other. If there are springs in only one leg, they will almost always be in the left leg, nearest the disc brake. This keeps the damping mechanism farther away from the heat generated by the disc brake, which will affect the viscosity of the damping oil. Having springs in just one leg doesn't make the fork unbalanced — the two sides of the lower legs still work together as a unit.

To get the best of both worlds, some forks use a combination of air and coil springs.

Spring rate

This is a measure of how much the suspension moves under pressure. Under the same force, a spring with a higher spring rate compresses less than one with a lower spring rate. If you are lighter, you use a spring with a lower spring rate than someone heavier.

Progressive spring rates

All suspension depends on the spring, either air or coil. Both types perform the same function: when you press on the spring, it shortens slightly. When you ride along on your bike, and you hit a rock, force is applied to the fork, which then compresses. One difference between air and coil spring forks is how they behave through their stroke. Coil spring forks are linear — that is, it takes roughly the same amount of force to compress the second half of the coil as it does to compress the first.

Air springs behave differently. When you pressurize your fork, you put a lot of air into a small space. The air dislikes being compressed in the first place, so when you hit a bump and compress the fork, squashing the air even more, it resists and pushes the fork back out again — doing the spring thing. But, as the fork compresses, the space that the air is in gets even smaller, and it dislikes being compressed even more. In other words, the beginning of the stroke takes less force to compress than the end. The disadvantage is that air forks are less active over small bumps.

Negative air springs

As well as the regular positive air spring, forks like the Rock Shox Sid have a second air spring, a negative one, which sits at the top of the fork leg and compresses upward (rather than downward). This allows you to tune the reaction of the fork to small bumps. Less negative air pressure makes the fork stiffer at the beginning of its travel, so that it doesn't bob so much when you climb out of the saddle. More negative air pressure allows the fork to move more at the beginning of its travel, soaking up small bumps.

Learn the language of suspension: damping

Whenever you hit a bump, your fork and rear shock (or both) compress, absorbing the shock. When you've gone over the bump, they spring back out again, ready for the next bump. But you don't want them to spring out quickly and bounce you off your bike (if we wanted to play that game we'd return to rigid bikes), so we "damp" the movement, by making the rebound extension happen more slowly than the original compression.

This is a good thing. However, you can take it too far. If the rebound happens too slowly, and you ride over a series of bumps, the fork compresses when you go over the first bump, and will not have had time to extend again by the time you hit the second bump. As you go over the series of bumps, the fork gets shorter and shorter, doing less and less suspending, until you're riding on a very short, rigid fork. This is called 'stacking up' and can be avoided by reducing your rebound damping. Damping adjustment affects your steering too — forcing your front wheel around a corner compresses your fork and, if you have too much damping, the fork stays compressed through the turn, tucking under the handlebars rather than helping to turn.

Suspension forks are designed so that you can control the speed of the movement, adjusting the damping to find the middle ground between too fast and too slow. At the ideal setting, your fork is always ready to respond to fresh forces, but it never moves more quickly than you can, so that you're always in charge. Ideal damping setting is an individual preference.

Early attempts at damping control were very basic. One design had what the manufacturers referred to as "friction damping," as if this was an asset. What it actually meant was the elastomers that did the springing rubbed against the insides of the tubes they were trapped in, slowing down the movement. I had a pair like this — they cost me a week's wages and wore out in three months — and I thought they were fantastic.

Each generation of suspension since then has become more sophisticated. Oil is the universal damping medium now. The same principle is used by all manufacturers, regardless of what three-letter acronym they use to convince you that their product is radical and innovative. I'll describe the process for suspension forks, but shocks work in exactly the same way.

Your fork contains damping oil that sloshes about in the fork leg. While your forks are extended, the oil remains at the bottom of the chamber. As the fork is compressed, the stanchions get pushed down through the oil. But between the two is a piston, a disc that blocks the flow of oil. Holes in the piston allow the oil to pass through, but oil doesn't really like being forced through holes, and it won't be hurried. The fork can only compress as fast as the oil will pass through the holes.

Once the fork is fully compressed, the springs start doing their job, and act to force the fork to extend again. In order for the fork to re-extend, the oil has to pass back through the holes in the piston — once more, only as fast as the oil will flow through the holes. The key to effective damping is controling the speed of the oil through the holes. This is done by changing the thickness of the oil — see the oil weight section opposite — or more easily by changing the size of the oil-flow hole. A bigger hole equals faster oil flow equals less damping.

Turning the damping adjustment knobs on your forks will open or close the oil ports, changing the speed at which the oil can pass through the piston, and so altering the speed at which your forks can respond to shocks.

Ideally, we'd like to control the movement of the oil through the holes separately in each direction, so that we can alter the rebound speed without affecting the compression speed. One way to do this is by mounting a thin, flexible washer on one side of the piston so that it covers a set of relatively large piston holes. When you hit a big bump, the fork compresses, pushing oil through the piston toward the washer. The force bends the washer out of the way, allowing the oil to flow freely. Once the spring begins to re-extend the fork, the direction of oil flow is reversed. From this side, the pressure of the oil will flatten the washer against the piston, blocking the holes and preventing oil flow. The addition of the washer means that the piston acts like a turnstile, allowing free flow of oil in one direction and not in the other.

However, you don't want to block the flow of oil completely, as this would simply lock the forks out. So a smaller hole is set in the middle of the piston, where it won't get blocked by the washer. This allows the oil to flow back, but it does so much more slowly. Controlling the size of this hole adjusts the rebound speed. The most common control set-up is a needle that gets pushed into the central hole as you turn the rebound adjustment knob. It makes the hole effectively smaller, and increases damping, so that the forks re-extend more slowly.

Piston

Hole in damping shaft

▲ **Damping shaft**

Rebound damping

After the preload adjuster, the most common adjustment that you'll find on forks is a rebound adjuster that controls the speed at which the fork re-extends after it's been squashed by hitting an obstacle. Here's an example of a rebound adjusting mechanism — this piston sits inside the fork stanchion. The rebounding oil is forced to flow through the hole in the damping shaft. The size of this hole is controled by turning the rebound damping knob, which pushes a rod up through the center of the shaft, gradually closing off the hole to reduce oil flow, thereby increasing the damping and slowing down the fork.

Compression damping

Compression damping affects how quickly the suspension responds to being compressed — if there is very little damping, the suspension reacts to every bump, which is good, but it will reach the end of its travel very quickly, bottoming out when you hit something big. The damping in forks is often controlled by damping oil being forced through a small hole as the fork compresses. A larger hole, or thinner oil, allows the fork to compress more quickly.

All forks have some kind of compression damping. As they get more expensive, this is more likely to be adjustable externally. The compression damping mechanism can also be used to lock out (turn off) the fork or shock, so it doesn't bob when you climb. Turning the lockout knob closes the hole through which the oil passes, effectively stopping the fork compressing. This design almost always "blows" — or automatically releases if it's put under a lot of pressure — if you forget to turn off the lockout and hit something big. This is to stop the fork getting damaged (and hopefully helping you out in the process).

Oil weight

Oil resists being forced to flow through small holes. The speed at which it moves depends on two things — how big the holes are and how thick the oil is. Large holes and thin oil means fast oil flow. Small holes and thick oil means slow oil flow. The thicker oil is, the less it likes squeezing through small holes.

The thickness of the oil is called its weight (wt). Thicker (gloopier) oil, say 15wt, is more reluctant to pass through small holes, and so it increases the rebound damping. Thinner oil, say 5wt, is lighter. This makes your forks faster. However, each fork is made for a specific weight of oil, and changing the performance of the fork by altering the weight is a precise science. Unless you are particularly heavy or light, use the oil weight recommended by your fork manufacturer, and adjust the damping speed by changing the size of the flow holes with the damping adjustment knobs.

Extreme temperature affects how runny the oil is. Heat makes the oil runnier, and it flows through the holes quicker, reducing damping. Very cold weather has the opposite effect. So increase the oil weight for very hot climates, and reduce it for cold ones. A change of 5wt should be enough, but you have to experiment.

Damping oil does get worn out over time. It picks up dirt and moisture from the inside of your forks. It needs to be changed periodically. It should last two years with normal use, more frequently if you're hard on your forks. New forks will sometimes have tiny metal scraps left over from the manufacturing process, which get picked up by the fork oil, so it's a good idea to schedule an initial oil change after six months or so.

Front suspension

Fork servicing isn't magic. It isn't even difficult, but it does need care and patience. It often needs very specific parts, which usually have to be ordered — there must be at least a million different spare suspension part numbers out there now. Don't assume you'll get spare parts for older forks. Some companies stock a longer back catalogue than others, but if your forks are more than about three years old, you're on shaky ground. That counts from when they were first made, so if you picked them up as a cheap end-of-line model, you'll arrive in obsolete land even sooner.

Steerer tube

Crown

Top cap

Compression adjusting knob

Damping

Stanchions

Lower legs or sliders

Bottom out bumpers

Rebound adjusting knob

Spring

▲ **Manitou Skareb**

Forks are generally harder to repair than to maintain — once something goes wrong or breaks, they need special parts and usually special tools as well. This is often best left to your bike shop or the fork manufacturer. If your bike shop doesn't do fork repairs, you can send your forks off to be serviced (see the list of suppliers at the back of the book, page 240). I have included a sample fork strip to demonstrate the principle of what your shop does as part of a service.

There are several designs of fork — air spring forks and coil spring forks being the main division. There isn't space here to go through a complete strip-down of every kind of fork, so I've included just a couple of examples. The main reference text is always the owner's manual. If you don't have the one your fork came with, print a new one off the Internet. Make sure you get exactly the right year and model — even if the fork looks the same, small details change from one year to the next.

How far should you go? Use the manual for guidance — be aware that stripping down your fork further than recommended may invalidate the warranty.

Take extra care with any fork that uses an air spring. Always be sure to release all the air pressure from the fork before you take anything apart. This is easy to forget but crucial — start undoing things under pressure, and they rocket off. If they don't hit and hurt you, you'll probably lose something vital.

You should be able to service forks while they're on the bike, but you'll probably find it easier if you remove them. Follow the instructions on pages 182–86 — and you might as well service the headset while you're there. Either way, you'll need to be able to clamp the forks upright to add oil to the tops, and to inject oil horizontally into the bottoms of the fork legs.

The most important constant maintenance for forks consists of only three things:

◆ Keep them clean, but don't jet-hose them. The most common cause of death for forks is dirt that works in between stanchions and seals, leaving scratches.

◆ Be conscious as you ride of any changes in the ride characteristic — nothing trashes forks faster than being used when something is a little loose.

◆ Ride them regularly. Forks get cantankerous if they're not ridden for a while.

There are two good reasons why people should carry out mild maintenance on their bikes more often than most do. The first is economic: the more expensive forks are to buy, the more expensive they are to fix. Catch a problem sooner rather than later, and you save yourself money. The second reason is safety. Suspension is good at keeping your wheels on the ground, maximizing your grip and steering, but if parts work loose and break free, you can be left with no control over your bike.

The very best time to clean your forks is just after your last ride, not just before your next one! Forks left dirty do not last as long as forks cleaned between rides. Find something wrong and you have time to fix it before going out next.

How suspension parts fit together

Fork designers keep us all on our toes by changing the locations of damping and preload-adjusters from year to year and model to model. Here's a couple of examples, but refer to your owner's manual to find which knob does what on your forks. Sometimes, generous designers label the knobs on the forks for you — this makes life a lot easier!

Marzocchi MX Comp

Manitou Skareb

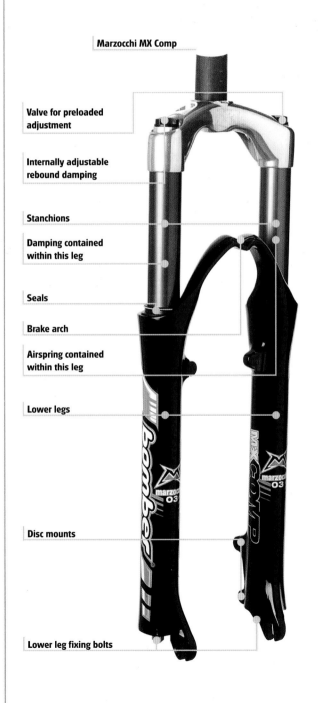

Valve for preloaded adjustment

Internally adjustable rebound damping

Stanchions

Damping contained within this leg

Seals

Brake arch

Airspring contained within this leg

Lower legs

Disc mounts

Lower leg fixing bolts

Compression damping adjusting knob

Preload adjuster

Stanchions

Coil springs contained within this leg

Brake arch

Lower legs

Damping contained within this leg

Lower legs

Disc brake mounts

Lower leg fixing bolts

Rebound damping adjusting knob

Setting up your forks properly

I still get shocked by how many people happily spend a chunk of cash buying a new set of forks but can't find an hour to set them up properly. It's not difficult, and it makes an expensive fork ride like an expensive fork.

Basic forks allow you to set the preload, which you use to alter the sag. As forks get more expensive, you are also able to adjust the rebound damping, the compression damping, the travel, and you can temporarily lock out the fork to make it rigid. All the different manufacturers put the controls for these adjustments in different places — say, the rebound knob at the top of the left leg, or at the bottom of the right leg. Before you go any further, dig out the owner's manual for your fork, and identify the adjustments you can make on it, and locate where the adjusters are.

When setting up and tuning your forks, it's important to change only one thing at a time. Don't be tempted to twiddle all the knobs and see what happens: you are as likely to hit upon a "just wrong" place as a "just right" place. Keep a note of the adjustments you make, so that once you find the adjustment to suit you can return to it.

Sag

First set up the sag, which is where the fork compresses a little under your weight. The best information about how much sag your fork needs should come from your owner's manual — as I mentioned earlier, if you haven't kept it, you can usually print another off the internet. As a general guideline, start with 20–25 per cent of your total fork travel for cross-country forks, and 30–35 per cent for downhill/freeride forks.

This is only a rough guide; your fork is designed for a specific amount of sag. There are still plenty of diehard XC racers who consider they have made enough of a concession by fitting suspension forks and run them so they hardly move at all. I don't understand this — it makes no more sense than fitting a nine-speed cassette and adjusting the end-stop screws so that only the middle five gears work. The worst part is that these guys do it to good-quality, lightweight, adjustable forks. Oh well.

Page 181 guides you through setting up your fork sag; page 190 describes setting up your shock sag.

Rebound damping

Once the sag is sorted, adjust the rebound damping. You'll need to take your bike outside and ride around for this bit. People like to lean on suspension forks, watch them spring back, and nod knowledgeably, but there's no substitute for getting out and seeing how your fork reacts to being properly ridden.

Most manufacturers have a pretty good idea of a starting point for you and will recommend it in the manual. I like to set my rebound damping as fast as I can before it's so fast that the bars come back up quicker than I do. I think that's the key — to match the fork's reaction speed to yours. The faster it is, the less often it gets caught out by a series of bumps, hitting the next before recovering from the last. But it's a very personal adjustment. Your rebound damping setting affects the bike's feel when cornering — if you have too much rebound damping, the fork stays compressed as you turn, digging the wheel into the corner rather than pushing you around it.

Find a baby dropoff that you can ride over repeatedly — 10cm (4 inches) or so is about right. Set your fork to the slowest rebound damping position (i.e., maximum damping equals slowest movement), and ride over the dropoff. Reset to the fastest damping position (least damping equals fastest movement), and ride off again. You'll feel your bike react differently, with the handlebars springing straight back toward you.

Repeat the dropoff, slowing the rebound damping down a little at a time — if your adjuster has distinct clicks, go one click at a time. You're aiming to find a position where you're completely in control throughout the cycle of the fork, but with as little damping as possible. Once you've found the right place, write down the adjustment so that you can find it again. I use a marker pen to draw a line on the fork and the knob, so that I can find the adjustment again by lining up the two marks.

Compression damping

If you have a compression damping adjustment, set this last. This adjustment affects how fast your fork compresses when it hits an obstacle. Again the right setting is tied up with your reaction speed. If you set up the preload correctly and are still bottoming out, you don't have enough compression damping. If the fork doesn't respond to small obstacles, you have too much compression damping. With many forks, your compression damping is preset and cannot be adjusted. I don't think this is a great loss, I've always found the preset levels to be fine. If you have both front and rear suspension, set up the front forks first, then set the back end to match. Set yourself a time and place where you can ride safely without looking where you're going, ideally somewhere fairly flat with a single obstacle you can ride over repeatedly without too much effort. You need to ride over the identical object a number of times to see the effect the adjustments are having.

Setting your sag for the best possible results

Use the steps below to measure your sag, and adjust the preload to give you the recommended sag. Remember that this is just a starting point though — you may want to fine-tune the preload for your riding style.

Once you've followed the steps, ride your bike to see how it feels. If you hit something hard, you'll go all the way through the travel of the fork to the point where the top part thuds against the bottom part. This is "bottoming out the fork." It's not a bad thing — if you don't hit that point during normal riding, you aren't using all the available fork travel. Play with the initial sag setting to aim to bottom out about once a ride.

SETTING YOUR SAG

Step 1: Work out your travel. If it's written in your owner's manual, use that measurement. This is one of those times when your owner's manual will come in really handy — it will have recommendations for sag, and it will tell you the total travel. Manuals for air shocks often give you a recommended air pressure for your weight, but it's worth testing the actual sag you get on your bike because it depends on your position on the bike, and the configuration of your shock.

Step 2: If you don't have the manual, work travel out like this: with the fork fully extended, measure the distance from the bottom of the fork crown to the top of the lower leg seal, i.e., check how much stanchion is showing.

Step 3: Release air pressure in air forks or remove coil springs in coil forks, and push the fork right down as far as it will go. Measure the same distance again. Take the second number from the first. This is your total travel. Replace coil springs, reinflate air chambers.

Step 4: Take a ziptie and loop it around one of your fork stanchions so it's fairly tight but can still be pushed up and down easily. Push it down so it sits just above the seal.

Step 5: Lean your bike against a wall and mount it carefully. Sit still on the bike, in your normal riding position. Don't bounce up and down. Get off the bike. Your weight on the bike has compressed the forks, pushing up the ziptie. Now measure the distance between the ziptie and the top of the seal. This is the sag.

Step 6: Adjust the air pressure or the coil-spring preload until the sag is the required proportion of the total travel.

Inspecting and maintaining your forks for fun and profit

Regular, careful fork maintenance will save you money — keeping your forks clean will help reduce servicing frequency. It's also a good time to inspect them, allowing you to pick up and sort out potential problems quickly.

All fork maintenance starts with a good clean. Disconnect the V-brakes and drop the wheel out of the frame, so that you can get to the forks properly. For disc brakes, push a wedge of clean cardboard between the disc pads, so that you don't accidentally pump the brake pads out of the calipers. Go through the steps below; if you find worn or broken components, it's time for a fork service. Don't ride damaged forks — they may let you down without warning.

Stanchions

Wipers/seals

V-brake mounts

Lower legs

Disc mounts

Dropouts

◀ **Marzocchi MX Comp**

- Start by washing the lower legs, stanchions, and fork crown. Plain water is fine, although if they're really grimy, use Finish Line or other similar bike cleaners.
- As you wash the dirt off, inspect the forks carefully and methodically. Start with dropouts. Check for cracks around the joint between the fork leg and the dropout, inside and out.
- Take a look at the condition of the surfaces that your wheels clamp onto, inside and out. These grip the axle and stop the wheel popping out of the fork. The serrations on the quick-release and axle make dents in the fork — make sure that these are clean, crisp dents, rather than worn craters that indicate the wheel has been shifting about.
- Check each fork leg in turn. You're looking for splits, cracks or dents. Big dents will weaken the fork, and prevent the stanchion from moving freely inside the lower legs. Cracks and dents both mean that it's new fork time.
- Take a look at disc and V-brake mounts. Check disc mounts for cracks, and check that all caliper fixing bolts are tight.
- Check the bolts at the bottoms of the fork legs — these hold everything together, so make sure they're not working loose. Look for signs that oil has been leaking out from under the bolts.
- Clean muck out from behind the brake arch — grit has a tendency to collect here.
- Inspect the wipers that clean the stanchions as they enter the lower legs. Tears or cuts will allow grit into the wipers, where they will scour your stanchions. The tops of the wipers are usually held in place with a fine circular spring that should sit in the lip at the top of the wiper.
- Check the stanchions. If grit gets stuck in the wipers or seals, it will be dragged up and down as your fork cycles, wearing vertical grooves in the forks. These grooves in turn provide a new route in for more dirt.
- Check all the adjuster knobs. They often stick out so that you can turn them easily, but this does make them vulnerable.
- Refit the wheel and reconnect the V-brakes. Pull the front brake on and hold one of the stanchions just above the lower leg. Rock the bike gently back and forth. You may be able to feel a little bit of flex in the forks, but you should not be able to feel the lower legs knocking. Lots of movement here means you need new bushings.
- Push down firmly on the bars, compressing the forks. They should spring back smoothly when you release the bars. If they stutter or hesitate returning, it's time for a fork service.
- Finally, finish off by polishing the lower legs. It makes the forks look better, which is important in itself, but also leaves a waxy finish that means dirt doesn't stick so well to the fork.

Cleaning and lubricating the stanchions

Wipers are the black rubber rings at the top of the lower legs into which the stanchions disappear. Your forks bob constantly up and down as you ride, and on a muddy day your stanchions will be constantly bombarded with grit. If this grit can work its way down into your seals, it will get dragged up and down by the action of the forks, scouring long vertical grooves in the stanchions, which will allow dirt into your fork and oil out of it.

The wipers serve as a first line of defence against unwanted grit, helping to keep it off the seals. Regularly clean any build-up of dirt off the wipers to stop dirt from working its way down to the seals, which are found below the wipers where they are pressed into the top of the lower legs.

Fork seals have to flex with the movement of the stanchions, forming a tight-fitting barrier to prevent dirt getting in or oil getting out. The seals mustn't fit too tightly though, or they will stop the fork from moving smoothly. Good seals are one of the most important qualities in a fork. Seals need to be replaced regularly, so ensure that this is done when you get your forks serviced.

Forks used to all come with fork boots, which are flexible rubber gaiters that were supposed to keep the stanchions clean. Besides being ugly, they had a tendency to trap moisture in the area around the top of the lower leg, just where you need it least. Very few forks come with boots now — wipers have replaced them and seals have become much more effective.

Wiper care

Check your instruction book for specific instructions — as an example, see below for instructions on how to clean and lubricate the seals on Marzocchi Bombers. Marzocchi forks have a well-deserved reputation for durability, but that doesn't mean you can ignore routine maintenance. It doesn't take much care and attention to keep them running sweetly.

CLEANING LOWER LEGS

Step 1: Use a small screwdriver to lever up the wipers. Don't tear the wipers — work around gradually, lifting a bit at a time. Check for scratches on the stanchions, which can be caused by dirt trapped in the wiper being scraped up and down by the fork action or by stones flying up and hitting the stanchions. Scratches and dents let oil seep out of the forks and let dirt in.

Step 2: Clean the visible parts of the stanchions, and the area between the stanchions and the brake arch, without forcing any dirt down onto the seal.

Step 3: Oil the stanchions with Teflon-based oil. You shouldn't need much — a couple of drops is enough, anything more will attract dirt. Replace the wipers — you will need to push and twist to seat them properly. Cycle the fork a couple of times — stand over it and push down hard on the bars to work the oil over the stanchions.

Simple, regular maintenance of Manitou Skareb Comps

As with any fork, persistent nurturing of the Skareb Comps has far more effect than intermittent guilt-ridden frenzies. Servicing forks needs more patience and experience than maintaining them, so have them serviced regularly by a Manitou agent. However, I've included instructions here, so you get a feel for what needs to be done. I like Manitou's Skareb Comps for their simplicity and reliability. Regular maintenance is fairly straightforward and needs no special tools: 2mm and 8mm Allen keys, a 20mm socket wrench, 5wt suspension oil and a syringe.

The fork has a steel coil spring in the left leg and a damping assembly in the right leg. The rebound adjusting knob is on the bottom of the right leg, the compression damping adjustment is at the top of the right leg, and both lower legs have an oil bath for lubrication. This arrangement keeps the entire damping mechanism as far away from the heat of the disc brake, which is mounted on the bottom of the left leg, as possible.

Damping performance depends on the viscosity of the damping oil, which is greatly affected by temperature. The damping oil level is critical, so check it twice a year. Replace it once a year, twice if you ride a lot. If you can't get the correct sag within the range of the preload adjuster with the stock spring, change it for a harder or softer one. You can carry out both of these tasks without affecting your warranty.

Servicing is more complicated, and involves three stages: taking the fork apart, cleaning the lower legs and stanchions, and reassembling with fresh oil. Manitou recommend that you get this done at least twice a year, or once every three months if you ride hard or cover a lot of miles. These more advanced procedures should be done by an authorized Manitou dealer, so either take your forks into your bike shop or send them away to one of the service centers listed on page 240.

MANITOU SKAREBS

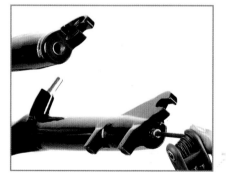

Step 1: Before you start, make a note of the rebound setting you are using. Turn the preload knob all the way clockwise, counting and making a note of how far you had to turn it. Use a 2mm Allen key to remove the rebound damping knob from the bottom of the fork, and put it aside somewhere safe.

Step 2: Looking at the fork from below. You see an 8mm Allen key bolt head from underneath where you removed the rebound damping knob. This is the end of the rebound adjusting rod and has to be wound into the fork leg to release the damping rod from the lower legs — turn it clockwise.

Step 3: Have a container handy to catch the old oil that drains out of the bottom of the forks. Use a 4mm Allen key to remove the bolt in the bottom of the left leg (on the right-hand side if you're looking at the fork from the front).

Step 4: Pull the stanchions out of the lower legs gently, keeping the lower legs over the container to catch the oil. Leave the lower legs draining while you clean and inspect the upper legs.

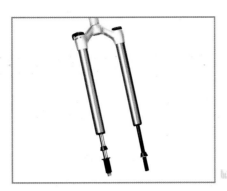

Step 5: Check for scours on the stanchions. Badly scratched stanchions need replacing — go to your bike shop for a second opinion. Clean the insides of the lower legs by wrapping a clean rag around a stick and winding it down in there. If the lower legs or stanchions are dirty or dry, you need to increase your servicing frequency.

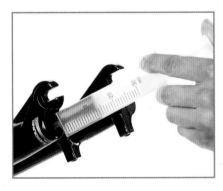

Step 6: Slide the stanchions a little way back into the lower legs. Next, syringe 15cc of 5wt oil back in through the hole in the bottom of each fork leg. It helps to prepare a syringe with 30cc in it. Hold the lower legs horizontally and squirt half the oil into each leg.

Step 7: Keeping the fork horizontal so you don't lose the oil (this bit can be messy if you aren't careful), slide the fork legs gently onto the stanchions. Next, slide the 8mm Allen key through the hole in the bottom of the right fork leg and use it to guide the bottom of the damping rod into the hole at the bottom of the fork. Thread it loosely into the fork leg.

Step 8: Wiggle the 4mm Allen key bolt through the bottom of the left-hand fork leg and feel for the threads. Start the bolt off by hand, then tighten it up firmly.

Step 9: Tighten the damping rod into the right-hand fork leg, and replace the rebound damping knob (2mm Allen key). Reset your preload position by turning it counterclockwise, thereby returning it to its original position.

Toolbox

Tools for changing your spring
- 2mm Allen key
- 20mm socket wrench — the caps have soft, narrow flats; don't try undoing them with an adjustable wrench, you'll tear the metal
- Replacement spring
- Suspension grease, like Rock Shox Judy Butter or similar

Tools to replace damping oil
- 2mm Allen key
- 20mm socket wrench
- 5wt suspension oil from your bike shop or motorcycle shop
- A tray to catch the old oil and clean cloths to mop up spillage
- Tape measure or narrow ruler

Tools to remove and lubricate lower legs
- 2mm, 4mm, and 8mm Allen keys
- Tray to catch old oil
- 5wt suspension oil
- Syringe to pour oil into lower legs

185

Manitou Skarebs: replacing damping oil and changing the spring

Your damping oil should be changed regularly — it gets forced constantly back and forth through the pistons and wears out, making your forks feel lumpy rather than smooth and responsive. This process isn't as difficult as it sounds.

The tricky part is pouring the old oil out of your forks — unless you've removed the forks from your bike, you'll need to turn your bike upside down, so the oil runs out the top of the fork. Once you've got the fork upended, pump the fork to squirt all the oil out of the damping mechanism. This can get messy, so have a clean cloth or paper towel on hand to mop up spillage. Springs don't need routine changing because they last for years. However, if you find yourself running out of preload adjustment, you'll need to replace the spring with a stiffer or softer one.

REPLACING THE DAMPING OIL

Step 1: Use a 2mm Allen key to remove the cover on the top of the right-hand fork leg (on the left-hand side as you look from the front). Use a 20mm socket to undo the head of the damping assembly. Wiggle it loose and pull upward to remove it. Lay it on a clean surface.

Step 2: Tip up the fork and pour out the old oil. You need to pump the fork in and out to flush it all out. Rinse the damping chamber by pouring in a little 5wt suspension oil, cycling the fork in and out a few times, then flushing this out too. Pour in some fresh 5wt oil, and cycle the shock ("compress and extend") to fill up the rebound assembly.

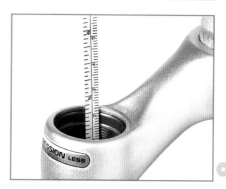

Step 3: Pull the stanchions gently up out of the lower legs until they're fully extended, then continue to fill until the surface of the oil is 115–125mm (4½–5 inches) from the top of the stanchion. This oil level is crucial, so make sure you measure carefully — from the surface of the oil in the stanchion to the top of the stanchion. Replace the top cap and tighten gently with 20mm socket. Replace the cover.

CHANGING THE SPRING

Step 1: The Skareb Comps have only one spring, located in the left-hand fork leg. The spring comes in four stiffnesses, from soft to extra firm. If you cannot get the right sag adjustment with the preload knob, change your spring for a softer or harder one. Remove the preload-adjuster knob with a 2mm Allen key.

Step 2: Remove the top cap with a 20mm socket wrench, extract the old spring, and wiggle it free from the top of the fork. This will expose the top of the old spring. Pull it out. Grease the new spring generously, and then drop it into the top of the stanchion.

Step 3: Refit the top cap firmly by hand — you shouldn't need to crank it down with the socket. Refit the preload-adjuster knob. Having fitted a different spring, you now need to reset your sag.

Rear suspension

Mountain biking — being highly competitive in sporting, technology and commercial terms — boasts as many different rear suspension designs as it does bike companies. And each proud designer knows their beautiful baby blows the others away. While the models differ in detail, it is possible to divide the majority into three types: cantilever, linkage, and URT (unified rear triangle). All three rise and fall in popularity over time. Within each type, there are bikes that have been designed with computer-aided whatsits and cutting-edge doodahs but still ride like dogs. Meanwhile, those you heard a convincing argument against last week still feel fast and furious.

▲ **Fox Float suspension unit**

Choosing a suspension bike can be stressful. Anybody with any experience has an opinion on what suspension you should consider, and they're all different. However, out there is a bike designed by someone who wants the same from a ride as you do. My advice is try to ride as many different designs as you can before making a decision.

The appropriate design for you depends on your build and riding style. Some people sit in the saddle as long as possible, using their energy economically (they might have a road-bike background). They may generally dislike designs where the position of the rear end affects the chain length, snapping back as they pedal. Others, maybe with a BMX or trail bike background, are up and out of the saddle with little excuse, using their shoulders and their body weight rather than their legs to propel the bike. They may waste loads of energy, but they like great short bursts of power.

Rear suspension design has two elements: frame shape and shock characteristic. All frames are based on the principle that the rear part of the frame is hinged so that the rear wheel moves relative to the main body of the frame. A lot of thought goes into manipulating the pivot and strut positions that make up the rear end in order to control the axle path (or, the position of the axle relative to the frame as it moves through its travel).

Trail forces come from different directions. When you land from a dropoff you apply force directly upward, and if this were the only force on the rear wheel the equation would be much simpler. But you're also driving the back wheel by pedaling, applying force to the wheel along the horizontal, along the chain from chainring to sprocket. If the hinge between the back and front of the bike lies between the chainset and the rear axle, then pedaling activates the suspension. The movement of the rear end as it reacts to the terrain causes movement in the pedals — "chain reaction." This isn't always a bad thing; in climbing, the pedaling tends to extend the suspension and dig the back wheel into the ground, giving you extra grip. Chain reaction is not so alarming, as long as it isn't huge. Your feet get familiar with dealing with the effect quickly, until you don't notice it. Successful suspension design makes the rear axle as responsive as possible to uneven terrain, while minimizing the extent to which pedaling compresses the shock and wastes your energy.

Once the frame has been constructed, the task of the rear shock is to control the speed at which the rear wheel moves along its axle path under force. The spring in the shock absorbs force, while the damping ensures that the spring re-extends at a controlable speed and doesn't buck you off the saddle. A perfect shock responds to small forces instantly, making the bike feel supple and helping to find whatever grip there is. It can also take a big blow without reaching the limit of travel.

This is a lot to pack into the back end of a bicycle, especially when, at the same time, people want everything to be light, strong, stiff and painted this week's hot color. Small wonder there are as many different "perfect" designs as there are designers. The evolution of suspension design has taken place in fits and starts, with some folks charging down cul-de-sacs, and others beetling away to refine proven designs. There is no right answer, and thus it would be a shame to waste too much riding time wondering if your pivots are in the "right" position.

Cantilever, linkage and URT

While it's difficult to categorize full suspension bikes precisely, most fall into one of three broad categories — cantilever, linkage and unified rear triangle (URT). There are examples of all three types that are a dream to ride, and others that are a nightmare.

Cantilever

Early full-suspension bikes were a cantilever design: the rear wheel is connected to a swingarm rotating around a single pivot near the bottom bracket, with the shock connected directly to the main frame. The design's strong advantages — a single pivot and few moving parts — make the frame light, durable, stiff, and strong without costing the earth. It is still in use — see the Santa Cruz Bullit.

The disadvantage of the cantilever design is it is difficult to control the effects of chain reaction. Wherever you place the pivot, the rear wheel moves in an arc around it so that, as the axle moves through its travel, the distance between axle and chainset changes appreciably.

Linkage

The linkage design adds extra pivots to the swingarm, changing the shape of the rear end as it moves through its travel. This adds weight and complication to the simple cantilever, but means the path of the axle can be precisely controled through the full travel of the suspension. This maximizes the proportion of pedaling energy that propels you forward, and minimizes the amount wasted compressing the shock. Every designer has a different take on the ideal axle path. Once you have linkages, you can mount the shock to the linkage rather than directly to the swingarm. This has the added advantage that varying the position of the shock alters the leverage and changes the amount of force needed to compress the shock. Many linkage designs allow you to shift the shock to suit your terrain and riding style. One classic example of a linkage bike is the Specialized FRS.

The disadvantage of linkage concerns extra pivots. They must all move smoothly. Otherwise the axle-path discussion is pointless because effectively you have an odd-shaped rigid bike. Sealed cartridge bearings make the best pivots. They must be good quality from the start, then regularly serviced, promptly replaced when they become pitted — and you should never jet-wash them.

URT — unified rear triangle

The unified rear triangle (URT) design is an attempt to sidestep the chain-reaction issue, by mounting the bottom bracket, chainset and front derailleur on the swingarm, so that the drivetrain is always the same size and shape, regardless of suspension position. This was heralded as the only way forward a few years back, and still has diehard fans. Many great bikes have been made this way, so the design's discrediting is undeserved. It will probably come back into fashion. The positioning of the chainset behind the main hinge means that the back end may tend to wallow when you stand up in the pedals, but its clean, simple design is appealing. URT is considered by some to be the ideal design for singlespeed bikes, where the distance between chainset and rear axle has to remain constant as there is no derailleur to take up chain slack.

Types of shock

As with suspension forks, rear shocks come in several different styles, while the two main components remain the same — some form of spring and some form of damping. The spring can be air or coil, and the damping can be air, oil or a mixture of oil and gas.

An air spring is stiffened by pumping more air into the spring chamber. The volume of air is small, so adding a tiny amount makes a big difference: use a suspension pump with a gauge for the job. Bleed air off either by using the bleed valve on the pump (if you have one), or by removing the pump and depressing the pin in the middle of the Schraeder valve, then using the suspension pump to go back up to the right pressure. Don't overpump the shock, you will damage it. The maximum pressure the shock will take is almost always printed on the shock body, otherwise check your manual.

Coil springs have a steel spring wound over a damping unit. The preload is adjusted by turning the plate that supports one end of the shock along a thread, squashing the spring. Springs don't have a huge weight range and work much much better if you don't put too much preload on them. Don't be tempted to crank up the preload-adjuster on a spring that's too soft to get the right sag. As a general rule, use no more than two turns of the preload-adjuster to get the right sag, unless your manual specifically says that you can use more.

Air shocks are slightly lighter than coil spring shocks, although using titanium springs rather than steel ones can decrease the weight difference. It is easier to adjust air shocks for a wide range of rider weights, whereas coil springs are only adjustable within the range of the spring — riders who weigh more or less than average will need to swap springs, whereas air can simply be added or released.

Coil and air shocks do feel different though. Coil springs are very supple and are often the preferred choice. I like air springs because I don't weigh much. If you carry a shock pump with you, it will cancel out most of the difference in weight between air and coil.

Suspension: measuring total travel

Travel is the total distance your suspension unit can move, from fully extended to fully compressed. More travel means that your shock unit can absorb larger shocks, stretching out the short, sharp impacts so that you can maintain control over your bike. Longer travel allows people to do stuff on bikes that would never have been possible five years ago — jumping off things and onto things, in ways that would previously have resulted in broken bikes and broken bones.

Longer travel isn't all good, though. Frames have to be beefier and heavier to maintain stiffness, as well as to withstand abuse. The shape of a long travel frame changes through the travel, making it tiring to ride long distances or to take on steep climbs. Cross-country frames with a medium amount of travel seek to find a compromise between soaking up uneven terrain, maximizing grip by keeping the rear wheel glued to the ground, and providing a comfortable, stable pedaling platform. Microtravel suspension — where the rear triangle moves 5cm (2 inches) or so — will absorb harsh trails, adding a bit of comfort with the minimum of weight penalty.

Like front suspension, rear shocks need to be set up so that when you sit on the bike the suspension settles slightly. This is important — it means that your rear wheel can drop down into dips, as well as fold upward to pass over lumps and obstacles in your path. This keeps you floating in a horizontal straight line, rather than climbing in and out of every irregularity on the trail, saving you energy.

Each manufacturer has their own ideas about how much of your total travel should be taken up by this initial sag, so you'll need to consult the shock handbook or the manufacturer's website to find out their recommendations. Since the sag is always given as a proportion of total travel, you'll need to know the travel as well before you can start setting your sag. If you don't know it already, use the steps below to measure it.

MEASURING TOTAL TRAVEL

Step 1: Stand the bike up and measure the distance from center to center between the shock eyelets. This is the extended length.

Step 2: Release the spring: for an air shock, take the valve cap off, push down the pin in the middle of the valve, pump the bike up and down a couple of times, and push the pin down again to release the rest of the air. For coil shocks, back off the preload-adjuster, as far as it will go, so that the spring dangles loose.

Step 3: Push the bike down to compress the shock and measure the distance between the eyelets again. Subtract the second measurement from the first, and that's your total available travel.

Setting up sag

Once you've worked out how much travel your bike has, put a small amount of air back in the shock, or remount the coil and put in a single turn of preload.

10% sag = total travel divided by 10
15% sag = total travel divided by 7
20% sag = travel total divided by 5
25% sag = total travel divided by 4
33% sag = total travel divided by 3

The next step is to calculate how much sag you're aiming to have. Different bike shapes and shock models work best with different amounts of sag, but as a rule, for cross-country racers it's 15–25 percent of total travel; for general cross-country, it's 20–30 percent; and for downhill/freeride, it's 30–35 percent. These are guidelines only — refer to your shock manual for recommendations. This gives you a starting point to use to tune to your preferences. Don't worry about that now, we take that into account at the test stage.

Now work out what sag you would like.

Coil shock

You'll need a friend to help you with this. Measure the distance between the shock mounting bolts. Sit on your bike, in your normal riding position (it helps to lean against a wall for this), and get your friend to measure the same distance again. Get your friend to repeat the measurement between the centers of the shock eyelets. Subtract this new measurement from the original unloaded shock length, and you have the sag. If the amount is more than you expected, add preload to the coil spring. If it's less than you expected, back off the coil spring, or bleed out air, until you have it about right.

Air springs are adjustable throughout the range of what you need, but coil springs have a much narrower range. For example, Fox Vanilla springs are designed for up to two turns of the preload-adjusting ring. Crank them up too much and they won't work properly. Leave them too loose and they bang around. Ideally, with the exact spring rate, you shouldn't need to use preload at all. If you can't get the adjustment you need from the spring you have, get a softer or a harder spring. Give the bike shop the details of your bike (make, model, and year) and spring (spring rate and travel as printed on the spring), as well as your weight, so that they can work out the correct spring for you.

Air shock

You can work out the sag on an air shock without pressuring an assistant to measure for you — the travel O-ring on the shock shaft will get pushed down as you compress the shock, and will then remain there when the shock re-extends, making it simple to measure how far you squashed the shock by sitting on the bike. You'll need a shock pump to add air and to measure the pressure inside the shock.

AIR SHOCK

Step 1: For air shocks, push the travel O-ring right up the shaft of the shock, so that it rests against the air sleeve.

Step 2: Sit in your normal position on the bike in normal riding clothes. Just sit, don't bounce or twiddle. Get off the bike. Your weight will have compressed the shock, pushing the travel O-ring along the shaft. Measure the gap between the air sleeve and the O-ring. This is your sag.

Step 3: If the measurement is less than you expected, release a little air from the shock. If it's more than you expected, add a little air — screw the shock pump onto the valve, enough so that you can hear a little air escaping then half a turn more. Add a little pressure. Remove the shock pump, and test again. Make a note of what pressure you ended up with!

Testing and adjusting rebound damping for the best setting

If you don't have this adjustment, it doesn't mean you don't have rebound damping, but rather that the manufacturer has decided what works best and they don't want you fiddling with it ...

First, get a feeling for the effect of the rebound damping adjustment before finding the right setting. Find a place where you can repeat a simple five-minute loop — nothing special, a parking lot will do fine. Ride the loop twice at the two extremes of the rebound damping adjustment to get a feel for the effect of changing the settings. Then set the rebound damping in the central position; for example, if it has a total 12 clicks, start with six clicks.

Find a clear, flat space without cars with a single baby dropoff — 50mm (2 inches) or 100mm (4 inches) or so — to ride repeatedly. The idea is you ride over the dropoff, the shock compresses, rebounds further than it started, and returns to its original position. If the shock springs back and kicks you on landing, the rebound is too fast, and you need to increase the damping. If you wallow on landing, it's too slow and needs to be reduced. At first you may want to make radical changes to the adjustment to learn its effect. Whatever you do, remember to keep a clear and constant note of all changes you make, and resist the temptation to fiddle randomly with combinations — if playing with the rebound damping, leave the sag alone.

Now for the test ride. Go out and play. You should bottom out the shock about once every ride. If not, you are not using the full travel, which is a waste. Play with the sag, a little at a time. This is where your personal taste and riding style come into play. If you stand a lot, up and out of the saddle, you may prefer a stiffer ride, at the lower end of your recommended sag range.

Maintaining rear suspension

Rear shocks have two levels of servicing: they need to be kept clean; and the moving parts need regular lubrication. The bushings that allow them to move must be kept clean and must be replaced when worn. They need to be checked regularly to ensure they're working properly. You can kill a shock very quickly by continuing to ride when something internal is broken. All this can be done with a few simple tools, and it is worth learning to do regularly.

Rear shocks often sit directly in the firing line for mush thrown up by your back wheel, and their performance deteriorates quickly if you ignore them. Conversely, keep them clean and greased, and they last a whole lot longer.

Deeper, internal servicing and tuning must be carried out by a shock servicer. Don't be tempted to continue ripping inside the shock once you are confident with the outer parts. Depending on make, the internal parts may be filled with nitrogen or stored under high pressure. Don't get involved. It's too easy to hurt yourself, and the action voids the warranty. Send the shock to the service center.

Luckily, there are enough specialists to do the job and, luckily again, once you've taken the shock off the bike, it is small enough to send easily. If there's one thing you can do to help this process, clean the shock before packaging. It is cleaned at the other end, but it's polite to wipe off last weekend's fun before putting it in a box. The correct service center depends on the make of shock; see the instruction manual or the list of suppliers on page 240. Servicers are quick too. You can usually get a shock back in the space between weekends.

Maintenance commandments

◆ When opening up the shock for regreasing, clean the bike before you start. Otherwise mud drops into the body of the shock — the rebound characteristics of mud are notoriously variable.

◆ Air shocks: DON'T forget to discharge all the air in the shock before you start working it. Open a unit that is still pressurized and it releases suddenly, flying into the air. Usually it hits you because you are undoing it. It hurts and you feel stupid.

◆ DON'T open up the damping cartridge inside the shock.

◆ Occasionally, air shocks get stuck in the squashed position. Let all the air out of the valve, then reinflate to the maximum pressure the shock is rated for. If this doesn't work, deflate again, and send to the servicer. DON'T open the air sleeve — let the specialist deal with it.

Coil springs have a pair of numbers printed on the coil: the first is the spring rate (stiffness); the second is the travel in inches. You need to know the vital statistics of your spring to change it for a stiffer or softer one.

Fitting and adjusting a Fox Float Air

I like the Fox Float Air shock. It works well, adjusts easily, and is simple to keep clean. Don't be tempted to go further than the level of servicing below. For that, send it to an authorized service center, or you void the warranty. The damping chamber is charged with pressurized nitrogen, which makes it dangerous to open and impossible to refill without a cylinder of nitrogen.

All types of shocks, both coil and air, are well worth keeping clean and well greased — it costs less to service if you don't let the internal parts wear out. Most shocks are centrally mounted above the rear wheel. Any mud, grit, and sand left over after your back wheel has sprayed a stripe up your back gets dumped onto your shock body. Clean this off regularly; grit will work its way in past any seals, scouring grooves in the central shaft, in turn allowing in more dirt.

This particular shock model allows you to adjust rebound-damping and travel, but other combinations are common on other bikes — preload and rebound is the most useful, although lockouts are great for climbing and roadwork. Some people like to be able to adjust their compression damping. Compression damping affects the speed at which the shock compresses; and rebound damping, the speed at which it springs back.

Greasing air sleeve

If you're happy with how your shock performs — it soaks up uneven terrain without consistently bottoming out — then measure and record the pressure before you start maintenance, so that you can reinflate to that pressure when the shock is reassembled. It's also worth checking and noting the rebound settings — count the clicks back to fully open (it's easy to knock the adjusting wheel during work). As ever when working with air springs, release all air pressure before starting work.

Fox Float suspension unit ▶

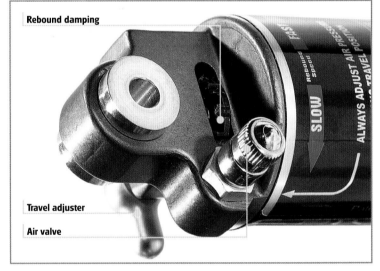

Rebound damping

Travel adjuster

Air valve

GREASING AIR SLEEVE

Step 1: Release air from the shock by removing valve cap and pressing down pin at center of valve. Pump bike up and down a couple of times through the whole stroke of the shock to expel air from the negative air spring. Release the air at the valve again. Undo the pivot fixing bolts at either end of the shock, usually using an Allen key and socket, or two Allen keys. Pull the aluminum reducers out of each end of the shock and clean them.

Step 2: Clamp the body end of the shock (the end with the air valve and any adjusting knobs or dials) into a vice. Protect the eye bolt with wood — otherwise you damage the shock. Take care not to crush the valve, or the lockout switch, or anything else down there. Stick a screwdriver, or similar, through the top eyelet to stop the air sleeve flying off when unthreaded.

Step 3: Undo the air sleeve by hand. This has a normal thread and undoes counterclockwise. A little gadget called a gator (available from auto supply stores) can grip the sleeve if stif. Don't use grips or pliers, which can damage the sleeve. The threads are very fine, so they take ages to unscrew. Persevere until you pull the sleeve free. Remove the screwdriver, and pull off the sleeve, along with the travel O-ring.

Step 4: Now the parts have been separated, clean them carefully. If things look fairly clean, just wipe with a clean rag. If things are a mess, you need to clean and degrease (check your degreaser is O-ring-friendly, something like Finish Line Ecotech 2 should be fine). If there's no grease at all, or the grease is discolored and dirty, you need to clean-and-grease more frequently.

Step 5: Next, grease. Good-quality, clean grease is essential. I like Pace grease from the UK, but there are plenty of alternatives — Rock Shox Judy Butter is great. There are three sets of O-rings. The two outer sets, at either end of the air sleeve (currently attached to the shock, just below the air sleeve threads), both need a light smear of grease — just a little, but ensure a constant bead all the way around.

Step 6: The same goes for the bearings and seal at the end of the air sleeve. The air sleeve threads also need a smear of grease. Make sure the threads run all the way around with no gaps.

Extra grease

Step 7: Be more generous with the O-ring and bearing in the middle of the shock, the one that sits in the middle inside the air sleeve. Pack an extra layer of grease into the shoulder above the body bearing, which gets dragged onto the bearing and O-ring during the shock cycle.

Step 8: Slide the air sleeve loosely back onto the body of the shock. However, you cannot push it home by hand — sliding the air sleeve over the middle O-ring traps air in the shock and prevents you from compressing it. For now, refit the travel O-ring. Clean and refit reducers.

Step 9: Refit the shock on the bike, using Loctite on the bolts if they came off easily because they must be refitted firmly. Keep the shock compressed while you refit the air sleeve. Locate end of the threads carefully, keeping the sleeve aligned with the shock. Turn the sleeve by hand until you feel it reach the thread limit. Tighten by hand. Inflate the shock to maximum pressure (300psi), then release air to the right pressure. Check all nuts and bolts.

Toolbox

Tools for cleaning and greasing air shaft
- Allen keys to remove shock from bike — usually 5mm or 6mm
- Screwdriver
- Plenty of good-quality shock grease, such as Rock Shox Judy Butter or Pace RC7 from the UK
- Plenty of clean cloth or paper towel
- Shock pump to reinflate once you're done

Fitting new reducers and bushings

Your shock is held in place by pivot bolts at either end. These need to move smoothly, so that the shock can rotate with the rear end of the bike as the shock moves through its travel. If the pivots become stiff, the shaft of the shock is forced to slide in and out of the shock body at an angle, wearing the seals and the shaft. Loose, sloppy pivots make your bike feel uncertain, since the back end hesitates before following the front end around tight turns.

Fox shocks

I don't understand why some people go through bushings more quickly than others. If you do, then learn to replace them. It's worth checking regularly, so you recognize replacement time — there should be no slop between the front and back ends of the bike.

▲ **Check for play by rocking the back end of the bike sideways**

▼ **Replace worn reducers**

Checking pivots for slop

Check the pivots for slop by holding the main frame still and rocking the back end of the bike. There should be no lateral movement, and definitely no knocking or clunking noises. If the pivots are worn, order fresh ones before you start, so you can refit them as you go along. See page 195.

It makes sense to replace the bushings at the same time as the reducers, while everything is open. This takes a little more work, but it is worth the effort.

Release the spring. Using an air shock, let all the air out. Then, back off the preload with a coil spring, so the spring is baggy. Undo the bolts at either end of the shock using either an Allen key and socket, or two Allen keys. Check the orientation of the shock so you can refit it correctly later. Remove the shock from the bike. The bike folds up when you take out the shock — support it so that no hoses or cables are stretched or kinked, and that your vulnerable paintwork is protected.

Pull the reducers from either side of each eyelet. The bushing is the part that lines the inside of the eyelet. You need to use the new one to push the old one out, installing itself in the process. It's a tight fit, so you need a vice for controled force. I've seen this done with a hammer, but it wasn't pleasant.

Support the far side of the eyelet with something hollow for the old bushing to push out into. A socket is ideal. Choose one where the hole is slightly bigger than the bushing, so the bushing does not touch as it pushes out.

Look closely at the eyelet. The bushing is slightly shorter than the width of the eyelet, maybe 0.5mm ($\frac{1}{50}$ inch). This creates a shoulder to rest the new bushing on, aligning it precisely. Sit one of the old reducers in the new bushing for protection.

Set up the shock in the vice, with all the parts in order: socket lined up with shock eyelet, shock, new bushing, old reducer. Carefully close the jaws of the vice. This pushes the new bushing in through the eyelet, forcing out the old bushing in the process so it ends up inside the socket. Leave the new bushing exactly flush on one side with a shallow shoulder left on the other side, so you can repeat the process next time.

Refit the reducers. Grease the part in contact with the bushing. Refit the shock to the bike, checking direction and orientation. Refit the bolts, using Loctite on the threads if they undid easily. Reset the sag by preloading the spring, or by refilling with air.

Pivot maintenance

The performance of the rear suspension depends utterly on the free movement of the pivots that join the struts and swingarms to the frame. All the hard work that went into designing and building the frame and shock is completely wasted unless you keep the pivots clean and lubricated. There are as many designs as designers, but they have one common enemy — the jet-wash. Never directly jet-wash at the side of your bike — you blow any lubrication out of the bearings.

Check the pivots twice a year by hanging the back of the bike up, taking off the back wheel, removing the rear shock completely, and moving the back of the bike through its travel. Don't kink or bend hoses or cables. Rock the back end of the bike sideways. There should be no movement.

If there's pivot slop, or if the rear end of the bike doesn't swivel freely, it's time for pivot maintenance. Details depend on your frame, so check the owner's manual. Usually pivot maintenance is not at all difficult.

Undo the bolts through the pivots, and disassemble carefully. Make a note of the position and orientation of any washers. Remove and inspect bushings or bearings. Bushings have to be ordered from your frame manufacturer, but sealed bearings are almost always common sizes so your bike shop or an auto supply center can supply fresh ones. You can also service bearings; use a sharp knife to peel off the plastic seals on both sides of the bearing, degrease, rinse, dry and repack with fresh grease. Refit the seals, pressing them gently into place with both thumbs. Hold the central part of the bearing, and rotate the outer part to check they run smoothly. Refit into the frame. Use Loctite on the bolt threads to stop them rattling free. Retighten the bolts firmly. Once you've refitted the bearings, and before you refit the shock, move the rear end of the bike through its travel again to check you've cured the problem. Check the fixing bolts are still snug after your first ride.

Troubleshooting forks

Symptom	Cause	Solution	Page
Forks have correct sag, but stop working over a series of bumps	Stacking up — forks haven't had time to re-extend between two obstacles	Reduce rebound damping	180
Reduce rebound damping	Bushes worn	Replace bushings — send to service center	194–5
Forks spring back with a jolt after an impact	Insufficient damping	Increase rebound damping	180
Forks suddenly start recoil too quickly, even though the adjustment is unchanged	Damping mechanism damaged	Replace damping mechanism — send to service center	183–6
Forks rebound slowly, even minimum rebound damping	Insufficient lubrication	Replace or replenish lubricating oil	183–6
	Oil weight too high	Use lower weight oil — try 5wt less than current	130
Forks leak oil from top of fork legs	Seals worn or damaged	Replace seals — send to service center	N/A
Forks leak oil from lower-leg fixing bolts	Fixing bolts working loose	Check tightness of fixing bolts	195
	O-rings on fixing bolts torn or missing	Replace O-rings	130
Shocks	Air shock bottoms out repeatedly	Not enough preload — increase air pressure	190

Bottom brackets and headsets

These two are the major bearings on your frame. The bottom bracket runs through the frame, connecting your cranks together and transferring the vertical force that you input through the pedals into rotational motion that drags your chain around your chainset. The headset connects your forks to your frame, keeping the front wheel securely attached while allowing you to rotate the bars to steer the bike.

Well adjusted and protected from the elements, the bottom bracket and headset will both run without complaint for years. But both bearings are susceptible to their environment. Dust, mud, salt, sand, rain — anything you might want to ride in, on, or through, in fact — will find its way into bearing surfaces and wear them out.

Both bearings need to be precisely adjusted. Play (side-to-side movement) in your bottom bracket causes sloppy shifting from your front derailleur, wears your chain and chainset, and gives you sore knees. Play in your headset means movement between frame and forks, leading to loss of vital control during braking and turning.

Overtight bearings are just as bad. Tight bottom brackets rob you of pedaling efficiency, making every pedal stroke that bit harder. Tight headsets make it difficult to turn the bars, forcing you to yank on them around corners.

This chapter leads you through the process of checking adjustments on both these major bearings. It also tells you how to adjust and service headsets, and how to replace bottom brackets. Headsets must be replaced once their bearing surfaces are worn, but it's best to take your bike to your shop for this — the job doesn't need doing very often, but it does require expensive tools. Bottom brackets used to be adjustable, but almost all of them are sealed units now, which means that when they become worn, you must remove and replace them.

Headset bearings allow your forks to rotate freely in your frame

Routine maintenance of the bottom bracket

The bottom bracket is the large main bearing that passes through your frame, between the cranks. Actually, it is a pair of bearings, one on each side bolted into threads cut on both sides of the frame. Like all the sealed parts of the bicycle, water and dirt will get in with enough time and abuse. This slows you down and wears out the bearings, so your bottom bracket needs regular, say annual, changing.

Back in the beginning, bottom brackets were sold in their separate parts: the axle that ran through the middle, the cups that bolted into the frame, and the bearings that sat in the gap between the two. The advantages of this system were that the gap between the bearings could be adjusted so that the bearings ran smoothly with no drag and that the parts could be regularly disassembled, cleaned, regreased, reassembled and adjusted. But we were all too lazy to do this often enough, so now almost all bottom brackets are sealed-in cartridges. They stay cleaner and, when they wear out, they have to be replaced as a unit.

Bottom brackets have a reverse thread on the right-hand side, so the cup on the chainset side of the bike has to be turned clockwise to remove it and counterclockwise to fit it. This is true of all mountain bikes and almost all other bikes. The exceptions are a few fancy Italian road bikes, which have a standard tighten-clockwise thread on both sides. These bikes serve to demonstrate why the reverse thread is necessary — bottom brackets with the Italian threading are prone to unravel under pressure from the pedals and require special attention from mechanics to stop this happening.

Different types of bottom bracket
Around the late 1990s, we'd finally come to settle on a standard fitting to attach cranks to bottom bracket axles when somebody came along with another improvement. History is now repeating itself with the appearance of a new bunch of designs. The standard for a while was called "square taper," which worked fine. Newer bottom brackets are splined and are generally lighter. Your bottom bracket type must match your crank type. There is no compatibility at all between the different types; you cannot exchange cranks or bottom brackets between systems.

All types are similar when it comes to getting them on and off though. In all cases, a bolt pulls the crank onto the axle, using either an 8mm or 10mm Allen key or a 14mm bolt. You remove the crank by clamping a tool into its threads, then wind in the center of the tool to push off the axle.

Square taper
A square-shaped axle fits into a similar hole on the crank. Since the axle and the hole in the crank are both tapered, as you tighten the bolt on the end of the axle, you push the crank farther onto the axle, wedging it firmly in place. The idea is simple, but if the crank comes just a little loose on the axle, it tends to loosen more, damaging the soft metal of the crank at the same time. This problem is particularly marked on the left-hand side — since the crank bolts both have a standard thread, the one on the left has a tendency to loosen as you put pressure on the pedals, whereas the right-hand one generally tightens itself. Check the bolts regularly.

Square taper

Cup

Crank bolts

ISIS

ISIS stands for International Spline Interface Standard. This is the type of bottom bracket used by Bontrager, Race Face, FSA and others. There are 10 splines on each side. The chainset has matching splines. To fit the chainset to the bottom bracket, slide it over the splines and tighten until the back of the chainset butts up firmly onto the shoulder on the bottom bracket axle.

Take care lining up the second crank — the cranks fit just as easily into each of the 10 splines, so make sure your cranks point accurately in opposite directions before you tighten down the bolts.

Cup

ISIS

Crank bolts

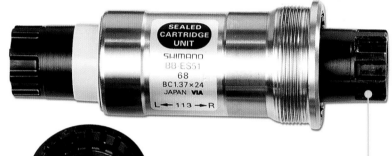

Shimano Octalink

Cup

Shimano Octalink

This is the Shimano splined bottom bracket. It has eight splines, rather than 10 as on an ISIS bottom bracket. ISIS bottom brackets and chainsets are not compatible with Shimano ones. When refitting chainsets, always carefully clean the splines on the chainset and bottom bracket, otherwise the chainset will work itself loose as you pedal. Retighten the crank bolts after the first 80km (50 miles).

Light, stiff, strong

Splined bottom brackets axles have a larger diameter than the older square taper types. The axle is a hollow tube, rather than a solid axle, making them lighter without compromising stiffness or strength. They need a larger diameter crank bolt, normally an 8mm Allen bolt, although recently a 10mm bolt has become more common.

Shimano Octalink

ISIS

Square taper

Bottom brackets: regular checking for play and wear

The bottom bracket suffers from being invisible much of the time. It is an essential bearing and is expected to turn smoothly even when you stamp on the pedals yet, because it can't be seen, it tends to be ignored. But a worn bottom bracket slows you down without noticing and also makes your chain and chainset wear quickly. Check regularly for play — the bottom bracket should spin freely and shouldn't rock from side to side at all.

Crouch on the right-hand side of the bike. Line up the right-hand crank with part of the frame — chainstay, seat-tube, down-tube, whatever. Hold the crank (not the pedal) in one hand and the frame in the other. Rock your hands gently toward and away from each other. You should not hear or feel any knocking or play between the crank and frame — no side-to-side movement at all. Repeat at other angles, lining the crank up each time with a part of your frame and rocking across the bike — you might get more knocking at one angle than another. Repeat on the other side.

Once you've checked both sides, decide whether the play comes from a worn bottom bracket, from the bottom bracket moving in the frame, or from the crank moving on the bottom bracket axle. If you can only feel knocking from one crank, most likely that crank is loose. Tighten the crank with a long 8mm (⅓ inch) Allen key, or if it's an older bottom bracket, a 14mm (%₁₆ inch) socket. This bolt must be firmly fitted or it will work loose — your work tool needs to be at least 200mm (8 inches) long, and you need to tighten hard. Extend short Allen keys by sliding them onto a longer tube. Tighten both sides while you're at it. Test again to see if the rocking has gone away. If the cranks still rock after tightening, you have a worn or loose bottom bracket.

You may be able to work out which bracket it is by looking into the gap between your left-hand crank and the frame as you rock the crank. You can only see the very end of the bottom bracket cup, since most of it is invisible inside the frame. There should be no movement at all between this sliver of bottom bracket cup and the frame. Check the right-hand side as well — this is trickier to see because the chainset is in the way. If the bottom bracket is loose in the frame, you can usually cure the problem simply by tightening it in the frame. You'll have to remove the chainset and crank; see pages 202–4. If the bottom bracket is worn out, you will see the axle shifting in the cup as you rock the crank. In this case, you have no option but to replace the bottom bracket; see pages 206–7.

Next, check that the bottom bracket bearings spin freely. Change into the smallest chainring at the front, then reach around to the back of the chainset and lift the chain off the smallest chainring. Drop it into the gap between the chainset and the frame below the front derailleur, so that the chain is not connected at all to the chainset. Spin the pedals. They should spin freely and silently. Grinding or crunching noises, or resistance mean it's time to change your bottom bracket. Lift the chain back onto the top of the smallest chainring and pedal forward slowly to re-engage the chain with the chainring.

◀ **Checking for bottom bracket play**

Creaking noises

This kind of noise from the bottom bracket area can spoil a perfectly good ride. Like all creaking sounds, investigate it right away — bicycles rarely complain unless something is loose, worn or about to snap. If your bicycle has the courtesy to give you warning creaks, it's worth your time to pay heed.

Fat-tubed aluminum bikes amplify the smallest sound. Anything with any tube fatter than you can get your hand around is, basically, a soundbox, and it will do its best to ensure you hear everything. The end result is that you start lusting after a narrow-tubed Italian steel racing bike, then suddenly you're visiting your mother for Christmas in full Lycra, duck shoes and aero helmets. Tighten your cranks instead.

Try these silencing measures, and then test to see if the creaking has gone away. If nothing works, note that frames transmit noises strangely, so creaks can sound as if they come from somewhere else. Common causes include handlebar and stem bolts, and rear hubs.

SORTING OUT NOISES

Step 1: Tighten both crank bolts clockwise. They both need to be tight — you will need a long (at least 200mm [8 inches]) Allen key, not just a multi-tool. The 8mm Allen key on multi-tools is for emergencies only.

Step 2: If that doesn't work, remove both crank bolts, grease the threads and under the heads, and refit firmly.

Step 3: Tighten both pedals. Remember that the left-hand pedal has a reverse thread — see the Pedals chapter for more details.

Step 4: Remove both pedals, grease the threads, and refit firmly. This sounds farfetched, but it does the trick more often than you'd imagine. Dirt or grit on the pedal threads will also cause creaking, so clean the threads on the pedal and inside the crank.

Step 5: Take hold of each pedal and twist it. The pedal should not move on its own axle. If it does, it could well be the source of the creak, and needs stripping and servicing (see the Pedals section). Spray a little light oil, like GT85, on the cleat release mechanism. Don't use chain oil — it's too sticky and will pick up dirt.

Step 6: Remove the crank and chainset, loosen the left-hand bottom bracket cup, tighten the right-hand cup firmly (remember it has a reverse thread), then tighten the left-hand cup (normal thread). Refit crank and chainset, and tighten bolts firmly. See pages 202–3 for more details.

Removing and refitting the cranks

Start on the left-hand side of the bike. Remove the Allen key bolt or 14mm Allen key that holds the crank on. Check inside the crank and remove any washers in there. Look into the hole to determine the kind of axle. If the bike is an older or entry level model, you will see the square end of the axle. On newer, more expensive bikes you will see the round end of a splined axle.

Use the appropriate crank-extractor — splined axles are fatter, so an older crank extractor, designed for square taper cranks, cannot push out the axle. It disappears down the hole into the middle of the axle instead. Crank extractors for splined axles have a fatter head and do not fit into older square cranks. If you do have a splined axle and an older crank extractor, Shimano makes a little plug to slip into the end of your splined axle, so that the square taper crank extractor will work: a TLFC15. Sometimes one comes packaged with new chainsets.

REMOVING A CRANK

Step 1: The crank bolts should be tightly fitted, so you will need a long Allen key (or 14mm socket) to undo the bolt. If you find the bolts come off without too much effort, tighten them more firmly next time!

Step 2: Hold the handle, or the nut end of the inner part of the tool and turn the outer part of the tool. You will see that turning one against the other means that the inner part of the tool moves in or out of the outer part.

Step 3: Next, back off the inner part of the tool so that its head disappears inside the outer part of the tool.

Step 4: Thread the outer part of the tool into the threads in the crank that you've revealed by taking off the bolt. The crank is soft in comparison to the tool so take care not to crossthread the tool and damage the crank, which will be expensive. Thread on the tool as far as it will go.

Step 5: Start winding in the inner part of the tool. It will move easily at first, but will then meet the end of the axle and stiffen. You need to be firm with it. Once it starts moving, turning the tool gets easier as it pushes the axle out of the crank.

Step 6: Once you've started the crank moving on the axle, the crank will come off in your hand. Pull it off the axle and remove the tool from the crank.

If your crank extractor is designed for fatter, splined axles, it will not work at all with square taper axles. The crank extractor has two parts. The outer part threads onto the crank; the inner part threads through the outer part and bears on the end of the axle. As long as the outer part is firmly fitted into the crank, as you thread in the inner part, it pushes the axle off the crank. The inner part of the tool will either have an integral handle, like the Park one in the picture on page 202, or it will have separate flats for a wrench. Either version works fine.

If at any time the outer part of the tool starts to pull out of the chainset, stop immediately. If you continue, you will strip the threads out of the chainset, and it will be difficult to remove the chainset without destroying it. Remove the tool from the crank, and check that you've removed all bolts and washers. If there are any accidentally left in there, remove them and try again. If you can find no reason why the threads are stripping, this might be a good time to beat a retreat to your bike shop and get your mechanic to have a go.

Once you've got the left-hand crank off, repeat the procedure for the chainset side, which works exactly the same way. Once you've done whatever you need to do in the bottom bracket, you need to refit the chainset and cranks. It's worth giving the area that's behind the chainset a good clean while the rings are off, and you might as well give the chainset a good scrub with degreaser too. Rinse it off well afterward. There's no need to oil it.

The same procedure is used to fit both crank and chainset. Fit the chainset first. Before starting, clean the axle and the hole in the chainset thoroughly. Make sure there's no dirt left on the tapers or between the splines, or you will get creaking. Apply antiseize to any titanium parts.

Refitting the crank and chainset

There are two different opinions about whether the axle should be greased before you fit the cranks onto it. Proponents on both sides of the discussion are often fiercely loyal to their points of view. The advantage of greasing the axle is that the lubrication allows the crank to be pulled further onto the axle, fitting it more tightly. Those who prefer not to grease the axle say that the grease layer allows the two surfaces to move against each other, leading to potential creaking and then allowing the parts to work themselves loose. Personally, I can be convinced by either argument, but have found that it makes more difference whether the axle and crank surfaces are clean than whether they are greased. New bottom brackets often come with antiseize already applied to the right-hand axle; this should be left on.

Inspect the surface of both the axle and the holes in the cranks. Square taper axles should be flat with no pitting. The crank hole is the place you're most likely place to find damage — the hole needs to be perfectly square and must fit smoothly over the axle. The most common problem is where loose cranks have rounded themselves off on the axle, smearing the shape of one or more of the corners of the square. Splined cranks will also be damaged by being ridden loose. Each spline should be crisp and clean. Replace damaged cranks immediately — they will never hold securely and will cause expensive damage to your bottom bracket axle.

Slide the chainset over the end of the axle. Line it up with the square or splined axle, and push on it firmly. Grease the threads of the fixing bolts, and add a dab of grease under the head of the bolt, which may otherwise creak. Fit the bolt and tighten firmly.

For the last part, line the crank up with the Allen key/socket wrench up, so they are almost parallel. Hold one in each hand and stand in front of the chainset. With both arms straight, use your shoulders to tighten the crank bolts. (This uses the strength of your shoulders and reduces the chance of stabbing yourself with the chainring if you slip.)

Next, fit the crank onto the other end of the bottom bracket axle. Line it up so that it points in the opposite direction to the one on the other side. This is simple with square tapers but takes a little care with splined designs — the bike feels very strange if you fit the crank to a neighboring spline. Tighten that crank on firmly too.

It's worth retightening all types of crank bolts after the first ride — you often find they work themselves a bit loose as they bed in. Both types of crank, square taper and splined, depend on the shape of the hole in the crank being exactly right. Riding with loose cranks stretches the shape, so the cranks will never fit firmly enough again, leaving replacement the only option. The material of the crank is softer than that of the axle, so it wears first, but if the worn crank is not replaced, it also eventually wears down the shape of the end of the bottom bracket axle.

◀ **Hold crank steady, retighten crank bolt firmly**

One-key release

Some chainsets come with standard one-key release. You can also buy them separately — they fit into standard crank threads.

These releases were invented so you could get the cranks off without using a crank extractor. They can also seize easily and can be fussy.

The one key release comes in a bag with no instructions. The large diameter washer (usually black) fits under the bolt head; the smaller one (usually white) sits on top between the bolt and the one-key release cap. The white one is vital; it allows the top of the bolt to turn easily against the inside of the one-key cap. The one-key release cap fits over the top of this washer so that the washer ends up trapped between the bolt and the cap. Both washers should be greased to help the bolt turn easily when fitting and removing the cranks.

Some one-key release bolts use a 6mm Allen key rather than the standard 8mm size. You'll need to get an extra long one from your bike shop to get enough leverage, or you can extend a standard one by sliding it into a longer tube.

FITTING A ONE-KEY RELEASE

Step 1: Start with the chainset side. When you come to fit the left-hand crank, make sure it lines up so that it points in exactly the opposite direction — this is easy on square tapers but takes a little more care with splined axles.

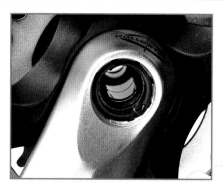

Step 2: Your one-key release kit comes with two washers. One fits neatly over the head of the bolt, the other sits underneath the bolt. Choose the washer that fits snugly over the threaded part of the bolt and sit it in the crank with a dab of grease.

Step 3: Thread the bolt into the axle, with the second washer pushed over the head of the bolt. This will also need a dab of grease to help the bolt turn against the one-key release cap when you come to take the crank off.

Step 4: Tighten the crank bolt firmly using an Allen key with at least 200mm (8 inches) of leverage. Hold the end of the Allen key and the end of the crank so that you get maximum leverage, and tighten very firmly. Otherwise your crank will work loose and fall off.

Step 5: Grease the threads of the one-key release cap and the inside surface, and tighten into the crank threads. A small peg wrench is perfect for this, but you can also use needle-nose pliers. If you have the special Shimano tool for tightening the backs of chainset bolts (TL-FC20), it has a one-key release cap wrench on the other end.

Step 6: To remove the crank, simply undo the crank nut. It will turn easily briefly, but will then jam against the inside of the one-key release cap. As you continue to turn, the bolt will push the crank off the axle.

Measuring the bottom bracket

Every model of every make of chainset is designed to work with a specific-length bottom bracket, which determines how far out from the frame the chainset sits. If it's too close, the chainrings will rub on the frame; too far out, and the front derailleur will struggle to reach the outer chainring.

Aligning the chainset correctly minimizes that angle of the chain in the outer rear sprockets, reducing chain wear.

Before removing your old bottom bracket, inspect it to see whether it is the right length. Even new bikes sometimes come fitted with the wrong length bottom bracket, so it's worth checking rather than automatically replacing it with the same length again.

◆ Check the chain line by shifting into your middle chainring and middle sprocket, and looking along the chain from behind the cassette. The chain should run straight, without an obvious kink where it meshes onto the sprocket and chainring teeth.

◆ Check the gap between the chainstay and chairings — there needs to be 2–3mm (around ⅛ inch) clearance to allow for chainring flex under pressure. If the chainrings rub on the chainstay, they'll wear it away.

◆ Shift into the smallest chainring and check the back of the front derailleur does not touch the frame. You need enough clearance here to adjust the front derailleur.

◆ Shift into the middle chainring and the smallest chainring at the back. If the chain rubs on the bottom of the outer chainring in this gear, the chainring needs to move outward.

If your current bottom bracket is the right length, replace with the same length. Estimating what length to use to correct any of the above problems can be tricky — it's worth taking your bike to your bike shop for help. Take your cranks off to measure the size of your current bottom bracket; once you've done that, you can measure your bottom bracket while it's still in the frame.

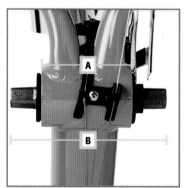

Bottom bracket shell width **(A)** is measured across the part of the frame that the bottom bracket fits into. Measure only the frame, not the flange of bottom bracket overlapping the edge of the frame. For example, if the frame is blue, measure across only the blue part, not across the silver bottom bracket. The two most common sizes are 68mm and 73mm. If your frame measures up any other size, measure again; there are other widths, but they are very unusual. The total axle width **(B)** runs from one end of the axle to the other (including the amount that sticks out each side) and is measured to the nearest millimeter. The differences between sizes are quite small — for square taper axles, Shimano make 107mm, 110mm, 113mm, 115mm, 118mm and 122mm lengths.

These may seem like a lot of similar sizes, but the difference between one size and the next will radically affect your shifting.

Toolbox

Removing chainset and crank:
- Crank bolt wrench — an 8mm Allen key, a 10mm Allen key or (for older bikes) a 14mm socket — you'll need one with a long handle (at least 200mm [8 inches]) to apply sufficient leverage
- Crank extractor — choose the correct type for your cranks — fatter version for splined cranks, standard size for square taper — you can use a standard size crank extractor with splined cranks if you use an axle end plug

Refitting chainset and crank:
- Crank bolt wrench (as above)
- Grease for crank bolt threads and heads

Fitting one-key release kit:
- Needle-nose pliers, narrow peg wrench, or the reverse end of the

Shimano chainset bolt tool (it took me years to find this use for the other end of my chainset bolt tool)

Removing and refitting bottom bracket:
- Tools to remove chainset and crank as above, plus:
- Bottom bracket tool — most will fit the standard Shimano bottom bracket tool
- ISIS type bottom brackets need a very similar tool, but the ISIS version has a larger hole in the middle to accommodate the fatter axle — ISIS bottom bracket tools will work fine on Shimano-type bottom brackets
- Big wrench to turn bottom bracket tool. Bottom brackets should be fitted firmly, so you will need a long wrench in order to be able to apply sufficient leverage — 300mm (12 inches) should be enough
- Grease or antiseize for bottom bracket threads

Removing the bottom bracket

The key here is remembering that the right-hand cup has a reverse thread, so it undoes backward. This is the same for all mountain bikes and most road bikes.

Before starting, check what kind of bottom bracket you have so you know the tool you need. Check the fitting. Almost everything is now a Shimano type splined fitting with 20 narrow splines in each cup. ISIS bottom brackets use the same size spline, but the hole in the middle of the tool must be bigger to fit over the fatter axle. ISIS tools work fine on Shimano-type bottom brackets though. Many of these bottom brackets have eight notches on the outside of the cup, and a few have only the notches. If your bottom bracket has both internal splines and notches around the outside of the bottom bracket, always use the internal splines to remove and refit — they make a more secure fitting, and the tool is less likely to slip and damage your frame or the notches. If you only have notches in the outside of the cup, use them, but get a tool that fits onto as many notches as possible because the type with a single hook, which only fits into one notch, is not enough. The instructions work in the same way, but use the notched tool instead of the splined one mentioned in the text.

REMOVING BOTTOM BRACKETS

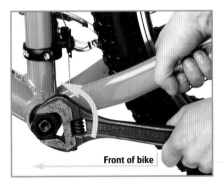

Front of bike

Step 1: Start on the left-hand side. Clean out all the splines on the bottom bracket cup so that the tool fits into them firmly. It's worth getting a little screwdriver and picking the dirt out of all the splines before you start — they're right down near the ground and tend to pick up all sorts of garbage, which can stop the tool from engaging with the full depth of the slots.

Step 2: Insert the tool, firmly clamp on a large adjustable wrench, and turn the tool counterclockwise to loosen the cup. It may be very firmly fitted. Take care not to let the tool slip off — it will damage the splines, and it's easy to hurt yourself. If the cup won't come out easily, clamp the tool onto the bottom bracket. This calls for ingenuity; you need to fashion a washer of a size that allows you to bolt the tool on with your original crank bolt.

Step 3: Remove the left-hand cup completely. Check the condition of the splines and the threads, especially the cheaper plastic cups. These work fine and are light, but the splines can get damaged easily.

Front of bike

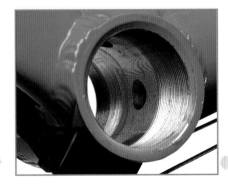

Step 4: Shift the tool onto the right-hand side and fit it firmly into the spline. Remove the tool by turning it clockwise. It can be tough to turn. Clamp on the tools if necessary. Bottom brackets often seize on, so a release agent like Shimano Get-a-Grip could be handy. If you use a release agent, make sure you're in a well-ventilated place. Spray or drip on, and leave the release agent to do its chemical magic for half an hour before you try to shift the cup again.

Step 5: Remove the body of the bottom bracket. Don't throw it away right away — you will need to measure it to get the right size for your new one.

Step 6: Once both sides are out, take a look at the inside of the frame. Clean it out carefully. If it holds lots of debris, work out where the dirt is getting in, and block up the hole. Make sure there are bolts in all the water bottle bosses, even if they have no cage mounted to them.

Refitting the bottom bracket

Check the new bottom bracket. The fitting threads are either metal on both sides, or metal one side and plastic the other. Grease the threads that will take a metal thread, but do not grease those that take plastic. All titanium threads need a generous coat of anti-seize.

Generally, the cups are marked "L" and "R." Usually, the body of the bottom bracket is the right-hand side, with a loose cup that attaches from the left. This is not universal though. If it's the other way around, reverse the fitting order. The bottom bracket threads are very fine, so it's important to take care when fitting that you don't "cross-thread" (thread in crookedly) the cups. Start each side by hand so that you can't force the threads to start unless they fit properly. Riding with a loose bottom bracket will damage the threads. New frames, and those that have been resprayed, may have paint stuck in the threads that prevents fitting the new bottom bracket. If the threads are damaged, get the frame to your bike shop. Unless they are really badly damaged, they can be recut with a tap (a big tool with the same size and shape thread as the bottom bracket, but with hard, sharp cutting blades instead of a plain thread).

REFITTING THE BOTTOM BRACKET

Front of bike

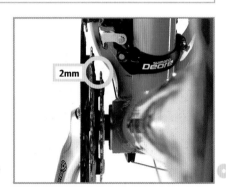

2mm

Step 1: Roll the left-hand cup a couple of turns into the thread on the left-hand side. Start fitting the right-hand side — the main body of the bottom bracket — into the right-hand side of the frame, tightening counterclockwise by hand. Once you've got it in a couple of turns, look from the left-hand end of the bottom bracket, to check that the axle is coming out exactly in the middle of the hole in the cup you just fitted.

Step 2: Tighten counterclockwise. It needs to be fitted really firmly — you need about 300mm (12 inches) of leverage and a good grunt home. Once the body of the bottom bracket is fitted firmly, tighten up the left-hand cup. Take care with plastic cups — they need to be fitted fairly firmly, but won't take as much force as the main body of the bottom bracket. Overdo it and you damage the plastic splines and make it difficult to remove next time.

Step 3: Refit the cranks as on pages 202–3. If you fit a new bottom bracket, watch as you fit the chainset side. Even if you've measured carefully, it's worth checking that the chainset doesn't jam on the chainstays as you tighten the crank bolt. You need at least 2mm ($^1/_8$ inch) of clearance between the chainset and the chainstay — if there's not enough, remove the bottom bracket and fit a longer one.

Stubborn bottom brackets

Sometimes bottom brackets get wedged in hard. Usually, it means they weren't fitted with enough grease or antiseize in the first place, or that they've simply been in there too long. Living by the sea in a salty atmosphere, doesn't help either. Try the following measures:

A good dose of release agent helps in three or four applications over a couple of days — especially if, in the middle of proceedings, you put everything back together and go for a good hard ride. A light spray like WD40 will work as a basic penetrant, although you can get something tougher at your hardware or auto shop. You can also get bike-specific release agent from your bike shop — Shimano makes one called Get-A-Grip that is frighteningly effective. All release agents contain various nasty chemicals, so use sparingly in a well-ventilated space and don't get any on your skin. Check once again that you are trying to turn the tool in the correct direction — it's easy to get confused. Looking from the right-hand side of the bike, the right-hand cup is removed by turning it clockwise — a reverse thread. Looking from the left-

hand side of the bike, the left-hand cup is removed by turning it counterclockwise — a normal thread.

Once you've soaked the bottom bracket thoroughly, try using as long a lever as possible on the tool. Find a tube that fits over the end of your adjustable wrench, and use that to increase your leverage, bracing yourself carefully so you don't slip and hurt yourself when the tool starts to move. Clamping the tool in place helps stop the tool slipping off and damaging you and the splines. You need to fiddle with the washers to clamp it successfully. Use the crank bolt and find a washer that stops the crank bolt from slipping into the hole in the center of the tool without interfering with the wrench flats.

If you have a vice and assistance from a friend, take off the wheels. Drop the tool into the vice and clamp it so the bike is held horizontally over the workbench. Use the bike as a lever and turn it to undo the tool.

Troubleshooting bottom brackets

Symptom	Cause	Solution	Page
One crank rocks from side to side, the other is firm	Loose crank bolt	Tighten crank bolt	201, 203
Both cranks rock from side to side	Bottom bracket unit loose in frame	Remove both cranks, tighten bottom bracket in frame, replace both cranks	202–3, 207
	Bottom bracket worn out	Replace bottom bracket	206–7
Cranks loosen repeatedly	Crank bolt loose	Tighten firmly — use a longer wrench for more leverage	201, 203
	Crank mating surface worn by being ridden loose	Replace crank	202–3
	New crank still loosens repeatedly	Replace bottom bracket	206–7
Creaking noises from bottom bracket area	Dry or loose interface between components	Remove cranks, clean interface between cranks and axle, replace, retighten firmly	201–3
	Bottom bracket loose in frame	Remove both cranks, tighten bottom bracket in frame, replace both cranks	201–3, 207
Bottom bracket works loose constantly	Insufficiently tightened in frame	Use a longer wrench on the bottom bracket tool for more leverage	201–3
	Bottom bracket shell stretched by riding with loose bottom bracket	For minor stretching, use Loctite threads to fill gaps. For major stretching, the only option is to replace frame	N/A
Front derailleur won't shift on to largest chainring	Bottom bracket too long	Replace with shorter one	206–7
Chainrings rub on frame	Bottom bracket too short	Replace with longer one	206–7
Chainring clearance looks fine but chainrings rub under pressure	More clearance needed to allow for chainring flex	Fit longer bottom bracket	206–7
	Chainring bolts loose or missing, allowing chainring to flex excessively	Tighten or replace chainring bolts	130

Headsets: Ahead or threaded

The headset is the bearing at the front of the bike that connects the forks to the frame. Like the bottom bracket, it's an "out of sight, out of mind" component. It is often ignored in favor of more glamorous upgrades, but it makes a huge difference to how your bike rides. The Aheadset design is almost universal on new bikes, although there are plenty of older bikes around that still have threaded headsets.

Aheadset or threaded headset?

You can identify which type of headset you have by looking at how your stem is attached to your forks. Older, threaded headsets have two large nuts between the stem and the top of the frame. The lower of the two nuts is an adjustable bearing race, used to alter the amount of space that the bearings have to roll around in. The upper of these two nuts is a locknut, used to wedge the bearing race in place once you've adjusted it correctly. Aheadset stems are bolted directly to the fork steerer tube where it emerges from the top of the headset. Aheadset stems will have one or two bolts used to adjust the bearings on the side of the stem, as well as a top cap bolt directly on top of the stem.

Design advantage

The appeal of the Aheadset over the older headset design is that the bearings are adjustable with one (or two) Allen keys, rather than with a pair of the heavy, bulky headset wrenches needed for threaded headsets — and nothing else. The old design does have the advantage of allowing you easily to make precise adjustments to the stem height without having to readjust the bearings afterward, but we've grown used to this. Besides the difference in adjustment methods, both the Aheadset and regular headset work in the same way: a set of bearings at either end of the headtube is adjusted to give enough space between the cups for the forks to steer freely, but not so much that the forks rock backward and forward in the frame. Ride mainly at ground level in fairly clean environments and your headset will live for years without complaint. Mud, water, sand and jumping shorten its lifespan. If you go through a lot of bearings or headsets, upgrade. Wet conditions require better seals and replaceable cartridge bearings. Lots of airtime necessitates bigger, beefier bearings and a longer headset that fits deeper into the frame.

Checking headset adjustment

Incorrect bearing adjustment and worn bearings both mean uncertain steering. A tight headset makes your steering feel heavy and wear quickly. A loose headset will rock and shudder as you brake.

ADJUSTING HEADSETS

Step 1: Pick the bike up by the handlebars and turn the handlebars. The bars should turn easily and smoothly, with no effort. You should not feel any notches.

Step 2: Drop the bike back to the ground and turn the bars 90°, so the wheel points to one side. Hold on the front brake to stop the wheel rolling, and rock the bike gently back and forth in the direction the frame (not the wheel) is pointing. The wheel might flex and the tire yields a bit, but there should not be any knocking or play. Turning bars sideways isolates headset play, avoiding confusion with movement you may have in your brake pivots or suspension.

Step 3: Sometimes it helps to hold around the cups, above and below, while you rock the bike — you shouldn't feel any movement at all.

Aheadsets: adjusting bearings

The bearings are adjusted for no play at all, while allowing the fork and bars to rotate smoothly in the frame without resistance. Check the bearings as below; if they're tight, or there is play, adjust them. You wear your bearings really quickly if you ride them either tight or loose.

It's vital to check that your stem bolts are tight after finishing this job — it's easy to get carried away with doing the adjustment and forget to finish the job off. Some people will tell you to leave your stem bolt slightly loose, so that in the event of a crash your stem will twist on the steerer tube rather than bending your handlebars. You should not do this. The consequences of your stem accidentally twisting on your steerer tube as you ride are far too serious and dangerous. Always tighten your stem bolts firmly. It is fine to slacken the topcap bolt off though — it's only needed for headset adjustment and can be a handy emergency bolt if something else snaps!

ADJUSTING AHEADSET BEARINGS

Step 1: Loosen the stem bolt(s) so the stem can rotate easily on the steerer. Undoing the top cap makes the headset turn more easily; tightening it eliminates play. Approach the correct adjustment gradually, testing for rocking. It is easier to get the adjustment right by tightening a loose headset than by loosening a tight one. If the headset is too tight, back off the top cap a few turns, hold on the front brake, and rock the bars gently back and forth.

Step 2: Slowly retighten the top cap, checking constantly, and stopping when you've eliminated all the play. Remember to check for play with the bars turned to one side, so that you can be sure that any knocking you feel is the headset, rather than the brake pivots or fork stanchions.

Step 3: Once you have the adjustment correct, align the stem with the front wheel and firmly tighten the stem bolts. Check the stem is secure by holding the front wheel between your knees and twisting it. If you can turn it, the stem bolts need to be tighter. Check the adjustment again and repeat if necessary — sometimes tightening the stem bolt shifts everything around.

Toolbox

Adjusting bearings:
- Allen key to fit stem bolts
- Allen key to fit top cap
- Both of these are almost always a 5mm or 6mm Allen key, although you may occasionally come across a 4mm Allen key fitting

Adjusting stem height:
- The same Allen keys as above, to fit your stem bolts and top cap

Servicing:
- Allen keys as above
- Tools to disconnect your brake cable, lever or disc caliper — almost always the same Allen keys as above — 4mm, 5mm or 6mm Allen key
- Degreaser to clean bearing surfaces
- Good-quality grease — preferably a waterproof grease such as Phil Wood

- Fresh bearings: Ball bearings for headsets are generally 4mm (5⁄32 inch), but take your old ones to your bike shop to match them up.
- Bearing races can be replaced by loose bearings, which are trickier to fit but roll more smoothly and last longer
- Cartridge bearings should be taken to the shop to be matched up for fresh ones — there are a few different types in use, all of which look very similar
- The most common type, for Shimano bearings, also fits in headsets made by other manufacturers

Cutting down steerer tube
This is the most tool-intensive job you can do to your Aheadset!
- All the servicing tools above
- Hacksaw
- Vice to hold steerer tube while you cut it
- Soft jaws or an improvised tube clamp to protect steerer tube from vice

Aheadsets: adjusting stem height

If your handlebar is set at the correct height, you are more comfortable and your bike is more stable and easier to steer. You can change the height in a couple of ways.

Swapping the stem is easiest — you can change both the length of the stem and the height. Check page 224 for tips. Make minor changes to the height of the stem by swapping the position of the washers on it. If you take off your stem and remove a couple of washers from the steerer tube, your stem sits lower when you refit it. Replace the washers above the stem before refitting the top cap — they push the stem down the steerer tube when you tighten the top cap. You'll end up with a little stack of washers protruding above your stem. Leave them there until you're satisfied with your position. Once you're happy, cut off the extra bit of steerer tube. Don't do this until you're sure you don't want to raise the stem — it's relatively easy to make the steerer tube shorter, but you can't make it longer again! You'll need to readjust the headset bearings again once you've reassembled the stem and refitted the top cap. Steel or aluminum washers can be replaced with flash carbon fiber ones for a marginal weight saving.

ADJUSTING STEM HEIGHT

Step 1: Remove the top cap. You'll need to undo the top cap bolt all the way and wiggle the cap off. This reveals that star-fanged nut inside the steerer tube. Lift off any washers that were sitting between the top cap and the stem. Check the condition of the top cap. If it's cracked or the recess where the bolt head sits is distorted, replace it.

Step 2: Loosen the stem bolts so that the stem moves freely on the steerer tube. Pull the stem up and off — you may need to twist it a little to help it on its way. Tape the entire handlebar assembly to the top tube so that hoses and cables don't get kinked under the weight of the bars.

Step 3: If you've hung the bike in a workstand, keep a hand on the forks so that they don't slide out of the headset. Add or remove washers from the stack under the stem. If you're adding washers, you can only add washers that came off above the stem.

Step 4: Replace the stem, then any leftover washers — everything that came off the steerer tube should go back on. The washers are all necessary because as you tighten the top cap, they push down onto the stem and then the bearings, adjusting the headset.

Step 5: Check the height of the washer stack above the top of the steerer tube. There should be a gap of 2–3mm (around $\frac{1}{8}$ inch). If possible, this should be a single washer, not a stack of thinner ones as individual washers have a tendency to get caught and stop you adjusting the headset properly. Add or remove washers from the top of the stack to achieve the desired 2–3mm gap.

Step 6: Replace the top cap, and go to "Aheadset: Adjusting bearings" on page 210. **Ensure the stem bolts are securely tightened.**

Headsets: regular maintenance to ensure a smooth ride

Headsets are remarkably simple to service, needing no special tools at all, just one (or two) Allen keys, degreaser or other cleaning agent and good quality grease.

Headsets, like bottom brackets, are frequently ignored, gradually deteriorating without you noticing. Regular servicing will help keep them turning smoothly and will make your bike feel more responsive. Cleaning the dirt out and replacing the grease with fresh stuff will help make the bearing surfaces last as long as possible. With the ball type, it's worth replacing the bearings at every service — new ones only cost a few dollars. Cartridge bearings are more expensive and can usually be resuscitated — see page 218 for help servicing them. Always take the old cartridge bearings along to your bike shop to match up new ones. The size and shape are crucial.

Check carefully for pitting once you've cleaned out the headset. Even very tiny pits are a sign that your headset needs replacing. The surface that suffers most is the crown race, the ring at the very bottom of the headset that's attached to your forks. Your bearings will quickly wear a groove in this, showing you where they run. The crown race should be completely smooth. You should be able to run a fingernail around the groove without it catching in any blemishes on the surface.

Headset replacement is a job for your bike shop. The new headset needs to be pressed into your frame, with the top and bottom surfaces exactly parallel; otherwise the headset will wear very quickly and bind at some handlebar angles. The cups are a tight fit, and so must be pressed in carefully to avoid damaging the shape of the head tube. Ignore anybody who tells you that it's OK to fit new headset cups by bashing them into the head tube with a block of wood.

Headset hints

Before you start, remove the front wheel altogether. It's easiest to do this job if you disconnect either the front brake lever from the front brake or the front brake lever from the handlebars. This way you won't damage the cable or hose when you remove the forks.

With cable brakes, disconnect the noodle from the brake (don't undo the fixing bolt, just quick-release it), line up the slots on the barrel-adjuster with the slot on the lever, pull the cable gently out, and wiggle the nipple free from its nest inside the brake lever.

With disc brakes, have a look at the lever. If it's fixed on with two bolts on either side of the handlebar, simply remove them both, untangle the hose from the other cables, and tape the lever to the forks to stop the hose getting snagged on anything. Otherwise, remove the handlebar grip on the front brake side, loosen the brake-fixing bolt, and slide the brake lever off the end of the bars.

Untangle the hose from any of the other controls, and tape or tie to the fork leg.

SERVICING HEADSETS

Step 1: Undo the Allen key on the very top of the stem, the top cap bolt. Remove the top cap completely, revealing the star-fanged nut inside the steerer tube. Undo the bolts that secure the stem while holding onto the forks, and the stem should pull off easily.

Step 2: Tape or tie the stem to the top tube out of the way (protect the frame paint with a cloth). Pull off any washers and set them aside. Pull the forks gently and slowly down out of the frame.

Step 3: The fork may not want to come out. Lots of headsets have a plastic wedge that sits above the top bearing race and that sometimes gets very firmly wedged in place. Release it by sliding a small screwdriver into the gap in the plastic wedge, and twist slightly to release the wedge. You could also try tapping the top of the fork with a plastic or rubber mallet. Don't hit it with a hammer — that's not the same thing at all.

Step 4: Catch all pieces as they come off, and note the orientation and order of bearing races and seals.

Step 5: Once you've got the fork out, lay out all the bearing races and cups in order. Check the bearing cup at the bottom of the head tube for any bearings or seals left in there. Clean all the races carefully: the ones attached to the frame top and bottom, the loose one off the top chunk of bearings when the fork came out, and the crown race still attached to the fork. If you have cartridge bearings, see the section on servicing the cartridges.

Step 6: Look carefully at the clean races, and check for pits or rough patches. Pitted bearing races mean a new headset. This needs special tools and so is a job for your bike shop. Otherwise, clean all the bearings and seals carefully. If you used degreaser, rinse it off, and dry everything. Grease the cups in the frame enough that the bearings sit in grease up to their middles. Cartridge bearings just need a thin smear to keep the weather out.

Step 7: Don't grease the crown race on the fork or the loose top head race. Fit a bearing ring into the cups at either end of the head tube and replace the seals. The direction the races face is crucial, so replace them facing the same direction they were. Slide the fork back through the frame and slide the loose top race back down over the steerer tube. If it had a plastic wedge, put it next, followed by any washers or covers in the order they came off.

Step 8: Refit the stem and any washers from above the stem. Push the stem firmly down the steerer tube.

Step 9: Make sure there's a gap of 2–3mm (around ⅛ inch) between the top of the steerer tube and the top of the stem, adding or removing washers if necessary. Refit the top cap, then adjust bearings (see page 216). Tighten the stem bolts securely, then refit your brake lever or cable and your front wheel. Check your stem is tight and facing forward. Also check that your front brake is working properly.

Checking the condition of the steerer tube

While you've got the forks out, it's worth checking the condition of the steerer tube. This will break if abused, so it is worth inspecting regularly. Adjustment of the bearings also depends on the stem being able to slide easily up and down the steerer tube when the top cap is tightened or loosened.

- Hold a ruler up to the steerer tube. The side of the ruler should lie flat against the length of the steerer. Any bends in the steerer will show up as gaps between it and the ruler. Gaps greater than 1mm (¹⁄₁₆ inch) mean that the steerer is bent and should be replaced.
- Feel along the surface of the steerer with your fingers. There should be no bulges, dips or irregularities in the diameter of the steerer.
- Check for cracks, especially down at the bottom of the steerer tube, near the crown race.
- Check that the crown race is a tight fit on the forks — you should not be able to move it with your fingers.
- Check the area that the stem bolts onto. It's important that this is clean and smooth. Some stems will damage the steerer if overtightened — replace if it is distorted.
- The top of the steerer must be smooth. If you've cut down the steerer, file the cut surface so that there are no overhanging snags of metal — these will get caught in the stem and prevent you from adjusting the bearings.

Aheadsets: cutting off excess steerer tube

With your stem at its maximum height, your stem top cap will sit directly on top of your stem. If you decide to move your stem downward, removing washers from below the stem, you'll have to replace them above the stem, so that they bear down on the top of it when you adjust the top cap. Excess steerer tube will then protrude above the stem.

Mechanically, this works perfectly well, but it's not particularly attractive and will hurt if you land on it in a crash. It's a bit of extra weight that you don't need to carry around too. So, once you're sure that you prefer the new, lower stem height — and do be sure because cutting off excess steerer tube is easy, making it longer again means buying a new pair of forks — cut off the protruding part. You'll also need to do this when fitting a new pair of forks — they are always supplied longer than you would ever need and are then cut down to length — this is much cheaper for suppliers than making a selection of different steerer lengths.

Start by very carefully marking the place to cut. It's easy to get confused and cut off too much, leaving you with a useless pair of forks. Marker pen works well. Assemble the fork completely, including the stem. Mark the point where the steerer tube comes up out of the top of the stem. Draw the line all the way around the top of the stem. Remove the forks from the bike again.

If you are shortening previously fitted forks, you need to check the position of the star-fanged nut inside the steerer tube. You can see it if you look down into the steerer tube from above — a short length of thread mounted in a domed, fanged plate. The fangs point slightly upward, so that, as you tighten the top cap, they are forced into the inside wall of the steerer tube. This means that the more you tighten the top cap, the firmer the star-fanged nut wedges itself in place.

The star-fanged nut needs to sit just inside the steerer tube so that the top of the nut is about 10mm (⅜ inch) below its top. When cutting down forks, you will often find that the current position of the nut is just exactly where you want to cut the tube. If this is the case, it's best to move the nut down the tube so that you can reuse it. Thread a long 6mm (¼ inch) bolt into the star-fanged nut, and tap it down gently with a hammer until it lies about 10mm (⅜ inch) below the level of the line you've marked. Be careful to knock it in straight, don't let it drift to one side.

Cutting the steerer tube

Now you're ready to cut the steerer tube. I like to hold the forks up against the bike as a final check that I've measured correctly before I start cutting.

The forks will need to be clamped securely while you cut them, but it's vital not to squash the steerer tube. Soft vice jaws, made of wood or plastic, work fine as long as you're careful not to overtighten the vice. If you have a scrap of wood (a block about 50mm x 50mm x 50mm [2 inches x 2 inches x 2 inches] is perfect) and a drill, cut a hole that's about the same diameter as the steerer tube (25mm [1 inch] should be fine) through the length of the wood. Then cut the wood in half across the middle of the hole, and along its length. You will end up with two blocks of wood, each with a semicircular channel. Place these on either side of the steerer tube so that you can clamp the steerer tube firmly in the vice without squashing it.

You need to cut the steerer tube 2–3mm (around ⅛ inch) shorter than the mark you've made. Draw a new line, all the way around the steerer tube — it's important that the cut is flat and square. Cut carefully, checking that you're not trying to cut through the star-fanged nut as well — you may find that you need to knock it through a little further. File off sharp edges because the stem needs to be able to slide freely over the steerer tube without scratching. Clean off any metal shavings and filings; these will play havoc with your headset bearings if they work their way in there.

If you're fitting new forks, or you cut the star-fanged nut off, you'll need to fit a new nut. They have two parallel-toothed plates. Both plates are slightly curved — the nut sits in the fork, so that the teeth point upward. Screw the new star-fanged nut onto a long (45mm or so) bolt — the usual size is 6mm, but some nuts take 5mm.

Protect the dropouts at the bottom of the fork by standing them on a piece of wood. Take special care if you have adjuster knobs or valves protruding from the bottom of the fork legs — support the forks so that these parts don't come into contact with hard surfaces, as they will bend or break. Tap the top of the bolt, knocking the star-fanged nut into the top of the steerer tube. Take care to keep it vertical. It should sit 10–20mm (⅜–¾ inch) below the top of the steerer tube.

Threaded headsets

The big advantage that the older style threaded headset has over new Aheadsets is that it is very easy to adjust the stem height without replacing any parts.

Adjusting stem height

Follow these instructions to change your stem height. Then check that the stem is tight by standing in front of the bike, holding the front wheel between your knees. Try to twist the bars around. If you can move them, the stem bolt is too loose. Retighten. If the stem is tricky to tighten, it may indicate that the steerer tube (the central part of the fork that extends up through the frame and onto which your stem is bolted) is damaged. Alternatively, the wedge at the bottom of the stem, the one that is pulled upward when you tighten the stem bolt, may have become twisted in the steerer tube. Either way, if you can't tighten your stem, get your bike shop to have a look at the stem and steerer tube, and to replace the forks if necessary. Also make sure that the front wheel is pointing straight forward; if not, loosen the stem bolt, twist it so the wheel and bars are at 90 degrees, and retighten.

ADJUSTING STEM HEIGHT

Safety mark

Step 1: Undo the expander bolt at the top of the stem. This almost always needs a 6mm Allen key, but you might need to pry off a rubber cap first. Undo it in four complete turns.

Step 2: As you turn the bolt, the head rises up out of the stem. Tap the Allen key with a rubber mallet or block of wood, so that the Allen key drops down flush with the stem again. This releases the wedge that holds the stem in place.

Step 3: Once the stem is loose, you can adjust its position. Make sure you don't raise it above the safety mark — an arrow or a row of vertical lines around the stem. They should not be visible; instead they should be hidden inside the headset. Retighten the 6mm Allen key bolt firmly.

Toolbox

The main reason for the demise of the once-ubiquitous threaded headset is that it requires a pair of expensive wrenches to adjust — unlike the Aheadset, which can be adjusted with an Allen key.

Tools for threaded headsets: adjusting stem height
- 6mm Allen key
- If the expander bolt is wedged firmly, a plastic hammer or a block of wood is needed to knock it down

Tools for threaded headsets: adjusting bearings
- Ideally, two headset wrenches — the most common size is 36mm, although older, 1-inch headsets need 32mm wrenches — it is possible to use an adjustable wrench on the top lock nut instead of a headset

wrench, but take time to tighten the wrench carefully onto the nut flats, since they are soft and easily damaged

Threaded headsets: adjusting bearings

You need two wrenches to adjust the bearings. The most common size, for 1⅛ inch headsets, is 36mm. You may also come across 1-inch headsets, which need a 32mm wrench, and even the rare 1½-inch headsets, which need a 40mm wrench. The adjustable nut is quite narrow, so you will need a special narrow headset wrench. The top nut is wider, so use an adjustable wrench if you only have one headset wrench.

To check your headset, pick the bike up by the handlebars, and turn the steering. The bars should turn easily and smoothly, with no effort. You should not be able to feel any notches. Drop the bike back onto the ground again, and turn the bars 90 degrees so that the wheel points off to one side. Hold on the front brake to stop the wheel rolling, and rock the bike gently backward and forward — in the direction the frame points, not the direction the wheel points. The wheel might flex, and you may feel the tire giving a bit, but you should not feel or hear any knocking or play. Sometimes it helps to hold around the cups, above and below, while you rock — you shouldn't feel any movement.

The top of the fork steerer tube is threaded and held into the frame with two big nuts. The lower of these has a bearing surface on the bottom in which the top set of bearings runs. Tightening the nut draws the fork up into the frame, squashing the bearing surfaces closer together and eliminating play between fork and frame. Loosening this nut increases the space the bearings sit in, allowing them to turn more smoothly. The correct adjustment is found by turning this nut to a position that eliminates play while still allowing the forks to rotate freely. Once you've found this magic position, the top nut can be locked down onto the adjusting nut, holding it firmly in position so that it doesn't rattle loose as you ride along. Once bearings have been correctly adjusted and the top nut firmly locked down, they should not work loose over time, so they will not need frequent readjustment. However, the bearings often settle a little bit after servicing, so they will often need readjusting. If you find yourself having to readjust your bearings often, check that the threads on the forks and the headset are in good condition. The threads will suffer if the headset is ridden loose, when both nuts will rub constantly over the fork threads.

Remove the stem, then the top locknut. Have a look at the threads inside the nut. They should be crisp and distinct, with sharp edges. The fork threads should be the same. Unscrew the lower adjusting nut and check the threads on it, as well as the fork threads that were concealed by the adjusting nut. If the threads are slightly damaged, reassemble the headset with Loctite on the threads to prevent the nuts from working loose. A new top locking nut will also help. However, if either the fork threads have been badly worn, or the nut has worn grooves in the surface of the fork, the fork should be replaced immediately.

ADJUSTING BEARINGS

Step 1: Hold the adjusting nut still with one wrench, and undo the top nut a couple of turns with the other. The two will be firmly locked together, so you have to be firm with the wrenches to get them moving. Once the top nut is loose, use the wrench to adjust the position of the adjusting nut — tighten clockwise to eliminate play in the headset, loosen counterclockwise to allow the bars to rotate freely.

Step 2: Ideally, you looking for the place where the adjusting nut is as loose as possible, without allowing the forks to rock in the frame. Turn the adjustable cup clockwise to eliminate rocking — counterclockwise to allow the headset to turn more freely. Test by holding the front brake on and rocking the bike forward.

Step 3: Once you've found the right place, hold the bottom nut still with the wrench to maintain the adjustment, and lock the top nut firmly down onto it. Test the adjustment again — you often find that locking down the top nut changes the adjustment, so that you have to repeat the procedure. Take care, as you do this not to overtighten the adjusting cup — if you wedge it down onto the bearing surface, you damage the bearings.

Servicing threaded headsets

Headsets will thank you for regular servicing. Pick up the bike by the handlebar, and twist it — the bar should move freely, with no crunching noises.

Check before you start that it's not too late for a service — leave it too long and you have to replace your headset. Replacement is a job that needs expensive and special tools, so it is worth getting your bike shop to do for you.

Turn your bars gently from one side to the other. If the headset is pitted, you will feel a notch as the headset passes through the "straight ahead" position — almost as if the headset is indexed. If this happens, it's new headset time. Otherwise, it's worth trying to service.

Release the front brakes, and free the cable from the front brake lever so that it hangs free. Take the front wheel off (you take the forks out in a while, and the wheel makes them heavy and unwieldy). Remove the stem — loosen the expander bolt on the top of the stem four turns, then knock the head of the bolt gently with a block of wood or a rubber mallet. Pull the stem up and out of the steerer tube, and tie or tape it to the top tube to keep it out of the way. Now you're ready to service the headset.

SERVICING HEADSETS

Step 1: Remove the top nut. It is wedged tightly against the lower nut, so you need two wrenches of the right size: one to hold the adjusting nut still, one to loosen the top nut. Slide off any washers. Lay out everything you take off in order so you know how to put them back together.

Step 2: Hold the fork still and undo the adjusting nut. When you've removed it, you should find that you can slide the forks out from the bottom of the frame. Make sure you catch any bearings or seals that come off, and note which direction they were facing in. Be particularly careful with bearing races — they must go back together in the correct order.

Step 3: Clean cups, bearings and seals carefully. To remove compacted grease and mud, scrub them with an old toothbrush and some degreaser. Rinse and dry afterward. Inspect the bearing surfaces carefully. Any kind of pitting means replacing the headset, a bike shop job. Pay particular attention to the crown race, the part that usually suffers first. If the bearings are dirty, replace them — fresh bearings make your headset last longer. Make sure you get the correct size.

Step 4: Grease the cups at either end of the head tube. There should be enough grease to cover the bearings up to their middles. Cartridge bearings are the exception: you do not need to grease the cups. Grease the threads on the adjusting and top nuts, and dab a little on the bottom surface of the top cup.

Step 5: Pop bearings and then seals into the cups, paying attention to the direction of the bearings. Slide the fork up through the frame and trap it in place by threading on the adjusting cup. Make sure it's flat as it goes on — it's easy to cross-thread by mistake. Tighten until the fork doesn't rattle around in the frame — no tighter for now.

Step 6: Replace any washers. If the fork has a slot cut down through the thread, orientate any washers with a tab so that the tab fits in the slot. Fit the top nut and tighten it down until it touches the adjusting nut. Grease the inside of the steerer tube and replace the stem. Check that it points straight forward and that the safety mark is inside the frame. Tighten the Allen key bolt at the top of the stem firmly. Replace front wheel and front brake, then adjust bearings as on page 216.

Headset bearing types and servicing cartridge bearings

When headsets are new, it makes little difference how they are made. As long as they are properly adjusted, cheap ones feel about the same as expensive ones. The difference shows up after a bit of hammering.

A major advantage of better headsets is usually in the sealing: cheap headsets allow in rain, mud and dust, and then deteriorate quickly. Once headsets start to get sticky, they retain everything that gets trapped in them as a paste. Soon this wears pits in the bearing surfaces, and then the bearings fall into the pits as you turn the bars, rather than rolling smoothly. Time for a new headset! Basic headsets use two rings of ball bearings, sealed above and below with a rubber washer. If you have this type and ride in wet or muddy conditions, build up a regular servicing habit to keep your bike running smoothly. Consider servicing your headset twice in winter and once more in summer.

A variation on the loose bearing idea is the needle bearing. Instead of a ring of balls, these use a ring of small rods fanning out from the center and sitting at an angle. Some people swear by them. Personally, I like my ball bearings round. If you have needle bearings, treat them in the same way as standard round bearings.

Cartridge bearing

Needle bearing

Ball bearing

Cartridge headset bearings are more expensive. Instead of loose bearings, the bearings are set top and bottom in cartridges that fit into the headset cups. The advantage of this system is that when you replace the cartridges, you replace the bearing surface as well as the bearings themselves. It's a very good idea for headsets, since replacing the cartridges is equivalent to replacing the headset. They are more expensive than buying ball bearings, but less expensive than buying a headset, especially when you take into account the extra time it takes to fit new headset cups, or to pay someone to do it for you.

There are several different types and shapes of cartridges, so take the old cartridge to the shop when you buy a new one. They can be serviced though — see below. The bottom race is worked harder than the top race, so swap the top and bottom races every service to get maximum life from them. Cartridge bearings can be replaced easily, with the advantage that as well as replacing the ball bearings, you also replace the bearing surface on which they run. If you can catch them before their condition gets too bad, they respond well to a cleaning and regreasing. This is only easy if they have a plastic seal — otherwise replace them.

SERVICING CARTRIDGE BEARINGS

Step 1: Using a very sharp knife, carefully peel back the seal on one side of the bearing. Take care not to bend the seal or cut it. Keep the knife as parallel to the seal as possible. Always push the knife away from your fingers. It's easy to slip and cut yourself — take care. Once you've lifted the seal, run the knife carefully around the seal, lifting it off without bending it. Repeat on the other side.

Step 2: Soak the bearing in degreaser and scrub all the old grease out. An old toothbrush is perfect for this. Dry the bearing; hairdryers work fine (I strongly recommend cleaning off all the grease and putting it away when you've finished and will not be held responsible for any failure to do so.) Clean the seals.

Step 3: Pack the bearing half-full with good quality bicycle grease. Spin the bearing to spread the grease evenly around the bearings. Refit the seals, easing them into place with both thumbs. Wipe excess grease off the outside of the bearing.

Troubleshooting headsets

Symptom	Cause	Solution	Page Aheadset	Page Threaded
Steering sluggish, unresponsive	Headset too tight	Loosen headset	210	216
	Headset clogged	Service headset	212–13	217
Front of bike rocks when braking	Headset loose	Tighten headset	210	216
Bike uncertain when cornering	Headset loose	Tighten headset	210	216
Headset rotates in distinct steps rather than smoothly	Bearings dirty or worn	Service headset, replace bearings	212–13, 218	217, 218
Headsets don't last long, wearing out frequently	Bearing surfaces pitted	Take to bike shop for new headset	N/A	N/A
	Headset cups not parallel in frame	Take to bike shop to have headset repressed into frame	N/A	N/A
		Take to bike shop to have faces of head tube reamed flat	N/A	N/A
Creaking noises when bars turn	Brake and gear cables flexing in cable stops	Check that all sections of casing have ferrules and oil ferrules	N/A	N/A
	Headset dry — insufficient or contaminated grease	Service headset, repack with plenty of good quality grease	212–13	217
Aheadset — top cap won't tighten any more, but headset still rocks	Not enough washers on steerer tube, so that top cap tightens directly onto top or steerer	Remove top cap, fit an extra washer above or below the stem, replace top cap, readjust, tighten stem securely	211	215
Aheadset — bearings work loose after adjustment	Stem bolts not tightened enough	Remove, clean and regrease stem fixing bolts, tighten firmly	211	224
	Steerer tube too slippery to grip stem	Remove stem, clean off excess grease, refit securely, test for stem tightness	211	215

Components

This is the part of bike mechanics where you get to express yourself! When you buy a new bike, the manufacturer makes guesses about what size and shape you'll be and chooses the "finishing gear" — handlebars, stem, seatpost and saddle — accordingly. These are really personal items, though, and getting the right size and shape for your needs makes a big difference to how comfortable you are when you're riding your bike.

Correct fit determines how efficiently your pedaling energy is transferred into forward — or downward and upward — motion. Appropriate choices will depend on your riding style too. Wide, high bars are great for maximum control on fast downhills, whereas flatter, narrower bars help you out on steep climbs by keeping your body weight low and over the front wheel.

This chapter will help you when you're swapping components, fitting them securely and adjusting them, so your bike is fast and efficient. Handlebars, stems, seatposts, bar ends and pedals are all covered — these are the parts that are most dependent on your body shape and riding style.

It's important to be able to fit and adjust these parts for yourself because only you can judge which positions are comfortable. Small changes, like rolling your bars a couple of degrees backward or forward, will instantly affect how comfortable and efficient you are. It's really handy to be able to make the final position adjustments yourself, allowing you to fine-tune the setup so that your bike is as ergonomically sound as possible.

The finishing gear can sometimes be where bike manufacturers save a little on the cost of making your bike. Upgrading these components can be an opportunity to save weight on your bike without spending a fortune. This chapter also includes a guide to servicing pedals, which usually get unfairly neglected so they turn a bit squeaky. Servicing them regularly isn't difficult and will double the lifespan of your bearings.

fi'zi:k pavé saddle, USE seat post

Handlebars

Renew your bars regularly, whether they show signs of cracking or not. Of all the components you use, these are the ones with a short shelf life. I like to use lightweight bars because I don't weigh much, and I like how they feel. I exchange bars every couple of years, but if I was heavier or harder on equipment, I'd replace them once or twice a year.

Removing and swapping bars means taking off grips, shifters and levers. The key is remembering not to scratch the bars. It's tempting to twist and pull, leaving a spiral scour all the way along. But if you want to break a handlebar, the easiest way is to scratch it, then stress the bar repeatedly. Sound familiar?

The other damage to watch out for is crash damage — especially if you ride with bar ends. Any bending at all means they must be replaced. Both ends of the bar should be exactly the same shape and point in completely opposite directions.

Also beware of causing scratches or cracks where the stem bolts onto the handlebars. Creaking noises are a warning — always take them seriously. Sometimes the sound is caused by dirt trapped between bars and stem; sometimes it means something is about to break. Check the section on stems for help cleaning out the stem.

A different-shaped bar makes a surprising difference to how the bike feels. Straight flat bars keep the front end of your body low, spreading your weight evenly between the front and back of the bike. The aerodynamic advantage is minimal unless you ride a lot on the road, but many people find this a comfortable position.

A little extra rise, say 20mm (¾ inch), makes the steering feel more precise. A slight sweep back on the bars, say 5 degrees, is easier on your wrists and shoulders. When you fit the bars, roll them until the sweep points up and back toward your shoulders. You can raise them too far — too much height at the front end makes climbing difficult because you struggle to keep the front end of the bike on the ground. When you refit the brake levers and shifters, spend a little time getting the angle right. I like mine set so that the brake levers are at 45 degrees to the ground, with the shifters tucked up as tight as possible underneath — but it's personal preference.

Manufacturers often save money by fitting heavier own-brand or no-brand bars on new bikes, so bars are a good place to start upgrading if you want to shave a little weight. Lightweight thin-gauge aluminum bars absorb vibrations from your bike, which helps stop your wrists from getting tired on long rides.

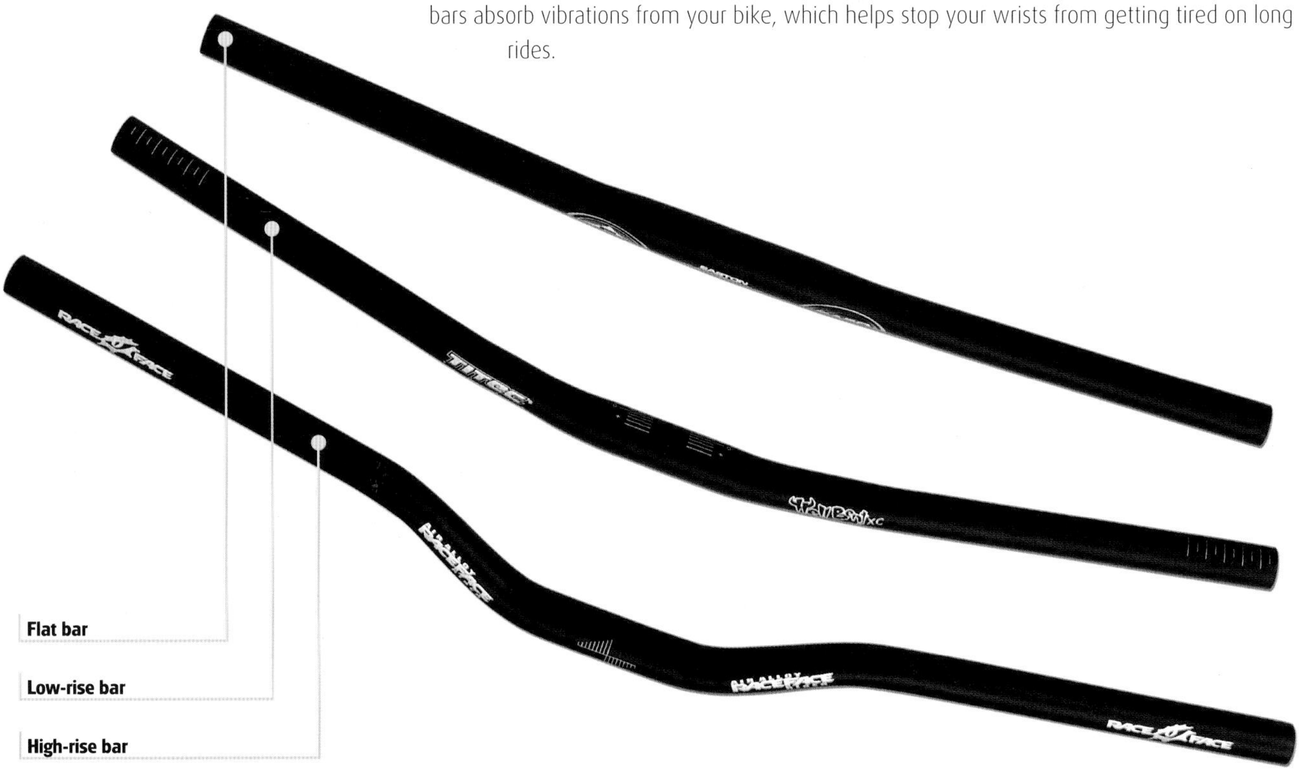

Flat bar

Low-rise bar

High-rise bar

Fitting new handlebars

Bars that have been bent in a crash need to be replaced immediately — they'll be weakened and will let you down when you least expect it. You may also be upgrading your bars for lighter or stronger ones — or for a new shape like a higher rise for more downhill control or a flatter bar to keep your weight over the front wheel when climbing.

If you have bar ends, undo the fixing bolt a few turns, and pull the bar ends off. Rolling around the bar as you pull often helps. Inspect the end of the bar where the bar end was bolted on while you're there. Bar ends provide enough leverage to bend the part of the bar that they bolt to in a crash. Never refit bar ends to damaged handlebars — the handlebar will be weakened and will snap at the worst moment. Replace the bar or ditch the bar ends.

Next, remove the grips. Slide something underneath so that you can lift the grip up a little. It's tempting to use screwdrivers because they're the right size and handy, but it's all too easy to scratch the bars with them. Chopsticks, being made of wood, are much better. Use hairspray, spray degreaser or warm soapy water to lubricate the under grips. Twist and pull to get the grip off.

▲ **Ease the clamp open slightly to avoid scratching the bars**

Unbolt and remove the shifter and brake lever. Take care not to scratch the bars at all because cracks can grow from tiny scratches. If the levers and shifters don't slide off easily, remove the fixing bolts altogether, and open up the clamp very slightly with a screwdriver — just enough to slide off the levers. Don't bend the clamps, though!

You may find that cables or hydraulic hoses are too short to slide the levers off without kinking them. Don't wrestle with them: undo the bolts that hold the handlebars onto the stem, and slide the handlebars along in the stem so the levers don't have to travel as far to slip off the end. Remove the handlebars.

Clean the face of the stem that the bars fit into — if dirt has worked its way in between the two parts, the bars won't clamp firmly onto the stem, and will creak as you ride. Grease the central part of the new bars.

Next, clean and grease the bolts that fix the bars onto the stem. The threads in the stem are soft and will strip easily if treated badly — this is expensive neglect because once you've stripped the threads, your only option is to replace the stem. So clean dirt out from the bolt threads and under the bolt head, then grease the threads and bolt head.

Refit the bars loosely onto the stem, then slide the brake and gear levers onto the bars. If the cables or brake hoses are short, you may need to pass the bars from one side to the other through the stem to get the controls onto the bars without kinking the cables. Next, refit the grips. They need to be a tight fit so that they don't suddenly slide off the ends of the bars as you ride (this sounds like it would be a comic moment, but is actually disastrous and painful). You'll have to lubricate them to slide them on, but whatever you lubricate them with then needs to stick the grips to the bars. The ideal product is motorbike grip glue, but it's often hard to find. Alternatives include hot soapy water, hairspray and degreaser. Don't use spray oil because it never dries properly. Set the bars in the center of the stem, tighten the stem bolts enough to hold the bars in place, then sit on your bike to work out the most comfortable angle for the bars to sit at. If the bars are swept or curved back, a good starting place is pointing the sweep up and back toward your shoulder blades. Small rotations of the bar can make a big difference, so take a bit of time playing with the angle. Once you have the bar position, rotate brake levers and shifters to a comfortable angle. You need to be able to grab and operate them with as little effort as possible. Experiment with different brake-lever angles. Set the levers so that you don't have to lift your fingers too far up to get them over the lever blades. Refit the bar ends if necessary.

Once you have everything in place ergonomically, go around and tighten all the fixing bolts. If your stem has a removable front face, be sure to tighten the bolts evenly so that there is an equal gap above and below the bars.

New bars are always supplied wide — don't be shy of cutting the ends off if you feel like you're riding a cruiser. For female cyclists, cutting a couple of centimeters off each end of the bars can make a bike feel much quicker, as women generally have narrower shoulders than men. Cut down the ends gradually — you can't stick bits back on if you go too far. File any sharp edges smooth after you've finished and refit bar-end plugs to protect you in crashes.

Fitting a new stem

The length and angle of the stem make a big difference to your comfort and sense of well-being, as well as to how well the bike steers.

Longer stems have the same effect as big steering wheels on cars: when they are too long the steering feels lazy, which is great for cruising but hard work for fast singletrack. Very short stems make the bike twitchy; the smallest hand movement translates into movement of your wheel, which is great for technical stuff but tiring for longer rides. The right stem length depends on your top tube length, your riding style and your body shape. Women are often more comfortable with a slightly shorter stem than men of the same size. Almost all stems are now the Ahead type. One advantage is you get two different-shaped stems in one: take it off, turn it over and refit it for a higher or lower position.

First check how the stem fits to the handlebar. It will either be a front-loader with two or four bolts, or a single-bolt type. Front-loaders are the easiest to deal with: the front of the stem can be completely removed, allowing you to change or flip the stem without too much fuss. With older single-bolt stems, the handlebars can only be removed if you strip all the controls off one side of the bars.

Single bolt/quill stems

Remove the grip on one side by sliding a chopstick between grip and bar, lubricate with a squirt of light oil, and twist to slide off. Loosen the bolts on the shifters and brake levers and slide them off without scratching the bars. If they're a tight fit, lever the clamps gently open with a screwdriver, without bending the clamps. The cables will often be too short to allow you to slide the controls off the end of the bar. Loosen the bolt that holds the stem to the handlebars and slide the bar sideways in the stem so that you can remove the controls without kinking the cables. Undo the bolt at the top of the stem four turns, and knock it back into the stem with a rubber mallet or block of wood. This releases the wedge nut at the bottom of the stem. Twist and pull to remove it. Clean carefully inside the steerer tube. Clean the central part of the handlebars, then smear a little grease on the part that will be trapped between bars and stem. Fit the new stem to your bars. Grease the inside of the steerer tube generously and fit the bars. Make sure they're pointing directly forward, then tighten the bolt at the top of the stem firmly. Gripping your front wheel between your knees, twist the bars to check that they're tight. Slide the shifters and brake levers back onto your bars, then twist the grips back onto bars, lubricating with hot water if necessary. Slide the controls back up to the end of the grip and tighten the fixing bolts.

Front-loader stems
Removing
These clamp onto the handlebars with two bolts, or a bolt and a hinge. When you've undone and removed the bolt(s), you can take the front of the stem off or fold it out of the way, releasing the handlebars completely.

REFITTING

Step 1: Clean both the stem and the handlebars where they clamp together. Any dirt left at this interface can cause annoying creaking. Once both are clean, spread a thin layer of grease on the part of the handlebar that's to be clamped in the stem. Grease the bolt threads with an extra dab of grease under the bolt head. Titanium bars, stems, and bolts need a generous dab of anti-seize.

Step 2: It's important to do bolts up evenly. With two-bolt stems, tighten both bolts until there is an even gap between the main part and the front of the stem, then tighten each bolt one turn at a time until both are firm. With four-bolt types, tighten in a cross pattern as shown above.

Step 3: Once the bolts are tight, check that the gap is even top and bottom and, for four-bolt types, that the gap is also even either side. This matters because the bolts will go in straight and be stronger. If one side has more gap, bolts enter the main part of the stem at an angle, stressing them and making them more likely to snap. If the front of the stem is hinged, fold over the hinge and tighten the bolt firmly.

Seatposts

Seatposts must be sized very accurately: the 30 different common sizes are sized in increments of 0.2mm (⁸⁄₁₀₀₀ inch). One size too big won't fit your frame; one size too small will fit but rock slightly at every pedal stroke, slowly destroying your frame. If you have your old seatpost, the right size is stamped on it. If in doubt, get your bike measured at the shop.

All seatposts have a minimum insertion line. This is usually indicated by a row of vertical lines printed or stamped near the bottom of the seatpost. The vertical lines must always be inside the frame. If you have to lift your seatpost high enough to see the marks, you need either a longer seatpost or a bigger bike. In the unlikely event that you have no markings on your seatpost, you need a length at least 2.5 times the diameter of the post inside the frame. Seatposts that are raised too high will snap your frame.

ADJUSTING SADDLE POSITION

Step 1: This is the most common type of saddle fixing. The saddle rails are clamped between two plates with a single bolt. The bottom of the lower plate is curved to match the top of the post. Loosening the bolt (6mm Allen key) allows you to slide the saddle backward and forward or to roll it to change the angle. Start with the top of the saddle horizontal, clamped in the middle of the rails. Remove and regrease the fixing bolt regularly.

Step 2: This design allows you to control the angle of the saddle precisely. To tip the saddle nose downward, loosen the back bolt slightly and tighten the front bolt firmly, one turn at a time. To lift the nose, loosen the front bolt one turn and tighten the back bolt. To slide the saddle along on the rails, loosen both bolts equally, reposition the saddle, then retighten the bolts equally. A ball-ended Allen key is handy here, as the front bolt can be tricky to access.

Step 3: This design has two small Allen keys at the back of the clamp. Loosen both to slide the saddle rails in the clamp or to roll the clamp over the curved top of the post.

SADDLE ANGLE

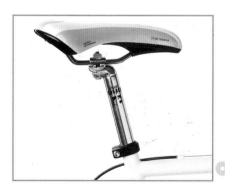

Step 1: Saddle angle is critical for a comfortable ride. Pedaling in this position, with the nose of the saddle tipped upward, will push you off the back of the saddle, lifting the front wheel off the ground when climbing. Your thighs will also get tired with the effort of pulling your body forward as you push down on the pedals.

Step 2: This position can help relieve the discomfort of a saddle that doesn't suit you, but it tips you forward toward the bars, causing wrist and shoulder pain. This position is also often a sign that your saddle is too high — try leveling it off and dropping your seatpost a few millimeters into the frame.

Step 3: A level saddle position is always the best starting point.

Bar ends and grips

Bar ends went through a flourish of popularity some years ago when everybody owned a pair and everyone famous had a signature model. There are less about at the moment. I'm sure it's an aesthetic thing: they look a little odd on riser bars.

Bar ends are most useful for climbing because moving your weight forward over the front wheel helps keep it on the ground. They're great for short bursts of standing up on the pedals too — the angle is more comfortable, allowing your shoulders to open out so that you can get loads of air into your lungs. And it's nice to have a variety of hand positions when you're out on a long ride so that you don't get stiff and locked into a single position.

The profusion of shapes available can be confusing. Generally, choose short stubby ones for climbing and longer curved types for altering your riding position. I like ones with a machined pattern on the metal for extra grip.

The extra leverage that bar ends give you can be enough to twist your handlebars in their mounting — alway check that your stem bolts are tight after fitting bar ends. Test that they will hold by standing in front of the bike with the front wheel between your knees. Push down hard on both bar ends. They shouldn't move on the bars, and neither should the bars move in the stem.

The end of your bar end, like handlebars, should always be finished off with a plastic plug. This protects you a little bit if you land on the end of your bar or bar end in a crash — an open end will make a neat round hole wherever it encounters parts of your body.

Just as vital for handlebar comfort are grips. There really are a lot of different choices here, so many that it's confusing rather than helpful. The most significant variable is grip thickness. Slim versions are lighter but less comfortable. Thick ones absorb more vibration, but this makes your bike feel less responsive — it's harder to feel what's going on if there's too much cushioning.

Your hand size also matters here. If you've got small hands, choose thinner grips. Dual density compounds, which have a softer, spongier layer over a firmer core, are a good compromise. Deep-cut patterns are better if your grips tend to get muddy, and if you tend to ride when it's very hot, as smooth grips get slippery when you sweat onto them.

Grips that bolt on rather than stick on, like those made by Yeti, are a little more expensive but they are more secure and are easier to get on and off if you swap bars frequently. Each end of the grip has a locking aluminum collar that you tighten on with an Allen key.

REFITTING BAR ENDS

Step 1: Undo the bar-end fixing bolt (almost always a 5mm Allen key). Slide the bar ends off the bars. They usually come straight off easily, but if they don't, ease the clamp open by removing the fixing bolt completely and opening the gap with a screwdriver. This avoids scratching the bars.

Step 2: Inspect the end of the bar and the bar end. Bar ends provide enough leverage for them to damage bars in a crash. If the end of the bar has been bent or dented, either replace the bar or choose not to refit the bar ends. Clean the interface and grease under the bolt head.

Step 3: Refit the bar ends, tightening the bolt just enough to keep them in place. Sit on the bike in your normal riding position and rotate the ends into a comfortable position. (It can help to close your eyes.) Check that both are pointing in the same direction, then tighten firmly. Stand in front of the bike and push down on the bar ends to check that they don't rotate on the bars, and to see that the bars don't rotate in the stem under pressure.

Cleats and pedals: Cleats

Cleat positioning is very important. Clamping your feet in one position then pedaling hard for a long period can quickly make your knees sore if the position isn't perfect. As a guideline, you should position your cleat so that the pedal axle sits under the middle of the ball of your foot. Draw a line on the side of your shoe marking the ball of your foot, clip into your pedals, and look down from above. Reposition your cleats until the line on your shoe falls over the centerline of your axle.

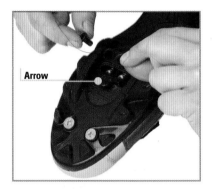

Arrow

▲ **Arrow pointing forward, writing facing outward**

Sit with the backs of your thighs on a table, letting your legs dangle. They probably don't hang straight or at the same angle. Set the angle of the cleats so that your feet are held as close as possible to the natural angle they hang at.

Go for a trial ride with a 4mm Allen key and keep adjusting your angle and position until your feet feel really comfortable, and you can clip in and out without your knees hurting. Your shoes shouldn't rub on the cranks as you pedal because you will wear away the metal and create a weak point in the crank — and scuff your shoes.

Set the release tension in your pedals. It's important that both sides of both pedals have the same tension. The most common adjusting bolt has a 3mm Allen key head. If you're not sure whether both sides of each pedal have equal tension, screw all four (both sides of both pedals) all the way in (clockwise), and then count out the clicks as the bolt turns. Start with the lowest tension that will still retain your feet, tightening gradually as you become confident. Properly adjusted cleats should avoid pain in knees and ankles. If you get sore knees when you cycle with cleats, get a medical opinion on your cleat position. Cycling physiotherapists are very valuable for this; if you find one, nurture him or her.

Eventually your cleats wear out. They start by being hard to clip in. Renew them at this point because they will soon become hard to clip out of. Fresh cleats don't wear the retaining mechanism so fast either. The other type of cleat wear comes from walking on it. Shoes with thick soles hold the cleats clear of the ground, but with thinner soles or worn thicker ones, the bottom of the cleat gets scuffed along the ground. This doesn't harm the cleat until it's worn almost through, but it does wear the heads off the Allen bolts that fix the cleat to the shoe. It's better to keep an eye on them and replace them before major work is needed to remove them.

Shimano cleats

Time cleats

Check the condition of your cleats regularly, especially if they touch the ground when you walk. The bolts wear down and become difficult to remove. Grease the bolt threads before fitting them and replace the cleats before the Allen key sockets get too worn to accept the key. Scrape out mud and grit before you fit in the key too. If the key sits deep in the hole, it is less likely to slip around it.

If you are forced to drill out the cleat, use lots of cutting oil, as cleat and cleat bolt metal is very hard. The drill bits must be good quality. Use a small bit to start with and gradually increase the size to 8mm. This separates the head of the bolt and the threaded parts. Once both heads are off, lift off the cleat upward. The threaded part can then be removed with vise-grips. Cleats only fit into the pedals for which they were designed. Do not try to ride with cleats that don't match — you may be able to get them to locate, but you won't necessarily be able to release them in a hurry.

Shimano cleats are fitted with the writing facing outward and the pointed arm of the cross pointing forward. The bolt hole in the cleat is larger than the diameter of the bolts, allowing you to alter the angle at which the cleat bolts into the shoe. Time cleats are fitted with the arrow facing outward and pointing forward. For a standard release angle, fit the cleat marked "L" and "G" to your left shoes and the one marked "R" and "D" to your right shoe. For a greater release angle, swap the cleats. Be aware that this means your joints will have to twist further to release your feet from the pedals — the standard fitting is recommended for tender knees.

Pedals and how to look after them

Clipless pedals are the standard for cross-country bikes. They're also commonly known as SPD pedals, after the original Shimano version. (SPD stands for Shimano Pedaling Dynamics.) There are many versions available from different manufacturers. There isn't a standard-shaped cleat, so only use the cleats made by your pedal manufacturer — you can sometimes make others clip in, but you might not be able to clip out in a hurry.

Pedals

Treat the threads of the pedals with grease or antiseize before fitting them. This treatment helps you to remove them and stops the cranks creaking as you pedal. Screw the pedals on firmly, or they will work loose and strip the threads, an expensive mistake to rectify. The thread that fixes the left-hand pedal is reversed, which means it screws on counterclockwise, and removes clockwise. This also means that the left-hand and right-hand pedals are not interchangeable.

This standard helps prevent the pedals from working loose and was originally adopted for fixed-wheel racing bicycles. Still in use today for track racing, these bikes have no ratcheting mechanism in the back wheel, so you can't freewheel. You brake by slowing down the pedaling. The reverse thread was vital. If the pedal bearings seized, the pedal, still being driven by the back wheel, would unwind from the cranks instead of snapping your ankle.

Pedals usually need more attention in the winter; seals are fine for summer but dirt works in as soon as it gets cold and muddy. Check by spinning the pedals on the axles. They should spin around at least twice with a good start. If not, it's time for a bearing service. Somehow, people neglect pedal bearings. I often come across otherwise well-cared-for bicycles with a pedal that almost needs a wrench to turn it. You might as well ride with the brakes dragging on the rim.

Often, one pedal continually needs more attention than the other. This is the side you fall off most, the side that gets stuck in the ground and picks up muck. Most mud falls off, but the rest is dragged in past the seals. Mud is not a good lubricant. I usually do both pedals in the same session, rather than just the sticky one. Once you have the tools out, doing both sides doesn't take much more effort than doing one.

Jet-washing destroys pedals faster than anything other than crashing. This is partly because people usually jet-wash from the side — the perfect angle to drive water and mud past seals that weren't designed to withstand pressure — and partly because the bindings accumulate mud so the pedals get extra spraying.

Pedals also suffer more than most other bearings. They get pushed as hard and are turned as often as bottom brackets, but in comparison their bearings are tiny and close together.

Toolbox

Tools for component upgrades
- Allen keys — 4mm (⁵⁄₃₂ inch), 5mm (⅛ inch) and 6mm (¼ inch)
- Degreaser to clean interfaces and bolts
- Grease
- Chopstick to remove grips
- Grip glue or hairspray
- Cloth or paper towel for cleaning

Tools to cut bars down
- Hacksaw
- Tape measure
- File to clean off cut ends

Pedal tools: to remove and refit pedals
- Almost universally: long 15mm (⅝ inch) wrench
- For older Time pedals: long 6mm Allen key
- Grease (or antiseize for titanium axles) — otherwise your pedals will creak, and will seize into your cranks

Pedal tools: Time Alium pedals
- 6mm Allen key
- 10mm socket wrench
- New cartridge bearing — order this from your bike shop
- Degreaser to clean axle
- Grease

Pedal tools: Shimano PD-M747 pedals
- 15mm pedal wrench
- Shimano plastic pedal tool
- Shimano bearing adjustment tool or 7mm wrench and narrow 10mm wrench
- 24 ³⁄₃₂ inch (2.5mm) bearings
- Degreaser to clean bearing surfaces
- Good-quality bicycle grease

Time Alium

These nice pedals clear mud quickly, and the cartridge bearings can be replaced without using any special tools. Before you start stripping the pedals down, check the condition of the pedal-release mechanism. The wide wire springs that clip around the cleat do eventually wear out, but luckily Time supply all the separate parts as individual spares — so you can rebuild worn pedals. I like this attitude.

Check for bearing wear by holding the pedal body and twisting it. The pedal should feel firm on the axle and should not knock from side to side — worn bearings won't turn smoothly under pressure, wasting your energy with every pedal stroke. Spin each pedal on its axle. They should turn silently and keep spinning half a dozen times. If the bearings are loose or binding, pick up a pair of new cartridges and rejuvenate your pedals.

REPLACING TIME ALIUM BEARINGS

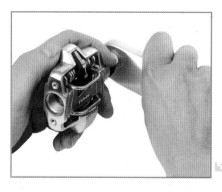

Step 1: Remove the pedals from the cranks, remembering that the left-hand pedal has a reverse thread. The original Time pedals had to be removed with an Allen key, which was a pain, but current models use an ordinary 15mm pedal wrench. Remove the bearing cover at the end of the pedal.

Step 2: This exposes the pedal bearing which is held in place with a 10mm nut. Hold the axle steady with a pedal wrench, and use a 10mm socket wrench to undo. Remove the nut, which untightens counterclockwise on both pedals.

Step 3: Pull the axle out of the pedal body. You may have to screw the axle back into the crank and pull on the body firmly to get it off.

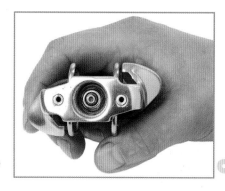

Step 4: There are very few parts inside this pedal. Clean the axle, the seals and the inside of the pedal body. Pay particular attention to the bearing surface at the inboard end of the pedal body. Replace or service the cartridge bearing. Cartridge bearings are not expensive, so replacement is a better option if the bearing doesn't spin easily.

Step 5: Replace the seal on the axle, with the soft flange facing toward the pedal. Grease the wide, shiny section of the axle, and slide it back through the pedal body. Push the cartridge bearing in from the other end. Spread a thin layer of grease on the surface of the bearing to help keep out the weather.

Step 6: Refit the nut, holding the axle still with your 10mm wrench. The nut has a plastic ring above the threads. This stops the nut from working loose but makes it stiff to turn as soon as the plastic engages with the axle threads. Tighten it down onto the axle but not so far that the pedal won't spin freely. Replace the axle cover. Don't overtighten: it holds nothing on, is made of plastic and will shatter easily.

Shimano PD-M747

Check pedal bearings by holding the pedal body, and twisting it sideways. The pedal should feel firm on the axle and should not knock from side to side. Spin each pedal on its axle. It should turn silently, and keep spinning freely.

If the pedals are knocking or binding, it's new bearing time. They're an unusual size: $\frac{3}{32}$ inch ($\frac{8}{1000}$mm). If your bike shop doesn't have them, try a bearing shop. If the bearing surfaces or cones are pitted or otherwise damaged, replace the whole axle. Take care not to swap the plastic sleeves between pedals — I usually do one pedal at a time to avoid confusion.

Remove both pedals from the bike, remembering that the left-hand pedal has a reverse thread and comes off clockwise. Follow the instructions below to replace the bearings. The final readjustment of the bearings can be a bit tricky — you have to reassemble the pedal and refit it to the cranks before you can be sure that your adjustment is correct. Sometimes it takes a couple of goes — adjusting the pedal bearings, reassembling the pedal, and checking the adjustment — before you're satisfied.

REFITTING THE PEDALS

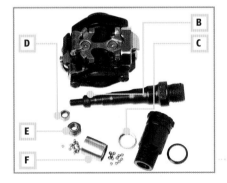

Step 1: To strip the pedal, you need the Shimano grey plastic pedal tool, that you can order through your bike shop. Clamp the tool in a vice and turn the pedal in the direction of the arrow printed on the tool. Wrap a cloth around the pedal for extra grip if necessary. The threads are plastic and strip if forced backward, so check the direction carefully.

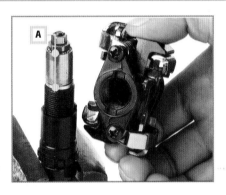

Step 2: Pull the pedal right off the axle. Take the axle out of the vice, remove the plastic tool, and clamp the pedal axle back in the vice, narrow end upward. You see the top row of bearings **(A)** trapped under the cone. The second set is between the steel tube and the washer below it.

Step 3: The top of the pedal has two wrench flats, 7mm and 10mm. Shimano has a neat cone-adjusting tool, which makes the job easier, but you can use ordinary wrenches. The 10mm must be narrow to fit in the space. First remove the locknut, then the cone; the lower one is the cone and takes a narrow 10mm wrench, the upper one is the locknut and needs a 7mm wrench.

Step 4: Remove the lock nut and cone. Pick off all the bearings, then pull off the steel tube. Pull the rubber spacer off the axle, then lift off the lower washer complete with bearings. Pull off the plastic sleeve and the rubber seal. Clean all parts carefully and check for pitted bearing surfaces. If they're worn out, replace the axle. **(B)** Rubber sleeve; **(C)** Lower washer; **(D)** Locknut; **(E)** Cone; **(F)** Steel washers

Step 5: Refit rubber seal and plastic sleeve. Dry the curved washer so that the grease sticks, and grease it. Place 12 $\frac{3}{32}$ inch ($\frac{8}{1000}$mm) bearings carefully on the washer, then slide it gently over the axle to rest on top of the plastic sleeve. Refit the rubber spacer. Grease the bearing surface in one end of the metal tube, then pack another 12 bearings onto it. Slide it carefully over the axle.

Step 6: Tighten the cone, curved side down, onto the axle by hand. Make sure it traps all bearings. Refit the locknut loosely. The cone must be tightened onto the bearings, so there is no play between the axle and the metal tube but so the tube can still turn freely. Holding the cone still, tighten the locknut onto it. This is fiddly: you may have to repeat the action several times to get it right. Refit the axle assembly into the pedal body, then use the grey tool to tighten firmly.

Choosing the right gear

Gear is the fun bit, full of things you buy because they're pretty colors. You always find that some buys make a permanent place for themselves in your life, whereas other stuff, which once seemed a good idea, is more trouble than it's worth.

Liquid

Cycling is hard enough work without being thirsty as well. A quart an hour is often thrown about as a guideline, but you should increase this in hot weather. Water bottles on your frame are a great low-tech solution, but protect the drinking nozzle if your trails take you through farms — muddy bottles don't bother me, but I don't like the thought of drinking farmyard debris.

Luggage

Most people carry everything on their backs or round their waists. I like to make an exception for tools, which I think are best carried in a seatpack under your saddle. They're usually oily, so you don't want them knocking around in your bag with clothes and sandwiches. And if you fall off, the last thing you want to land on is your toolbag. For day rides, hydration systems with luggage capacity — as pioneered by CamelBak — are great. If you live somewhere wet, make sure you get something waterproof — no point in carrying an extra layer all day then having to wring it out before you put it on. For hot climes, concentrate on getting enough air circulating between bag and back to keep you as cool as possible. Larger bags take heavier loads, so look for wider breathable straps. Bags with lots of little pockets are more expensive, but it is worthwhile having different compartments so you can keep spare socks separate from sandwiches.

Mudguards

If you live somewhere dry and dusty, skip this section. I do like cycling in all those places that don't have mud, and I agree it can be fun — especially because the weather is usually sunny — but I always worry that it's just not real. So, for real cyclists who get muddy, a word about mudguards.

I think that a front "crudguard", some variation on the theme of a piece of plastic strapped securely to your downtube (or equivalent), is an essential piece of gear. I have eaten too many pieces of tire-grated cowpie in my life already, and if not eating any more comes at the price of fixing an ugly piece of plastic to my bike, it's worth it. The guard also helps to stop bits of stuff from your front tire getting flicked up into your eyes. Even if you wear glasses, the angle of approach from the back of your tire is perfect to slip lumps of crud under the bottom of your glasses. Strap on a front guard today. If you can't bear to spend hard cash on a plastic moulding, cut a waterbottle in half, punch some holes in it, and ziptie it on. Guards can also make great emergency shovels and, with a good wash, make a lovely camping plate too.

Back mudguards aren't quite so useful, but if it's cold as well as wet, they make the leap into the essential items basket. I can't bear spray from my back wheel hitting the gap at the top of my jacket collar, trickling cold rain down my back. Again, I will put up with ugly plastic on my bike if it helps keep me warm and dry. And when I get home, I won't give up my place by the fire to a colder person with a prettier bike.

Computers

I'm definitely of two minds about these. Computers are the kind of thing I go cycling to escape, so I will only attach them to my bike reluctantly. On the other hand, they are very useful for map reading, allowing you to pace off distances and to estimate how far you have to go before looking for a turning. They can also be useful for structured training routines and all that kind of thing. The simpler models usually have everything you need. You can get models that will read your altitude and heart rate, but mostly I'd rather not know about these things. It's up to you though — if it matters to you, you need one.

Lights

Night rides are fun. They bring on some kind of ancestral night vision that often let you ride sections faster at night because all the extraneous information your brain normally processes is invisible. I like it best when there's enough moon to see by — otherwise you'll need lights. The faster you go, the more powerful you need your lights to be — you need to be able to see far enough ahead to have time to react to things that appear in your pool of light **before** you arrive at them. And here's a safety message — don't do anything dangerous. If you can't see there, don't go there!

With lights under 5W in power, you have to move fairly slowly, even if there's a bit of moon. All batteries also contain a heap of environmentally unpleasant stuff, and we use far too many of the disposable ones as it is, so treat yourself to at least 10W of rechargeable units. Make sure they're strapped on securely.

Conclusion

It can sometimes feel like bicycles change all the time, with designers thinking up new ways to make them lighter, stronger and faster. However, underneath the surface gloss, the principles stay pretty much the same — a couple of wheels, a couple of brakes, some gears, a seat to sit on, and something to point you in the right direction. Once you've worked out how derailleurs work, for example, the same procedures apply whether you're dealing with seven sprockets on your cassette or ten.

The Internet makes it easy to keep your instruction manuals up to date with components that are changing fast, like suspension technology and disc brakes. Most big manufacturers keep copies on their web sites for you to download. You can also look at shiny pictures of new products at the same time, which is what makes it worthwhile for the manufacturer to run the web site.

Once you're confident with the basics set out in this book, some indispensible reading will help if you want to take things further. I learned to build wheels using *The Bicycle Wheel* by Jobst Brandt (Avocet, 3rd edition, 1998), and it's still the clearest explanation of how bicycle wheels actually work. Two indispensible workshop reference books are *Sutherland's Handbook for Bicycle Mechanics* by Howard Sutherland (Sutherland Publications, 6th edition, 1995) and *Barnett's Manual — Analysis and Procedures for Bicycle Mechanics* (Velopress, 2000). Both pack in a huge amount of clear, precise technical information. Magazines are also great for keeping you up to date on the newest products — I like the British *Singletrack* because it has the best pictures.

I've added the glossary to this chapter to help you when you need stuff from your bike shop. Bicycles are covered in parts with similar names but quite different functions.

Finally, I hope this book has made you more confident about fixing your bicycle, has helped you understand how it works, and has inspired you to get out and ride it more.

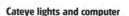

Cateye lights and computer

Glossary: the language of bikes

From Aheadset to Ziptie, this list covers most of the odd word and phrases that you are going to need in order to talk about bicycles and their mysteries. It's easy to get confused since many of the names that refer to specific parts also have more general meanings. Stick with these definitions and you should be okay.

◆ **Aheadset:** The bearing that clamps the fork securely to the frame, while allowing the fork to rotate freely so you can steer. The now-standard Aheadset design works by clamping the stem directly to the steerer tube of the forks, allowing you to adjust the bearings by sliding the stem up and down the steerer tube with an Allen key.

◆ **Air spring:** Used in both suspension forks and shocks, an air spring consists of a sealed chamber pressurized with a pump. The chamber acts as a spring, resisting compression and springing back as soon as any compressing force is released. Air has a natural advantage as a spring medium for bicycles — it's very light.

◆ **Antiseize:** This compound is spread on the interface of two parts, preventing them sticking together. It is vital on titanium parts, since the metal is very reactive, and will seize happily and permanently onto anything to which it is bolted.

◆ **Axle:** The axle is the central supporting rod that passes through wheels and bottom brackets and around which they can rotate.

◆ **Balance screws:** These are found on V-brakes and cantilevers and allow you to alter the preload on the spring that pulls the brake away from the rim so that the two sides of the brake move evenly and touch the rim at the same time.

◆ **Bar ends:** Handlebar extensions that give you extra leverage when climbing and permit you to use a variety of hand positions for long days out.

◆ **Barrel-adjuster:** This is a threaded end-stop for the outer casing. Turning the barrel moves the outer casing in its housing, changing the distance the inner cable has to travel from nipple to cable clamp bolt, and so altering the tension in the cable.

◆ **Bleeding:** The process of opening the hydraulic brake system, allowing air to escape, and refilling the resulting gap with oil. Bleeding is necessary because, unlike brake fluid, air is compressible. If there's air in your system, pulling the brakes on squashes the air, rather than forcing the brake pads onto the rotors.

◆ **Bottom bracket cups:** These threaded cups on either side of the bottom bracket bolt onto your frame. The right-hand cup has a reverse thread and is often integral to the main body of the bottom bracket unit.

◆ **Bottom bracket:** The main bearing connects the cranks through your frame. Often ignored because it's invisible, the smooth running of this part saves you valuable energy.

◆ **Bottoming-out**: This suspension term means that the fork or shock has completely compressed to the end of its travel. Sometimes accompanied by a loud clunk, bottoming-out is not necessarily a problem — if you don't do it at least once every ride, you're not using the full extent of the travel.

◆ **Brake arch:** On suspension forks, this is a brace between the two lower legs that passes over the tire and increases the stiffness of the fork. It is called a brake arch even if your brakes are down by your hub.

◆ **Brake blocks:** These fit onto your V-brake or cantilever brakes. Pulling the brake cable forces them onto your rim, slowing you down.

◆ **Brake pads:** On disc brakes, these hard slim pads fit into the disc calipers and are pushed onto the rotors by pistons inside the brake caliper. They can be cable or hydraulically operated. Being made of very hard material, they last longer than you'd expect for their size, and, unlike V-brake blocks, do not slow you down if they rub slightly against the rotors. Contamination with brake fluid renders them useless instantly.

◆ **Brake pivot:** This is the stud on the frame or forks onto which cantilever or V-brakes bolt. Brakes rotate around the pivot so that the brake blocks hit the rim.

◆ **B-screw:** This component sits behind your derailleur hanger and adjusts its angle. Set too close, the chain rattles on the sprockets; set too far, your shifting is sluggish.

◆ **Burn-in time:** New disc brake pads need burning in; they never brake powerfully fresh from the box. Burn new pads in by braking repeatedly, getting gradually faster, until the brakes bite properly.

◆ **Cable stop:** This part of the frame holds the end of a section of outer casing but allows the cable to pass though it.

◆ **Cable:** This steel wire connects brake and gear levers to shifters and units. It must be kept clean and lubricated for smooth shifting and braking.

◆ **Caliper:** This mechanical or hydraulic disc brake unit sits over the rotor and houses the brake pads.

◆ **Cantilever:** (1) This older rim brake type connects to your brake cable by a second, V-shaped cable; (2) A suspension design that sees the back wheel connected to a swingarm that pivots around a single point. These designs are simple and elegant.

◆ **Cantilever brake:** *See* cantilever.

◆ **Cartridge bearing:** These sealed bearing units are more expensive than ball bearings, but they are usually better value since the bearing surface is part of the unit, and so is replaced at the same time.

◆ **Casing:** Usually black, this flexible tube supports cables. Brake and gear casings are different: a brake cable has a close spiral winding for maximum strength when compressed; a gear casing has a long spiral winding for maximum signal accuracy.

◆ **Cassette:** This is the cluster of sprockets attached to your back wheel.

◆ **Chain-cleaning box:** This clever device makes chain cleaning less of a messy chore, increasing the chances of you doing it. (Now you just need a chain-cleaning box-cleaning box.)

◆ **Chainring:** This is one of the rings of teeth your pedals are connected to.

◆ **Chainset:** *See* crankset.

◆ **Chainsuck:** A bad thing! When your chain doesn't drop neatly off the bottom of the chainring, but gets pulled up and around the back, it jams between chainring and chainstay. Usually caused by worn parts, chainsuck is occasionally completely inexplicable.

◆ **Clamp bolt:** This holds cables in place. There is usually a groove on the component, indicating exactly where the cable should be clamped.

◆ **Cleat:** Bolted to the bottom of your shoe, this metal key-plate locks securely into the pedal and releases instantly when you twist your foot.

◆ **Clipless pedal:** This pedal is built around a spring that locks onto a matching cleat on your shoe. It locks you in securely and releases you instantly when you twist your foot.

◆ **Coil spring:** Usually steel but occasionally titanium, coil springs provide a durable, reliable conventional spring in forks and rear shocks.

◆ **Compression damping:** This is the control of the speed at which forks or shock can be compressed.

◆ **Cone:** This curved nut has a smooth track that traps bearings while allowing them to move freely around the axle without leaving no room for side-to-side movement. The amount of space available for the bearings is adjusted by moving the cone along the axle, which is then locked into place with the locknut.

◆ **Crank:** Your pedals bolt onto cranks. The left-hand one has a reverse pedal thread.

◆ **Crank extractor:** This tool removes cranks from axles. There are two different kinds available — one for tapered axles, the other for splined axles.

◆ **Crankset:** The crankset is made up of three chainrings that pull the chain around them when you turn the pedals.

◆ **Cup-and-cone bearings:** These bearings roll around a cup on either side of the hub, trapped in place by a cone on either side. So that the wheel can turn freely with no side-to-side movement, set the distance between the cones by turning the cones so that they move along the axle threads.

◆ **Damping:** Damping controls how fast a suspension unit reacts to a force.

◆ **Derailleur hanger:** The rear derailleur bolts onto this part. This is usually the first casualty of a crash, bending when the rear derailleur hits the ground. Once bent it makes shifting sluggish. Luckily, hangers are quick and easy to replace, but there is no standard size; take your old one when you buy a new one, and get a spare for next time too.

◆ **Disc brake:** This braking system uses a caliper, mounted next to the front or rear hub, that brakes on a rotor or disc bolted to the hub. Hydraulic versions are very powerful. Using a separate braking surface also means the rim isn't worn out with the brake pads.

◆ **Dish:** Rims need to be adjusted to sit directly in the centerline of your frame, between the outer faces of the axle locknuts. Adding cassettes or discs to one side or other of the hub means the rim needs to be tensioned more on one side than the other to make room for the extra parts.

◆ **Dishing tool:** This tool allows you to test the position of the rim relative to the end of the axle on either side of the hub.

◆ **DOT fluid:** The fluid used in DOT hydraulic brakes. Higher numbers — i.e., 5.1 rather than 4.0 — have higher boiling temperatures.

◆ **Drivetrain:** This is a collective name for all the transmission components: chain, derailleurs, shifters, cassette and chainset.

◆ **Duct tape:** Like the Force, it has a dark side and a light side, and it holds together the fabric of the universe.

◆ **Elastomers:** This simple spring medium is usually found only in cheap forks now.

◆ **End cap (cable end cap):** This is crushed onto the ends of cables to prevent them from fraying and stabbing you when you adjust them.

◆ **End-stop screw:** Used on derailleurs, this part limits the travel of the derailleurs, preventing them from dropping the chain off either side of the cassette or chainset.

◆ **Eye bolt:** On cantilever brakes, the stud of the brake block passes through the eye of the bolt. Tightening the nut on the back of the bolt wedges the stud against a curved washer, holding the brake block firmly in place.

◆ **Ferrule:** This protective end cap for outer casing supports it where it fits into barrel-adjusters or cable stops.

◆ **Freehub:** This ratcheting mechanism allows the back wheel to freewheel when you stop pedaling. It's bolted to the back wheel, and has splines onto which the cassette slides. This is the part that makes the evocative "tick tick tick" as you cycle along.

◆ **Freewheel:** This older version of the sprocket cluster on the back wheel combines the sprockets and ratcheting mechanism in one unit. Freewheels are rarely used for multispeed bikes now; the cassette/freehub set-up is far stronger, as it supports the bearings nearer the ends of the axle. Freewheels are often found on singlespeed bikes.

◆ **Front derailleur:** This part moves the chain between the chainrings on your chainset.

◆ **Gear ratio:** Calculated by dividing chainring size by sprocket size and multiplying by wheel size in inches, the gear ratio determines the number of times your back wheel turns with one revolution of the pedal.

◆ **Guide jockey:** The upper of the two jockey wheels on the rear derailleur, this part does the actual derailing, guiding the chain from one sprocket to the next as the derailleur cage moves across beneath the cassette.

◆ **Hop:** This term describes a section of the rim where the spokes don't have enough tension and bulge out further from the hub than the rest of the rim.

◆ **Hydraulic brakes**: Usually disc brakes, these use hydraulic fluid to push pistons inside the brake caliper against a rotor on the hub. Because brake fluid compresses little under pressure, all movement at the brake lever is accurately transmitted to the caliper.

◆ **Indexing:** The process of setting up the tension in gear cables so shifter click moves the chain across neatly to the next sprocket or chainring.

◆ **Instruction manuals:** Often ignored or thrown out, these contain vital information. Keep them and refer to them!

◆ **International Standard:** This term refers to both rotor fitting and caliper fitting. International Standard rotors and hubs have six bolts. International Standard calipers are fixed to the bike with bolts that point across the frame, not along it.

◆ **ISIS:** This is a standard for bottom brackets and chainsets and has 10 evenly spaced splines.

◆ **Jockey wheel:** These small black-toothed wheels route the chain around the derailleur.

◆ **Lacing:** This technique is used to weave spokes to connect the hub to the rim. This part of wheelbuilding looks difficult, but it is easy once you know how.

◆ **Link wire:** Used in cantilever brakes, this connects the pair of brake shoes to the brake cable. It is designed to be failsafe; if the brake cable snaps, the link wire falls off harmlessly rather than jamming in the tire lugs and locking your wheel. You are still left with no brake though . . .

◆ **Lockring:** Used on bottom brackets and barrel-adjusters, this is turned to wedge against frame or brake lever to stop the adjustment you've made from rattling loose.

◆ **Lower legs:** The lower parts of suspension forks, these attach to brake and wheel.

◆ **Mel:** Mel is a bicycle mechanic in need of tea and cookies.

◆ **Mineral oil:** This hydraulic brake fluid is similar to DOT fluid and must only be used with systems designed for mineral oil. It is greener than DOT, and less corrosive.

◆ **Modulation:** This is the ratio between brake lever movement and brake pad movement, or how your brake actually feels.

◆ **Needle bearing:** Similar to a ball bearing, a needle bearing is in the shape of a thin rod rather than a ball. Since there is more contact area between bearing and bearing surface than with the ball type, they are supposed to last longer, but they can be tricky to adjust. They are usually found in headsets, although some very nice bottom brackets also use needle bearings.

◆ **Nest:** This hanger or stop in a brake lever or gear shifter holds the nipple on the end of the brake or gear cable.

◆ **Nipple**: (1) This blob of metal at the end of a cable stops it slipping through the nest; (2) This nut on the end of a spoke secures it to the rim and allows you to adjust the spoke tension; (3) This perfectly ordinary part of a bicycle causes the pimply youth in the bike shop to blush furiously when asked for it by women.

◆ **Noodle:** This short metal tube guides the end of brake cable into V-brake hanger.

◆ **Octalink:** This is the name of the Shimano eight-splined bottom bracket/chainset fitting.

◆ **One-key release:** The combination of axle bolt and special washer fits permanently to the bike and doubles as a crank extractor.

◆ **Pawl:** This part allows you to freewheel: a sprung lever inside ratcheting mechanism in the rear hub is flicked out of the way when the ratchet moves one way, and catches on the ratchet teeth the other way.

◆ **Pinch bolt:** In this version of a clamp bolt, the cable passes through a hole in the middle of the bolt, rather than under a washer beside the bolt. Occasionally it is found on cantilever straddle hangers.

◆ **Pinch puncture:** This happens when the tire hits an edge hard enough to squash the tube on the tire or rim and puncture it. It is also known as snakebite flat because it makes two neat vertical holes a rim width apart. Apparently this is what a snake bite looks like, although I've never had a problem with snakes biting my inner tubes.

◆ **Pivot:** (1) This bearing on a suspension frame allows one part of the frame to move against another; (2) This is also a rod or a bearing around which part of a component rotates.

◆ **Post mount:** Brake calipers are mounted with bolts that point along the frame, rather than across. These are less common than the alternative, the International Standard mount, but easier to adjust.

◆ **Preload:** This initial adjustment made to suspension springs to tune forks or shock to your weight is usually made by tweaking the preload adjustment knob, or by adding or removing air from air springs.

◆ **Presta valve:** Also known as high pressure valves, these are more reliable than Schraeder valves, which are designed for lower pressure car and motorcycle tires. Their only disadvantage is that they cannot be inflated at gas stations.

◆ **Rapid-rise (low-normal):** In this rear derailleur, the cable pulls the chain from larger to smaller sprockets, then, when cable tension is released, the spring pulls the chain back from smaller to larger sprocket.

◆ **Rear derailleur:** This mechanism is attached to the frame on the right-hand side of the rear wheel. It moves the chain from one sprocket to the next, changing the gear ratio, when you move the shifter on your handlebars. It makes odd grinding noises when not adjusted properly.

◆ **Rebound damping:** Rebound damping controls the speed at which the fork or shock re-extends after being compressed.

◆ **Reservoir:** This reserve pool of hydraulic damping fluid is housed in a chamber at the brake lever. Having this reservoir of cool fluid a distance away from the hot rotor and caliper, helps to minimize fluid expansion under heavy braking.

◆ **Reverse thread:** The spiral of the thread runs the opposite way to normal: clockwise for undoing; counterclockwise for tightening.

◆ **Rotor:** Bolted to the hub, this is the braking surface of a disc brake.

◆ **Sag:** This is the amount of travel you use sitting normally on your bike. Setting up suspension with sag gives a reserve of travel above the neutral position.

◆ **Schraeder valve:** This is a fat, car-type valve. The inventor, Franz Schraeder, is buried in a magical spot at the Cirque de Gavarne in the French Pyrenees.

◆ **Seal:** A seal prevents dirt, mud and dust from creeping into the parts of hubs, suspension units, headsets, bottom brackets, and any other components where the preferred lubricant is grease rather than mud.

◆ **Seatpost clamp:** These plates and bolts connect the seatpost firmly to your saddle.

◆ **Shim:** This thin piece of metal is used to make two parts fit together precisely. The washers between IS (International Standard) calipers and the frame are shims because they hold the caliper precisely in position.

◆ **Shimano joining pin:** Once split, Shimano chains must only be joined with the correct joining pin. Attempting to rejoin the chain using the original rivet will damage the chain plates.

◆ **Singlespeed (1x1):** This state of peace is obtained through self-liberation from the complexities of modern life by throwing away your gears.

◆ **Snakebite flat:** *See* pinch puncture.

◆ **Socket:** Shaped like a cup, this wrench holds the bolt securely on all the flats.

◆ **Splines:** These ridges across a tool or component are designed to mesh with a matching part so that the two parts turn together.

◆ **Split link:** This chain link can be split and rejoined by hand without damaging the adjacent links.

◆ **Sprocket:** This toothed ring meshes with the chain to rotate the rear wheel. The cassette consists of a row of different-sized sprockets.

◆ **Stanchions:** This upper part of the suspension forks slides into the lower legs and contains all the suspension extras, including springs, damping rods and oil.

◆ **Standard tube:** For those who don't need tubelessness, this normal inner tube is designed to fit into a normal tire.

◆ **Star fanged nut (star nut, star-fangled nut):** This nut is pressed into the top of the steerer tube. The top cap bolt threads into it, pushing down on the stem and pulling up on the steerer tube.

◆ **Stationary pad:** In disc brakes with one piston, the piston pushes a pad against the rotor, which in turn pushes the rotor against the stationary pad, trapping the rotor between moving and stationary pads.

◆ **Steerer tube:** This single tube extends from the top of the forks through the frame and has the stem bolted on the top.

◆ **Stiff link:** The plates of the chain are squashed too closely together to pass smoothly over the sprockets, and they jump across teeth rather than mesh with the valleys between teeth.

◆ **Straddle wire:** This connects the two units of a cantilever brake via a straddle hanger on the brake cable.

◆ **Stress relief:** You can achieve this by squeezing the spokes to settle them into place as you build a wheel.

◆ **Swingarm:** This is the rear of a suspension frame, to which the back wheel attaches.

◆ **Tension jockey:** The lower of the two jockey wheels on the rear derailleur is sprung so it constantly pushes backward, taking up slack in the chain created by the different teeth size combinations of sprockets and chainrings.

◆ **Toe-clips:** These survive today only in ghost form as the missing clip in clipless pedals. An unfortunate loss is the accompanying toe-strap, which was occasionally a priceless emergency item. (*See* ziptie.)

◆ **Toe-in:** To prevent squeaking, rim brakes are set up so the front of the brake block touches momentarily earlier than the back.

◆ **Top cap:** This disc, on the top of your stem, is bolted into the star-fanged nut in the steerer tube. Provided the stem bolts are loose, adjusting the top cap pushes the stem down the steerer tube, tightening the headset bearings. Always retighten the stem afterward!

◆ **Travel:** Travel is the total amount of movement in the fork or shock. The longer the travel, the heavier and beefier the fork or shock must be.

◆ **Triggershifters:** This gear shifter features a pair of levers; one pulling, the other releasing, the cable.

◆ **Truing wheels:** The process of adjusting the tension in each spoke prevents the rim from wobbling from side to side when the wheel spins.

◆ **Tubeless:** In this weight-saving tire design, the bead of the tire locks into the rim, creating an airtight seal that needs no inner tube.

◆ **Twistshifters:** These gear shifters work by twisting the handlebar grip. Turning one way pulls through cable, while turning the other way releases cable.

◆ **Tire boot:** Stuck onto the inside of a tire, this patch prevents the inner tube from bulging out of big gashes.

◆ **URT:** Unified Rear Triangle. In this suspension frame design, bottom bracket, chainset and front derailleur are located together on the swingarm (rear end of the bike), so the movement of the swingarm never affects the length of the chain.

◆ **UST:** Universal Standard for Tubeless. This is an agreed standard for the exact shape of rims and tire beads. UST tires and rims made by different manufacturers lock together neatly for an airtight seal.

◆ **V-brake:** In these rim brakes, two vertical (hence "V") units connected by the brake cable, hold the blocks.

◆ **Virtual pivot:** In suspension, this is when the swingarm is made of a series of linkages that combine to rotate around a position. Rather than a physical location on the frame, this position may be a point around which the frame would rotate if it was a simple swingarm.

◆ **Wheel jig:** This frame for holding a wheel during truing has adjustable indicators that can be set close to the rim to allow you to estimate how round and straight the rim is.

◆ **Ziptie:** The tool for whenever you need to connect one thing to another thing.

A-Z List of Suppliers

The Internet is a fantastic source of information, as well as places to find different and specialized parts. Whether you are looking for a seatpost, a chainset or a grip, if you can't get it at your local bike shop, it's bound to be out there, on the Net.

Bikes

Bianchi
Iconic Italian machines.
www.bianchi.com

Cannondale
U.S.-made road, hardtail and full-suspension bikes and components.
www.cannondale.com

Cove
Hardcore bike manufacturer based on Vancouver's famous north shore.
www.covebike.com

Dawes
A name everyone knows. Good value hardtails.
www.dawescycles.com

Gary Fisher
Bikes from one of the pioneers of mountain biking. Now owned by Trek.
www.fisherbikes.com

Giant Bicycles
One of the biggest bike firms in the world.
www.giantbicycles.com/uk

GT
Former bike superpower, now back after a few hiccups.
www.gtbicycles.com

Klein
Another pioneering bike firm that now comes under Trek's umbrella.
www.kleinbikes.com

Kona
Colorful designers from Vancouver offer everything from singlespeeds to downhill beasts.
www.konaworld.com

Marin
Longstanding firm with many models designed by the British Formula One guru Jon Whyte.
www.marinbikes.com

Orange
Gritty northern bikes made for real mountain bikers.
www.orangebikes.com

Rocky Mountain
Canadian bikes from the champions of the freeride movement.
www.bikes.com

Santa Cruz
Santa Cruz have done much to popularize quality full-suspension bikes.
www.santacruzbikes.com

Scott
Hardtails and full-suspension bikes designed in Europe.
www.scott-europe.com

Specialized
The other Big "S." Specialized make everything from BMX bikes to top-end road bikes.
www.specialized.com

Trek
Huge company that makes anything from Lance Armstrong's bike down to entry level MTBs.
www.trekbikes.com

Whyte
Named for their F1 designer
Jon Whyte. Eclectic
full-suspension MTBs.
www.whytebikes.com

Bars/Stem/Seatposts

Answer
Components from the
company who own Manitou.
www.answerproducts.com

Bontrager
Frame building guru turned
component manufacturer.
www.bontrager.com

Easton
Hi-tech aluminum and
composite component
company.
www.easton.com

Race Face
Canadian components with
a bomber-strong reputation.
www.raceface.com

Specialized
Components from shoes to
grips to tires.
www.specialized.com

Titec
Makers of bars, stems, saddles
and more.
www.titec.com

USE
The original suspension
seatpost. Rigid ones too.
www.use1.com

X-Lite
British firm doing bars, stems
and more.
www.x-lite.com

Bottom Brackets

Shimano
The Microsoft of the bike
industry. Making gears,
shifters and components
for nearly everything.
www.shimano.eu

FSA
Full Speed Ahead —
components ranging from
BBs and cranks to stems.
www.fullspeedahead.com

Race Face
Canadian components
with a bomber-
strong reputation.
www.raceface.com

Brakes

Avid
Makers of the most popular
cable disc brake and now a
hydraulic one.
www.avidbike.com

Clarks
Clarks, known for their
cables, now with a
hydraulic disc brake.
www.clarkscyclesystems.com

Formula
Italian disc brake company
and one of the earliest
disc companies.
www.formula-brake.it

Hayes
They make disc brakes
for Harley Davidson and
now bicycles.
www.hayesdiscbrake.com

Hope
British-made hubs, headsets,
and hydraulic brakes.
www.hopetechnology.com

Magura
Huge German disc
brake company.
www.magura.com

Chainsets

FSA
Full Speed Ahead —
components ranging from BBs
and cranks to stems.
www.fullspeedahead.com

Middleburn
British-made hubs and cranks.
www.middleburn.co.uk

Race Face
Canadian components with a
bomber-strong reputation.
www.raceface.com

Ritchey
Bike and component
company set up by one
of the early mountain
bike pioneers.
www.ritcheylogic.com

Shimano (see above)
www.shimano.eu

Gears and Shifting

SRAM
You might know their
"Gripshift" product better than
the name. They make triggershifters too now.
www.sram.com

Forge MTB
Small British firm converting
Shimano bar-end shifters
into thumbshifters.
www.forge-mtb.com

Shimano
www.shimano.eu

Grips

ODI
Possibly the biggest name in
mountain bike grips.
www.odigrips.com

ATI
Another name big in BMX and
Mountain bike grips.
www.rideati.com

Lizard Skins
Chainstay protectors, grips,
gloves and shock boots.
www.lizardskins.com

Ritchey
Bike and component company
set up by one of the early
mountain bike pioneers.
www.ritcheylogic.com

Wilderness Trail Bikes
Another collection of early
mountain bike pioneers
developing MTB tires and
components.
www.wtb.com

Specialized
Components from shoes to
grips to tires.
www.specialized.com

Headsets

Chris King
The Rolls Royce of hubs
and headsets.
www.chrisking.com

Cane Creek
Makers of nice headsets,
wheels, shocks and more.
www.canecreek.com

FSA
Full Speed Ahead —
components ranging from BBs
and cranks to stems.
www.fullspeedahead.com

Ritchey
Bike and component company
set up by one of the early
mountain bike pioneers.
www.ritcheylogic.com

Shimano
The Microsoft of the bike
industry.
www.shimano.eu

Pedals

Crank Bros
New kids on the block with
their innovative four-sided
"Eggbeater" pedal design.
www.crankbros.com

Time
Classic mud-shedding pedals.
www.timesport.fr

Ritchey
Bike and component company
set up by one of the early
mountain bike pioneers.
www.ritcheylogic.com

Shimano
The Microsoft of the bike
industry.
www.shimano.eu

Wilderness Trail Bikes
Collection of early mountain
bike pioneers developing MTB
tires and components.
www.wtb.com

Saddles

Brooks
Classic British leather saddle
company. Now owned by Selle
Royal.
www.brookssaddles.com

Selle Italia
Makers of the Flite saddle.
www.selleitalia.com

Selle Royal
Championing their gel insert
saddles, they also own
Fizik saddles.
www.selleroyal.com

Terry
Pioneers of the "saddle with a
hole" for both sexes.
www.terrybicycles.com

Specialized
Components from shoes to
grips to tires.
www.specialized.com

SDG — Speed Defies Gravity
From tough saddles to crazy
fake tigerskin ones.
www.sdgusa.com

Wilderness Trail Bikes
Collection of early mountain bike
pioneers developing MTB tires and
components.
www.wtb.com

Suspension Forks

Fox
New kids on the block for forks,
but with a whole lot of shock
experience behind them.
www.foxracingshox.com

Manitou
Long-time suspension fork manufacturers, now making rear shocks too.
www.answerproducts.com

Marzocchi
Italian fork giants, loved by XC riders and freeriders alike.
www.marzocchi.com

Pace
British-made suspension forks for the cognoscenti.
www.pace-racing.co.uk

Rockshox
The company that started it all back in the Eighties.
www.rockshox.com

USE
Makers of a very different "anti dive" single-sided suspension fork.
www.use1.com

White Brothers
Well-known motocross firm who also make mountain bike forks.
www.whitebrothers.com

Tires and tubes

Continental
German rubbermeisters.
www.conti-online.com

Hutchinson
French tire-makers.
www.hutchinsonrubber.com

Michelin
The other French tire company. Popular with racers.
www.michelin.com

Nokian
Lesser-known tire company from Finland. They even do ice tires.
www.nokiantyres.com/bike

Panaracer
A company that's been around nearly as long as the mountain bike.
www.panaracer.com

Specialized
Components from shoes to grips to tires.
www.specialized.com

Tioga
Another firm who've been making mountain bike tires for ages.
www.tiogausa.com

Wilderness Trail Bikes
Collection of early mountain bike pioneers developing MTB tires and components.
www.wtb.com

Wheels/Hubs/Rims

Cane Creek
Makers of nice headsets, wheels, shocks and more.
www.canecreek.com

Chris King
The Rolls-Royce of hubs and headsets.
www.chrisking.com

Hope
British-made hubs, headsets and hydraulic brakes.
www.hopetechnology.com

Mavic
Probably the top name in rims and wheelsets.
www.mavic.com

Middleburn
British-made hubs and cranks.
www.middleburn.co.uk

Hadley
Top-quality U.S. hubs.
www.nwmtb.com

Shimano
The Microsoft of the bike industry.
www.shimano.eu

Wilderness Trail Bikes
Another collection of early mountain bike pioneers developing MTB tires and components.
www.wtb.com

Tools and service

Park Tool
Blue-handled tools seen in nearly all bike shops.
www.parktool.com

Pedro's
Once a bike lube company, they now also make a full range of tools.
www.pedros.com

Web sites

Bikebiz
The bike trade web site, full of useful info, addresses and details.
www.bikebiz.co.uk

Bikemagic
News and reviews with useful "localizer" feature, so you can find riders and shops nearest you.
www.bikemagic.com

MBUK.com
The web site of Britain's most popular magazine.
www.mbuk.com

MTBR
Mountain Bike Review — a site where you can read lots of consumer reviews of bikes and components by the people who bought them.
www.mtbr.com

Singletrackworld
The web site of *Singletrack* magazine: news, reviews, classifieds and one of the busiest forums on the Internet.
www.singletrackworld.com

What MTB
Web site of the magazine that tests every mountain bike product they can get their hands on.
www.whatmtb.co.uk

Index <small>Page numbers in **bold** refer to illustrations or photographs</small>